BEYOND RIGIDITY

BEYOND RIGIDITY

THE UNFINISHED SEMANTIC AGENDA OF *NAMING AND NECESSITY*

SCOTT SOAMES

OXFORD
UNIVERSITY PRESS

2002

OXFORD

UNIVERSITY PRESS

Oxford   New York

Athens   Auckland   Bangkok   Bogotá   Buenos Aires   Cape Town
Chennai   Dar es Salaam   Delhi   Florence   Hong Kong   Istanbul   Karachi
Kolkata   Kuala Lumpur   Madrid   Melbourne   Mexico City   Mumbai
Nairobi   Paris   São Paulo   Shanghai   Singapore   Taipei   Tokyo   Toronto   Warsaw

and associated companies in
Berlin   Ibadan

Copyright © 2002 by Scott Soames

Published by Oxford University Press, Inc.
198 Madison Avenue, New York, New York 10016

Oxford is a registered trademark of Oxford University Press, Inc.

Library of Congress Cataloging-in-Publication Data
Soames, Scott.
Beyond rigidity : the unfinished semantic agenda of Naming and necessity / by Scott Soames.
p. cm.
Includes bibliographic references and index.
ISBN 0-19-514528-3
1. Kripke, Saul A., 1940– Naming and necessity. I. Title.
BD417.S63 2001
160—dc21   2001036845

1 3 5 7 9 8 6 4 2

Printed in the United States of America
on acid-free paper

Preface

In *Naming and Necessity*,[1] Saul Kripke argued that proper names and natural kind terms are rigid designators, and that, in part because of this, their meanings are not given by the descriptions that speakers associate with them. In so doing, he told us what the meanings of these expressions are not; however, he did not provide a positive account of what their meanings are. I do so in this book.

In the first part of the book (chapters 1–8), I argue that for a great many proper names, meaning and reference coincide. This view is, of course, not new, having been championed by John Stuart Mill, as well as by a number of contemporary neo-Russellians, most notably Nathan Salmon.[2] I myself have long been a defender of the Millian view that the meanings of most linguistically simple proper names are their referents, and of the Neo-Russellian view that the proposition semantically expressed by an attitude ascription containing such a name in its content clause reports a relation between an agent and a singular, Russellian proposition. In this book I ground these views in a larger, explanatory conception of meaning, and of semantic content, together with an accompanying account of how the semantic content of a sentence relates to information conveyed and asserted by utterances of the sentence in different contexts. A central feature of this account is the explanation it provides of how sentences containing names or indexicals may be used to convey, and even assert, propositions the contents of which exceed the semantic contents of the sentences uttered.

In chapter 1, I describe two main items of the unfinished semantic agenda of *Naming and Necessity*: the development of a positive theory of the meaning, and semantic content, of proper names, and the proper extension of the central semantic theses about names to the more linguistically diverse, and philosophically significant, class of natural kind terms. In chapter 2, I show how Kripke's argument that proper names are rigid designators, and therefore are not synonymous with nonrigid descriptions associated with them by speakers, can be extended to rule out the possibility that names are rigidified descriptions, or descriptions that are required to take wide scope in modal contexts. In chapter 3, I develop an account of meaning that justifies the claim that the meanings of many, but not all, proper names are their referents. In chapter 4, this account is refined in order to account for the ambiguity of many proper names, and it is generalized to include the semantic contents of indexicals. In chapter 5, I discuss an important class of exceptions to the theses about proper names developed in earlier chapters. Here I discuss a rich and varied class of linguistically complex phrases that I call *partially descriptive names*. These names, though not, strictly speaking, rigid designators, are nearly so, in the sense that they always designate the same object, when they designate anything at all. In addition, many of them are standardly recognized as names, and they can be shown to display most of the important features of linguistically simple proper names. I argue that partially descriptive names are equivalent to certain quite special definite descriptions that combine direct reference to their referents with partial descriptions of them; the semantic contents of these expressions are amalgams of their referents plus additional descriptive information carried by the phrases as a whole. Chapters 6–8 are concerned with propositional attitude ascriptions, particularly those containing names or indexicals in their content clauses. I argue that it is possible to reconcile the combination of (i) a Millian account of the semantic contents of simple names and indexicals and (ii) a Russellian treatment of attitude ascriptions with (iii) Fregean intuitions about the information conveyed, and even asserted, by utterances of both simple sentences and attitude ascriptions containing such expressions.

The remainder of the book is concerned with the second main piece of unfinished business left to us by *Naming and Necessity*—the task of applying the semantic insights gained from the study of proper names to natural kind terms. Although I have long been persuaded of the basic correctness of the anti-descriptivist account of these terms developed by Saul Kripke and Hilary Putnam, I have also been puzzled by central aspects of it.[3] Kripke, in particular, models his treatment of natural kind terms on his account of proper names. For example, he characterizes both as rigid designators, and claims that, because of this, identity sentences involving such terms, including sentences expressing theoretical identifications, are necessary if true. Over the years, this characterization of natural kind terms has come to be regarded by many as axiomatic of the Kripke-Putnam view. This is puzzling, since the only definition of rigid designation that Kripke ever gives applies solely to singular terms, whereas natural kind terms come in a variety of syntactic and semantic types—including mass nouns, count nouns, and adjectives, all functioning as predicates. This raises the question of what it might mean to characterize such a predicate as rigid designator.

This question is addressed in chapter 9, where I argue that there is no natural way of extending the concept of rigidity from singular terms to predicates that vindicates the central doctrines of *Naming and Necessity*. In particular, I argue that there is no natural concept of rigidity applicable to predicates according to which (i) all natural kind predicates are rigid, whereas familiar descriptive predicates, like *is a bachelor*, are not, and (ii) theoretical identification sentences involving rigid predicates must be necessary, if true. If this is right, then we need to find some other way of characterizing the semantic similarities between natural kind predicates and proper names. I do this in chapters 10 and 11, where I provide a different, more limited vindication of the claim that the semantics of natural kind terms guarantee that certain theoretical identification sentences involving them are necessary, if true. According to the view I develop, rigidity is not the key to the semantics of natural kind terms in general; nor is it central to bringing out the most important properties they share with proper names.

The views presented in this book have been in the works for a number of years, during which time I have benefited greatly from the contributions of many people and several institutions. The idea for the book originated in a series of lectures, "Logic in Natural Language," that I gave at the Lingua 98 conference, held in January 1998 at the department of informatics of the Federal University of Pernambuco in Recife, Brazil. In "Reference, Intentionality, and the Aims of Semantics," presented to a group of cognitive scientists, I tried to trace certain technical disputes in semantics—for example, disputes about propositional attitude ascriptions containing names or indexicals—to foundational questions about the nature of linguistic meaning, and its relation to information conveyed and asserted by utterances of declarative sentences. It was at this time that I developed the ideas behind both the approach to linguistic meaning and communication elaborated in chapter 3 and the application of that approach to attitude ascriptions containing proper names given in chapter 8. Later versions of this material provided the basis for lectures at the University of California at Santa Barbara in April 1999, at the Center for the Study of Language and Information at Stanford University in May 1999, and at the conference on Methods in Philosophy and the Sciences at the New School for Social Research in December 1999.

My first presentation of material from chapters 9 and 10 was at an international conference on the work of Saul Kripke held at the Instituto de Investigaciones Filosóficas, Universidad Nacional Autónoma de México, in Mexico City in October 1996. Later versions of this material were presented in lectures at the Graduate Center of the City University of New York in March 1997, at Harvard University in April 1997, at UCLA in November 1997, at Pernambuco in January 1998, at Cornell University in April 1998, at the University of California at Davis in November 1998, at Stanford University in March 1999, at Arizona State University in March 1999, at California State University at Northridge in May 1999, and at Ohio University in October 1999.

In addition, an early version of the book manuscript as a whole (minus chapter 5) was presented during a yearlong graduate seminar at Princeton that I taught jointly with David Lewis during the 1999–2000 academic year. I am much indebted to David and other participants in that seminar, including Mark Johnston, Kit Fine, Jonathan Vogel, Cian Dorr, Benj Hellie, Michael Nelson, and Jonathan McKeown-Green for extremely valuable input that helped shape the final formulations of many of my views.

Although the main ideas presented in this book have not appeared in print before, parts of chapters 2 and 7 contain material originally published elsewhere. With the exception of its final section, which is new, chapter 2 is an updated and expanded version of "The Modal Argument: Wide Scope and Rigidified Descriptions," *Nous*, vol. 32, 1998, 1–22. In addition, one section of chapter 7 includes some material that originally appeared in "Beyond Singular Propositions?," *The Canadian Journal of Philosophy*, vol. 24, 1995, 515–550.

Finally, I would like to express my gratitude to those who have made systematic contributions to this work. These include the philosophers Ali Kazmi, Michael Thau, James Pryor, and Jeff King, all of whom read early versions of the manuscript and provided numerous comments that resulted in substantial contributions to the final product.

The same is true of Kent Bach and the members of the Bay Area Philosophy of Language Discussion Group, which devoted three sessions in the spring of 1999 to parts of the book. My student Jeff Speaks proofread the penultimate version of the manuscript and made many helpful suggestions for final revisions. I would also like to express an intellectual debt to my friend and former colleague Saul Kripke, whose seminal contributions to the field both inspired and provided the theoretical framework for the present work.

Finally, special thanks are owed to the Center for Advanced Study in the Behavioral Sciences in Stanford, California, where I wrote the first draft of the book during the 1998–1999 academic year. My year there was financed in part by Princeton University, from which I was on sabbatical, and in part by the Andrew W. Mellon Foundation. I am grateful to these institutions for providing me the time, free of competing distractions, to focus on this work.

Princeton, New Jersey   Scott Soames
Spring 2001

Contents

BEYOND RIGIDITY

1

The Unfinished Semantic Agenda
of *Naming and Necessity*

This book is concerned with rigid designation in particular and, more generally, with the unfinished semantic agenda that has been left to us by Saul Kripke's *Naming and Necessity*. Kripke's strategy in *Naming and Necessity* is to begin by articulating semantic doctrines covering the simplest case, proper names, and then to extend his theory to the more complex and potentially significant case of natural kind terms. Along the way, questions about the modal and epistemic status of sentences containing proper names and natural kind terms come in for extended discussion. Modal considerations give rise to doctrines about the truth conditions of sentences in a rich and substantial sense— namely, as conditions that possible states of the world must satisfy if sentences are to be true when taken as descriptions of those states. Epistemic considerations raise fundamental questions about the semantics of attitude ascriptions like *x knows/believes/asserts that S*.

These modal and epistemic considerations take us to the heart of the semantic enterprise. The simplest and most fundamental question to be answered by a semantic theory is *What do sentences say or express (relative to various contexts of utterance)*? This, in turn, is closely related to the question *What do speakers say, and what beliefs do they express, when they assertively utter sentences of their language*? A semantic theory that tells us what sentences say helps us answer this latter interpretive question about speakers, in virtue of principles like (1).

 A sincere, reflective, competent speaker who assertively utters S in a context C typically asserts (among other things) what S says in C.

This principle presupposes a relational analysis of the attitude of saying or asserting—an analysis that sees it as a relation between speakers, who do the asserting, and the semantic contents of sentences, which are the things asserted. Once this analysis is accepted, it is natural to view propositional attitude reports in accord with (2) and (3).

2. An individual i satisfies *x says (asserts) that S*[1] relative to a context C iff i stands in a certain relation R, the assertion relation, to the semantic content of S in C.

3. An individual i satisfies *x v's that S* (where v = 'believes,' 'knows,' 'proves,' etc.) iff i stands in a certain relation R' to the semantic content of S in C.

I will call the semantic content of a sentence relative to a context, the proposition semantically expressed by the sentence relative to that context. My working hypotheses will be (i) that the central task of a semantic theory is to specify a function from sentence-context pairs to propositions semantically expressed by the sentence in those contexts; (ii) that propositions are the objects of propositional attitudes in the sense of principles (2) and (3); and (iii) that a sentence, when set in a context C, is true with respect to an arbitrary possible world-state w iff the proposition expressed by S in C is true with respect to (i.e., when taken as a description of) w. According to this framework, the semantic analysis of an expression is a theory about the propositions expressed by sentences containing the expression. This theory has immediate consequences for the truth conditions of sentences, including propositional attitude ascriptions, containing the expression. This is the perspective from which I investigate proper names, natural kind terms, and related expressions.

Let us begin with a summary of central theses about proper names defended in the first two lectures of *Naming and Necessity*.

Theses About Proper Names

T1. Proper names are rigid designators: a proper name that designates an object o does so with respect to all world-states in which o exists, and never designates anything else.

T2. Proper names are nondescriptional: (i) they are not synonymous with descriptions or clusters of descriptions associated with them by speakers; (ii) the referent of a name with respect to an arbitrary world-state w is not determined semantically via the satisfaction of any description or descriptive condition at w; instead, (iii) the referent of a name is initially fixed at the actual world-state and, once fixed, is stipulated to remain the same with respect to all other world-states.[2]

T3. The referent of a proper name is initially determined in one or the other of two ways: by an ostensive baptism or by a stipulation that it is to be whatever satisfies a certain description. Later, when the name is passed from speaker to speaker, the way in which the reference was initially established usually doesn't matter. Typically, speakers farther down the historical chain use the name to refer to the initial referent whether or not they associate properties with the name that (uniquely) apply to it.

T4. Identity sentences in which different names (or other rigid designators) flank the identity sign are necessary if true. Nevertheless, often the truths expressed by these sentences are knowable only a posteriori.

In chapter 2 I will look closely at the arguments behind theses T1 and T2, and examine certain descriptivist counterclaims—that names are equivalent to rigidified descriptions, or that names are equivalent to descriptions that are required to take wide scope over modal operators. For the moment, however, let us assume that the arguments for T1 and T2 go through, and that these theses are correct. If they are correct, then presumably the semantic content of a proper name is not the same as that of any description, and the proposition semantically expressed by a sentence containing a name is not the same as the proposition expressed by any corresponding sentence in which a description has been substituted for the name.

This is an interesting negative result. However, it is not accompanied by any corresponding positive result. Nowhere in *Naming and Necessity*, or anywhere else, does Kripke tell us what the semantic content of a name is; nor does he tell us precisely what proposition is expressed by a sentence containing a name. The perplexing nature of this gap in his analysis may be brought out by the following speculation: If the semantic content of a name is never the same as that of any description, then it seems reasonable to suppose that names don't have descriptive senses, or descriptive semantic contents, at all. Moreover, if names don't have descriptive semantic contents, then it would seem that their only semantic contents are their referents. From this it follows that coreferential names have the same content. If we add a plausible principle of compositionality, we are led to the view that sentences differing only in the substitution of one of those names for another must have the same semantic content, and so must semantically express the same proposition. However, this conclusion plays havoc with thesis T4. For, on this line of reasoning, if a and b are proper names, and the sentence $a = b$ is true, then it semantically expresses the same proposition as the sentence $a = a$. But then, since the proposition expressed by $a = a$ is surely knowable a priori, so is the proposition expressed by $a = b$.[3]

This conclusion conflicts with T4. We can therefore be sure that, at least at the time of *Naming and Necessity*, Kripke didn't accept it. What is not completely clear is why he didn't. The alleged necessary aposterioricity of the truths expressed by identity sentences in which different names flank the identity sign is discussed at some length at the end of lecture 2 of that work.[4] The view Kripke presents there goes essentially as follows: Let $a = b$ be a true identity sentence involving proper names. These names may either be ordinary names like *Cicero* and *Tully*, or names like *Hesperus* and *Phosphorus*—where understanding the latter may involve associating them with specific reference-fixing descriptions. Either way, Kripke argues, the evidence available to a competent user of the names—just by virtue of understanding them—is insufficient to determine that the names are coreferential. He illustrates this by noting that there is a possible state of the world in which speakers are in an evidentiary situation qualitatively identical with the one in which we actual speakers find ourselves, and yet in the merely possible situation the names are used to refer to different things. For example, there is a possible state of the world in which speakers fix the referent of the name *Hesperus* just as we do in the actual world—by pointing to a bright object that appears in the evening in a certain part of the sky in certain seasons. Furthermore, speakers in that possible state fix the referent of the name *Phosphorus* by pointing to a bright object that appears in the morning in certain seasons. From a qualitative point of view, these speakers are in the same evidentiary situation with respect to their uses of the names as we are. Yet in their state the names are used to refer to different things.

Kripke intends this example to show that the evidence available to agents in any of these possible states of the world, simply by virtue of being competent users of the names, is insufficient to show that the names are coreferential. We may express this idea as follows: Let E be the collection of possible world-states in which the epistemic situation of agents regarding their uses of the terms *Hesperus* and *Phosphorus* is qualitatively identical with our actual epistemic situation. One might then think that any proposition which fails to be true in all members of E is a proposition which is not determined to be true by the qualitative evidence available to us, and so is one that we do not know a priori, simply on the basis of our mastery of the relevant terms or concepts. Let us suppose this is right. Well, one proposition that fails to be true in all members of E is the proposition that the names *Hesperus* and *Phosphorus* are coreferential in our language; another closely related proposition is the proposition that the identity sentence *Hesperus* = *Phosphorus* expresses a truth in our language. Thus, we are in a position to conclude that the metalinguistic claim that the sentence *Hesperus* = *Phosphorus* is true in our language is something that is not knowable a priori; rather, it is something that we can come to know only on the basis of empirical investigation.

So far so good. However, there is a problem. The lesson Kripke explicitly draws from the example is not that a certain metalinguistic claim is knowable only a posteriori but, rather, that the claim that Hesperus is Phosphorus is knowable only a posteriori. This can be seen from the following passage in which he sums up his argument.

> *The evidence I have before I know that Hesperus is Phosphorus is that I see a certain star or a certain heavenly body in the evening and call it 'Hesperus', and in the morning and call it 'Phosphorus'. I know these things. There certainly is a possible world in which a man should have seen a certain star at a certain position in the evening and called it 'Hesperus' and a certain star in the morning and called it 'Phosphorus'; and should have concluded—should have found out by empirical investigation—that he names two different stars, or two different heavenly bodies. At least one of these stars or heavenly bodies was not Phosphorus, otherwise it couldn't have come out that way. But that's true. And so it's true that given the evidence that someone has antecedent to his empirical investigation, he can be placed in a sense in exactly the same situation, that is a qualitatively identical epistemic situation, and call two heavenly bodies 'Hesperus' and 'Phosphorus', without their being identical. . . . So two things are true: first,*

that we do not know apriori that Hesperus is Phosphorus, and are in no
position to find out the answer except empirically. Second, this is so be-
cause we could have evidence qualitatively indistinguishable from the evi-
dence we have and determine the reference of the two names by the posi-
tions of two planets in the sky, without the planets being the same.[5]

The problem with this passage is that Kripke's conclusion does not
follow from his argument as stated. The proposition that Hesperus is
Phosphorus is, as Kripke rightly insists, true in all possible states of
the world. So it is true in all members of the class of world-states E in
which agents are in an epistemic situation qualitatively identical to
ours. And since it is true in those worlds, the principle that only propositions true in all members of E are known a priori does not rule out
that it may be knowable a priori.

The point I am making depends on sharply distinguishing between
(4a) and (4b).

4a.   Hesperus = Phosphorus
4b.   'Hesperus = Phosphorus' expresses a truth in our language.

When explaining the necessity of (4a), Kripke uses his example of the
possible world-state whose agents are in an epistemic situation qualitatively identical to ours to remind us that the contingency of (4b) is
irrelevant to the necessity of (4a). According to Kripke, the agents in
his imagined world-state use the sentence *Hesperus = Phosphorus* to
express a proposition different from the proposition we actually use it
to express. The fact that the proposition they use it to express is false
in their world-state does not show that the proposition we actually use
it to express is false when evaluated in their world-state, or any other.

What Kripke fails to point out is that the same reasoning applies
to the epistemic status of the two examples. Proposition (4b) is knowable only a posteriori. But that has no obvious bearing on the question
of whether proposition (4a) is a priori. The agents of Kripke's imagined
world do not know the proposition they use the sentence *Hesperus =
Phosphorus* to express, for the simple reason that the proposition they
use the sentence to express is false in their world. But this does not
show that the different proposition we use the sentence to express isn't
known by us; nor does it show that it isn't known by us independent
of empirical investigation. For this reason, Kripke's conclusion—that

it is not knowable a priori that Hesperus is Phosphorus—does not follow from the considerations he adduces.

More precisely, it does not follow from these considerations alone. Perhaps if Kripke's explicit remarks were supplemented with some further principles, the gap in the argument could be filled. What is needed are principles connecting an agent's understanding and accepting a sentence, on the one hand, with the agent's believing or knowing the proposition expressed by the sentence, on the other.[6] One principle of this sort is the following.[7]

> *Strong Disquotation*
>
> A sincere, reflective, rational individual i who understands S is disposed to accept S iff i believes the proposition expressed by S, and thereby satisfies *x believes that S*.

Agents in an epistemic situation qualitatively similar to our situation before the astronomical discovery understand, but are not disposed to accept, *Hesperus is Phosphorus*, and so they don't believe what they express by the sentence. Similarly, prior to the astronomical discovery we didn't accept the sentence, so at that time we didn't believe that Hesperus is Phosphorus. Moreover, the evidence available to both of us by virtue of our understanding the terms is such that we would not have been **justified** in accepting the identity sentence on the basis of that evidence. With this in mind, one might formulate the following principle involving disquotation and justification:

> *Strong Disquotation and Justification*
>
> A sincere, reflective, rational individual i who understands S and is in possession of evidence e would be justified in accepting S on the basis of e iff i's possession of e, and i's reasoning correctly about it, would be enough to ensure that i would be justified in believing the proposition expressed by S, and hence that i satisfies *x would be justified in believing that S*.

If these two principles are accepted, then Kripke's argument can be reconstructed as follows:

(i) Since there are possible situations in which *Hesperus is Phosphorus* expresses something false, even though the agents in those situations are perfect reasoners who have evidence qualitatively identical with the evidence available to us simply on the basis of our linguistic competence, the evidence available to us simply on the basis of our linguistic competence does not justify our accepting the sentence.

(ii) So, by the strong disquotation and justification principle, the evidence available to us simply by virtue of our competence, plus our reasoning correctly about it, is not enough to justify us in believing that Hesperus is Phosphorus.

(iii) If the belief that Hesperus is Phosphorus were justifiable a priori, then it would be justifiable by virtue of the evidence available to us by virtue of our linguistic competence, plus our reasoning correctly about it.

(iv) Thus that belief is not justifiable a priori. Hence, it is not knowable a priori that Hesperus is Phosphorus.

Although this argument fills the gap in the passage from Kripke, it is not transparently sound. One potential problem is that step (i) seems to rely on a questionable general principle—namely, that if an agent could have evidence qualitatively identical with my evidence for accepting a certain sentence S, even though S is false in that agent's situation, then I would not be justified in accepting S on the basis of the evidence I possess. But consider my qualitatively identical twin in a merely possible world who lives a life identical with mine up until last night, at which time his brain is removed, placed in a vat, and artificially stimulated so as to have experiences qualitatively identical with my actual experiences. If today my twin were to accept *I am not a brain in a vat*, he would be accepting something false. If the general principle implicit in (i) were correct, this would mean that I am not justified in accepting *I am not a brain in a vat*. It is, however, far from obvious that I am not justified.

Second, and even more significant, the strong disquotational principles on which (ii) depends are troublesome in their own right. The central difficulty is illustrated by the case of puzzling Pierre, presented by Kripke in "A Puzzle About Belief," which appeared in 1979, nine years after Kripke delivered the lectures which became *Naming and Necessity*.[8] Kripke's Pierre is a Frenchman who grows up in Paris, speaking French. He sees picture postcards of London and forms the belief that London is pretty, which he expresses by saying *Londres est jolie*. Later, he moves to London, learns English not by translation but by the immersion method, and lives in an unattractive part of the city. On the basis of his experience he forms a belief that he expresses by saying *London is not pretty*. It is not that he has given up the belief he formed in Paris on the basis of the picture postcards. He still affirms *Londres est jolie* when speaking French to old friends, even though he does not accept the English sentence *London is pretty*. The reason for this disparity is that he doesn't realize that *Londres* and *London* are names of the same city. This doesn't mean that he fails to understand the two sentences. He understands the former as well as he and his French-speaking friends did while he was living in France, which was certainly well enough to assert and communicate his belief that London is pretty, and he understands the latter as well as monolingual native speakers of English, who surely count as competent speakers, do. Moreover, since the sentences are translations of one another, they express the same proposition. But now we have a problem. By the strong disquotation principle (right-to-left direction) we get the result that Pierre does not believe that London is pretty, because he understands but does not accept *London is pretty*. By a corresponding strong disquotational principle for French (left-to-right direction), together with an appeal to a standard translation from French to English, we get the result that Pierre does believe that London is pretty. Since this is a contradiction, we have an apparent reductio ad absurdum of the strong disquotational principles.[9]

One way of putting the general idea behind the strong disquotation principles is that in order to believe a proposition, one must be disposed to accept every sentence one understands that expresses that proposition. As Kripke's Pierre example illustrates, this idea overlooks the possibility that an individual might understand two sentences that express the same proposition, without knowing that they do, and so might accept one of the sentences while not accepting the other.[10]

Another illustration of this possibility is provided by the following example, due to Nathan Salmon.[11] Salmon asks us to imagine an individual, Sasha, who learns the words *catsup* and *ketchup* by independent ostensive definitions, perhaps by being given, at different times, bottles with these words on the labels to season his foods. As a result of these experiences Sasha comes to learn what catsup is and what ketchup is. However, since the occasion never presents itself, no one ever tells him that the two words are synonymous (which of course they are). Because of this, Sasha does not accept the identity sentence *Catsup is ketchup*—either because he suspects that there may be some, to him indiscernible, difference between the two, or because he thinks it improbable that different words would be used for the same condiment. Though this is unusual, it does not disqualify him from understanding the two terms. As Salmon emphasizes, nearly all of us learn one of the terms ostensively, before learning the other. The order in which the terms are learned doesn't matter, and if either term may be learned in this way, then surely it is possible that someone like Sasha could learn both ostensively, without being told that they are synonymous. But if this is right, then there will be sentences S_c and S_k which differ from one another only in the substitution of one term for the other such that Sasha understands both while being disposed to accept only one, say S_c. But then by strong disquotation we get the result that *Sasha believes that S_c* is true whereas *Sasha believes that S_k* is not true—which is impossible, given the synonymy of the two sentences.

Indexicals provide further problems of a similar sort. For example, imagine the following case: Professor McX, dazzled by the performance of his school's quarterback, points at the player and says, "He is the finest athlete in school." The quarterback's friend overhears the remark, and when he sees him in their next class, tells him, "Our math teacher, Professor McX, believes that you are the finest athlete in school." The friend's remark is, of course, true; McX **does** believe this. However, McX, who overhears the remark while not recognizing his student as the player he saw, denies it. Speaking to the quarterback, McX says, "You, the finest athlete in school? Don't be silly. You are a math genius, and they are never good athletes." Since the professor is not disposed to accept *You are the finest athlete in school* in this context (in which the student/quarterback is the referent of *you*), the context-relativized principle of strong disquotation (needed for sentences containing indexicals)

Context-Relativized Strong Disquotation

A sincere, reflective, rational individual i who understands S is disposed to accept S in a context C iff i believes the proposition expressed by S in C, and thereby satisfies *x believes that S* in contexts that incorporate the same world-state and assign the same semantic values to context-sensitive expressions as C.

gives the incorrect result that McX does not believe the proposition expressed by *You are the finest athlete in school* in contexts in which the student/quarterback is the addressee.

The upshot of all this is that there are serious doubts about the strong disquotational principles. We need not, at this point, regard these principles as definitely refuted, but neither should we accept them.[12] However, if we don't accept them, then the gap in Kripke's argument that the statement *Hesperus is Phosphorus* is an example of the necessary a posteriori remains unfilled. More generally, his discussion of thesis T4 in *Naming and Necessity* provides no compelling argument for the claim that identity statements made using sentences in which different but coreferential proper names flank the identity sign are standardly knowable only a posteriori.[13]

How bad is this? Many, I think, take it simply to be a datum that one can know that Cicero is Cicero, or that Hesperus is Hesperus, without knowing that Cicero is Tully, or that Hesperus is Phosphorus. In the presence of my proposed relational analysis of propositional attitudes and attitude ascriptions, this alleged datum leads to the conclusion that sentences which differ only in the substitution of coreferential proper names may semantically express different propositions. And if the sentences $a = a$ and $a = b$ express different propositions, then at least the observation that the proposition expressed by the former is knowable a priori won't force the conclusion that the proposition expressed by the latter must also be knowable a priori. Thus, even though Kripke hasn't given us a persuasive argument that the proposition expressed by $a = b$ is knowable only a posteriori, accepting the alleged datum would at least allow one to block the most obvious line of argument to the effect that it must be knowable a priori.

But now there is a difficulty to be faced. We need some positive account of the contributions made by proper names to the propositions semantically expressed by sentences containing them. Moreover, if the alleged datum is to be accepted, then this account must make clear precisely in what respect the propositions semantically expressed by sentences containing different but coreferential proper names differ. What makes this task so daunting is that the old solution to this problem—the view that names have descriptive semantic content—seems to have been thoroughly discredited by the arguments of Kripke and others. If this is right—if the idea that names have descriptive semantic content really has been discredited—then, given the alleged datum, one

cannot identify the semantic contents of names either with their referents or with descriptive information that may vary from one coreferential name to another.

It is not clear what alternatives remain. In what other ways do
coreferential names differ? Often, they have different syntactic, phono-
logical, and orthographic properties, and in theory one could appeal to
these differences to distinguish the different propositions semantically
expressed by sentences containing different names. Surely, however,
we don't want to say that speakers using names that differ syntactically,
phonologically, or orthographically can never assert or believe the
same proposition.

Thus we are left with a dilemma. On the one hand, we may accept
the alleged datum that typically, when sentences differ only in the substitution of one proper name for another, it is possible to assert and
believe the proposition semantically expressed by one of the sentences
without asserting and believing the proposition semantically expressed
by the other. If we do this, then we must give some positive account
of propositions and propositional attitudes that explains how this is
possible. This problem is exceedingly difficult if, as Kripke seems to
have shown, proper names do not have descriptive semantic contents.
On the other hand, we may reject the alleged datum and identify the
semantic contents of names with their referents. If we do this, we will
be led to maintain that sentences which differ only in the substitution
of coreferential names semantically express the same propositions, and
that attitude ascriptions involving such sentences are truth-conditionally
equivalent. The difficulty for this approach is to explain how, if it is
correct, speakers succeed in using such sentences to convey different
information and express different beliefs, which they clearly do, and
why speakers often do not regard attitude ascriptions involving such
sentences to be truth-conditionally equivalent, which they frequently
do not. Dealing with this dilemma is one of the two most important
pieces of unfinished semantic business left to us by *Naming and Necessity*. A central part of my task in chapters 2–8 will be to resolve it.

The second major unresolved semantic problem that we have in-
herited from *Naming and Necessity* is an extension of the first. Until
now I have been concentrating on proper names, reviewing Kripke's
theses T1–T4, and stressing the important questions left unanswered
by them. At this point, it is good to remind ourselves that the semantic
model that Kripke presented was never intended to be confined to

proper names alone. On the contrary, much of the significance of his work is owing to the fact that he intended to include the rich and heterogeneous class of natural kind terms in its scope. Unfortunately, this aspect of his semantic model was never fully specified. As a result, it has remained incompletely developed and poorly understood. Thus, the second important piece of unfinished semantic business left to us by *Naming and Necessity* is that of understanding how to extend the model of proper names to other classes of expressions, including natural kind terms of different grammatical categories.

I have already summarized the four central theses about proper names defended in the first two lectures of *Naming and Necessity*. In lecture 3, similar theses are defended for natural kind terms. For example, Kripke argues at length that natural kind terms like *gold, tiger, cat, water, heat*, and *light* are not synonymous with clusters of descriptions standardly associated with them by speakers. As in the case of proper names, two ways are given by which the reference of a term may initially be fixed. One way involves direct presentation of samples of the putative kind, together with the stipulation that the term is to be understood as applying to all and only instances of the unique natural kind (of a certain sort) of which nearly all members of the sample are instances. The other way of fixing the reference of a natural kind term involves the use of a description that picks out the kind, or members of the kind, by some, usually contingent, properties. Later, when the kind term is passed from speaker to speaker, the way in which the reference was initially fixed normally doesn't matter—just as with proper names.[14] As a result, speakers farther down the linguistic chain may use the term to apply to instances of the given kind, whether or not the descriptive properties they associate with the term really pick out members of that kind.

In addition, scientific investigation may lead to the discovery of properties that are necessary and sufficient for membership in the kind. These properties are expressed in theoretical identity sentences that express truths that are necessary but a posteriori. Examples of such sentences specifically discussed in *Naming and Necessity* are *Water is H_2O* (pp. 126–129), *Flashes of lightning are flashes of electricity* (p. 132), *Light is a stream of photons* (pp. 129–130), *Gold is the element with atomic number 79* (pp. 123–125), *Cats are animals* (pp. 122–123), *Whales are mammals* (p. 138), *Heat is the motion of molecules* (pp. 99–100).

The parallels between Kripke's treatment of proper names and his discussion of natural kind terms are evident. However, there are special complications that arise in the discussion of natural kind terms. Among the most important of these are questions about rigidity, and related questions about the modal properties of certain identity sentences. As in the case of proper names, natural kind terms are said to be rigid, and the putative rigidity of these terms is used to support the corollary that theoretical identity sentences involving them are necessary, if true. For example, in discussing theoretical identifications involving natural kind terms, Kripke says *"Theoretical identities, according to the conception I advocate, are generally identities involving two **rigid** designators and **therefore** are examples of the necessary aposteriori."*[15] Another example occurs in the discussion of the mind/body identity theory, where he maintains that *pain* and *c-fiber* stimulation are rigid designators, and adds *"So it seems that the identity theorist is in some trouble, for, **since we have two rigid designators, the identity statement in question is necessary.**"*[16] Again, this remark carries the implication that any identity sentence involving rigid designators will be necessary, if true.

However, there is a difficulty here that has not been widely appreciated. Kripke gives no separate definition of what it means for a natural kind term to be rigid; nor does he provide distinct arguments to show that such terms are rigid. This is a problem because his explicit definition of rigidity tells us only what it is for a singular term to be rigid.[17] If all natural kind terms were just ordinary singular terms, each purporting to designate a single object, then this definition could be applied directly to them, without qualification. However, as Kripke recognizes, natural kind terms fall into a variety of syntactic and semantic categories.

For example, he says, *"According to the view I advocate, then, terms for natural kinds are much closer to proper names than is ordinarily supposed. The old term 'common name' is thus quite appropriate for **predicates** marking out species or natural kinds, such as 'cow' or 'tiger.' My considerations apply also, however, to certain mass terms for natural kinds, such as 'gold', 'water' and the like."*[18] A little later, summing up his views, Kripke adds:

> . . . *my argument implicitly concludes that certain general terms, those for natural kinds, have a greater kinship with proper names than is generally realized. This conclusion holds for certain for various species names,*

whether they are count nouns, such as 'cat,' 'tiger,' 'chunk of gold,' or
mass terms such as 'gold,' 'water,' 'iron pyrites.' It also applies to certain
terms for natural phenomena, such as 'heat,' 'light,' 'sound,' 'lightning,'
and, presumably, suitably elaborated, to corresponding adjectives—'hot,'
'loud,' 'red.'[19]

It appears from these passages that Kripke intends his general theses about natural kind terms—including, presumably, the claim that
they are rigid—to apply in some form to terms of various syntactic
and semantic categories. This raises a number of fundamental questions. Included among the questions with which I will be concerned
are the following:

(i)   What is it for a predicate to be a rigid designator?

(ii) Are natural kind predicates, like *cow, tiger, animal, chunk
      of gold, flash of lightning,* and *drop of water* rigid?

(iii) What sorts of sentences count as identity sentences involving
      predicates? What are their logical forms? In particular, can
      they be taken to be universally quantified conditionals and
      biconditionals—*All A's are B's*/$\forall x (Ax \supset Bx)$, *All and only
      A's are B's*/$\forall x (Ax \leftrightarrow Bx)$?

(iv) Are theoretical identity sentences involving rigid natural
      kind predicates guaranteed to be necessary if true?

(v)   Is there any semantic property of natural kind predicates,
      other than rigidity, that guarantees theoretical identity sen-
      tences involving predicates possessing that property are nec-
      essary if true? If so, are the necessary truths expressible by
      such sentences knowable a priori, or only a posteriori?

(vi) What are the most important ways in which natural kind
      predicates are semantically similar to proper names?

Extending Kripke's semantic model from names to natural kind predicates in order to answer these questions is the second important piece
of unfinished semantic business left to us by *Naming and Necessity.*
This will be my task in chapters 9–11.

Rigid Designation and Its Lessons
for the Semantic Contents
of Proper Names

This chapter is concerned with Kripke's doctrine that proper names are rigid designators, and the challenges it poses to analyses that treat the meanings of names as given by definite descriptions associated with them by speakers. We will begin with a brief review of Kripke's arguments against descriptivism about names, and with the isolation of one of these arguments—the so-called modal argument—as depending crucially on the claim that names are rigid. After an explanation of this claim and its role in the modal argument, the bulk of the chapter will be devoted to examining and refuting the leading attempts to circumvent the argument and reinstate descriptivism. The main lesson to be drawn from these failures is that the considerations underlying Kripke's original modal argument can be strengthened and extended so as to constitute a decisive objection to all standard forms of descriptivism about the meaning of names, no matter how sophisticated or convoluted. This objection invites the conclusion that no proper names have the semantic contents of definite descriptions. However, it does not quite establish it. Although the conclusion does seem to hold for the great majority of proper names that have attracted the attention of philosophers, at the end of the chapter we will discuss a distinctive class of proper names that may well constitute a special and highly restricted exception to it.

Three Arguments Against the Descriptivist Picture

In *Naming and Necessity*, Saul Kripke gives three types of argument against semantic theories that analyze the meaning of proper names, and the manner in which their reference is determined, in terms of the meaning, or denotation, of descriptions associated with those names by speakers. The first type consists of **semantic arguments** designed to show that, typically, the referent of a proper name n, as used by a speaker s, is not linguistically determined to be the denotation of any description, or set of descriptions, associated with n by s. The second type consists of **epistemic arguments** designed to show that what is known or believed by someone who knows or believes that which is expressed by a sentence s containing a proper name n is different from what is known or believed by someone who knows or believes that which is expressed by a sentence which results from substituting a description for n in s. The third type consists of **modal arguments.** These are intended to show that sentences containing names typically have different truth conditions than corresponding sentences containing descriptions, in the sense that sentences of these two types are typically true in different possible states of affairs.

One of Kripke's semantic arguments is based on the observation that in some cases a speaker's use of a name n may uniquely refer to an object o, even though the speaker has no uniquely denoting description at all associated with n. Names of famous people of whose accomplishments most speakers are only dimly aware provide examples of this type. For example, many people have heard the name *Cicero* and know that it refers to a famous Roman, but know little else about him. Nevertheless, such speakers can use the name to refer to a specific man, even though they are not able to provide any description that picks him out uniquely.

The reason they are able to do this, as Kripke points out, is that the linguistic mechanism determining the reference of a speaker's use of a name is typically the historical chain of transmission in which the speaker stands. The standard case goes roughly as follows: A name is introduced and, once introduced, is passed from one speaker to another. Each time it is passed to a new speaker, the person acquiring the name intends to use it to refer to whomever or whatever that person's sources use it to refer to. Often when this happens, the person acquiring the name picks up substantial information about its referent in the process. However, this is not always so, and in some cases considerable misinformation may be passed along. Because of this, speakers' answers to the question

Q.   To whom or what are you using the name n to refer?

are not always reliable. As Kripke has shown, there are cases in which
speakers use a name n to refer to an object o even though the descriptions elicited by Q (a) do not pick out any object uniquely,[1] or (b) pick
out some unique object other than o.[2] He takes cases like these to refute
descriptive theories that claim the referent of an arbitrary proper name
n, as used by a speaker s, is linguistically determined to be the unique
object (if there is one) satisfying the descriptions that s takes to be
definitive of s's use of n.

Some descriptivists have objected that Kripke's conclusion is pre-
mature. Although they agree that his semantic arguments show that in
most cases the referent of a name for a speaker is not fixed by the
descriptions the speaker would most readily give in answer to Q, they
insist that there may be other descriptions that fill the bill. Consider,
for example, Kripke's own theory about the historical chain of transmission by which reference is normally determined. Surely that theory
could be put in the form of a description. But then, if the theory is
right, that description fixes reference. And so, it might be claimed,
descriptivism is vindicated after all.

However, things are not so simple. First, the historical-transmis-
sion account of reference sketched by Kripke leaves many questions
unanswered, and falls short of being a complete and explicit theory.
For example, we know that sometimes a name is introduced with a
certain referent, is passed on to others, and at some stage in the historical chain of transmission loses its initial referent and acquires a new
one, without anyone in the chain intending to change the reference of
the term.[3] There is nothing in Kripke's discussion that explains precisely how this happens, or that specifies the conditions that have to be
met in order for it to occur. This does not, of course, falsify his guiding
idea. However, as he was the first to admit, it does show that his idea
does not amount to a fully explicit theory that accounts for all instances
of a speaker's use of a name referring to an object.[4] Consequently, no
description extracted from it constitutes the linguistic mechanism by
which the referents of names are definitively determined.

Second, even if one had a complete, explicit theory from which
one could extract a definitive reference-fixing description, in order to
vindicate descriptivism one would still have to show that ordinary
speakers somehow possess this description, and use it to establish the

Cf. Devitt or the 'principled distinction'

references of names. This problem is by no means trivial. Surely ordinary speakers cannot produce on demand a fully accurate and explicit description that covers all cases. Moreover, even in the unlikely event that they could somehow be shown to implicitly grasp such a description, this would not be enough. Speakers often have many descriptions associated with a name they use. What, if anything, makes one of those descriptions privileged, in the sense not only of managing to apply to what the name really refers to, but also of playing the central role in determining the reference of the name in the first place? Unless the descriptivist can answer this question, there is no vindication of descriptivism.

Finally, the question of how the reference of names is fixed is less important philosophically than related questions about the meaning or semantic content of names, and of sentences containing them. Kripke approaches these questions by investigating the epistemic and modal properties of sentences containing names, and using these properties to argue that the most straightforward versions of descriptivism about the semantic contents of names can't be correct. Unless these arguments can be answered, there will be little to recommend descriptivism.

To Kripke or to Soames?

This brings us to Kripke's epistemic arguments against descriptive theories of names. These arguments are designed to show that the epistemic status of (the propositions semantically expressed by) sentences containing names typically is different from the epistemic status of (the propositions semantically expressed by) corresponding sentences containing descriptions. For example, if D is the description associated with a name n by speakers, then the proposition semantically expressed by the sentence *if n exists, then n is D* (or *if there is/was such a thing as n, then n is/was D*) is typically not knowable a priori even though the proposition expressed by *if D exists, then D is D* (or *if there is/was such a thing as D, then D is/was D*) is knowable a priori. This supports the conclusion that D does not, in fact, have the same meaning (semantic content) as n.

One example of this type is provided by the name *Christopher Columbus* and the description *the first European to discover America*. Although this description represents the most important thing that most people think about Columbus, the claim that if there was such a person as Columbus, then Columbus was the first European to discover America clearly rests on empirical evidence, and thus is the sort of proposition that could, in principle, be shown to be false by further

① Columbus = 1st European to discover America

② FETDA = FETDA

empirical investigation. (In fact, Kripke notes that it may well be false.) Consequently, it is not knowable a priori, and the semantic contents of sentences containing *Columbus* are not the same as the semantic contents of corresponding sentences containing the description *the first European to discover America*. Kripke contends that the same could be said for other descriptions that speakers associate with this name.

The third and final type of argument used by Kripke against description theories of names is the **modal argument**. This argument is based on the observation that the modal profile of sentences containing names often differs from the modal profile of corresponding sentences containing descriptions. This fact is used to show that the meanings (semantic contents) of names are not given by the descriptions associated with them by speakers. This argument is both the best-known, and the most criticized, of Kripke's arguments against descriptivism. For this reason it is worth looking at closely.

This argument is encompassed in the following generalized form.

The Modal Argument (Generalized Version)

(1) Proper names are rigid designators.

(2) Therefore proper names do not have the same meanings (semantic contents) as nonrigid descriptions. Thus, if n is a proper name, and D is a nonrigid description, then the sentences *n is F* and *D is F* typically do not have the same meaning (semantic content) or semantically express the same proposition.

(3) Since the descriptions commonly associated with names by speakers are nonrigid, typically the meanings (semantic contents) of names are not given by those descriptions. Thus, if n is a name and D is a description associated with n by speakers, then the sentences *n is F* and *D is F* typically do not have the same meaning (semantic content) or semantically express the same proposition.

The most important step in the argument is the first one, which requires establishing that names are rigid designators. The way this is done can be illustrated using the name *Aristotle*.

To say that *Aristotle* is a rigid designator is to say that it denotes the same thing in (or at, or with respect to) all possible worlds.[5] Before

Possible Worlds / as unactualised properties the world could have instantiated

evaluating this claim, I will say a word about what possible worlds are, and what talk about them amounts to. As Kripke understands the notion, a possible world is not another universe; rather, it is a way the universe could have been. Following him, I take a possible world to be a maximally complete property that the universe could have had (instantiated). The actual world is also such a property; it is a maximally complete property that the universe does have. To say that a proposition p is true in (or at, or with respect to, or according to) a possible world w is to say that p would have been true if w had obtained—that is, p would have been true if w had been instantiated. On this conception, talk about possible worlds can be used to illuminate ordinary modal discourse without providing a reductive analysis of it. Ordinary sentences containing modal notions like *could, would, possibly,* and *necessarily* are systematically connected with truth-conditionally equivalent sentences that talk about possible worlds, but since possible worlds themselves are defined as properties the universe could have had, there is no attempt to provide a reductive analysis of ordinary modal notions in terms of nonmodal notions.

The upshot of this is that talk of a possible world need not be thought of as committing one to contentious and implausible metaphysical claims about the existence of real, but nonactual, concrete universes spatiotemporally disconnected from our actual universe, and ordinary statements about what could or could not have been the case need not be thought of as surprising assertions about the goings-on in concrete universes with which we have no connection. Some philosophers do think of possible worlds, and modal talk in general, in that way. Though I take this to be a mistake, the main arguments I will give in this chapter can be reconstructed from that point of view. What I wish to emphasize is that nothing so elaborate or contentious is either required or intended. My talk of possible worlds is nothing more than talk of ways the universe could have been, which, like Kripke, I take to be relatively innocuous metaphysically.[6]

Back to the modal argument, and to the claim that a name like *Aristotle* is a rigid designator. To say that *Aristotle* is a rigid designator is to say that it denotes the same thing in (or at, or with respect to) all possible worlds. The reason we think it does this is that we think the truth-values, at different worlds, of sentences containing the name always depend on the properties of one and the same individual at those worlds. For example, we take the sentence *Aristotle was a philosopher* to be true at a world (state) w iff a certain individual—the person who was actually Aristotle—was a philosopher in w. Since a sentence α *is F* is true at an arbitrary world (state) w iff the denotation of α at w is in the extension of F at w, we conclude that for any arbitrary world (state) w, *Aristotle* denotes in w the individual who was Aristotle in the actual world (state).

The key point here is the claim that the truth-value of the sentence *Aristotle was a philosopher* at a world (state) w always depends on whether or not the person we call *Aristotle* in the actual world is a philosopher in w. Why do we think this? Couldn't people in w have given the name *Aristotle* to some other person, and thus taken the sentence to be about him? Of course they could; but that is irrelevant. When we say that the sentence *Aristotle was a philosopher* is true at w, we are saying that the sentence, as we actually understand it, is true when taken as a description of how things stand, according to w. In other words, to say that a sentence is true at a world (state) w is to say that the claim or proposition we actually use the sentence to express would be true if w obtained. Thus, our ultimate ground for thinking that the name *Aristotle* is a rigid designator is our conviction that there is a certain individual x, such that for every possible world (state) w, the proposition that Aristotle was a philosopher is true at w iff x was a philosopher at w, and similarly for other propositions.[7] This feature of the name differentiates it from a description like *the teacher of Alexander*. The proposition that the teacher of Alexander was a philosopher is true at an arbitrary world (state) w iff one and only one person taught Alexander at w, and that person was a philosopher at w. Since different people teach Alexander at different worlds, the description *the teacher of Alexander* is not rigid. Hence, by the modal argument, it does not give the meaning (semantic content) of the name *Aristotle*.

Descriptivists' Attempts to Circumvent the Modal Argument

As I noted earlier, the modal argument was just one of several arguments given by Kripke against description theories of proper names. As such it was never intended to constitute, all by itself, a decisive refutation of all such theories. Rather, it was intended to be used in conjunction with the other arguments to produce that result. Nevertheless, the modal argument has been the main focus of attention for proponents of descriptivism, who have developed two main strategies for challenging it.

Both strategies claim that names are semantically equivalent to descriptions, but descriptions of a certain special sort. According to the first strategy, names are equivalent to descriptions that are semantically required to take wide scope over modal operators occurring in the same sentence.[8] This strategy amounts to a denial that names are rigid designators, plus an alternative proposal to account for the semantic data on which the doctrine of rigidity is based. According to the second strategy for challenging the modal argument, names are semantically equivalent to rigidified descriptions, and thus are rigid designators. Since speakers have at their disposal the linguistic resources to convert ordinary nonrigid descriptions into corresponding rigid descriptions, proponents of the second strategy take the meanings of proper names to be given by the rigidified descriptions that speakers associate with them.[9] My aim in this chapter will be to examine these two strategies in more detail, to demonstrate that they won't work, and to explain why. Once this is achieved, I will summarize the reasons for thinking (a) that the semantic content of a name is never identical with that of any (nonparasitic, purely qualitative) description, and (b) that the semantic contents of the overwhelming majority of linguistically simple proper names do not even include substantive descriptive elements.

The Analysis of Proper Names as Wide-Scope Descriptions

Recall the conclusion reached earlier about the grounds for thinking that the name *Aristotle* is a rigid designator. We think that *Aristotle* is rigid because we believe that which is expressed by principle (GR).

$$(\exists x) \sqcap \langle P_a \rangle \longleftrightarrow Px$$

GR.   There is a certain individual x, such that for every possible world w, the proposition that Aristotle was a philosopher is true at w iff x was a philosopher at w, . . . and so on for other propositions expressed using the name *Aristotle*.

Note that (GR) contains an occurrence of the name *Aristotle*, embedded under a modal quantifier—one ranging over possible worlds. Suppose we replace this occurrence of the name with a nonrigid description, *the G*, which denotes the man Aristotle in the actual world, and which is required to take wide scope over all modal predicates, operators, and quantifiers in the same sentence. This replacement of the name *Aristotle* by a wide-scope description gives us a simulated rigidity principle, (SR i), the content of which is explicitly given by (SR ii).[10]

(SR.) (i) There is a certain individual x, such that for every possible world w, the proposition that the G was a philosopher is true at w iff x was a philosopher at w, . . . and so on for other propositions expressed using the name *Aristotle*.

(ii) [the y: Gy] (there is a certain individual x, such that for every possible world w, the proposition that y was a philosopher is true at w iff x was a philosopher at w, ... and so on for other propositions expressed using the name *Aristotle*)

Since the description *the G* denotes Aristotle, principle (GR) is true iff (SR) is true. The proponent of the wide-scope analysis now asserts that the name *Aristotle* is synonymous with the wide-scope description *the G* that appears in (SR).[11] Thus, he maintains that our original reason for taking the name *Aristotle* to be rigid—namely, (GR)—really is nothing more than (SR), which simulates rigidity. On this view, the semantic intuitions underlying the original rigidity claim are compatible with a treatment of proper names as having descriptive semantic contents.

Moreover, the proponent of this analysis argues that facts about propositional attitudes show that names really do have descriptive meanings, and that propositions semantically expressed by sentences containing names are identical with those expressed by sentences containing descriptions. The argument is based on the widely held view that often it is possible to assert or believe the proposition semantically expressed by a sentence *a is F* without asserting or believing the proposition semantically expressed by a corresponding sentence *b is F*, even though the two sentences differ only in the substitution of coreferential names. For example, it is widely presumed that one can assert and believe the proposition semantically expressed by the sentence *Hesperus is seen in the evening* without asserting or believing the proposition semantically expressed by the sentence *Phosphorus is seen in the evening*, despite the fact that the names *Hesperus* and *Phosphorus* are coreferential. Proponents of description theories claim that the explanation of this putative fact is that speakers associate the names with different, nonequivalent descriptions, *the E*, and *the M*, respectively; hence the proposition semantically expressed by *Hesperus is seen in the evening* is just the proposition expressed by *the E is seen in the evening*, and the proposition semantically expressed by *Phosphorus is seen in the evening* is just the proposition expressed by *the M is seen in the evening*. Everyone agrees that one can assert and believe one of these descriptive propositions without asserting or believing the other. According to the descriptivist, a similar treatment can standardly be given to other pairs of coreferential proper names.

The driving force behind the wide-scope analysis is the desire to preserve this explanation of the behavior of names in propositional attitude constructions, while also explaining their behavior in modal constructions. In propositional attitude ascriptions, the different descriptions associated by speakers with codesignative names are invoked to explain the apparent possibility of *substitution failure*. In modal constructions, the wide scope given these descriptions is used to explain the apparent rigidity of names and the accompanying guarantee of *substitution success*.[12]

That, as I see it, is the basic idea behind the wide-scope analysis. I will now try to state the analysis a bit more precisely. In doing so, we let S(n) be a sentence of English containing an occurrence of a name n; we let d be a description and S(d) be the result of substituting d for each occurrence of n; similarly, we take S(x) to be the result of replacing each occurrence of n with the variable 'x.' According to the analysis, the proposition semantically expressed by S(n) is the proposition expressed by S(d), on an interpretation in which each occurrence of d (that replaces an original occurrence of n in S(n)) is given wide scope over every modal operator, modal predicate, and modal quantifier in S(x), except those for which doing this would involve removing d from the scope of some propositional attitude verb. When S(n) contains no modal operators, modal predicates, or modal quantifiers, it semantically expresses whatever proposition (or propositions) is (or are) expressed by S(d).[13]

Let us now consider some examples. If the semantic content of the name n is given by the description *the G*, then the proposition semantically expressed by *n is F* is the proposition expressed by *(the x: Gx) Fx*—for example, the proposition that the president of the United States is a Democrat. Similarly, the proposition semantically expressed by (*necessarily*) *John believes that n is F* is the proposition expressed by (*necessarily*) *John believes that* [(*the x*: *Gx*) *Fx*]. However, the propositions semantically expressed by *necessarily n is F* and *necessarily if n is F, then something is both F and G* are the propositions expressed by (*the x*: *Gx*) *necessarily* [*Fx*] and (*the x*: *Gx*) *necessarily* [*Fx* ⊃∃ *y* (*Fy* & *Gy*)].

Finally, two points of clarification. First, the analysis states that sentences of different sorts that contain names semantically express the same propositions as sentences of various kinds containing descriptions. For this reason it is worth saying a word about what I am assuming about propositions. In addition to being expressed by sentences, I assume that propositions are both bearers of truth or falsity and objects of attitudes, such as believing and asserting. To say this is just to say that there are some things that can be asserted and believed, and that what is asserted and believed may also be true or false (either necessarily or contingently). That there are such things seems to be one of the evident commitments of our ordinary, prephilosophical speech. For present purposes, the expression *propositions* is simply a name for these things, whatever they turn out to be. In giving the arguments that follow in this chapter, I will make only the most minimal use of further theoretical assumptions about the structure of propositions and about the nature of the relations, such as belief and assertion, that we bear to them. Thus my arguments will not depend on controversial positions on these issues.

Second, I want to stress that the wide-scope analysis that is the target of these arguments states something more than the claim that names are semantically equivalent to descriptions that may take wide scope in modal constructions. Rather, it states that names are semantically equivalent to descriptions that must take wide scope in modal constructions (of the sort indicated above). The view is not that a modal sentence containing a name is ambiguous, with one reading in which the associated description takes wide scope over the modal operator and another reading in which it does not. Rather, the analysis asserts that such a sentence is unambiguous, having only the reading in which the description takes wide scope. This feature of the analysis is needed to account for certain obvious differences between the behavior of names and ordinary descriptions in modal constructions. For example, as Kripke has pointed out, there is clearly a sense in which (i) the teacher of Alexander might not have taught Alexander, and so might not have been the teacher of Alexander, and (ii) someone other than the teacher of Alexander might have been the teacher of Alexander; however, there is no sense in which (i) Aristotle might not have been Aristotle or (ii) someone other than Aristotle might have been Aristotle.[14] In these examples the occurrences of *the teacher of Alexander* that follow the modal operators *might not have been* and *might have been* in the two sentences remain within the scope operator, and the sentences express truths on that interpretation. If *Aristotle* were equivalent to a nonrigid description that could be given any scope, then there would be corresponding senses of *Aristotle might not have been Aristotle* and *Someone other than Aristotle might have been Aristotle* in which they express truths. The fact that these sentences do not have such interpretations shows that any analysis according to which *Aristotle* is analyzed as being equivalent to a nonrigid description, must be one in which the description is not allowed to take small scope in examples like this. It is precisely to account for the lack of ambiguities like this that the wide-scope analysis has been formulated as it has.

With this in mind, we are now ready to criticize the analysis.

Arguments Against the Wide-Scope Analysis

$$Fn \rightarrow \exists y (Fy \wedge Gy)$$

The Basic Argument According to the analysis, the proposition semantically expressed by the sentence *if n is F, then something is both F and G* is the proposition semantically expressed by the sentence *if the G is F, then something is both F and G.* This gives us premise 1 of our argument.

$(the\ x : Gx)\ Fx$ $FG \rightarrow \exists y (Fy \wedge Gy)$

P1. The proposition that if n is F, then something is both F and G = the proposition that if the G is F, then something is both F and G. $\langle Fn \rightarrow \exists y (Fy \wedge Gy)\rangle = \langle FG \rightarrow \exists y (Fy \wedge Gy)\rangle$

$((the\ x : Gx) Fx)$

Next we add premise 2.

P2. The proposition that if the G is F, then something is both F and G is a necessary truth $\Box$ [((the x: Gx) Fx) $\supset \exists y$ (Fy & Gy)].

Clearly, C ought to follow from P1 and P2.

C. The proposition that if n is F, then something is both F and G is a necessary truth □ [Fn ⊃ ∃y (Fy & Gy)].

However, on the wide-scope analysis, it does not follow, since, according to the analysis, C is just claim C′.

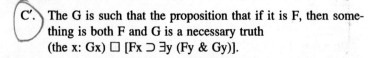

C′. The G is such that the proposition that if it is F, then something is both F and G is a necessary truth
(the x: Gx) □ [Fx ⊃ ∃y (Fy & Gy)].

The problem for the wide-scope analysis is that whereas the argument from P1 and P2 to C is clearly valid, the analysis wrongly characterizes it as invalid. According to the analysis, both P1 and P2 are true, while C (i.e., C′) may be false (when F and G are unrelated and the property expressed by G is not an essential property of the thing to which G actually applies).

The reason that the wide-scope analysis has this consequence is that it treats linguistic constructions containing modal operators like *necessarily*, or modal predicates like *is a necessary truth*, as inherently shifty. In each case, the modal element combines syntactically with an argument A, a sentence in the case of the operator *necessarily*, a noun phrase in the case of the predicate *is a necessary truth*. When the argument A contains no proper names, the modal element is applied to the proposition expressed, or denoted, by A (depending on whether A is a sentence or a noun phrase). However, when A does contain a proper name, the modal operator, or predicate, is not applied to the proposition expressed or denoted by A; rather, it is applied to a different proposition.[15]

To simplify matters, let us focus simply on the modal predicate *is a necessary truth*. According to the wide-scope analysis, this predicate can be seen as expressing a modal property of propositions. When the predicate is combined with a term α that denotes a proposition p, the resulting sentence *α is a necessary truth* attributes the property of being necessarily true to p, provided that α does not itself contain any proper names. However, when α does contain a proper name, the sentence *α is a necessary truth* does not attribute any property to the proposition denoted by α. For example, if α is the proposition that Fn, and the name n is associated with the description *the G*, then the sentence *α is a necessary truth* is interpreted as saying *there is a unique individual o which is G, and which is such that the (singular, Russellian) proposition that o is F has the property of being a necessary truth.*[16]

This is why the wide-scope analysis of names is forced to treat some arguments with the apparent (grammatical) form (I) as invalid.

I.
  (i) $\alpha = \beta$
  (ii) α is a necessary truth
  (iii) β is a necessary truth

When α contains no proper names but β does, the analysis treats (ii) as predicating the property of being necessarily true of a certain proposition p; the analysis views (i) as identifying p with proposition q; yet the analysis denies that (iii) predicates the property of being necessarily true of q. Because of this, (i) and (ii) may be characterized as true, while (iii) is characterized as false. (An analogous point holds for examples using the operator *necessarily*.)

The lesson to be drawn is clear. The wide-scope analysis purports to provide a correct description of the meanings of English sentences containing proper names, definite descriptions, and modal expressions. The fact that it wrongly characterizes obviously valid arguments as invalid shows that it fails to do this. This failure is not mitigated by the fact that the semantics it provides these sentences is conceptually coherent. There could be a language that worked in the way characterized by the wide-scope analysis, and in such a language many arguments of the (grammatical) form (I) would be invalid. But English as we now understand it is not such a language. It is not even clear that we should be willing to describe such a language as containing proper names in the sense that English does. Because of this, the wide-scope analysis fails to throw light on how names actually function in English or other natural languages.[17]

The argument just given focuses on the modal predicate *is a necessary truth*. The argument shows that names cannot be analyzed as nonrigid descriptions that are required to take wide scope over this modal predicate in sentences of the form *the proposition that S is a necessary truth*. Equivalences like those in E can be used to generalize this result to modal sentences of different but related forms.

E.
  (i)   The proposition that S(n) is a necessary truth iff that S(n) is a necessary truth

Cf. Horwich

$\langle \Box Sn \rangle \longleftrightarrow \Box Sn$

(ii) That S(n) is a necessary truth iff it is a necessary truth that S(n)

(iii) It is a necessary truth that S(n) iff it is necessarily true that S(n)

(iv) It is necessarily true that S(n) iff necessarily S(n)

Any attempt to salvage the wide-scope analysis by blocking the descriptions allegedly associated with names from taking wide scope in sentences of the form *the proposition that S(n) is a necessary truth*, while requiring them to take wide scope in other modal sentences, would force one to deny at least one of the equivalences in E. The obviousness of these equivalences is an argument against any such modification of the wide-scope analysis.

A Variation on the Argument Before leaving this argument, I would like to call attention to an implicit assumption I have invoked. I have assumed that the descriptive contents attributed by the analysis to proper names are also expressed in English by ordinary descriptive phrases of the form *the G*. This is worth mentioning because some proponents of the wide-scope analysis have denied it.[18] And, of course, if, for some n, there is no synonymous description, *the G*, then we will not be able to formulate any true premise of the form P1, and the above argument will be blocked. In addition, some proponents of the wide-scope analysis have used the possibility that names may have descriptive contents, even if they do not have the same contents as any ordinary descriptive phrases, to support a surprising and mysterious doctrine—namely, that it makes no sense to attribute modal properties to propositions expressed by sentences containing names.

This mysterious doctrine can be motivated as follows: Suppose that the name n has a wide-scope descriptive content which is not the content of any ordinary descriptive phrase in English. In that case we will not be able to formulate any true claim of the form *'n is F' expresses the proposition that the G is F*. We can say, truly, that *n is F* expresses a proposition, and we can correctly identify that proposition by saying *that proposition is the proposition that n is F*. By using the sentence *n is F*, we can entertain this proposition, and we can make a variety of judgments about it. Strangely, however, we cannot assess its modal profile, its truth or falsity in different possible worlds. For if we try to do this, we find ourselves asking some such question as *Is it the*

case that in world w, n is F?. But in asking this question we have
embedded n under a modal operator, thereby causing the descriptive
content of n to "hop over" the content of the operator and take wide
scope.

This has the effect of transforming our question into one different
from the one we intended. We intended to ask about the truth-value in
w of the proposition expressed by *n is F*. We ended up asking about
the truth-value in w of the singular Russellian proposition consisting
not of the descriptive content of n together with the property expressed
by F, but of the individual denoted by that descriptive content in the
actual world, together with the property expressed by F. Moreover, the
proponent of the mysterious doctrine asserts, there is no other way in
which we can ask the question we intended. Instead, we must face the
fact that we simply cannot ask questions about the modal profiles of
propositions expressed by sentences. The best we can do is raise questions about the **truth-values** of propositions expressed by larger sentences containing modal operators under which the proper names are
embedded.[19]

How should we respond to this strange doctrine? Let us begin by
supposing, for the sake of argument, that proper names have nonrigid,
wide-scope descriptive contents which are not the contents of any descriptive phrase in English. If so, then propositions expressed by sentences containing names will not be expressible by us in any other way.
For example, it may be that the proposition expressed by the sentence *n
is F* is not expressed by any other sentence in our language. Still, there is
nothing to prevent us from describing that proposition. Indeed, we have
already done so—it is the proposition expressed by the sentence *n is F*, a
proposition that consists of the descriptive content of the name n together
with the property expressed by F. Since we can describe the proposition
in this way, nothing prevents us from using our description to ask about
its modal profile. For example, we may ask, "What is the truth-value of
the proposition expressed by the sentence *n is F* in world w?" This question does, of course, contain a modal phrase. However, since the name n
occurs within quotes in the question, it is not given wide scope over that
phrase. The alleged descriptive content of the name is not even a constituent of the propositional content of the question, so there is nothing here
to be given wide scope.

Thus we have succeeded in doing what the mysterious doctrine
tells us can't be done. We have asked an intelligible question about the

modal profile of a proposition expressed by the sentence *n is F*. More-over, it is not difficult to see how to go about answering it. We know that the proposition expressed by this sentence consists of the allegedly nonrigid descriptive content of the name together with the property F. We also know that, in general, any proposition expressed by a sentence α *is* Φ is true at a world w iff the denotation in w determined by the content of α is something which in w has the property expressed by Φ. Since we have been told that the name n has a descriptive content, we know that the denotation determined by this content at a world is whatever individual, if any, uniquely possesses the relevant descriptive characteristics at that world. Surely this is something that is determinable in many cases—for if it is determinable in the actual world which individual corresponds to the descriptive content of a name, there is no reason the same shouldn't hold true for other possible worlds. But this just means that often we can determine correct answers to questions about the modal profile of the proposition expressed by *n is F*.

With this in mind, all that remains for us to do is to reformulate the original counterargument (I) against the wide-scope analysis, so that it applies even to those versions of the analysis which maintain that names have wide-scope descriptive contents that are not the contents of any descriptive phrases in English. The first premise of the reformulated argument is P1a, which surely is undeniable.

 P1a. The proposition that n is F = the proposition expressed by the sentence *n is F*.

Next consider claims (1) and (2).[20]

 1. The proposition expressed by the sentence *n is F* is true at world w.

2. The proposition that n is F is true at world w.

According to the wide-scope analysis, (1) will be characterized as true iff the descriptive content ascribed to n picks out, at w, an individual that has at w the property expressed by F; (2) will be characterized as true iff that same descriptive content picks out, in the actual world, an individual that has that property at w. If the descriptive sense ascribed to n picks out different individuals at different worlds (as it must, if the appeal to wide scope is to have a point), then for some worlds, the corresponding claims (1) and (2) will be characterized as having different truth-values. Because of this, the wide-scope analysis will fail to characterize the pair of inferences, (i) from P1a and (1) to (2), and (ii) from P1a and (2) to (1), as jointly valid. Since in fact they are both valid, the wide-scope analysis fails.

A Related Confusion It is illuminating to note that essentially the same failure can be expressed in a slightly different way. As before, we begin with the undeniable premise P1a, to which we add the trivial truth P2a.

> P2a. For all worlds w, the proposition that n is F is true at w iff
>   the proposition that n is F is true at w.

$$(\forall w) \langle T_w F n \rangle \leftrightarrow \langle T_w F n \rangle$$

From these two premises, Obv is an obvious consequence.[21]

> Obv. For all worlds w, the proposition expressed by the sentence
>   *n is F* is true at w iff the proposition that n is F is true
>   at w.

According to the wide-scope analysis, however, P1a and P2a are true, while Obv is false.

To see this, imagine that n is synonymous with the wide-scope description, *the G*. (If there is no such ordinary description available in the language, let *the G* be *the x: x = n*, where the name is taken to have a descriptive content that is uniquely satisfied by different individuals at different worlds.) Then, according to the wide-scope analysis, Obv is equivalent to (3).

> 3. (the x: Gx) (for all worlds w) [the proposition expressed by
>   (*the x: Gx*) [*x is F*] is true at world w iff the proposition that
>   x is F is true at w]

But when G expresses a property that different objects may have at different worlds, (3) will be false (for some F). Since, according to the wide-scope analysis, (3) is equivalent to Obv, the analysis mischaracterizes it as false (and the inference from P1a and P2a to Obv as invalid).

This failure of the analysis is related to a persistent confusion about its content. A striking feature of the relationship between rigidity and wide scope is the frequency with which the two are confused.[22] In particular, the wide-scope analysis has often been mischaracterized, even by proponents, as claiming that names are rigid. Although this is a mistake, it is an understandable one. Recall our earlier discussion of the name *Aristotle*, in which I mentioned that the wide-scope analysis can account for the truth of the principle GR, which constituted our original grounds for taking the name to be rigid.

GR.   There is a certain individual x, such that for every possible world w, the proposition that Aristotle was a philosopher is true at w iff x was a philosopher at w, . . . and so on for other propositions expressed using the name *Aristotle*.

What I did not point out at the time was that in order to get from GR to the claim that *Aristotle* is rigid, we need an instance of Obv involving that name.

Obv$_A$.   For all worlds w, the proposition expressed by the sentence *Aristotle was a philosopher* is true at w iff the proposition that Aristotle was a philosopher is true at w; ditto for other examples involving the name.

Together, GR and Obv$_A$ entail R.

R.   There is a certain individual x, such that for every possible world w, the proposition expressed by the sentence *Aristotle was a philosopher* is true at w iff x was a philosopher at w, . . . and so on for other propositions expressed using the name *Aristotle*.

This is what is needed for the rigidity of *Aristotle*—for it is R that guarantees that the sentence *Aristotle was a philosopher*, as we now understand it, will be true at a world w iff a certain individual—the person who was actually Aristotle—was a philosopher in w. Given that a sentence α *is F* is true at an arbitrary world w iff the denotation of α at w is in the extension of F at w, we conclude that for any arbitrary world w, *Aristotle* denotes in w the individual who was Aristotle in the actual world.

Although the wide-scope analysis accommodates GR, it characterizes Obv$_A$, and R, as false. Thus it wrongly characterizes names like *Aristotle* as nonrigid. The fact that proponents of the analysis have not always recognized this suggests that they, too, may have simply taken Obv for granted, thereby implicitly endorsing as genuine some of the pretheoretic semantic intuitions denied by the analysis.

Argument 2 The second argument against the wide-scope analysis is a simple variation of the first that does not employ any premise explicitly identifying propositions. Instead, it is based on the following scenario: Bill assertively utters the sentence *If n exists, then n is F*, where F expresses some essential (but hidden and nonobvious) property of the bearer of the name n—such as the property of originating from a certain bit of genetic material. Suppose further that the bearer of n is the unique object with the property expressed by G, that speakers associate the nonrigid description *the G* with n, and that there is no necessary connection between the properties expressed by G and F.[23] In such a case the following premises, P1 and P2, will be true, and recognized as such by the wide-scope analysis.

$$A_B (\exists n \rightarrow Fn)$$

P1. Bill asserted that if n exists, then n is F.
P2. It is a necessary truth that if n exists, then n is F.

$$\Box (\exists n \rightarrow Fn)$$

However, C, which in fact follows from P1 and P2, may wrongly be characterized as false.

C. Bill asserted a necessary truth

$$\exists p (A_B p \wedge \Box Tp)$$

This is clear when the argument is symbolized (in accord with the wide-scope analysis) as follows:[24]

P1′. Bill asserted [that : n exists $\supset$ Fn]
P2′. (the x: Gx) [$\Box$ (x exists $\supset$ Fx)]
C′. $\exists p$ [Bill asserted p and p is a necessary truth]

The key point is that, according to wide-scope analysis, P2 does not attribute necessity to that which Bill is said, in P1, to have asserted. According to the analysis, the truth of P2 requires the necessity of that which is expressed by the open formula (*x exists $\supset$ Fx*), relative to an assignment to the variable 'x' of the unique object which actually has the property expressed by G. By contrast, the truth of P1 requires Bill to have asserted that which is expressed by the sentence (*n exists ⊃ Fn*). But, according to the wide-scope analysis, that which is expressed by this sentence is not identical with that which is expressed by the formula (*x exists ⊃ Fx*), relative to any assignment of an object to 'x.'[25] Rather, it is a descriptive proposition involving the sense of the name n. Since this proposition is not necessary, C is characterized as false in a situation in which P1 and P2 are characterized as true. As a result, the analysis wrongly characterizes as invalid an argument which is in fact valid. Because of this, the interpretations of sentences provided by the analysis are incorrect.[26]

[Argument 3] The third argument against the analysis is based on examples of a slightly different type.

$$\Box\left[(A_B\langle Fn\rangle \wedge Fn) \rightarrow (A_B p \wedge Tp)\right]$$

4. Necessarily, if Bill asserts (believes) that n is F, and n is F, then Bill asserts (believes) something true.

5. Necessarily, if Bill asserts (believes) that n is F, and everything Bill asserts (believes) is true, then n is F.

$$\Box\left[A_B\langle Fn\rangle \wedge ((\forall p)A_B p \wedge Tp)\right] \rightarrow Fn$$

Although these sentences express obvious truisms, many of them are wrongly characterized as false by the wide-scope analysis.

The problem arises because different occurrences of the name n are assigned different scopes, and so end up being evaluated at different worlds. Note that in each sentence the modal operator takes the entire conditional in its scope. According to the wide-scope analysis, both occurrences of the name are replaced by occurrences of an equivalent description—*the G*.[27] Since one of these occurrences is in the content clause of a propositional attitude verb, its scope remains confined to that clause; since the other occurrence is not in the scope of any propositional attitude verb, it is assigned wide scope over the modal operator.[28]

The resulting symbolizations are the following:[29]

4′. (the x: Gx) □ [(Bill asserts/believes [that: (the y: Gy) Fy] & Fx) ⊃ ∃p [(Bill asserts/believes p) & p is true]]

5′. (the x: Gx) □ [(Bill asserts/believes [that (the y: Gy) Fy] & (p) [(Bill asserts/believes p) ⊃ p is true]) ⊃ Fx]

These examples pose two problems for the wide-scope analysis.

The first is that each asserts the existence in the actual world of a unique individual with the property expressed by G. However, it is not obvious that any such existential claim is entailed by the original English sentences. More generally, the wide-scope analysis is incompatible with the existence of meaningful proper names that (i) do not denote any individual existing in the actual world, but (ii) sometimes occur embedded under modal operators (outside the scope of propositional attitude verbs) in true sentences of English . If proper names of this sort exist in English, then the wide-scope analysis is false.[30]

The second problem posed by these symbolizations involves cases in which the description *the G* is a nonrigid designator. For example, suppose that in the actual world o is the unique individual that has the property expressed by G, and that w is a possible world satisfying the following conditions: (i) o has the property expressed by F, but not the property expressed by G, in w; (ii) in w, Bill asserts the proposition expressed by *the G is F*; (iii) Bill doesn't assert anything else (or anything else true) in w; and (iv) either there is no unique object in w having the property expressed by G, or whatever uniquely has that property in w is such that in w it does not have the property expressed by F. The existence of such a world w falsifies (4'). (5') is falsified by a world w' in which (i) Bill believes the proposition expressed by *the G is F*; (ii) all of Bill's other beliefs in w' are true in w'; (iii) there is a unique object in w' that has the property expressed by G, and, in w', that object has the property expressed by F; but (iv) in w' o does not have the property expressed by F. Since (4') and (5') are analyses that would be assigned to (4) and (5) by the wide-scope analysis, the analysis incorrectly characterizes these obvious truths of English as false.

On the basis of all these arguments, I conclude that the wide-scope analysis of proper names is incorrect.

The Analysis of Names as Rigidified Descriptions

I now turn to the other main descriptivist challenge to Kripke's modal argument. This is the view that proper names are synonymous with rigidified versions of the descriptions associated with them by speakers. On this view, names are rigid designators; hence no appeal to wide scope is needed to account for the substitutivity of codesignative names in modal constructions. However since codesignative names may be associated with different descriptive information, they are not intersubstitutable everywhere; most notably they are not intersubstitutable in propositional attitude constructions.

In assessing this view it is crucial to understand how, according to it, names are to be rigidified. There are two main alternatives in the semantic literature, only one of which is promising for the rigidification analysis. The view in question involves using the actuality operator to construct definite descriptions. Syntactically, *actually* combines with a sentence or formula to form a more complex sentence or formula. Semantically, *actually* is an indexical, like 'I,' 'now,' and 'here.' As such, its content—that which it contributes to propositions expressed by sentences containing it—varies from one context of utterance to another. For example, the sentence *I am hungry now*, used by me at time t, expresses a proposition that is true at an arbitrary world w (and time t*) iff at w Scott Soames is hungry at t; the same sentence used by Saul Kripke at t′ expresses a different proposition, one that is true at an arbitrary world (and time) iff Kripke is hungry at t′ in that world. Similarly, the sentence *Actually Kripke wrote* Naming and Necessity used by anyone in the actual world, A_w, expresses a proposition that is true at an arbitrary possible world iff in A_w Kripke wrote *Naming and Necessity*; the same sentence used by a speaker at a different world w* expresses a proposition that is true at an arbitrary world iff in w* Kripke wrote *Naming and Necessity*.

It will be apparent from this explanation that whenever S is a true sentence, *Actually S* is a necessary truth. The corresponding fact about descriptions is the following: whenever a definite description *the x: Fx* denotes an individual o in the actual world, the rigidified description *the x: actually Fx* denotes o in all possible worlds in which o exists (and never denotes anything else). This follows directly from the standard semantics of *the* and *actually*. According to the semantics of *the*, the denotation of a description *the x: Sx* at an arbitrary world w is the unique object, if any, existing at w that satisfies the open formula Sx at w.[31] Where Sx is the formula *actually Fx*, an object satisfies it at w iff in the actual world the object has the property expressed by F.

The position we are considering now claims that ordinary proper names are synonymous with rigidified descriptions of this sort. For example, it might be claimed that the name *Aristotle*, as used by a particular speaker, is synonymous with the description *the actual teacher of Alexander*, which in turn is understood as *the x: actually x taught Alexander*. Several criticisms of this view can be extracted from the existing literature. I will mention them very briefly, and then put them aside in order to focus on a new criticism.

One of these criticisms concerns the question of whether proper names (like variables relative to assignments) designate their referents even with respect to worlds (and times) at which those individuals don't exist. David Kaplan and Nathan Salmon have argued, quite persuasively, that proper names should be understood in this way.[32] The most striking examples employed in their arguments exploit the parallels between temporal and modal semantics, and involve sentences like *Plato is dead* and *Locke anticipated Kripke*. The first of these is a sentence of the form *n is F*. On the usual view, such a sentence is true at a time t iff n designates at t something that is in the extension of F at t. But then, since *Plato is dead* is true now, the name *Plato* must now designate something—and what else than the now nonexistent Plato? Kaplan and Salmon generalize this point to cover a variety of cases, including modal examples. If they are right, then proper names are not equivalent to descriptions that have been rigidified using the actuality operator—since these descriptions designate an object at a world only if the object exists at that world.[33]

A second criticism is based on Kripke's original epistemic and semantic arguments against description theories. The epistemic arguments were designed to show that typically the sorts of descriptions D associated by speakers with a name n are such that the proposition expressed by *if n exists, then n is D* is not knowable a priori, even though the proposition expressed by *if D exists, then D is D* is knowable a priori. These arguments illustrate the difficulty of identifying the contributions made by proper names to propositional attitude ascriptions with the contents of descriptions that speakers typically associate with the names. Since these arguments typically seem to hold even when D is an *actually*-rigidified description, it is difficult to find specific descriptions that allow the analysis to get off the ground.

A third point can be made regarding Kripke's original semantic arguments. For nearly all ordinary proper names, these arguments eliminate the possibility of identifying the semantic content of a name with most of the descriptions speakers typically associate with it, whether rigidified or not. In light of this, a number of theorists seem to have concluded that the only hope of avoiding the standard semantic arguments is to appeal to metalinguistic descriptions that incorporate the insights of Kripke's historical transmission theory of how reference is fixed. Thus, it has sometimes been suggested that the content-giving description associated with a name n is a description of the form *The x: actually x stands at the beginning of a historical chain of transmission of such and such type ending with this use of the name 'n.'* (Imagine *such and such type* being filled out with a correct account of the way reference is actually determined, and imagine the referent of *this use of the name 'n'* being determined by the context of utterance.) However, it seems clear that no such proposal can be correct, since descriptions of this sort do not, in general, give the contents contributed by names to propositional attitude ascriptions. If they did, then when I attributed to someone the belief that Venus is a star, I would be attributing to that person a belief about a certain one of my uses of the name *Venus*, as well as a belief about the specific sorts of historical chains that connect uses of names to their bearers. Clearly no such beliefs are being attributed to the ancient Babylonians when I say that they believed Venus was a star.

A fourth criticism that I will simply mention can be extracted from Keith Donnellan's observation that names, unlike definite descriptions (whether rigidified using the actuality operator or not), are routinely exportable from positions within the scope of propositional attitude verbs.[34] For example, if t is a name, such as *Boris*, then (6b) is entailed by (6a) (together, perhaps, with the premise *there is such a person as t*); however when t is an arbitrary description, such as *the shortest spy* or *the person who is actually the shortest spy*, there often is no such entailment.

6a.   Ralph believes that t is a spy.
6b.   There is someone x such that Ralph believes that x is a spy.

Donnellan's point may also be put by saying that if t is a name, knowledge of the proposition expressed by *t is F* is always *de re* knowledge of the referent of t that it "is F," whereas this is not generally true when t is a definite description. Consequently, no name is synonymous with any description D that fails to support exportation in the manner of (6), or that occurs in a sentence *D is F* that expresses a proposition knowledge of which need not be *de re* knowledge of the denotation of D. In making these points, Donnellan was not concerned with distin-

en rapport

guishing names from *actually*-rigidified descriptions.[35] However, since the *actually*-rigidified descriptions standardly proposed as candidates for giving the semantic content of names often fail Donnellan's tests, his observations can be taken to show that these proposals are incorrect.

Considerations like these show that there are strong reasons, independent of special assumptions about the semantics of *actually*, for doubting that names are semantically equivalent to *actually*-rigidified descriptions. I want, however, to waive these difficulties for the moment in order to concentrate on a further problem which, by itself, is sufficient to show that the contents of proper names are not given by rigidified descriptions of the form *the x: actually Fx*. The problem involves the interaction of modal and propositional-attitude constructions; it is based on the elementary observation that not only individuals in the actual world, A_w, but also inhabitants of other worlds, share many of my beliefs. For example, I, along with many others in the actual world, believe that Aristotle was a philosopher; and it is not unreasonable to suppose that we also believe of the actual world, A_w, that Aristotle was a philosopher in it—that is, we believe of the way, A_w, that the concrete universe really is (a maximally complete property the universe instantiates), that relative to it, Aristotle was a philosopher.[36] A similar point holds for a great variety of different possible worlds w. In w, I, along with others, believe that Aristotle was a philosopher; in addition, we may also believe of the world w that Aristotle was a philosopher in it—that is, we may believe that relative to that way that the universe might have been, Aristotle was a philosopher.[37] However, in w we need not have any beliefs about the actual world, A_w, which may be different in many respects from w.

This fact provides the basis for the following argument against the analysis of proper names as *actually*-rigidified descriptions.

P1. It is possible to believe that Aristotle was a philosopher without believing anything about the actual world A_w—that is, about the way the universe really is (the property it really instantiates). In particular, there are worlds w* in which agents believe that Aristotle was a philosopher, without believing of A_w that anything was F in it, and hence without believing of A_w that the unique thing that was F in it was a philosopher.

P2. Necessarily, one believes that the actual F was a philosopher iff one believes of the actual world, A_w, that the unique thing that was F in it was a philosopher.

C1. It is not the case that, necessarily, one believes that Aristotle was a philosopher iff one believes that the actual F was a philosopher.

P3. If the content of *Aristotle*, as used in a context C, were identical with the content of *the actual F*, as used in C, then (i) the contents of (propositions expressed by) *Aristotle was G* and *The actual F was G* in C would be the same; (ii) the propositions expressed by α *believes that Aristotle was G* and α *believes that the actual F was G*, in C, would be necessarily equivalent; and (iii) C1 would be false.

C2. The content of *Aristotle*, as used in a context, is not the same as the content of *the actual F* as used in that context.

Each premise in this argument is true. First consider P1. Surely it is a datum that agents could have believed that Aristotle was a philosopher even if things had been quite different from the way they in fact are. Must these agents also have had beliefs about the actual world—that is, about a certain maximally complete property the universe actually instantiates? In asking this, I am, of course, asking about the world (world-state) that I call 'actual' here and now, the world (world-state) provided by the context for my present remarks. Presumably, in some merely possible world (world-state) the agents there have no direct acquaintance, or epistemic contact, with this world (world-state) that I am now calling 'actual'; nor, in many cases, will they possess any uniquely identifying descriptions of it.[38] As a result, often there will be no way for them to form beliefs about the actual world.[39]

They may, of course, have beliefs about worlds (world-states) they call 'actual,' but that is another matter. An agent who sincerely, and assertively, utters, in a possible world w, a sentence *Actually the earth is round* expresses his belief of w that with respect to it, the earth is round. We may even decide that whenever an agent believes a proposition p, at a world w, he also believes of w that p is true with respect to it. Such a principle would explain how all of us in the actual world have beliefs about the actual world.[40] However, it does not provide a way for agents in other worlds to share those beliefs.

Next consider P2 and P3. These premises are based on the standard Kaplan-style indexical semantics for *actually*,[41] plus an account of propositional attitude ascriptions as reporting relations to the propositions expressed by their content clauses. The relevant semantic ideas are given in (7).[42]

> 7. For any possible context of utterance C, the sentence *the actual F was G* expresses in C a proposition that says of the world, C_w of C, that the unique thing that "was F" in it "was G." The proposition expressed by *Jones believes that the actual F was G*, in context C, is true when evaluated at an arbitrary world w, iff Jones believes, in w, the proposition expressed by *the actual F was G* in C. Hence, the proposition expressed by *Jones believes that the actual F was G*, in C, is true when evaluated at an arbitrary world w, iff in w, Jones believes of C_w that the unique thing that "was F" in it "was G." It follows that when the actual world, A_w, is the world of the context, the proposition expressed by *Jones believes that the actual F was G* is true at an arbitrary world w iff in w Jones believes, of A_w, that the thing that was F in it was also G.

In addition to being highly plausible in itself, (7) is something that the proponent of the view that names are *actually*-rigidified descriptions can scarcely afford to deny. His view requires that *actually* be an operator which rigidifies a description while allowing it to retain its descriptive content. This requirement dictates that the content of *the x: actually Fx*, as used in a context C, be a descriptive condition involving the property expressed by F which, when applied to an arbitrary world w, is satisfied by the unique individual in w that has the property expressed by F somewhere—not in w (unless $w = C_w$), but in the world given by C. Thus, where C_w is the world of the context C, the proposition expressed by *the actual F was G* "says" that the unique thing such that it "was F" in C_w "was G," whereas the proposition expressed by *the F was G* "says" something different—namely, that the unique thing that "was F" also "was G." Since it is possible to believe one of these propositions without believing the other, this is enough to establish C1.[43]

In justifying the move from C1 to C2, P3 and (7) embrace an account of the semantics of propositional attitude ascriptions which has the consequence that expressions with the same content in a context C can be substituted for one another in attitude ascriptions without change in the truth conditions of those ascriptions with respect to C. As before, this view is both plausible in itself and difficult for the descriptivist to deny. His view is that proper names are synonymous with, and hence have the same contents in the same contexts as, *actually*-rigidified descriptions. The main point of appealing to descriptions in the first place was to provide names with the content needed to explain their apparent contributions to attitude ascriptions. This would be lost if the descriptivist were now to deny that expressions with the same content are intersubstitutable in attitude constructions.[44] As a result, P2 and P3 should be accepted. But then, since the argument is valid, and each of the premises is true, it follows that proper names are not equivalent to descriptions rigidified using the actuality operator.[45] Hence, this version of descriptivism is false.

It is worth noting that this result is robust, and cannot be avoided by appealing to technical variants of the standard actuality operator. Consider, for example, a related operator *actually**, which is just like the operator we have been discussing, except for the fact that occurrences of *actually** can be coindexed with occurrences of standard modal operators, *necessarily* or *it is possible*, when the former occurrences fall within the scope of the latter. When *actually** occurs in a sentence without any such modal operator, the sentence . . . *actually** S . . . has the same truth conditions, and expresses the same proposition, as . . . *actually S.* . . . However, when another modal operator with which *actually** is coindexed appears, this is not so. For example, the sentence (8a) is understood as making the claim (8b), as opposed to the claim (8c) or (8d).[46]

8a.   Necessarily$_i$. . . . the x: actually$^\dagger_i$ Fx. . . .
8b.   For all worlds w, ... the x: in w Fx. . . .
8c.   Necessarily . . . . the x: actually Fx. . . .
8d.   For all worlds w . . . . the x: in A_w Fx. . . .

When premise 2 of my argument is reformulated using the coindexed *actuality** operator, rather than the usual *actuality* operator, the true premise, P2, is transformed into premise P2*, which is equivalent to P2**.

P2*. Necessarily$_i$ one believes that the actually† F was a philosopher iff one believes of the actual world, A_w, that the unique thing that was F in it was a philosopher.

P2** For all worlds w, in w one believes of w that the unique thing that is F in it was a philosopher iff in w one believes of the actual world, A_w, that the unique thing that was F in it was a philosopher.

Since P2* is false, the proponent of the view that names are synonymous with rigidified descriptions might be tempted to identify the contents of names with those of descriptions rigidified using the indexed *actuality** operator, rather than with the contents of descriptions rigidified using the more familiar, unindexed, *actuality* operator. On this modified view, the second premise of my argument fails; as a result, one cannot refute the modified view by deriving corresponding versions of the destructive conclusions C1 and C2.[47]

From the perspective of the descriptivist, the view that proper names are synonymous with *actually** rigidified descriptions has three desirable features. First, like the standard actuality operator, *actually** is a genuine rigidifier in the following sense: if *the x: Fx* is a nonrigid description that denotes o with respect to a context C and world C_w of C, then *the x: actually* Fx* is a rigid designator of o in that it denotes o with respect to C and w, for every world w in which o exists, and never denotes anything other than o. This follows from the fact that (i) the denotation of a description *the x: Sx* with respect to a context C and world w is whatever uniquely satisfies Sx with respect to C and w, and (ii) when *Sx* is *actually* Fx*, and *actually** is unindexed, its semantics are just the semantics of the standard actuality operator. Second, like descriptions rigidified using the standard actuality operator, the content of *the x: actually* Fx* includes the descriptive content of F (whether *actually** is indexed or not). Hence, if names are analyzed as synonymous with descriptions of this form, then the different descriptive contents of coreferential proper names may be used to block substitution of coreferential names in attitude ascriptions. Third, unlike belief ascriptions containing the standard actuality operator, some belief ascriptions containing *actually**—namely, those containing occurrences of the operator that are coindexed with occurrences of a modal operator the scope of which includes the entire ascription—may be true even though the believers in question have no beliefs about the actual world. Hence, if names are analyzed as synonymous with descriptions containing the *actually** operator, a sentence like (9a) can be given an interpretation (9b) in which it is equivalent to (9c), and hence is true, even though (9d) is false.

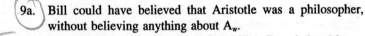

9a.   Bill could have believed that Aristotle was a philosopher, without believing anything about A_w.

9b.   It could have been the case$_i$ that Bill believed that [the x: actually$\dagger$ Fx] was a philosopher, without believing anything about A_w.

9c.   There is a possible world w such that in w, Bill believes of w that the unique thing that is F in it was a philosopher, without believing anything about A_w.

9d.   It could have been the case that Bill believed of A_w that the unique thing that is F in it was a philosopher without believing anything about A_w.

Despite these apparently attractive results, the view that names are synonymous with *actually**-rigidified descriptions is clearly incorrect. Although the view accommodates the fact that (9a) has an interpretation in which it is obviously true, it does so at the expense of assigning (10a) a corresponding interpretation in which it is equivalent to (10b) and (10c), and therefore is false.

10a.   There exists an x (Aristotle) such that necessarily one believes that Aristotle was a philosopher only if one believes something that is true iff x was a philosopher.

10b.   There exists an x (Aristotle) such that necessarily$_i$ one believes that [the x: actually$\dagger$ Fx] was a philosopher only if one believes something that is true iff x was a philosopher.

10c.   There exists an x (Aristotle) such that for all worlds w, in w the following is true: one believes of w that the unique thing that was F in it was a philosopher only if in one believes something that is true iff x was a philosopher.

Since (10a) is intuitively true, whereas (10b) and (10c) are false, the view that names are synonymous with *actually**-rigidified descriptions is incorrect. More generally, the view has the unacceptable consequence that when a belief ascription containing a name like *Aristotle* is embedded under a modal operator, the ascription is to be understood in one of two ways: Either *actually** is understood as unindexed, in which case the ascription is true at the relevant worlds only if the agents in those worlds believe certain things of the actual world A_w (and my original argument against such analyses holds), or *actually** is understood as indexed to the modal operator, in which case the ascription may be true at the relevant worlds without the beliefs in question being about one and the same individual—namely, the person who actually was Aristotle. In point of fact, the English belief ascriptions in question don't have either of these interpretations. Instead, they are understood as being true at arbitrary worlds only if the agents' beliefs in those worlds are about the individual who was Aristotle in A_w, even though the beliefs themselves are not about A_w. The view that names are synonymous with *actually**-rigidified descriptions cannot accommodate this fact. Since the same seems to be true of all versions of the view that assimilate names to descriptions rigidified using one or another kind of actuality operator, the lesson to be learned is that names are not synonymous with any descriptions of this kind.

Nevertheless, it must be admitted that there is another possible version of descriptivism that is immune both to Kripke's original modal argument and to all further arguments given here. According to this version, proper names have the same contents as descriptions rigidified using David Kaplan's *dthat*-operator.[48] This operator combines with a singular definite description D to form a singular term *dthat D*, the content of which in a context is just the denotation of D in the context. Rigidified descriptions of this sort designate their referents even in worlds in which the referents do not exist; they also may be used to express propositions that are routinely asserted and believed at alternative possible worlds by agents who have no propositional attitudes about the actual world. This is all to the good. However, the price of this success is too great for any genuine descriptivist to bear. When the *dthat*-operator is applied to a description D, it completely obliterates the descriptive content of D, and leaves the rigidified description *dthat D* with no descriptive semantic content at all. As a result, coreferential *dthat*-rigidified descriptions have the same content, and the goal of distinguishing coreferential names by associating them with different descriptive contents is thwarted.

Conclusion

This concludes my discussion of descriptivist challenges to Kripke's modal argument. If I am right, these challenges are unsuccessful. The original modal argument showed that proper names do not have the meanings (semantic contents) of ordinary nonrigid descriptions. The arguments given here show that they also do not have the meanings (semantic contents) of either wide-scope descriptions or descriptions rigidified using an actuality operator. In addition, these arguments illustrate a general lesson about the importance of paying attention not just to modality, nor just to propositional attitudes, but to the interaction of the two.

The theoretical notion linking these concerns is that of semantic content. The semantic content of a name is that which it contributes to propositions expressed by sentences containing it, relative to contexts of utterance. Since sentences inherit their modal profile (truth conditions) from the propositions they express, which in turn are the objects of assertion and belief, any positive account of the semantic content of a name (relative to a context) is responsible to both modal facts and facts about the attitudes. Looking at the modal facts alone, one can get the impression that the descriptivist's problems can be solved either by rigidifying his descriptions or by giving them wide scope over modal operators. Once the attitudes are added to the picture, it is clear that this is a misimpression. Similarly, if one looks only at Kripke's semantic arguments about how reference is fixed, one can get the impression that a descriptivist account of semantic content might be made to work by identifying the semantic content of a name (relative to a context) with a metalinguistic description based on the historical transmission theory. As before, this can be shown to be a misimpression by looking at a wider range of facts. Not only would such a view be subject to the difficulties inherent in rigidification, but it could not begin to account for the contents of ordinary assertions and beliefs expressed by sentences containing names. In short, when one looks at all the facts, the proper conclusion is that ordinary proper names typically do not have the semantic contents of descriptions.

Does this mean that no name whatsoever has the same the semantic content as any description? Not quite. Nothing we have said up to now rules out the possibility that some names might have semantic contents that are partially descriptive and partially nondescriptive. For example, consider the following possible theory.

A Partially Descriptive Theory

A partially descriptive name n is semantically associated with both a descriptive property P_D and a referent o. The referent o is determined in part by having the property P_D and in part by the same nondescriptive mechanisms that determine the reference of ordinary nondescriptive names—for instance, by a historical chain of transmission leading back to o. The semantic content of n includes both o and P_D. The proposition expressed by *n is F* is the same as that expressed by [*the x: Dx & x = y*] *Fx*, relative to an assignment of o to 'y.'[49] This proposition is true at a world w iff o has the properties expressed by D and F at w. To believe this proposition is to believe of o that it has both properties.[50]

According to this theory, the property expressed by D that is included in the semantic content of n need not uniquely pick out the object designated by n, which is determined, in part, nondescriptively—for instance, by the historical chain of transmission of the name from one speaker to another. This feature of the theory allows it to escape some of Kripke's semantic arguments against standard versions of descriptivism. However, the theory is subject to a substantial constraint that seriously limits the range of reasonable candidates for such an analysis: For any given name n and associated description D, the property expressed by D must apply to the object standing at the end of the historical chain of transmission, if there are to be any true sentences of the form *n is F*.

The modal argument further limits the range of potentially acceptable analyses. Here it is useful to consider names like *Trenton New Jersey* and *Princeton University*. Unlike the majority of proper names, these are among the comparatively few cases in which a reasonable argument can be made that understanding them involves associating them with specific and substantial descriptive contents—the property of being located in New Jersey, in the case of *Trenton New Jersey*, and the property of being a university, in the case of *Princeton University*. If this is right, then, according to the partially descriptive theory, the semantic content of the name *Trenton New Jersey* is a propositional constituent incorporating both the property of being located in New Jersey and the city Trenton, whereas the semantic content of *Princeton University* is a propositional constituent that includes both the property of being a university and the well-known institution of higher learning itself.

With this in mind, let us focus on the second of these two cases. Consider a possible world w in which Princeton is founded as a college (as it was in the actual world) but never becomes a university. Is the claim that Princeton University exists true, when taken as a description of w? If so, then *Princeton University* is rigid, and its semantic content cannot be the one ascribed to it by the partially descriptive theory. However, the rigidity intuition does not seem as robust in this case as it does with the great majority of ordinary proper names. Rather, it seems reasonable to suppose that in w there is no such thing as Princeton University, even though the thing which actually is Princeton University exists in w, while being only a college. If this is right, then (11a) may be treated as ambiguous, having one reading in which it is equivalent to the false (11b), and one reading in which it is equivalent to the true (11c).[51]

11a.   In w, Princeton University exists.
11b.   In w, [the x: x is a university and x = p] x exists.
11c.   [The x: x is a university and x = p] in w, x exists.

Similarly, *Princeton University could have existed without being Princeton University* should be ambiguous, having both a reading in which it is obviously false, and a reading in which it expresses a truth. Admittedly, the latter reading is harder to hear. However, its existence seems to be indicated by the coherence and apparent correctness of *Since Princeton University could have existed even if it had remained a college and never became a university, it (Princeton University) could have existed without being Princeton University*.[52]

If this account of the case is correct, then *Princeton University* is not, strictly speaking, a rigid designator. However, according to the partially descriptive theory, it is still namelike in two important respects. First, as with other names, it conforms to the modal principles (12a) and (12b).

> (12a) If n is a name that designates o, then n never designates any object other than o, with respect to any world.
>
> (12b) If n and m are names, and *n = m* is true, then *Necessarily if n and m exist, then n = m* is true.

Second, like other names, it conforms to the epistemic principle (13).

> (13.) If n is a name that designates an object o, then believing the proposition semantically expressed by *n is F* involves believing of o that it "is F."

Conformity to these principles is what justifies classifying partially descriptive names as names.

Is the partially descriptive theory acceptable, then, for at least some names? If so, how extensive is its range of application? We have not, as yet, said enough about semantic content to give a definitive answer to these questions. In the next two chapters I will try to remedy this defect by giving an account of semantic content and its relation to the information that speakers use sentences to assert and convey. I will argue that although speakers often use proper names to assert and convey descriptive information about the referents of those names, in the case of most (linguistically) simple proper names—such as my name, or the names of the readers of this book—there is little or no specific descriptive information that a speaker must associate with a name in order to understand it, or to be a competent user of it; hence there is little or no descriptive information that is part of the semantic content of such a name.[53]

There are, however, apparent exceptions to this rule. For example, it is plausible to suppose that the (linguistically) complex names *Princeton University* and *Trenton New Jersey* are associated with substantial descriptive information that must be grasped by any competent speaker who understands and is able to use them correctly. It is arguable that a similar point might be made about the names *Hesperus* and *Phosphorus*, as well as the name *Superman*—not as we use it to name a fictional character, but as it is used inside the fiction. Certainly, there is some plausibility in the suggestion that anyone who doesn't know

No'

that *Hesperus* is associated with the appearance of a celestial body in the evening sky and *Phosphorus* is associated with the appearance of such a body in the morning sky doesn't understand the two names. Similarly, it is not unreasonable to think that any character in the fiction

No.

who didn't know that *Superman* names someone with super powers wouldn't count as understanding the name. Because of this, it is an open question—for now—whether the partially descriptive theory fits these special names. I will return to this question in chapter 5, after I have sketched a set of principles for identifying the semantic content of a term.

3

The Meaning of Names

Two Conceptions of Meaning

In this chapter I will develop an account of the meaning of names and of simple sentences containing them. I will begin by making the simplifying assumption that ordinary proper names are unambiguous, and I will ignore any context sensitivity that may exist in simple sentences containing them. In chapter 4, I will extend the account to include these complicating factors. In this chapter, however, I will sketch the leading ideas behind what I hope will prove to be an intuitively plausible view of meaning and semantic content in as direct a form as possible.

In giving this view, I need to distinguish two different conceptions of meaning. According to the first conception, the meaning of a sentence is its semantic content. This can be thought of as that which the sentence "says," which in turn is closely related to what speakers say, and convey, when they assertively utter the sentence. The main difference between these two is that what a sentence says, the information (proposition) it semantically encodes, is invariant from context of utterance to context of utterance (provided that the sentence is unambiguous and contains no indexical expressions). As such, the constant information semantically encoded by a sentence must be carefully distinguished from the varying information it is used to convey in different contexts. If, as I will argue, an unambiguous, noncontext-sensitive sentence can sometimes be used to assert propositions that go beyond the information the sentence semantically encodes, then that information must also be distinguished from the varying information the sentence is used to assert in different contexts.

On this conception of meaning, the meaning (semantic content) of an expression is that which it contributes to the semantic content of sentences containing it. I will argue that, subject to one minor caveat, the semantic contents of many proper names, including most linguistically simple names of people and places, can be identified with their referents. In this sense of meaning, simple proper names that refer to the same thing typically have the same meaning, while names that are not coreferential have different meanings.[1]

There is also another conception of meaning. On this second conception, the meaning of an expression is information grasp of which explains speakers' ability to understand it, and to be able to use it competently. I will argue that on this conception of meaning, most simple, ordinary proper names have meaning only in an extremely minimal sense—one in which different names have nearly the same meaning, no matter what they refer to. We may express this by saying that the competence conditions associated with these names do not vary significantly from one name to another.

Although these two theses—that the semantic content of a name is its referent and that essentially the same competence conditions are associated with different names—hold for the vast majority of simple proper names, there appears to be a significant class of exceptions for which the theses do not hold. I call these "partially descriptive names," and suggest that the linguistically complex names *Princeton University*, *Trenton New Jersey*, *Princess Diana*, *Professor Saul Kripke*, and *Mr. Terry Thomas* are among them. I argue, briefly at the end of this chapter and in more detail in chapter 5, that the competence conditions associated with these names include descriptive information specific to each, and that their semantic contents should be understood as consisting of this descriptive information together with their referents. To this end I will sketch a theory of how both the referent of a partially descriptive name and the descriptive information associated with it are incorporated into the propositions semantically expressed by sentences containing the name.

The Semantic Content of a Sentence Versus the Information It Is Used to Convey

Let us begin with some general observations about semantic content, its relation to the overall subject of language use. A central fact about our use of language is that we utter sentences to convey or impart information. Some of this information is asserted by utterances of the sentence, some is conversationally implicated by Gricean implicatures, and some is communicated by virtue of special, idiosyncratic features of speakers and hearers in particular contexts. Because of this, the information carried by an assertive utterance of one and the same sentence often varies greatly from context to context. Clearly, not all of this information is part of the semantic content of the sentence. If s is a sentence that doesn't contain indexicals or other context-sensitive elements, then the semantic content of s (i.e., the proposition it semantically expresses) should consist of information that a competent speaker who assertively utters s asserts and intends to convey in any context in which s is used nonmetaphorically (without irony, sarcasm, and so on) with its normal literal meaning.

This suggests the following constraint that must be satisfied in order for a proposition to be semantically expressed by an unambiguous, noncontext-sensitive sentence:

> C. A proposition p is semantically expressed by s **only if** p is included in the information a competent speaker would assert and intend to convey by an assertive utterance of s in any normal context, in which s is used nonmetaphorically, without irony or sarcasm, and so on, with its literal meaning by conversational participants who understand s.

Three points of clarification are needed to understand this constraint. First, when I speak of information that a speaker would assert by an utterance of a sentence, I am using the notion of assertion to designate the most general and inclusive speech act of a set of closely related speech acts. As I am using the notion, **to say that s**, **to state that s**, **to claim that s**, and **to tell someone that s** are all ways of asserting that s, and hence of committing oneself to the proposition that s.[2] Constraint C tells us that only propositions asserted in this sense by utterances of s in all normal contexts qualify as candidates for being semantically expressed by s.

Second, in this discussion I am focusing on a sense of meaning, or semantic content, for sentences that corresponds to the notion of the proposition semantically expressed by a sentence, as it is used in familiar semantic theories. In so doing, I am ignoring certain potential complications. Consider, for example, the sentence *that damn McDuff got tenure*. Although I take no position on this point, some might argue that to assertively utter this sentence in an arbitrary context is both to assert that McDuff got tenure and to convey the information that one

Soames ignores emotivist implications

has a low opinion of McDuff, or that McDuff is damnable, where the information conveyed is no part of any proposition asserted by the utterance. If this view is correct, then condition C will exclude this evaluative information about McDuff, or about the speaker's attitude toward McDuff, from the semantic content of the sentence—in the sense of the proposition semantically expressed—even though this information is clearly tied to the meaning of one of the words in the sentence. If cases like this prove to be genuine, then there will be a third sense of meaning of a sentence that includes both the proposition it semantically expresses (its semantic content in the sense of C) and its conventional implicatures.[3] In my discussion I will ignore this complicating factor.

The third point of clarification involves the range of contexts involving assertive utterances of s that are contemplated in C. C tells us that the proposition semantically expressed by s is asserted by assertive utterances of s in all contexts in which s is used *nonmetaphorically (without irony, sarcasm, and so on) with its literal meaning*.... The idea is that the proposition semantically expressed by a sentence s is standardly among the things asserted by utterances of s, except in special cases in which this presumption is defeated by some obvious fact about how s is being used in the context—such as its being used metaphorically, ironically, or sarcastically. Since this list of exceptions does not purport to be exhaustive, principle C is not fully precise. Fortunately, it need not be in order to serve the purposes to which we will put it. Nevertheless, it may be useful to flag the kinds of concerns that give rise to the contemplated list of exceptions.

Consider a familiar and elementary example of irony. One utters *Sam is a fine friend* in a case in which it is obvious to all that the description *fine friend* doesn't apply to Sam, because he has behaved badly. As a result, the speaker does not assert the proposition that is semantically expressed by this sentence—the proposition that Sam (really) is a fine friend; rather, the speaker asserts something like the negation of that proposition. It is not that the sentence is used with a nonliteral, ironic meaning. On the contrary, it is used with its literal meaning, and the speaker exploits the fact that the literal meaning is obviously inappropriate to the situation in order to assert something different.

Something similar seems to be at work in at least some cases of metaphor as well. I once heard a highly opinionated, rather dogmatic, workaholic, public intellectual described as thinking of himself as "God's fountain pen." The speaker was obviously not asserting that the intellectual took himself to be a fountain pen, as would be indicated by the literal meaning of the sentence. Rather, she was exploiting the literal meaning, and relying on her hearers to recognize that she couldn't seriously intend to assert that which the sentence literally meant. Instead, she trusted them to take her to be asserting something different from, but suggested by, the proposition semantically expressed by the sentence. The suggestion was that the man, rather immodestly, took himself to be an instrument for the communication of ultimate truth, in the sense that he took his opinion on virtually any matter of public concern to be both vitally important and the last word on the subject.

Examples like these indicate that the normal presumption that the semantic content of a sentence is among the propositions asserted by an utterance of it may sometimes be defeated by Gricean conversational implicatures to the contrary—implicatures that arise from special features of the context and their relation to the sentence uttered.[4] The particular implicatures just discussed involve Grice's "Maxim of Quality," which requires one to speak the truth, and in particular not to say that which one believes to be false. Grice implicitly appeals to this maxim when he discusses a speaker A's ironic remark that someone is a "fine friend." Grice says:

> It is perfectly obvious to [the speaker] A and his audience that what A has said or has made as if to say is something he does not believe, and the audience knows that A knows that this is obvious to the audience. So, unless A's utterance is entirely pointless, A must be trying to get across some other proposition than the one he purports to be putting forward. This must be some obviously related proposition; the most obviously related proposition is the contradictory of the one he purports to be putting forward.[5]

Grice applies similar reasoning to examples involving metaphor like the one given above.

I believe that these Gricean explanations are broadly correct. However, in saying this, I want to disavow a certain suggestion that might easily be read into them. The suggestion is that the pattern of reasoning that shows p to be conversationally implicated in a given case is one that conversational participants in the situation actually go through—if not consciously, then unconsciously. I see no reason to believe this. In my view, the importance of the Gricean pattern of reasoning is that it shows how certain types of information could, in principle, rationally be extracted from utterances of specific sentences in certain types of conversational situations. The idealized model of fully rational conversational participants who explicitly work out the implicatures of utterances in a Gricean fashion plays an important role in defining and specifying the information that is implicitly contained in those utterances by virtue of the fact that the conversational goal to which they contribute is the efficient and cooperative exchange of information. When we apply this model to actual speaker-hearers, we should not think of them as explicitly appealing to Grice's maxims, or as reproducing the reasoning used in the model; rather, we should view them (i) as attempting to exchange information cooperatively and efficiently, and (ii) as succeeding at this by virtue of the fact that the information they do extract, and expect others to extract, from specific utterances conforms to the model. What psychological mechanisms are causally responsible for their ability to do this is not a matter for a priori philosophizing.[6] *Exportation to φ of Mind*

The normal presumption that the semantic content of a sentence is among the propositions asserted by an utterance of it may sometimes be defeated by Gricean conversational implicatures to the contrary. This suggests that the list of exceptions in principle C should be understood to include contexts in which it is conversationally implicated that the speaker is not intending to commit himself or herself to p. This is made explicit in the following modification of C:

> C+. A proposition p is semantically expressed by s **only if** p is included in the information a competent speaker would assert and intend to convey by an assertive utterance of s in any context c in which s is used with its literal meaning by conversational participants who understand s, provided that (i) s is not used metaphorically, ironically, or sarcastically in c, and (ii) the presumption that the speaker intends to commit himself or herself to p is not defeated by a conversational implicature to the contrary.[7]

I leave it open here whether the inclusion of the clause about conversational implicatures renders mention of metaphor, irony, and sarcasm redundant, or even whether further exclusions may, ultimately, be needed for special cases.

Subject to these qualifications, I take C+ to be an acceptable principle that is ready to be put to use. In what follows, C+ will play a role in explaining why certain descriptive propositions do not qualify as information semantically expressed by sentences containing proper names. However, there is also a more ambitious task to be faced. In the end we would like to be able not simply to exclude certain propositions as candidates for being the semantic content of a sentence, but also to identify the proposition that the sentence semantically expresses. In order to do this, we need to be able to eliminate certain propositions that satisfy C+ from further consideration.

It is tempting to think that the way to do this is simply to identify the proposition semantically expressed by s with the proposition asserted, and intended to be conveyed, by all assertive utterances of s in normal contexts involving competent speakers. The problem with this thought is that often there may be no unique proposition satisfying this condition. For example, suppose that p satisfies the condition, and that q is a distinct proposition that is a trivial, a priori, and necessary consequence of p. Then it may turn out that not only p but also q will be asserted and intended to be conveyed by utterances of s across contexts involving competent speakers. Nevertheless, it can't be that both qualify as the proposition semantically expressed by s. Thus, some further condition is needed if we are to identify a unique proposition as being the one that s semantically expresses.

With this in mind, consider the case of a conjunctive sentence, *Sam is at work and Susan is at the market*. Someone who assertively utters this sentence asserts the conjunctive proposition that Sam is at work and Susan is at the market. But surely such a person also asserts the proposition that Sam is at work. Thus both the conjunctive proposition and the initial conjunct satisfy C+. Crucially, however, there is an explanatory priority here. The reason the speaker is counted as asserting that Sam is at work is that this proposition is a trivial consequence of the conjunctive proposition the speaker asserts.

The same could be said about the sentence *Ramona opened the mail*. A person who assertively utters this sentence asserts not only the proposition that Ramona opened the mail, but also the proposition that someone did. However, as before, the reason this latter proposition is asserted is simply that it is a trivial consequence of the proposition that Ramona opened the mail, which is what the speaker means by the utterance.

Implicit
Assertions

Examples like these motivate the following strengthened version
of C+.

 SC1. A proposition p is semantically expressed by a sentence s
only if p satisfies C+, and there is no other proposition q
such that the fact that q satisfies C+ explains why p does
as well.

If SC1 is correct, then the proposition that someone opened the mail is
eliminated as a candidate for being the semantic content of *Ramona
opened the mail*, and the propositions corresponding to the individual
conjuncts are eliminated as candidates for being the semantic content
of *Sam is at work and Susan is at the market*.

If the facts about explanatory priority mentioned in SC1 are clear
and unproblematic, it may be possible to use SC1 to discriminate the
semantic contents of even such obviously equivalent sentences as *snow
is white* and *the claim that snow is white is true*. It is clear that anyone
assertively uttering *snow is white* asserts a certain proposition p about
snow—the proposition that snow is white. Since the claim that p is
true is a trivial consequence of p, it may be plausible to count the claim
that p is true as also being asserted by such an assertive utterance.
However, if this is the explanation of why the claim that p is true is
asserted in this case, then the explanatory priority of p ensures that it
satisfies the instance of SC1 involving the sentence *snow is white*,
whereas the claim that p is true does not. (Of course the situation is
just the reverse when the instance of SC1 involving the sentence *the
claim that show is white is true* is considered.)

Depending on how robust the facts of explanatory priority invoked
by SC1 are, it may be possible to strengthen the principle still further,
so as to provide a necessary and sufficient condition for a proposition
to be the semantic content of a sentence.

 SC2. A proposition p is the proposition semantically expressed
by a sentence s **if and only if** (i) p satisfies C+, and (ii) for
any other proposition q satisfying (i), the fact that p satisfies (i), explains why q does as well, and not vice versa.

There is, of course, a need to extend C+, SC1, and SC2 to cover ambiguous and context-sensitive sentences, to which I will turn in chapter 4.

For now, I want to emphasize that my aim in putting forward these principles is to give a preliminary account of the relationship between the notion of the meaning of a sentence s, the proposition it semantically expresses, on the one hand, and the information asserted and conveyed by utterances of s in normal contexts, on the other. I am **not** claiming that the notions of asserting and conveying information are conceptually prior to the semantic notions, or that they can be used to **define** the semantic notions. Principles C+, SC1, and SC2 are **not** definitions. Rather, their function is to **connect** certain semantic notions with certain pragmatic notions so that intuitions about each can be brought to bear on hypotheses about the other. The basic idea is, I think, commonsensical. The meaning of an unambiguous, noncontext-sensitive sentence, the proposition it semantically expresses, is information that would be asserted and conveyed in virtually any normal context involving competent speakers and hearers in which the sentence is used with its standard, literal meaning.

An Example Involving Names

Let us apply this idea to sentences containing names. Suppose I were to assertively utter the sentence (1) to a graduate student in the philosophy department at Princeton.[8]

1. Carl Hempel lived on Lake Lane in Princeton.

In the situation I have in mind, I expect the student to have heard the name *Carl Hempel* before; I expect the student to know that it refers to a well-known philosopher of science; I expect the student to know that I know this (and to know that I expect all this of him). In light of this, I intend my utterance to be understood by the student as committing me to the claim that the well-known philosopher of science Carl Hempel lived on Lake Lane in Princeton. I intend my utterance to convey this information, and, depending on the situation, I might even intend my utterance to assert it. In addition, I might judge it to be likely that the student knows other things about Mr. Hempel as well, for example, that he was once a member of the Vienna Circle. Hence I might judge it to be likely that my utterance would impart the further information that a former member of the Vienna Circle lived on Lake Lane in Princeton, even though this additional information might not be part of what I asserted, or committed myself to in uttering the sentence. Of course, it is clear that an utterance of (1) wouldn't assert or convey the same information to every competent speaker of English; one doesn't have to know that Carl Hempel was a philosopher at all in order to understand and be a competent user of the name. So if I uttered (1) to a boyhood friend of his, who knew him by his legal name, but lost touch with him at an early age before he went into philosophy, then my utterance would convey quite different information.

What information would be asserted and conveyed to competent speakers by assertive utterances of the sentence in all normal contexts? Surely such information would include little or no substantial descriptive information about Mr. Hempel. Many hearers would know something about his philosophy, but others would not. Some would know what he looked like at a certain age, but not everyone would. Some would have knowledge of his family background, but many would not. In short, although most speakers who had enough familiarity with the name to be able to use it could be expected to possess some substantive descriptive information about Mr. Hempel, little, if any, of this descriptive information would be common to all such users.

One might make the case that the information that Carl Hempel was a human being must be possessed by all competent users of the name. But even this is doubtful. It seems possible that a speaker might understand and competently use the name to refer to Mr. Hempel even if the speaker suffered from the misimpression that Mr. Hempel was an intelligent extraterrestrial, and as a result never intended to communicate that Mr. Hempel was a human being. If this is right, then it seems reasonable to suppose that the semantic content of (1) does not include the information that Mr. Hempel was human. Does it include the information that he was some sort of intelligent organism—as opposed to a highly sophisticated robot controlled by advanced beings from outer space? Conceivably, though it is hard to be sure. In any case, it is reasonable to suppose that the semantic content of (1) includes very little or no significant descriptive information about Mr. Hempel beyond the information that he lived on Lake Lane in Princeton. In what follows, I take no stand on whether some extremely general sortal is standardly included in the semantic content of a name.[9]

How, in light of this, should we characterize the proposition semantically expressed by (1)? It can't be a substantive descriptive proposition—since there is insufficient common descriptive information asserted and conveyed to competent speakers across contexts. What is common to all these contexts is that the property of living on Lake Lane in Princeton is ascribed to one and the same individual. The source of this ascription lies in the conditions governing what it is to be a competent user of an arbitrary proper name n.

Competence Conditions for Proper Names

In order to be a competent user of a name n of an object o, two things are required. (i) One must have acquired a referential intention that determines o as the referent of n. Two ways in which this may be done are by picking up n from others who used it as a name of o, and intending use n to refer to the same thing they did, or by being independently acquainted with o and introducing n as a name for o. (ii) One must realize that to assertively utter **n is F** is to say of the referent, o, of n that it "is F."

To say of an object o that it is F is to assert the singular, Russellian proposition that predicates F-hood of o. Hence these competence conditions guarantee that this singular proposition will be among the propositions asserted when a competent speaker assertively utters **n is F**.

Evidence that this is the right result is provided by the observations O1 and O2.

O1. If n is a proper name of an object, and Ralph is a competent speaker who assertively utters the sentence **n is F** in a normal context, then the ascription **Ralph asserted that n is F** will be true.

O2. The ascription **Ralph asserted that n is F**, together with the claim **n exists**, entails **There is an object x such that Ralph asserted that x is F**, which attributes to Ralph the assertion of a singular, Russellian proposition.

$$A_R F n \rightarrow A_R F x$$

Thus, if a competent speaker assertively utters **n is F**, then that person asserts, among other things, the singular, Russellian proposition that predicates the property expressed by F of the referent of n (provided that the referent of n exists).

This means that the singular proposition attributing to Mr. Hempel the property of having lived on Lake Lane in Princeton is asserted by utterances of (1) in all normal contexts in which speakers and hearers qualify as competent users of the relevant expressions. Hence this proposition is a prime candidate for being the proposition semantically encoded by the sentence.[10] Since there seems to be no better candidate, it is reasonable to identify the proposition semantically expressed by (1) with this singular, Russellian proposition.[11] This proposition is the semantic content of the sentence despite the fact that often what motivates one's assertive utterance of it, and what one wishes to convey, includes descriptive material that goes beyond what is semantically encoded by the sentence itself.

Next let us consider pairs of coreferential proper names. It is a fact that Carl Hempel was known to his friends and colleagues as 'Peter Hempel.' Thus, we may apply the reasoning we just went through to sentence (2).

(2.) Peter Hempel lived on Lake Lane in Princeton.

When we do this, we reach the conclusion that (2) semantically expresses the very same proposition as (1). This does not mean that utterances of the two sentences would assert and convey the same information to competent speakers in every context. In some contexts, for example, among my Princeton colleagues, they would, but in many other contexts they would not. Thus, I would choose one or the other of these two semantically equivalent sentences, depending on what I wanted to communicate to various audiences.

Now consider the identity sentence (3).

(3.) Peter Hempel was Carl Hempel.

Applying the same reasoning to this sentence, we conclude that it semantically expresses the singular proposition in which the identity relation is predicated of a pair consisting of an object and itself. However, since in this case the proposition is trivial, it is never what prompts one to assertively utter sentence (3).[12] Rather, we use (3) to convey different information in different contexts. For example, in speaking today to a new student who was introduced last September to an emeritus professor named 'Peter Hempel,' I might assertively utter (3) with the intention of conveying, and even asserting, the information that the man Peter Hempel, to whom the student had been introduced, was the famous philosopher of science Carl Hempel. Different information would be conveyed to other hearers in other contexts. But no descriptive information is asserted and conveyed in all the contexts in which (3) might be uttered.

What is common to all of these contexts is that one of the propositions asserted by the speaker's utterance of (3) is the trivial Russellian proposition that predicates the identity relation to the pair consisting of Mr. Hempel and Mr. Hempel. The assertion of this proposition in a context is typically the result of two facts. First, the speaker's primary goal in assertively uttering (3) is standardly to assert and convey something that could be explicitly expressed by a sentence of the form *the such and such, Peter Hempel, was the so and so, Carl Hempel*. But just as any assertion of a conjunction counts as an assertion of both conjuncts, so any assertion of a proposition explicitly expressed by a sentence *the such and such, n, was the so and so, m* also counts as a *de re* assertion of the pair, o_m and o_n, that the former was the latter (where o_m is the referent of m and o_n is the referent of n). When the names n and m are *Carl Hempel* and *Peter Hempel*, this, as we know, is just the assertion of the singular, Russellian proposition that predicates identity of Mr. Hempel and himself. Second, no matter what assertion the speaker is primarily trying to make, a normal speaker who assertively utters a sentence intends to assert whatever propositions are determined by the competence conditions governing the use of his words. Since in the case of (3) these conditions determine the assertion of the singular, Russellian proposition identifying Mr. Hempel with Mr. Hempel, the assertion of this proposition is something the speaker intends. Thus the proposition semantically expressed by (3), its meaning or semantic content, is this Russellian proposition, free of extra descriptive information that varies from context to context.[13]

Meaning, Semantic Content, and Speakers' Intuitions

Keeping these points in mind, let us now examine the relationship between true claims made by our semantic theory about meanings, or semantic contents, on the one hand, and speakers' judgments about meanings, or semantic contents, on the other. We may use the pairs of sentences (1, 2) and (3, 4) to illustrate this relationship.

4. Carl Hempel was Carl Hempel.

According to the view I advocate, (1) and (2), as well as (3) and (4), semantically express the same proposition—that is to say, the two members of each pair mean the same thing. Suppose now that someone were to suggest that we test this claim by consulting the semantic intuitions of competent speakers who are familiar with the expressions used in these sentences, and hence understand them. Would all, or nearly all, such speakers judge that the sentences mean the same thing?

No, they would not. Some speakers might be competent users of the names without realizing that they are coreferential. Presumably, they would not judge either pair of sentences to mean the same thing. Even among speakers who know the names to be coreferential, many might recognize that the sentences often would be used to communicate different information and, on that basis, judge the paired sentences to differ in meaning. In the case of (3) and (4) this intuition could be expected to be very robust, since the information carried by an utterance of (3) would nearly always be different from the information carried by an utterance of (4).

Many regard this as decisive evidence against the semantic claims I have been making. I do not. The claim that a sentence s semantically expresses a proposition p is, roughly speaking, a claim about the common informational content asserted and conveyed by utterances of s in different normal contexts. When ordinary speakers are asked what sentences mean, often they do not address themselves to the question of what information is **invariantly** asserted and conveyed across contexts involving competent speakers. Instead, they focus on what they would typically use the sentences to convey, or what information they would typically gather from assertive utterances of them. Similarly, when asked whether two sentences mean the same thing, often they do not ask whether the information **invariantly** asserted and conveyed across normal contexts by one of the sentences is the same as the information **invariantly** asserted and conveyed across normal contexts by the other. Instead, they focus on whether there are contexts in which they would use the sentences to assert or convey different information, or contexts in which different information would be imparted to them by utterances of the two sentences. Thus it is not surprising that the answers that speakers give to certain semantic queries differ from those provided by a correct semantic theory.

I believe that one reason why many semantic theorists are reluctant to accept this conclusion is that they are wedded to a faulty conception of what it is to understand a sentence, and of how propositions that are not semantically expressed by a sentence end up being communicated by an utterance of the sentence in a context.[14] The defective story goes something like this: A hearer who understands a sentence s that has been assertively uttered immediately computes what s means, and thereby becomes directly acquainted with its semantic content—the proposition it semantically expresses. This is the proposition asserted in the context. The hearer then combines this proposition with several other propositions—with auxiliary propositions presupposed as part of the common background information in the context, with general conversational maxims about the cooperative exchange of information, and with hypotheses about what the speaker might have been trying to get across. The hearer infers from all of this a variety of further propositions that are pragmatically implicated by the utterance. The sum total of the proposition that is both asserted and semantically expressed by the sentence, plus the implicatures generated by this inferential process, constitute the information carried by the speaker's utterance.

I have three main objections to this story. First, its talk of computing the meaning, or semantic content, of a sentence one has heard uttered is, I suspect, often empty. In many cases it is not clear that there is such a computation in any significant sense. Rather, a person hears an utterance of a sentence s; the person combines s with other sentences that express obvious background information in the context, and immediately infers (comes to accept) $s_1, \ldots, s_n$. The propositions expressed by these sentences constitute the information the utterance provides the hearer. Some of these propositions may even count as asserted by the speaker. On this picture, it is possible for two sentences to have the same semantic content, despite the fact that assertive utterances of them in a given context would give rise to different inferences—different sequences $s_1, \ldots, s_n$. It may even turn out that such utterances result in different assertions.[15]

This leads to my second objection. The account of communication to which I object assumes that the semantic content of the sentence uttered, exhausts that which the speaker says (asserts) in the context. In the next section, I will argue that a single assertive utterance may result in more than one assertion, and the totality of what is asserted often includes nonsemantic information.

Finally, the defective account of communication mistakenly accords the grasp of propositions semantically expressed by sentences a privileged place in the individual psychologies of language users. A language user who hears a sentence uttered in conversation is faced with the task of extracting information from it that the speaker wishes to convey. Although there are good reasons for theorists to abstract a common element from the information conveyed to competent language users by utterances of the sentence in all normal contexts, and to treat this information as the proposition semantically expressed by the sentence, there is no obvious practical reason why an ordinary hearer must always separate out this semantic information and treat it in a special way. A competent speaker/hearer who is familiar with a particular proper name or natural kind term can typically be expected to associate it with a substantial amount of descriptive material in the form of pictures, images, stereotypes, descriptions, and so on. Because of this, the totality of information the language user associates with sentences containing the name or natural kind term will vastly outstrip what the theorist recognizes as the semantic content of the sentence.

What is required for communication is **not** that language users have internalized some semantic theory that allows them to distinguish one of the many pieces of information carried by an utterance as the proposition semantically expressed by the sentence uttered. Rather, what communication requires is (i) that there be substantial uniformity among speakers and hearers regarding the salient information extracted from utterances in various contexts, and (ii) that among the pieces of information carried by an utterance in an arbitrary context is the proposition that the sentence semantically expresses. From this perspective, the meaning of a sentence is an abstraction from the information that is asserted and conveyed by utterances of the sentence in different normal contexts; it is not something that individual speakers need to separate out and identify in order to causally generate the conveyed information in the first place.[16]

If what I am saying is correct, then we ought to give up the assumption that individual speakers have internalized semantic theories that provide them with the means of identifying the propositions semantically expressed by sentences and distinguishing them from other propositions the sentence may be used to assert or convey. Having done this, we have no reason to expect that whenever two sentences semantically express the same proposition, competent speakers who under-

stand the sentences will recognize that they express the same proposition, and thus mean the same thing. There are many examples in the
literature, involving not just proper names and natural kind terms, but
expressions of all different sorts, which show that it is quite possible
for a competent speaker to understand a pair of sentences that mean
the same thing without realizing that they do.[17]

The mistaken idea that this is not possible is very much like Russell's old idea that if two expressions that function logically as names
both refer to the same thing, then it is impossible for anyone who
understands them not to realize that they are coreferential. In both cases
the error lies in thinking that what something means is fully transparent
to a person who understands it, so that such a person cannot in any
significant way be ignorant or mistaken about it. The cure for this error
is to recognize that semantic claims about the expressions of a language
are not claims about the individual psychologies, or states of mind, of
language users; rather, they are social claims about the conventions and
commonalities found in a linguistic community.

The claim that the semantic content of a name is its referent is
often expressed by saying that the meaning of a name is its referent. In
this sense of 'meaning,' linguistically simple coreferential names have
the same meaning, even though competent users of such names may
fail to recognize that they do. One reason that this may initially sound
strange involves a potential confusion implicit in much of our pretheoretic talk about meaning. Sometimes when we talk about the meaning
of an expression, we have in mind that which the expression contributes to the information semantically encoded by sentences containing
it—the information asserted and conveyed by assertive utterances of
the sentence across different normal contexts of utterance. This is the
sense in which the meaning of a typical proper name is its referent. I
have tried to explain how it is that coreferential names can have the
same meaning in this sense even if competent users of the name often
do not realize that they do.

However, other times when we talk about the meaning of an expression, we have in mind some information about the expression
knowledge of which is responsible for our coming to understand it.
Here it is important to realize that in this sense of meaning, individual
names have meanings only in a very attenuated way. As indicated earlier, the competence conditions for most ordinary names are essentially
the same. A speaker is a competent user of a name n for an object o

iff (i) the speaker has acquired a referential intention that (somehow) determines o as referent of n[18] and (ii) the speaker knows that assertively uttering *n is F* involves saying of the referent of n, that it "is F." Knowledge of this very general sort, together with exposure to particular names and the formation of particular referential intentions, is what explains our linguistic competence with the vast majority of the linguistically simple names that we are competent to use.[19] Given this, one can easily see how a speaker can fully satisfy the competence conditions for two different names that refer to the same thing, and have the same semantic content, without realizing that they do.

Information: Asserted, Conveyed, and Imparted

Up to now, I have relied on an intuitive understanding of what it is for an utterance to convey information, and what it is for information to be asserted. It is time to say a word about what these notions have in common, and how they differ. I take it that they do differ, since I assume that it is possible for a speaker to assertively utter a sentence with the intention of conveying p, even though the speaker's utterance is not (and is not intended to be) an assertion of p. Instead, the speaker may intend merely to imply, suggest, or implicate p. By contrast, a speaker who asserts p thereby intends to convey p, in the sense that I am using these terms (except perhaps in unusual situations in which the speaker is seriously mistaken about what he is asserting, and so does not realize that he is asserting p). Thus, the information asserted by an utterance is standardly a part of the information that the speaker intends to convey by the utterance. In both cases—that of asserting p and that of merely intending to convey p—the speaker undertakes a commitment to p, in the sense of endorsing p as something to be accepted by members of the conversation, of being responsible to defend p, and of being accountable if p turns out to be false.

It may seem that in speaking of the information a speaker asserts or intends to convey, I always have in mind a situation in which the speaker believes some proposition p and assertively utters a sentence in the hope of getting the other conversational participants to share this belief. I do not. There certainly are many situations that fit this pattern, but there are also situations that do not. For example, sometimes (as when answering a question in an oral examination) one asserts and intends to convey a proposition p even though one hopes that one's hearers (the examiners) already believe p.[20] On other occasions (for example, in the midst of a heated debate) one may assert p even though one is pretty sure that one's audience is not prepared to accept p. As Paul Grice has noted, even in these cases the speaker standardly intends that the other conversational participants should come to believe, on the basis of the speaker's remark, that the speaker believes p.[21]

However, there also seem to be cases in which this condition is not met. Grice himself gives an example in which a mother tries to get her son to confess (assert) that he performed a certain action, when the mother already believes that he committed the action, believes that he believes that he committed the action, and is known by the child to have these beliefs.[22] Another example in which the condition is not met is provided by a presidential press secretary who asserts p even though he knows that it is clear to everyone that he doesn't believe what he is saying. Even in these cases, however, the speaker commits himself to p, in the sense of endorsing p as something to be accepted by members of the conversation; of being responsible to defend p; and of being accountable if p is shown to be false. Intending to undertake such a commitment is a necessary condition for intending to convey p, and hence for asserting p, in the senses of these expressions that I have in mind.

Assertively uttering a sentence with the intention to assert or convey p involves doing so with the intention of committing oneself to p. Typically, but not always, this involves getting one's audience to come to believe, on the basis of one's remark, that one believes p. This, in turn, will often provide one's hearers with a reason to believe p themselves, and normally the speaker intends that this should be so. However, even in those special cases in which this latter intention is absent, I will characterize the speaker as asserting, or intending to convey, p.

We next need to look more closely at the relationship between semantic content, asserted information, and conveyed information. There is, I think, a widespread presumption that if a sentence s is assertively uttered in a normal context c, then the proposition asserted by such an utterance is simply the semantic content of s in c. In addition, it is sometimes assumed that although an utterance may convey various kinds of information, what it asserts is typically the information that the speaker is most concerned to communicate and that the audience is most interested in. This naive view of the relationship between assertion, semantic content, and conveyed information is expressed by N.

N. If s is a sentence, p is the semantic content of s (in a context c), and s is assertively uttered (in c) with its normal literal meaning (without metaphor, irony, sarcasm, or defeating conversational implicatures), then p both exhausts that which is asserted by such an utterance and constitutes the information that the speaker is primarily interested in conveying.

I will first present some hypothetical scenarios that show that N is false. After that, I will look more closely at why N fails, and what this shows about the relationship between semantic content, information that is asserted, and information that is merely conveyed.

The Introduction

I meet a stranger (who has never heard of me and of whom I have never heard) for the first time, and I introduce myself. I say, "I am Scott Soames." In so doing, I convey the information that my name is 'Scott Soames.' Although this is not the semantic content of the sentence I utter, it is the information that I was primarily interested in conveying. (The stranger might even have asked "What is your name?," but this is not necessary.) Moreover, I am successful in conveying this information, as is evidenced by the fact that later, in reporting the conversation to a third party, the stranger says, "He **told me** [said] that his name was 'Scott Soames.'"

The Emergency

I am in an auditorium, attending a lecture. Two university officials enter the room, interrupt the lecturer, and announce, "There is an emergency. We are looking for Scott Soames. Is Professor Soames here?" I stand up, saying, as I do, "I am Scott Soames." My intention in saying this is to communicate the information that I am the person they are looking for. Although this is not the semantic content of the sentence I uttered, they immediately grasp this, and the three of us leave the auditorium. Later, another member of the audience reports what happened to a third party. He says: "Two university officials interrupted the lecture and announced that they were looking for Scott Soames. Professor Soames **said** [told them] that he was the person they were looking for, and the three of them left."[23]

The Party

The scene is the Princeton philosophy department's party held at the beginning of the academic year to introduce new people to one another, and to regular members of the Princeton community. Among the guests is Peter Hempel. At a certain point Paul Benacerraf gestures in Mr. Hempel's direction and asks one of our new graduate students, Mary, "Have you been introduced to Peter Hempel?" Mary says that she hasn't, and the following conversations ensues:

> Mary: "Who is Peter Hempel?"
> Paul: "Peter Hempel is Carl Hempel."
> Mary: "You mean the famous philosopher of science?"
> Paul: "Yes."
> Mary: "Why do you call him 'Peter' instead of 'Carl'?"
> Paul: "His friends and colleagues call him that."

Paul's primary intention in assertively uttering *Peter Hempel is Carl Hempel* is to convey the information that the man Peter Hempel who is standing over there is the famous philosopher of science Carl Hempel. Paul succeeds in doing this despite the fact that this information is not the semantic content of the sentence he assertively uttered. The reason he succeeds is that he has good reason to assume (i) that Mary has in the past encountered the name *Carl Hempel*, and has come to associate it with the property of being a famous philosopher of science; (ii) that Mary can see that he (Paul) is gesturing at a man standing over there and referring to him as *Peter Hempel*; (iii) that Mary knows that he (Paul) is assuming these things; and (iv) that she knows that he (Paul) knows that she can see all this. Having acquired the information conveyed by Paul, Mary later reports the conversation to another new student by saying, "Paul **said** [told me] that the man, Peter Hempel, standing over there is the famous philosopher of science Carl Hempel."

In each of these examples, a sentence is assertively uttered with the primary intention of conveying information that goes well beyond its semantic content in the context. In each case, the speaker relies on his audience to interpret his utterance in light of certain obvious facts or assumptions in the conversation. In the first case, I assume that my hearer will recognize the obvious fact that in saying "I am Scott Soames," I am using my name to refer to myself, and hence will conclude that my name is 'Scott Soames,' and that I intend to communicate this. In the second case, I assume that my hearers will combine my utterance with the immediately preceding announcement of the university officials, and thereby conclude that I am the person they are looking for (and that I realize and intend to communicate this). In the third case, the speaker, Paul, relies both on what is perceptually obvious and on reasonable assumptions about what his audience already knows to support the inference to what he is trying to convey.

These cases show that N is false—the information a speaker primarily intends to convey by an utterance often exceeds the semantic content of the sentence uttered in the context. In fact, these cases suggest something stronger: in each case the speaker is described as saying something that goes well beyond the semantic content of the sentence uttered. In "The Introduction," the stranger describes me as having **told him** that my name is 'Scott Soames.' In "The Emergency," a member of the audience describes me as having **said** that I am the person they are looking for. In "The Party," Mary describes Paul as having **said** that the man Peter Hempel, standing in a certain place, is the famous philosopher of science Carl Hempel. Since to say, or to tell someone, that so and so is to assert that so and so (in the sense that I am using that term), these scenarios contain attitude ascriptions—(5), (6), and (7)—that characterize speakers as having asserted propositions that go substantially beyond the semantic contents of the sentences they uttered.

5. He told me that his name was 'Scott Soames' (said by the stranger in "The Introduction").
6. Professor Soames said he was the person they were looking for (said by a member of the audience in "The Emergency").
7. Paul said that the man Peter Hempel, standing over there, is the famous philosopher of science Carl Hempel (said by Mary in "The Party").

These attitude ascriptions sound natural and appropriate in the scenarios sketched above; they are just the sorts of things that speakers are inclined to say in ordinary conversations. There are two possible explanations for this. The first, and simplest, explanation is that the ascriptions in these scenarios are natural and appropriate because they truly describe what the agents (me in the first two cases, and Paul in the third) have said. The second possible explanation disputes this. It claims that the attitude ascriptions are, strictly speaking, false, and hence that those who assertively utter them in the scenarios say something false. Nevertheless, the explanation continues, these falsehoods are unimportant to (and perhaps not even noticed by) them, because their primary intentions are to use (5), (6), and (7) to convey certain truths. In "The Introduction" the stranger assertively utters the literally false (5) to convey the true proposition that I conveyed the information that my name is 'Scott Soames'; in "The Emergency," the member of the audience assertively utters the literally false (6) to convey the true proposition that I conveyed the information that I was the person they were looking for; in "The Party," Mary assertively utters the literally false (7) to convey the true proposition that Paul conveyed the information that the man Peter Hempel, standing over there, is the famous philosopher of science Carl Hempel.

In short, the second possible explanation preserves a close connection between the semantic content of a sentence in a context and the proposition asserted by an utterance of it in that context; but it does this at the cost of diminishing the significance of what is asserted for ordinary communication, and of delivering results about the truth-value of assertion ascriptions that conflict with ordinary intuitions. By contrast, the first possible explanation allows for a looser relationship between the semantic content of a sentence in a context, on the one hand, and (the totality of) what is asserted by an utterance of a sentence in the context, on the other. Doing this allows it to respect the ordinary intuition that those who assertively utter (5), (6), or (7) in the hypothetical scenarios are not guilty of saying anything false.

This seems to me to be a virtue of the first explanation. In the absence of any independent, compelling motivation for preferring the second account, it ought to settle the matter. This position is strengthened by the fact that the point illustrated by (5)–(7) is an extremely general one that has nothing special to do with proper names, indexicals, or any of the semantically contentious issues that are of special concern here. On the contrary, the phenomenon of asserting more than

the semantic content of the sentence one utters in a context is all but
ubiquitous. The following four scenarios illustrate this.

Coffee, Please

A man goes into a coffee shop and sits at the counter. The waitress
asks him what he wants. He says, "I would like coffee, please."
The sentence uttered is unspecific in several respects—its semantic
content does not indicate whether the coffee is to be in form of
beans, grounds, or liquid, nor does it indicate whether the amount
in question is a drop, a cup, a gallon, a sack, or a barrel. Nevertheless, it is obvious from the situation what the man has in mind,
and the waitress is in no doubt about what to do. She brings him
a cup of freshly brewed coffee. If asked to describe the transaction,
she might well say, "He ordered a cup of coffee" or "He said he
wanted a cup of coffee," meaning, of course, the brewed, drinkable
kind. In so doing, she would, quite correctly, be reporting the content of the man's order, or assertion, as going beyond the semantic
content of the sentence he uttered.

Smoking and Drinking

Interviewing for the position of butler in the home of a wealthy,
conservative family, Jeeves is asked whether he has any personal
habits or idiosyncrasies that might be offensive to the family. He
answers, "Well, I enjoy a cigarette after breakfast every morning,
and a brandy before retiring in the evening." What he means, of
course, is that he enjoys **smoking** a cigarette and **drinking** a glass
of brandy. That is what he says, and is taken to say, despite the
fact that the semantic content of the sentence he utters (its meaning
in the language) is unspecific regarding the precise manner in
which he enjoys the cigarette or brandy. Surely it is possible to
enjoy these things in other ways, and if the context were different
enough from the usual ones, the same sentence could be assertively
uttered, with its normal literal meaning, without indicating smoking or drinking at all. Thus, Jeeves's assertion about smoking ciga-
rettes and drinking brandy is another instance in which what is
asserted substantially exceeds the semantic content of the sentence
uttered.

The President and the Intern

Bill is talking with Monica. He says, "You should sign a statement asserting p," where it is obvious to both of them that p is false, that each knows p to be false, and that Bill's motive is to conceal certain facts that neither of them wants others to know. In light of this, it is correct to describe Bill as having told Monica to lie, or as having said that she should lie. These attitude ascriptions are true, despite the fact that no assertive utterance of Bill's was such that the sentence uttered had the semantic content in the context that Monica should lie.

The Terrorist

A terrorist has planted a small nuclear device in a crowded stadium downtown. There is no time to evacuate the building or the surrounding area. In speaking to the negotiator, he says, "I will detonate the bomb if my demands are not met," knowing that it is obvious that if he does so, thousands of people will die, and intending to communicate precisely that. The negotiator reports to his superior that the terrorist said that he will kill thousands of people if his demands are not met. This report seems correct.

Like the earlier scenarios, these examples illustrate that what an assertive utterance of a sentence s counts as asserting depends not only on the semantic content of s, but also on the obvious background assumptions in the conversation and the speaker's intentions about how the speaker's remark is to be interpreted in light of them. The end result is that someone who assertively utters a sentence often succeeds in asserting more than the proposition semantically expressed by the sentence in the context.[24]

Having appreciated this point, one must be careful not to exaggerate it. In order for p to be asserted by an utterance of a sentence, it is not enough that conversational participants be in possession of information which, together with the speaker's utterance, might, after long or careful consideration, support an inference to p. Rather, the speaker must have reason to believe both that p is a potentially direct, immediate, and relevant inference for all conversational participants, and that the conversational participants recognize this belief of the speaker.[25]

The speaker must know and intend that his hearers will take him to be committed to p on the basis of his assertive utterance, and the speaker must know and intend that the hearers are in a position to recognize this intention of the speaker. Typically this means that p must be something the relevance of which to the conversation is potentially obvious to all.

For example, suppose I were to assertively utter (8), with the intention of communicating information about David Lewis in a conversation with my Princeton colleagues in which we had been talking about various members of our department.

8.   There is an article about David in the *New York Times*.

If my hearers were to accept the remark as true, then they would be in a position to draw many conclusions of the form

9.   There is an article about D in the *New York Times*.

on the basis of the fact that there are a many descriptions D that they know apply to David Lewis. Any of these conclusions might reasonably be included in the information that my utterance of (8) provides them. However, not all of these conclusions are included in the information asserted by my utterance.

A reasonable candidate for what I asserted in this case is (10a).

10a.   There is an article about our colleague David Lewis in the *New York Times*.

There are several reasons why it is plausible to think that (10a) might qualify as being asserted, whereas various other, more detailed, examples of the form (9) do not. For one thing, the background fact appealed to in inferring (10a)—namely, the fact that David is our colleague—is something my audience and I are certain of, and that each knows the others are certain of. In addition, this fact is both significant to us and relevant to the conversation at hand. (Remember, we had been talking about various members of the department.) Partly for these reasons, I would expect this fact to be readily accessible to my audience when thinking about David. In particular, I would expect it to be among the first things to come to mind if my audience were to reflect on who I am talking about in an attempt to understand what I said. Thus, when I assertively utter (8) to my colleagues, I would expect them to be able to resolve any doubt they might have regarding whom I am talking about by reasoning as follows: "Which person named 'David' is Scott talking about? It must be someone we all know, whose appearance in the *New York Times* would be both relevant to the conversation and of interest to us, and whom Scott expects us to be able to identify without further help. Our colleague David Lewis is the obvious choice. So Scott must be saying that there is an article about our colleague David Lewis in the *New York Times*."[26]

In light of this, the proposition expressed by (10a) is a good candidate for what is asserted by my utterance of (8) in the context imagined, even though many related propositions that might come be judged to be true by the conversational participants on the basis of my remark are not. Still, it might be objected, (10a) may not be the only good candidate for what is asserted in the context. One can imagine filling out the story of my conversation in such a way that for each of the propositions in (10a–g) a good case could be made that it was asserted.

10b. There is an article about our friend David Lewis in the *New York Times*.

10c. There is an article about the philosopher David Lewis in the *New York Times*.

10d. There is an article about our friend and colleague David Lewis in the *New York Times*.

10e. There is an article about our colleague, the philosopher David Lewis, in the *New York Times*.

10f. There is an article about our friend, the philosopher David Lewis, in the *New York Times*.

10g. There is an article about our colleague and friend, the philosopher David Lewis, in the *New York Times*.

In the scenario imagined, it is not as though one of these richer propositions (or sentences) (10a)–(10g) must have flashed before my mind as I was assertively uttering (8). Nothing like that need have happened. Instead, we may suppose that all I was aware of were the words I was saying, which, somehow, I understood to be about a particular individual of my acquaintance, David Lewis. The facts that David is a philosopher, that he is our colleague, and that he is our friend were not things I consciously considered, or explicitly focused on, though they certainly were things I assumed, and knew to be both relevant to the conversation and obvious to us all. Because of this, each of the inferences from (8) to one of the propositions in (10) might well seem to qualify as potentially direct, obvious, relevant, and more or less immediately available to all the conversational participants; and each of the propositions in (10) might seem to be something that I could take my audience to be in a position to recognize me as being committed to on the basis of my remark.

Does that mean that my assertive utterance of (8) resulted in the assertion of each of the propositions in (10)? Perhaps. But there is also another way of viewing the matter. On this alternative view, it is determinate (i.e., there is a definite fact of the matter) that in assertively uttering (8), I asserted the singular proposition, p, that it semantically expresses; it is also determinate (i.e., there is a definite fact of the matter) that I asserted more than p; but it is indeterminate (i.e., there is no definite fact of the matter) precisely which propositions other than p I did assert. There are two main ideas behind this view: (a) often when one assertively utters a sentence *n is F*, one asserts more than simply the proposition that predicates the property expressed by F of the referent of n (i.e., the proposition the sentence semantically expresses); (b) in many of these cases there seems to be no uniquely correct way of specifying precisely what extra (descriptive) content gets into one's assertion. The chief advantage of viewing this extra assertive content as being to some degree indeterminate is that it gives full weight to both of these highly plausible ideas.[27]

It is important to realize that not all examples need to be treated in the same way. Let us restrict ourselves to cases in which the speaker assertively utters *n is F*, it is determinate that the speaker asserts the proposition p it semantically expresses, and either it is determinate that the speaker also asserts something more or it is indeterminate whether or not he does, where this something more involves descriptive content that goes beyond that of p (and involves propositions that are not necessary consequences of p). There are three subtypes of this sort of case that are worth considering:[28]

(i)   Cases in which the something more that is asserted is fully determinate—that is, cases in which there are (descriptively enriched) propositions $q_1, \ldots q_n$ (which are not necessary consequences of p), such that it is determinate that the speaker's utterance is an assertion of each q_i, and for all other relevant propositions z, it is determinate that the speaker's utterance is not an assertion of z. (Relevant propositions are those that are distinct from $q_1, \ldots, q_n$, and also not necessary consequences of p.)

(ii) Cases in which the something more that is asserted is partially determinate and partially indeterminate—that is, cases in which there are (descriptively enriched) propositions $q_1, \ldots q_n$ (which are not necessary consequences of p), such that it is determinate that the speaker's utterance is an assertion of each q_i, and there are other (descriptively enriched) propositions $q_1^{\dagger}, \ldots q_n^{*}$ (also not necessary consequences of p), such that for each $q_i^{\dagger}$ it is indeterminate whether or not the speaker's utterance is an assertion of it.

(iii) Cases in which the something more that is asserted is wholly indeterminate—that is, cases in which there are (descriptively enriched) propositions $q_1^{\dagger}, \ldots q_n^{*}$ (which are not necessary consequences of p), such that for each $q_i^{\dagger}$ it is indeterminate whether or not the speaker's utterance is an assertion of it, and for all other (descriptively enriched) propositions z, it is determinate that the speaker's utterance is not an assertion of z.

Although each of these types may well exist in real life, I suspect that type (ii)—where the extra asserted information is partially determinate and partially indeterminate—is the most common form. Up to now I have ignored the complications introduced by full or partial indeterminacy in my discussion of particular examples. I will continue to adopt this simplifying perspective except when the philosophical issues under discussion dictate otherwise. The reader should bear in mind, however, that when the model I am constructing is applied to real-life cases, substantial doses of indeterminacy should be expected.

With all of this in mind, we may return to my original example of an assertive utterance of

1. Carl Hempel lived on Lake Lane in Princeton.

to a graduate student in the philosophy department. In this case we may imagine that I assertively utter the sentence with the intention of asserting (perhaps among other things) that the well-known philosopher of science Carl Hempel lived on Lake Lane in Princeton. In addition to this, I may judge it to be likely that my audience will gain further information from my utterance—for example, information that a former member of the Vienna Circle lived on Lake Lane in Princeton. That is, I may expect the student to whom I am speaking to be in a position to draw this conclusion from my remark together with other things he already knows. However, I do not take myself to have asserted this, or even to be committed to defending it. The reason I don't, is that my hearer in the context has little reason to think that I expect him to know that Mr. Hempel was a member of the Vienna Circle, or to draw the relevant inference. Thus, even if I judge it to be likely that the student will conclude from my utterance that a former member of the Vienna Circle lived on Lake Lane in Princeton, this is not information I intend to convey by my utterance, in the sense in which I use that term here. It is information that I may hope will be imparted by my utterance, but it is not something that my utterance commits me to.

Finally, I should say a word about the difference between what is asserted by an utterance and what is merely conveyed, or implied. In both cases the speaker commits himself to a proposition. However, the nature of the commitment is different. I will not try to define this difference by providing necessary and sufficient conditions for drawing the distinction. Instead, I will illustrate the distinction by indicating some ways in which one might convey p without asserting p. The following examples illustrate different ways in which a speaker may imply p without asserting p.

Example 1

A and B are discussing the veracity of a story provided them by C. A asks, "Can we trust C on this?" B replies, "He has lied to us before." In assertively uttering this sentence B is not (or need not be) saying that they can't trust C to be telling the truth in this case. However, he is implying this. B does so by asserting something— that C lied before—the truth of which provides a substantial reason to believe that C can't be trusted now. B may or may not regard this as definitely establishing that C can't be trusted now, but B is suggesting that this claim is true, and to that extent B is committed to it. In this case, the commitment to that which B implies is weaker than B's commitment to what he asserted.

Example 2

Mary says that she is a member of an otherwise all male group of adults, and that some member of the group is a barber who shaves all and only those men in the group who don't shave themselves. She does not say that she is the barber, but what she says (together with the obvious background assumptions that she is a woman and that every adult in the group is either a man or a woman, but not both) entails this proposition. Because of this, it would be correct to describe **Mary** as implying this, provided that she recognizes the entailment and intends at least some in her audience to be able to work it out. Here, the proposition p that she implies is not asserted because the inference from her utterance to p is not immediate or obvious enough for her audience. However, it is something that she recognizes herself to be committed to, since she recognizes that its truth is required by what she did say, and expects at least some of her audience to be able to see this.

Example 3 (Gricean Conversational Implicature)

A is standing by his car on the side of the road. He tells B that he is out of gas. B says, "There is a gas station around the next corner." In so doing, B implies (implicates) that he knows, or has good reason to believe, that the station is open and that A can buy gas there. If that were not so, B's comment would not be relevant or responsive to A's obvious interest in the conversation. Thus, the presumption that B is being cooperative supports an inference to the claim that B has good reason to believe that there is a gas station around the corner that is open, and that A can buy gas there. However, this claim about himself is not something that B says or asserts. Of course, one might describe B as having implied that there is a gas station around the corner that is open, and that A can buy gas there. He does imply this proposition, in the sense of committing himself to the claim that it is at least likely to be true. However, as was the case in example 1, this commitment to what he implies (or suggests) is weaker than B's commitment to what he asserted.[29]

As these examples illustrate, even an expansive conception of what is said (asserted) by an utterance—of the sort I advocate—is compatible with the usual distinction between what is said by a speaker and what the speaker merely implies, suggests, or implicates. When speaking of the information carried by an assertive utterance of a sentence in a context, one must distinguish (i) the semantic content of the sentence uttered in the context; (ii) what the speaker says (asserts) by uttering the sentence; (iii) what the speaker implies, implicates, or suggests; (iv) what the speaker hopes or intends his utterance to impart to his audience; and (v) what the audience does acquire from the utterance. In this section, I have argued that (i) is standardly included in (ii), but that in the case of many utterances, (ii) is not exhausted by (i). In the case of ordinary, linguistically simple proper names, I have argued that although their semantic contents are their referents, speakers and hearers associate these names with varying descriptive information in different contexts, and this descriptive information is often included in the information of types (ii) (v) carried by utterances of sentences containing the names.

If this is right, then an austere, nondescriptive account of the semantics of many ordinary proper names is fully compatible with the recognition that these names may carry substantial descriptive information in different contexts. That is not all. From the perspective developed here, it seems plausible that the driving force behind descriptive accounts of the meanings (semantic contents) of such names is precisely the failure to distinguish the different types of information that an utterance may carry. I hope that drawing the necessary distinctions will help dissipate that force. Having said this, I should add that the goal is not the destruction of descriptivism; there are too many genuine descriptivist insights about our use of language in general, and names in particular, for that. Rather, the goal is to do justice to those insights by freeing them from confused conceptions about semantic content, and replacing those confusions with a clearer, more austere, nondescriptive conception of the semantic content of a name.[30]

Partially Descriptive Names

At the end of chapter 2 we considered the possibility that certain special names, such as *Princeton University*, *Princeton New Jersey*, and *Trenton New Jersey* might have semantic contents that include not just their referents but also substantial descriptive information.[31] The account of semantic content just sketched leaves room for partially descriptive names, and these particular names seem to be reasonable candidates for this status. For example, it would seem that part of what it is to understand and be a competent user of the name *Princeton University* is to realize that its referent is a university. If this is right, then normal (nonmetaphorical, nonironic, nonsarcastic), assertive utterances of **Princeton University is F** in contexts involving competent speakers and hearers who understand the name can be expected to result in assertions the content of which includes the information that the institution in question is a university (provided there are no defeating conversational implicatures to the contrary).[32] This is reflected in the observation that (11a) entails (11b), and that what a speaker says in assertively uttering the former commits him to that which is expressed by the latter.

$$11a \rightarrow 11b$$

11a. Princeton University is in New Jersey.
11b. There is at least one university in New Jersey.

A similar point holds for (12a) and (12b).

$$12a \rightarrow 12b$$

12a. Trenton New Jersey is a small city, whereas Princeton New Jersey is a small town.
12b. There is at least one small city and one small town in New Jersey.

The relationship between (12a) and (12b) reflects the fact that part of what it is to understand and be a competent user of the names *Trenton New Jersey* and *Princeton New Jersey* is to realize that their referents are located in New Jersey. Moreover, if we turn (11a) and (12a) into attitude ascriptions by prefixing the words *John believes (or asserted) that*, it appears that the descriptive contents of the partially descriptive names are included in the propositions John is said to believe, or to have asserted (on one natural reading of these ascriptions). Thus, there seems to be a natural reading of *John believes (or asserted) that Princeton University is in New Jersey* on which it is true only if John is committed to (11b), and there seems to be a natural reading of *John believes (or asserted) that Trenton New Jersey is a small city and*

Princeton New Jersey is a small town on which it is true only if John is committed to (12b).

For reasons like these, a good case can be made that the semantic contents of the sentences in (13) are something like the propositions expressed by the formulas in (14) (relative to assignments of the referents of the names to 'y').

$13a \rightarrow 14a \qquad 14a \rightarrow 14b$

13a.   Princeton University is F.
13b.   Trenton New Jersey is F.
14a.   [the x: x is a university & x = y] (x is F)
14b.   [the x: x is in New Jersey & x = y] (x is F)

On this view, *Princeton University* and *Trenton New Jersey* conform to the following partially descriptive theory of names.

| *A Partially Descriptive Theory* |

A partially descriptive name n is semantically associated with both a descriptive property P_D and a referent o. The referent o is determined in part by having the property P_D and in part by the same nondescriptive mechanisms that determine the reference of ordinary nondescriptive names—for example, by a historical chain of transmission leading back to o. The semantic content of n includes both o and D. The proposition expressed by a sentence *n is F* is the same as that expressed by the sentence *[the x: Dx & x = y] Fx*, relative to an assignment of o to 'y.' This proposition is true at a world w iff o has the properties expressed by D and F at w. To believe this proposition is to believe of o that it has both properties.[33]

Further examples of the many different kinds of names that seem to fit this theory are given in (15). (In each case the proposed semantic content of the name is the semantic content of the description that follows it, relative to an assignment of the referent of the name to 'y').

15a.   *Professor Saul Kripke (the x: Professor x & x = y), Princess Diana (the x: Princess x & x = y), Justice Antonin Scalia (the x: Justice x & x = y)*

15b. *Mr. Terry Thomas (the x: Male x & x = y), Miss Ruth Bar-*
      can (the x: Female x & Unmarried x & x = y), Mrs. Marilyn
      Frankfurt (the x: Female x & Married x & x = y)

15c. *New York City (the x: City x & x = y), Mexico City (the x:*
      City x & x = y), Princeton Township (the x: Township x &
      x = y), Park Avenue (the x: Avenue x & x = y), Griffith Park
      (the x: Park x & x = y)

15d. *Mount Rainier (the x: Mountain x & x = y), Lake Crescent*
      (the x: Lake x & x = y), Puget Sound (the x: Sound x & x =
      y), the Columbia River (the x: River x & x = y), the Olympic
      Peninsula (the x: Peninsula x & x = y), Snoqualmie Falls
      (the x: Waterfall x & x = y), Whidbey Island (the x: Island
      x & x = y)

15f. *The Empire State Building (the x: Building x & x = y), the*
      Brooklyn Bridge (the x: Bridge x & x = y), the Eiffel Tower
      (the x: Tower x & x = y), St. Patrick's Cathedral (the x:
      Cathedral x & x = y), Yankee Stadium (the x: Stadium x &
      x = y), Fort McHenry (the x: Fort x & x = y)

These and other examples will be discussed further in chapter 5, when
we look more closely at the theory of partially descriptive names, and
possible alternatives to it. There, we will discuss the analysis of some
potentially problematic examples, raise certain general challenges to
the theory itself, and offer a final evaluation of how best to understand
this significant class of partially descriptive, but still namelike, expressions. For now we simply note the existence of this special class of
names, and distinguish it from the majority of ordinary linguistically
simple proper names—such as *Carl Hempel, Saul Kripke, Scott
Soames*—the semantic contents of which can more happily be identified with their referents.[34]

Appendix: Direct Reference and the Problem of "Empty Names"

Let n be a name for which the associated negative existential, *n doesn't
exist*, could naturally be used to express a truth. Examples of such
names are *Socrates, Sherlock Holmes*, and *Santa Claus*. Since the negative existential sentences corresponding to these names would normally
be taken to be true, many philosophers would maintain that these

Empty Names

names lack referents. But then, on the account of semantic content I have offered, it might seem that both these names and the negative existentials containing them lack semantic contents. To say that the negative existentials lack semantic contents is to say that they fail to semantically express propositions, and so are meaningless. But if that is so, then it may seem hard to account for the evident fact that these sentences may be used to assert truths, and express true beliefs. This, in a nutshell, is the problem posed by "empty names" for Millian theories that identify the semantic content of a name with its referent (or for mixed theories, such as the partially descriptive theory just discussed, that take the referent of a name to be an essential component of its semantic content).

This problem is a large and difficult one, with a number of perplexing aspects. The problem is addressed from a nondescriptivist, and even Millian, perspective by a substantial and growing literature.[35] I will not attempt here to add anything new to that literature, or even to summarize it. However, I do want to draw from it to say a word about why I do not think that "empty names" pose an insuperable problem to the account of the semantic content of names developed here. The reason they don't can be summed up in two general theses: First, most "empty names" are not really empty; they turn out to have referents of certain sorts after all. Second, the propositions asserted, and the beliefs expressed, by an utterance of a sentence containing an "empty name" are not limited to those semantically expressed by the sentence uttered.[36]

The second of these theses should be fairly obvious. It is merely an application to empty names of a general point over which I have been laboring for much of this chapter. However, the first thesis, about the real referents of "empty names," needs more explanation.[37] Consider first the name *Socrates*. As it is generally agreed, *Socrates* refers to Socrates. However, since Socrates no longer exists, the negative existential *Socrates doesn't exist* is true. On my view, this sentence semantically expresses a singular proposition in which the property expressed by the predicate is predicated of the referent of the name. For our purposes, this proposition can be thought of as being made up of the constituents Socrates and the property of not existing. We may even grant that since Socrates once existed, but no longer does, this proposition once existed, but no longer does. This proposition—the proposition that Socrates doesn't exist—is, of course, different from the proposition that Plato doesn't exist, which is the proposition semantically expressed by *Plato doesn't exist*. The two names, *Socrates* and *Plato*, refer to different things, even though there exists nothing that is the referent of either name; and the two negative existentials *Socrates doesn't exist* and *Plato doesn't exist* have different propositions as their semantic contents, even though there exist no propositions that are their semantic contents. Because of this, these sentences are meaningful, even though there exist no propositions which are their meanings.

All of this is coherent once we admit that it is possible for certain objects to have certain properties at times when those objects don't exist. Socrates now has the property of being designated by *Socrates* (as well as the property of not existing), even though Socrates does not now exist. Similarly, the proposition that Socrates doesn't exist is such that it now has the properties of being a proposition and of being semantically expressed by certain sentences, even though it doesn't now exist. It also now has the property of being true, of being believed by me, and of being asserted by utterances of *Socrates doesn't exist*. In this way, the Millian can accommodate obvious facts involving sentences containing names of once existent, but no longer existing, objects, To say that *Socrates* now refers to an object that once existed but no longer does, is to say that there once existed an object o such that *Socrates* now refers to o, even though o does not now exist. To say that *Socrates does not exist* now semantically expresses a proposition that once existed but no longer does, is to say that there once existed a proposition p such that *Socrates does not exist* now expresses p, even though p does not now exist.

This account generalizes to sentences containing names of objects that do not exist now, but will exist in the future, as well as to objects that have never existed and will never exist, but which could have existed. The main complication in extending the account in this way involves the difficulty of naming merely future, or merely possible, objects. Typically, the names we use to designate objects that no longer exist are descendants of names introduced by past speakers whose acquaintance with the objects facilitated their ability to name them. Since the names we use to refer to past objects inherit their reference from those earlier speakers, we seldom are in the position of having to introduce an entirely new name for such an object. However, this is precisely the position we find ourselves in, if we wish to employ a name for a merely future, or merely possible, object.

Two requirements must be met if such naming is to be successful. First, we must be able to single out a unique, merely future, or merely possible object o to be the bearer of the name. Second, we must be sufficiently acquainted with o, prior to the introduction of the name, to entertain *de re* thoughts about o—that is, to believe of o that it is so and so—and perhaps even to assert singular propositions involving o. This second condition, though vague (what counts as sufficiently acquainted?), is not easy to satisfy.[38] Certainly, it is not enough to possess an arbitrary definite description that picks out a unique object. We cannot successfully introduce a new name, *Newman 1*, simply by announcing that its (present) bearer is to be the first child born in North America in the twenty-second century. Since we are not now in a position to have *de re* thoughts, or make *de re* assertions, about that individual, and since no linguistic ceremony can change this fact, we cannot use a sentence *Newman 1 is F* to say of that individual that it "is F." As we have seen, it is part of the competence conditions for any genuine name n of an object o that to assertively utter *n is F* in a normal context is to say of o that it "is F." Since *Newman 1* does not satisfy this condition, it does not qualify as a name of the object designated by the description used to introduce it.[39]

Though it is difficult to satisfy the requirements for naming merely future, or merely possible, objects, a few plausible cases have been offered in which these requirements seem to be met. For example, consider the following two scenarios drawn from earlier discussions by Nathan Salmon and David Kaplan.[40] In the first case one observes a particular male sperm cell and a particular ovum that are about to be united. Knowing what is going to happen, one names the child who will result from this process *Newman*. (For the sake of argument, imagine that we can control the process of uniting and later development so that we now know everything will be normal, the process will not result in twins, and so on.) It is plausible to think that in this case one succeeds in naming the future child. If this is right, then *Newman* now refers to an individual who does not yet exist, but will exist in the near future. The Millian may then maintain that the propositions that Newman does not exist, that Newman will exist, and that Newman will be a boy also do not yet exist, but will exist before long. These propositions are now true; they are now semantically expressed by the sentences *Newman does not exist*, *Newman will exist*, and *Newman will be a boy*; and they may now be believed and asserted. In this way, the account of sentences containing names of objects existing only in the past can be extended to sentences containing names of objects existing only in the future.

The second scenario is just like the first except that this time we know, when observing the particular sperm cell and the particular ovum, that although they could be united in such a way as to lead to the birth of a child, in fact they will never be united, and will never develop into a human zygote. Despite this, we can consider the possible child that would have resulted from their uniting (under the circumstances we have in mind). We might even call it *Noman*. It is plausible to think that in this way one could name an individual that doesn't exist, and will never exist, but could have existed. If this is right, then analogues of points just made about *Newman*, and sentences containing it, can be made about *Noman*, and sentences containing it. In this way, the account of sentences containing names of objects existing only in the past, or only in the future, can be extended to sentences containing names of objects that never exist, but could have existed. All of these sentences can be handled in a Millian framework in which the semantic content of a name is its referent.

Another kind of "empty name" that does not belong to any of the categories we have considered so far consists of names that occur in fiction or legend—names such as *Sherlock Holmes* and *Santa Claus*. The most promising account of these names that I know of has been developed by Nathan Salmon, building on earlier insights of Saul Kripke, Peter van Inwagen, and others.[41] The idea, in a nutshell, is this: Among the things that exist are stories, legends, novels, chapters, plays, movies, and the like. These are abstract objects created by authors. Fictional characters are constituents of these objects. Like the fictions of which they are part, fictional characters are a special kind of real, existing object; they, too, are abstract objects. Typically, however, they are created with the special purpose of being depicted as, or playing the role of, something quite different. For example, *Sherlock Holmes* is the name of a fictional character (an abstract object) that is depicted in the Conan Doyle stories as a brilliant detective.

Like most linguistically simple names, *Sherlock Holmes* refers to an object that is its semantic content, and sentences containing it semantically express singular propositions in which properties are predicted of that object. However, sentences containing fictional names also have certain specialized uses. When Conan Doyle used such sentences in writing the stories, he was not attempting to assert the propositions they semantically express, or any other propositions. Rather, he was engaging in a kind of pretense; he was, in effect, pretending to assert the propositions that make up his stories. By contrast, when we say, in talking about the stories, *Sherlock Holmes was a brilliant detective*, we may well intend to assert something, though not, of course, the singular proposition p that simply predicates the property of being a brilliant detective of the abstract object designated by *Sherlock Holmes*. Rather, what we assert is the proposition that according to the stories, Sherlock Holmes was a brilliant detective—a proposition that is true iff p follows from the propositions that make up the Holmes stories together with whatever background propositions may be taken as presupposed in reading them (e.g., commonplace facts about the world that are so obvious that they need not be mentioned in the stories themselves). Finally, one can use sentences containing fictional names to assert the propositions they literally express. One can say, *Whereas Scotland Yard really is the headquarters of the London Police, Sherlock Holmes is not really a man, but only a fictional character*. Someone who assertively utters this sentence intending to make a claim about the real world, independent of the fiction, truly says, of the abstract object named by *Sherlock Holmes*, that it is not a man but a fictional character.

Finally, consider *Sherlock Holmes doesn't (really) exist.* If one says this, meaning that according to the stories, Sherlock Holmes doesn't exist, then of course what one says is false. Similarly, if one says this, intending to make a statement about the real world to the effect that the character Sherlock Holmes doesn't exist, then again what one says is false—since characters, like the stories they are part of, exist. However, there are several other propositions that one might naturally intend to assert by uttering *Sherlock Holmes doesn't (really) exist*. For example, one might intend to assert (i) that there is no person in real life who has the properties that the character Sherlock Holmes is portrayed to have in the stories; (ii) that the character Holmes that appears in the stories is not a real person (in the way Napoleon, who appears in the novel *War and Peace*, is a real person), but rather is only a character; or (iii) that there is no one who both is the character Holmes that appears in the stories and has the properties that Holmes is portrayed to have there.[42] All of these propositions are true, and our ability to assert them by uttering the negative existential poses no serious problems for the Millian.

Presumably, what holds for *Sherlock Holmes* holds for *Santa Claus* as well. It makes no difference whether the character plays a role in a novel, short story, play, myth, or legend. Salmon's general framework can be applied straightforwardly in all of these cases. Whether or not it can successfully be applied to every "empty name"—including those such as *Vulcan* that occur in serious theories that turn out to be false, as well as apparently nonreferring names that arise from more innocent mistakes in ordinary discourse—is an open question.[43] Although I find Salmon's approach promising, I take no position regarding whether it is complete as it stands, or whether it needs further supplementation or modification. That is a matter for future investigation.

My aim in including this appendix on "empty names" was not to present, or report, a definitive solution to all the various problems they present, but rather to forestall a certain, not uncommon, objection to the Millian view of the semantic content of names developed in this chapter. The objection is that since empty names have no referents, the Millian must hold that they have no semantic content, that the sentences containing them are meaningless, and that assertive utterances of negative existentials fail to assert truths. Since these results are clearly incorrect, the objection continues, the Millian account of semantic content must be wrong. In this appendix I have attempted to answer this objection by showing that "empty names" do not require the Millian to hold any of the obviously incorrect positions attributed to him. Quite the contrary; a promising account of empty names is available to the Millian.

4

Ambiguity and Indexicality

Ambiguity

In the previous chapter I argued that in the case of most linguistically simple proper names, the semantic content of a name can be taken to be its referent. In coming to this conclusion, I made use of the simplifying assumption that names are unambiguous in the sense that each name refers to at most one individual. This assumption was implicit in the observation that when one becomes a competent user of a name, one learns that to assertively utter a sentence containing it is to say or assert something of the referent of the name. If names referred to more than one individual, there would be no such thing as **the** referent of a name, and this observation could not be maintained as stated. The assumption that a name unambiguously refers to at most one thing was also needed when I identified the semantic content of a sentence, *n is F*, with information asserted and conveyed across normal contexts in which it is assertively uttered with its standard, conventional meaning. If n were ambiguous, in the sense of having different conventionally determined referents, then surely there would be no information invariantly asserted and conveyed across all normal contexts in which the sentence is assertively uttered with one or another of its conventional meanings.

Thus, we must confront the question of whether ordinary proper names are ambiguous. This question is often ignored by formal semantic theories, which standardly treat the expressions undergoing semantic evaluation as unambiguous. What in ordinary language is recognized as ambiguity is represented in standard semantic models by homonymy. So, instead of saying that the word 'bank' is ambiguous, one says (in the model) that there are two words—*bank₁* and *bank₂*—with different meanings that share the same spelling and pronunciation. Although this can be a useful technique, it is important to realize that it is nothing more than that. As far as formal semantic theories are concerned, one could get the same effect by characterizing the single word

No

'bank' as ambiguous between two interpretations, introducing into the theory's representation of contexts of utterance a new parameter specifying the interpretations carried by ambiguous words in the context, and relativizing the notion of the semantic content of a name, or other ambiguous expression, to these newly enlarged contexts.

For our purposes, it doesn't matter which of these techniques is adopted in the statement of a formal semantic theory. Here it is important to realize that our purposes are not the same as those of such theories. The job of a semantic theory is descriptive; it aims to specify the semantic content of sentences and other expressions relative to arbitrary contexts. In order to accomplish this task it is neither necessary nor desirable to treat all contexts as circumstances in which sentences are uttered or even used by individuals in the context. Rather, an abstract conception of contexts is standardly employed according to which a context is thought of as a perspective from which a sentence may be interpreted, whether or not anyone occupying that perspective uses or utters the sentence.[1] Our purpose is different, and essentially foundational. It is to investigate how the semantic content of a sentence, or expression, relative to a context of utterance, C, is related to the information that the sentence, or expression, is used to assert and convey to competent speakers in a class of contexts in which it is "used in the same way" as it is in C. For this purpose, a context of utterance should always be thought of as a context of use, which is understood to be a context in which a sentence, or expression, is used by an agent.

What is important for the foundational account of semantic content developed in chapter 3 is our ability to say something about the conditions in which an ambiguous expression of natural language is being used with one interpretation rather than another. According to that account, the semantic content of a sentence is a proposition that the sentence is used to assert and convey across a wide range of contexts of utterance; the semantic content of an expression is that which it contributes to the semantic content of sentences containing it. In order to apply this idea in drawing conclusions about the semantic content of an ambiguous expression, we need to be able to distinguish contexts in which the expression is used with one semantic content from those in which it is used with a different semantic content. Thus, if proper names can be ambiguous, we need to make explicit assumptions about when an ambiguous name is used with one content and when it is used with another.

As for the question of whether proper names really are ambiguous, it seems to me that there is a perfectly good sense in which many of them are; they are ambiguous in that they conventionally apply to different individuals. This is not true of all names, since undoubtedly some names are unique to their bearers, and thus apply unambiguously to a single individual. For these names the argument in chapter 3 can be given as stated. However, many other names are shared by more than one person or thing. For example, there are many different people named 'John Smith.' We may put this by saying that the name 'John Smith' is ambiguous in the sense that it refers to many different individuals. Just as the word 'bank' is ambiguous in that it may apply to a financial institution or to a riverbank, so the name 'John Smith' is ambiguous in that, when used with one semantic content, it applies to one individual, whereas when it is used with a different content, it applies to a different individual.

With this in mind, we need to restate some of the principles used in the argument of the previous chapter. One of those principles was the claim that when one becomes a competent user of a name n, one learns that to assertively utter *n is F* is to say of the referent of n that he (she/it) has a certain property—the property expressed by F. This must be restated as a principle about what is involved in coming to be a competent user of a name, when that name is used with one of its conventional meanings (semantic contents). The relativized principle states that when one acquires a proper name n, as it is used with one of its semantic contents, one learns that to assertively utter *n is F* is to say of the referent of n, as used with that content, that he (she/it) has a certain property—the property expressed by F (provided that n has a referent). A similar relativization is needed to describe the way in which speakers typically acquire competence with a name from hearing the name used by others. In such cases the speaker intends to use the name with the same reference and semantic content that it carried in the remarks made by others which constitute the speaker's sources for the name.

Another principle that needs to be restated is the claim that the semantic content of a name is that which it contributes to the information asserted and conveyed by utterances of sentences containing it in all normal contexts involving conversational participants who understand the name. The relativized replacement for this principle states, roughly, that the semantic content of a name, as it is used in a certain context C, is that which it contributes to the information asserted and conveyed by sentences containing it in all normal contexts in which it is used with the same semantic content it has in C. Combining this principle with the argument in chapter 3, one gets the result that—partially descriptive names aside—the semantic content of an ordinary, linguistically simple proper name, as used in a context C, is the individual to which the name, as used in C, refers.

Having restated the argument in this way, we can now see that the route to this conclusion involves appeal to an assumption that so far has not been made explicit. Our task is to determine the semantic content of an ordinary, linguistically simple name n as used in a context C in which someone assertively utters *n is F*. The conclusion we arrive at is that the semantic content of n, as used in C, is its referent. This conclusion depends on the claim that when we consider all normal contexts in which n is used with the same meaning (semantic content) it has in C, we will see that the only thing contributed by n to what is asserted and conveyed in all these contexts is its referent. But in order to reach this conclusion, we must specify those contexts in which n is used with the same semantic content it has in C.

In essence, the dialectical situation is this. In giving the argument that the semantic content of an ordinary, linguistically simple name is its referent, we identify the content it has, as used in a context C, with that which the name contributes to a certain proposition asserted and conveyed by assertive utterances of a simple sentence containing it in all normal contexts involving speakers who understand the name. In order for this strategy to work, we must restrict the contexts of utterance in question to those in which the name, and other expressions in the sentence, are understood in the same way they are in C—that is, to those contexts in which they are used with the same semantic content they have in C. But this requires us to make explicit the conditions that are necessary and sufficient for a name to be used with the same semantic content in two contexts.

The first half of this task is obvious. Surely, it is a necessary condition for n to be used with the same semantic content in two contexts that it refer to the same thing in both. For example, 'Aristotle' is the name both of a great philosopher of antiquity and of a famous shipping magnate of the twentieth century. Because of this, the English sentence

1. Aristotle was a great philosopher.

is ambiguous. Used in a context with one semantic content, it expresses a truth about the greatest student of Plato; used with a different semantic content in another context, it expresses a falsehood about a famous business tycoon. Clearly, this ambiguity results from the fact that the name 'Aristotle' contributes something different to the semantic content of the sentence in the two contexts. Thus, differences in the referent of a name, as used in two contexts, are differences in its semantic content, as used in those contexts.

However, this is not enough. We still need to specify a sufficient condition for a name to be used with the same semantic content in two contexts. One thing should be clear from the outset: if the fact that an ordinary, linguistically simple name is used to refer to the same thing in two different contexts is sufficient for it to have the same semantic content in those contexts, then the argument identifying the semantic contents of these names with their referents will go through. For surely, if we consider all potential normal contexts of utterance in which n is used in a sentence *n is F* to refer to a specific object o, we will find that the singular proposition ascribing F-hood to o exhausts the common information asserted and conveyed across all such contexts. However, one might wonder whether n is used with the same semantic content (meaning) in all these contexts. That is, one might wonder whether— special cases involving partially descriptive names aside—it is a sufficient condition for n to be used with the same semantic content in two contexts that it refer to the same thing in both.

I believe both that it is, and that this is what we ordinarily think. Consider my name, for example. In ordinary life, we typically regard different people who use it to refer to me as using it with the same meaning, even though what they believe about me varies greatly from person to person. Certainly, we do not take the English sentence

2. Scott Soames writes philosophy,

when understood as talking about me, to be ambiguous, with a semantic content (meaning) that varies from speaker to speaker, depending on how much or how little they know about me. Nor do we think that there is any one thing which distinguishes me from everyone else that any speaker must know in order to master my name. This is not to deny that different speakers may use the sentence to convey different information. Of course, different speakers may mean different things by the sentence, in the sense of using it to assert, convey, or impart different information. But that doesn't make (2) an ambiguous sentence of English.

This brings out an important feature of the argument of the previous chapter. The argument that the semantic content of *Scott Soames* is simply me, its referent, rests on the premise that it is necessary and sufficient, for this name to be used with the same semantic content (meaning) in two contexts of utterance, that it refer to the same person in both. Moreover, this premise is virtually as strong as the conclusion itself. Thus the weight of the argument rests squarely on this premise.

As I have indicated, I believe that it will support this weight. There are three main things to be said in its favor. First, it accords better than any alternative principle with what we ordinarily think about meaning. As I have said, we don't ordinarily regard sentences containing proper names to differ in meaning simply because speakers may associate the names they contain with different information about the objects the names refer to. This intuition is, I believe, strengthened when we carefully distinguish the meaning of a sentence, as used in a context, from (the totality of) what speakers assert by uttering it, from what they imply or suggest, from what information they intend to impart to their audience, and from what they actually succeed in imparting.

Second, the crucial premise fits the competence conditions underlying our mastery of ordinary, linguistically simple names. As we have seen, there is no descriptive information that uniquely picks out the referent o of such a name n that everyone must acquire in order to become a competent user of n as a name of o. Rather, two things are required to become such a user: (i) One must have acquired a referential intention that determines o as referent of n—often by picking up n from others who used it to refer to o and intending to refer to the same thing they did, or by being independently acquainted with o and resolving to use n to refer to o. (ii) One must realize that to assertively utter *n is F* is to say of the referent of one's use of n that it "is F." These competence conditions have the effect of associating specific information with uses of sentences containing names in particular contexts. For example, let C be a context in which the referential intentions governing the use of n in C determine that n refers to o. The competence conditions associated with an utterance of *n is F* in C will determine that the singular, Russellian proposition attributing the property expressed by F to o is asserted. In other words, this proposition will be determined to be asserted by semantic conditions a speaker/hearer must grasp in order to understand the sentence, as it is used in the context. This notion of being a proposition the assertion of which in a context is entirely determined by the semantic conventions associated with the sentence, as used in the context, is essentially that of the semantic content of the sentence in the context. But then, since what n contributes to the semantic content of *n is F* in C is just its referent, o, the semantic content of n, as used in C, is simply o, and the premise is supported (along with the conclusion of the argument).

That is not all. The competence conditions support the premise in another way. Condition (i) of those conditions tells us that in acquiring the referential intention one associates with the name, it is sufficient to pick up the name from others with the intention of using it to refer to whatever they refer to.[2] When one picks up a name in this way, it is not required that one intend to associate the name with the same descriptive information that one's sources do, and a speaker picking up a name from others normally would not dream of forming such an intention. Since, presumably, the speaker acquiring the name intends to use it in the same way (i.e., with the same meaning) as those from whom the speaker acquired it, this already suggests that it is sufficient for sameness of semantic content that two uses of an ordinary, linguistically simple name refer to the same thing. From here it is a short step to the conclusion that the semantic content of such a name, as used in a context, is not a set of descriptive conditions for determining reference, but rather the referent itself.

The final thing to be said in favor of the crucial premise, as well as the conclusion to which it leads, is that these claims are part of an overall theory of linguistic meaning and language use that, I believe, conforms very well to the totality of linguistic facts that constitute the data for any such theory. In light of this, the discussion in chapter 3 should not be seen as an attempt to construct a proof of a surprising and controversial conclusion—that the semantic contents of most ordinary, linguistically simple names are identical with their referents—from a set of uncontroversial and independently plausible premises. Rather, it is an attempt to motivate that theoretical identification while showing how to defuse common objections to it. For example, by making explicit the relationship between the semantic content of a sentence and that which speakers intend to assert, convey, or impart by uttering it in different circumstances, we were able to explain why speakers sometimes have a tendency to confuse these different types of information, and how this confusion may prevent them from recognizing that in most cases involving ordinary, linguistically simple names, substitution of coreferential names preserves semantic content. The strength of the resulting view is comparable to the strength of other well-supported theoretical hypotheses; it lies in the fact that it does a good job of explaining and accommodating the totality of apparently obvious facts about its subject matter—in this case, facts about our use of ordinary, linguistically simple proper names.

Indexicality

It is now time to extend our foundational semantic model to indexicals. Unlike linguistically simple proper names, different indexicals typically have different meanings in the sense of being associated with different rules governing their use that must be grasped by competent speakers of the language. These rules constitute competence conditions for understanding individual indexicals, and they parallel what it is that speakers understand about the category of names in general. In the case of any name n, a competent speaker who understands n knows that one who assertively utters *n is F* in a context C says of the referent of n, as used in C, that he/she/it has a certain property—the property expressed by F (provided that n has a referent). Moreover, it is reasonable to suppose that someone who knows what a name is, has at least an implicit understanding that names standardly get their referents by stipulation, after which they are passed on to others by historical chains of transmission.

The case of indexicals is a little more complex. Here, there are different rules of the same general type associated with different indexical expressions. For example, to know the meaning of the first-person singular pronoun 'I' is to know that speakers use it to refer to themselves, and that someone x who assertively utters *I am hungry* (*tired, happy,* . . .) says of x that x is hungry (tired, happy, ...). Similarly, one who knows the meaning of 'today' knows that speakers who use it on a given day d use it to refer to d, and that someone who assertively utters *Today the Red Sox beat the Yankees* (*won the pennant,* . . .) on d, says of d that it is a day on which the Red Sox beat the Yankees (won the pennant, . . .). Further, to know the meaning of 'he' (when used as a demonstrative) is to know that its referent in a context is a contextually salient male m who is demonstrated by the speaker, and that someone who assertively utters *He is brilliant* (*intelligent, well-informed,* . . .) says of m that m is brilliant (intelligent, well-informed, . . .). Similar rules are associated with other indexicals.[3]

Although different names do not have different meanings in the sense of different rules mastery of which explains linguistic competence, they may have different meanings in the sense of semantic contents.[4] The semantic content of a name is that which it contributes to what sentences containing it "say"—that is, to their semantic contents. I have argued that for most linguistically simple names n, the semantic content of n (as used in a context C) is its referent (as used in C). This conclusion can also be extended to indexicals. As in the case of names, the semantic content of an indexical expression e, as used in a sentence containing it in a context C, is that which e contributes to the semantic content of the sentence, relative to C. However, unlike names, the competence conditions associated with indexicals dictate that the semantic content of an indexical is something that varies from context to context.

Consider, for example, the first-person singular pronoun as it occurs in a sentence *I am F*. There is no such thing as "what this sentence says" independent of the context of utterance in which it is used. The competence conditions associated with the first-person singular pronoun guarantee that when I assertively utter the sentence, I use it to say something about me, whereas when you assertively utter it, you use it to say something about you. One might be tempted to suppose that there is some more general thing that the sentence "says" in every context—namely, the proposition expressed by *the speaker is F* (or some such thing). But this will not do. Our notion of "what a sentence says" is tied to what speakers who assertively utter the sentence say. Typically, when I assertively utter *I am F*, I don't assert that I am speaking or using language at all. Further, the proposition that I assert when I assertively utter such a sentence may be true in a possible circumstance in which no one is using language, and someone may believe this proposition without believing anything about me being a speaker. For example, if now I assertively utter

3. I am tired

x=y explains x = x or vice versa?

then what I assert is something that could have been true even if I never said a word, as well as something a person could believe without believing that I ever spoke. Thus the proposition I assert is not metalinguistic, and there is no metalinguistic information which one can identify with what the sentence says. Nor is there any other information that remains invariant from context to context that could qualify as the semantic content of the sentence.

Because of this, there is no alternative to relativizing the semantic content of an indexical sentence to contexts of utterance. As in the case of names, we take our guide from the competence conditions of the relevant expressions. For example, if I am right about the first-person singular pronoun, someone who understands sentence (3) knows that a speaker x who assertively utters it uses 'I' to refer to x, and says of x that x is tired. This means that no matter in what normal context (3) is assertively uttered (with its standard literal meaning), one of the propositions asserted in the context will be the singular proposition that predicates tiredness of the speaker. This much, and only this much, is guaranteed by the semantic information carried by the competence conditions. Of course, in many contexts assertive utterances of (3) will result in the assertion of other propositions as well. But the assertion of these additional propositions is not tied in such an intimate way to the semantic information that speakers must grasp in order to qualify as competent users of the sentence. This provides the rationale for taking the proposition semantically encoded by (3), its semantic content, relative to a context with x as agent, to be the singular proposition that x is tired.[5] This proposition is the semantic content of the sentence relative to the context because it is the proposition the assertion of which is guaranteed simply by the application of certain semantic conventions—the competence conditions—associated with the sentence to the utterance of the sentence in the context.[6]

With this in mind, we are now in a position to generalize the constraints on semantic content given in chapter 3. The most straightforward way of doing this is as follows.

C+ₐ. A proposition p is semantically expressed by a sentence s relative to a context of utterance C **only if** p is information a competent speaker would assert and intend to convey by an assertive utterance of s in any context C' in which (i) s is used with its literal meaning by competent speakers and hearers who understand s; (ii) all indexicals in s have the same referents in C' that they do in C; (iii) all ambiguities in s are resolved the same way in C' that they are in C; (iv) s is not used metaphorically, ironically, or sarcastically in C'; and (v) the presumption that the speaker intends to commit himself or herself to p is not defeated by a conversational implicature in C' to the contrary.

SC1$_a$. A proposition p is semantically expressed by s relative to a context C only if p satisfies constraint C+$_a$, and there is no other proposition q such that the fact that q satisfies C+$_a$ explains why p does as well.

SC2$_a$. A proposition p is the proposition semantically expressed by s relative to a context C if and only if (i) p satisfies constraint C+$_a$, and (ii) for any other proposition q satisfying (i), the fact that p satisfies (i) explains the fact that q does so as well, and not vice versa.

On this account, the semantic content of an indexical sentence s relative to a context of utterance C is (roughly) that which would be asserted and conveyed by an assertive utterance of s in any normal context in which the reference of all indexicals in s is the same as their reference in C. For example, the semantic content of

4. You are in danger

relative to a context of utterance C in which x is the person addressed is that which would be conveyed and asserted by an assertive utterance of (4) in any normal context C' with x as addressee. Moreover, the common content that would be asserted and conveyed in all those contexts is the singular proposition in which the property of being in danger is predicated of x. This is "what the sentence says" relative to a context in which x is the person addressed; the semantic content of 'you' relative to such a context is just x. Similar reasoning applies to other indexicals. In general, the semantic content of an indexical relative to a context is its referent relative to that context.[7]

It is worth noting that essentially the same result can be gotten from alternative formulations of C+, SC1, and SC2.

C+$_b$. A proposition p is semantically expressed by a sentence s relative to a context of utterance C in which s is assertively uttered with its normal literal meaning **only if** the assertion of p is determined by the application of the semantic conventions (competence conditions) that must be grasped by any speaker who understands s, as it is used in C—provided that C is a context in which s is not used metaphorically, ironically, or sarcastically, and in which the presumption that the speaker intends to commit himself or herself to p is not defeated by a conversational implicature to the contrary.

SC1$_b$. A proposition p is semantically expressed by s relative to a context C in which s is assertively uttered with its normal literal meaning **only if** p satisfies constraint C+$_b$, and there is no other proposition q such that the fact that q satisfies C+$_b$ explains why p does as well.

SC2$_b$. A proposition p is the proposition semantically expressed by s relative to a context C in which s is assertively uttered with its normal literal meaning **if and only if** (i) p satisfies constraint C+$_b$ and (ii) for any other proposition q satisfying (i), the fact that p satisfies (i) explains the fact that q does so as well, and not vice versa.

These groups of constraints give the same results regarding the semantic contents of sentences in normal contexts in which they are used with their literal meanings, since the only propositions asserted by assertive utterances of s in all such (possible) contexts involving competent speakers (in which the referents of indexicals plus the resolutions of ambiguities are the same as they are in C; in which s is used nonmetaphorically, nonironcially, nonsarcastically; and in which there are no relevant conversational defeaters) will be propositions the assertion of which in C is determined by the application of the semantic competence conditions associated with s, as used in C (and vice versa). Either way, with C+$_a$, SC1$_a$, and SC2$_a$ or with C+$_b$, SC1$_b$, and SC2$_b$, we get the result that the semantic content of an indexical relative to a context is its referent relative to the context.

It is, of course, important to remember that an assertive utterance of a sentence containing an indexical might convey, and even assert, more than "what the sentence says" relative to the context. Examples of this were given in the hypothetical scenarios presented in the previous chapter ("The Introduction," "The Emergency," etc.). However, none of those examples made crucial use of nonsemantic descriptive information directly associated with an indexical. For an example that does this, we may consider an assertive utterance of (5), in which the use of the demonstrative 'he' is accompanied by a demonstration of a man standing close to the edge of a pool in which children are splashing.

5. He is going to get wet.

In a case like this it may be perfectly correct to take the speaker as asserting (among other things) the proposition that the man standing near the pool is going to get wet—even though this proposition is not the semantic content of the sentence relative to the context.

A similar example is provided by (6).

6. There will be an exam in this class tomorrow.

Imagine a situation in which a teacher is standing in front of her class on Monday morning. She directs the students' attention to the calendar, says "Sunday was the last day of May," and turns the calendar to June. Then she assertively utters (6). In such a case, the teacher can correctly be described as having said that there will be an exam in her class on Tuesday, June 2, even though this assertion contains information about the day of the exam—for instance, that it is a Tuesday and that it is the second day of June—that is not part of the semantic content of the sentence, (6), that she uttered in the context.[8]

The lesson to be learned from this discussion is that the relationship between the semantic content of a sentence, as used in a context, and that which the speaker asserts by assertively uttering it is very much the same in the case of sentences containing indexicals as it is in the case of sentences containing names. Indexicals require an explicit relativization of the notion of content to context (though it can be argued that ordinary ambiguity also requires something like this). Once this is done, the main points about the semantic contents of names made in chapter 3 carry over to the semantic contents of indexicals as well.

The Theoretical Significance of Semantic Content

When speakers learn a language, they learn how to use its expressions to assert and convey information. It is because expressions have certain rules conventionally associated with them that they can be used systematically by speakers of the language to communicate the information that they are used to carry. For example, the rule for names is that to assertively utter a sentence containing a name in a context C is to say or assert something of the referent of n, as used in C (provided the name has a referent). As we have seen, the rules for individual indexicals are similar but more specific (in that they do more to specify what the referent of a particular indexical is in a context). A speaker who assertively utters a sentence in a context implicitly makes use of these rules to assert and convey information.

However, not all information that a sentence is used to communicate in a given context of utterance is information that is conventionally associated with it by the rules of the language. This extra, nonsemantic information comes in a variety of types from a variety of sources; some of it is asserted, some is implied or suggested, and some is merely intended to be imparted to those hearers who happen to have the requisite background knowledge to extract it. Moreover, the semantic content of a sentence in a context need not be the most important information that the speaker wishes to communicate; nor must it always play a psychologically privileged role in supporting an inference to that information. Rather, the semantic content of a sentence relative to a context is information that a competent speaker/hearer can confidently take to be asserted and conveyed by an utterance of the sentence in the context, no matter what else may be asserted, conveyed, or imparted. It is a sort of minimal common denominator determined by the linguistic knowledge shared by all competent speakers, together with contextually relevant facts such as the time, place, and agent of the context; the identity of individuals demonstrated by the speaker; and the referents of the names, as used in the context. As such, the semantic content of a sentence functions as a sort of minimal core around which speaker/hearers can structure the totality of information the sentence is used to communicate in a given context.

The semantic content of a sentence s in a context also plays an important role in our understanding of propositional attitude ascriptions of the form *x asserts/believes/means/expects/hopes that s*. I will turn to this topic in chapters 6–8. Before doing that, however, it is necessary to say more about the subject of partially descriptive names, previously broached in chapters 2 and 3. It is this to which we turn in chapter 5.

5

Partially Descriptive Names

Near the end of chapter 3, I used the expressions *Princeton University* and *Trenton New Jersey* to illustrate the phenomenon of partially descriptive names, and to motivate the following theory of such names.

The Partially Descriptive Theory

A partially descriptive name n is semantically associated with both a descriptive property P_D and a referent o. The referent o is determined in part by having the property P_D and in part by the same nondescriptive mechanisms that determine the reference of ordinary nondescriptive names—for instance, by a historical chain of transmission leading back to o. The semantic content of n includes both o and D. The proposition expressed by a sentence *n is F* is the same as that expressed by the sentence *[the x: Dx & x = y] Fx*, relative to an assignment of o to 'y.' This proposition is true at a world w iff o has the properties expressed by D and F at w. To believe this proposition is to believe of o that it has both properties.[1]

The following additional examples were given of names that seem, potentially at least, to fit this theory. (In each case the proposed semantic content of the name is roughly that of the description that follows it, relative to an assignment of the referent of the name to 'y').

1a. *Professor Saul Kripke* (*the x*: *Professor x & x = y*), *Princess Diana* (*the x*: *Princess x & x = y*), *Justice Antonin Scalia* (*the x*: *Justice x & x = y*)

1b. *Mr. Terry Thomas* (*the x*: *Male x & x = y*), *Miss Ruth Barcan* (*the x*: *Female x & Unmarried x & x = y*), *Mrs. Marilyn Frankfurt* (*the x*: *Female x & Married x & x = y*)

1c. *New York City (the x: City x & x = y), Mexico City (the x: City x & x = y), Princeton Township (the x: Township x & x = y), Park Avenue (the x: Avenue x & x = y), Griffith Park (the x: Park x & x = y)*

1d. *Mount Rainier (the x: Mountain x & x = y), Lake Crescent (the x: Lake x & x = y), Puget Sound (the x: Sound x & x = y), the Columbia River (the x: River x & x = y), the Olympic Peninsula (the x: Peninsula x & x = y), Snoqualmie Falls (the x: Waterfall x & x = y), Whidbey Island (the x: Island x & x = y)*

1e. *The Empire State Building (the x: Building x & x = y), the Brooklyn Bridge (the x: Bridge x & x = y), the Eiffel Tower (the x: Tower x & x = y), St. Patrick's Cathedral (the x: Cathedral x & x = y), Yankee Stadium (the x: Stadium x & x = y), Fort McHenry (the x: Fort x & x = y)*

It is time to look at these examples more closely, and to use them to explore important issues concerning the partially descriptive theory.

The examples in (1a) and (1b) involve combining ordinary names of people with titles of different sorts. Most of these examples are straightforward. However, even these simple cases raise potentially significant issues. One of the most important and general of these is illustrated by the contrast between the genuine partially descriptive names, *Professor Saul Kripke* and *Princess Diana*, on the one hand, and the examples, *Professor Longhair* and *Queen Latifah*, which are stage names of popular entertainers, on the other. Professor Longhair is not a professor, Queen Latifah is not a queen, and their stage names are not partially descriptive names, in the sense of the present theory. Presumably, the stage names were chosen because of their descriptive connotations, which are in some way derivative from genuine partially descriptive names. However, these descriptive connotations are not part of the semantic contents of the names, and they are not standardly included in the assertions made by utterances of sentences containing the stage names. From a semantic point of view, these stage names are like ordinary (i.e., nondescriptive) proper names; their semantic contents can be identified with their referents. The fact that they have the form of phrases that could be used as genuine partially descriptive names does not prevent them from having a reading in which they are semantically simple.

A second general issue is illustrated by (2).

2a.   Prior to 1980, Justice Scalia was neither a judge nor a justice.

This sentence has a natural interpretation in which it is true, and is obviously not equivalent to (2b) (when the latter is taken relative to an assignment of Antonin Scalia to 'y,' and the description [*the x: Justice x & x = y*] is given small scope).

2b.   (prior to 1980) ([the x: Justice x & x = y] $\sim$ Judge x & $\sim$ Justice x)

There are two obvious ways of accommodating this fact within the framework of the partially descriptive theory. According to the first way, the occurrence of *Justice Scalia* in (2a) is taken to be a genuine partially descriptive name which is given wide scope over the temporal operator *prior to 1980*, to produce the logical form (2c) (taken relative to an assignment of Scalia to 'y').

2c.   [the x: Justice x & x = y] ((prior to 1980) ($\sim$Judge x & $\sim$ Justice x))

According to the second way, the occurrence of *Justice Scalia* in (2b) is taken to have a reading in which it is an ordinary, nondescriptive name of Antonin Scalia (on a par with the stage name *Queen Latifah*), and no scope maneuvers are needed. Although both approaches avoid analyzing (2a) as being (unambiguously) equivalent to (2b), the former approach has the virtue of explaining the parallel between the examples in (2) and those in (3).

3a.   Prior to 1992, John's wife was unmarried.
3b.   (prior to 1992) ([the x: Wife-of x, John] $\sim$ married x).
3c.   [the x: Wife-of x, John] ((prior to 1992) $\sim$ married x).

Just as (3a) has a reading in which it is equivalent to (3c) rather than to (3b), so (2a) has a reading in which it is equivalent to (2c) rather than to (2b). The ability to treat (2a) and (3a) in the same way constitutes a substantial advantage of the scope approach.

Nevertheless, allowing partially descriptive names to take different scopes in a sentence will not, by itself, solve all problems of the sort we are concerned with here. This point is illustrated by (4a).

4a. Princess Diana is dead.

Since the sentence is simple, we don't have multiple scope possibilities, and the only analysis made available by the partially descriptive theory would seem to be (4b) (when 'y' is assigned Diana as value).

4b. [the x: Princess x & x = y] x is dead.

But, it might seem, (4b) can't possibly be true (relative to the assignment of Diana to 'y'). Even if the quantifier phrase is allowed to range over all past and presently existing individuals, (4b) can be true now only if the quantifier phrase now denotes Diana and Diana is now dead. What is it for someone to be dead? I imagine it is for that person to have existed in the past, but not to exist now. If that is right, then an individual can satisfy the predicate *dead* at a time t, even though the individual does not exist at t. So far, so good. However, the predicate *dead* is rather unusual in this respect. Most predicates—such as *weighing over 100 pounds*, *being located at a certain place*, *having a certain occupation or social position*, *being a professor*, or *being a princess*— apply at a time t only to things that exist at that time. If, at t, an individual weighs over 100 pounds, or is located in Princeton, or is a professor, or is a princess, then that person exists at t. But if that is right, then even though Diana is now dead, she is not now a princess, in which case (4b) is not true now, since the quantifier it contains is (now) nondenoting (relative to an assignment of Diane to 'y'). But if all this is right, then (4b) cannot be the analysis of (4a), and the partially descriptive theory would seem to be in trouble.

Although the puzzle posed by this example is real, it doesn't pose a serious threat to the partially descriptive theory. The reason it doesn't, is that the same puzzle arises in cases in which it is evident that we have genuine semantically descriptive phrases, such as *my mother*, which, for our purposes, may be taken to be equivalent to [*the x: Mother x, me*]. Just as (4a) is now true even though no one who is now a princess is Diana, so (5a) is now true even though no one who is now a mother is my mother.

What of: President Reagan is dead.

5a.   My mother is dead.

Similarly, just as there is a puzzle in seeing how (4b) can be true now, so there is a puzzle in seeing how (5b) can be true now.[2]

5b.   [the x: Mother x, me] x is dead.

But since, surely, something like (5b) must be the analysis of (5a), there must be a solution to this puzzle. Presumably, whatever that analysis is, it can be applied to (4) so as to preserve the idea that something like (4b) is the analysis of (4a). One possibility is that in certain special cases like these, a past-tense operator is (implicitly) inserted in the descriptive phrase, so that the occurrence of *my mother* in (5a) is understood as equivalent to [*the x: in the past* (Mother *x*, *me*)], and the occurrence of *Princess Diana* in (4a) is taken to be equivalent to [*the x: in the past* (Princess *x* & *x* = *y*)] (relative to an assignment of Diana to '*y*').[3] But whether or not this explanation ultimately proves to be the right one, the parallel between (4) and (5) shows that whatever worries there may be about these cases do not undermine the partially descriptive analysis of names like *Princess Diana*.

In addition to the general issues we have considered, certain individual names raise more restricted issues about their precise descriptive content. Consider, for example, the pair *Miss Ruth Barcan* and *Mrs. Marilyn Frankfurt*, which I have rendered as roughly equivalent to (*the x: Female x & Unmarried x & x = y*), and (*the x: Female x & Married x & x = y*), relative to assignments of Ruth Barcan and Marilyn Frankfurt, respectively, to the variable '*y*.' The titles *Miss* and *Mrs.* have undergone significant changes in use in the last 50 years, and may even be dying out, or at least becoming greatly restricted. Nevertheless, I believe that there was a period of time, not very long ago, in which they carried more or less the descriptive content I have indicated.

Consider first *Miss Ruth Barcan*. This was the maiden name (plus title) of the famous modal logician Ruth Barcan Marcus. After her marriage to Mr. Marcus, she was no longer known as *Miss* at all. Instead, she took her husband's last name and was known as (*Mrs.*) *Ruth Marcus* or (*Mrs.*) *Ruth Barcan Marcus*. After her divorce she retained her husband's name. However, had she shed her married name in favor of her former surname, as many women do, she could, I believe, have correctly been addressed as *Miss Ruth Barcan* once again—though in such cases it may be more natural to drop the title altogether.[4] If this is right, then it lends some support to the particular descriptive content I have proposed.

The case of *Mrs.* is more complicated. One complication involves widows who have not remarried. Typically in such a case, it remains correct, and often appropriate (depending on the wishes of the woman in question), to continue to refer to the wife of the late Mr. Jones as *Mrs. Jones*. Since it seems wrong to say that the widow of Mr. Jones is still married, this suggests that the content of *Mrs. Judy Jones* cannot be precisely that of [*the x*: *Female x* & *Married x* & *x = y*] (relative to an assignment of Judy Jones to 'y'). Perhaps the content is simply that of [*the x*: *Female x* & (*Married x or Widow x*) & *x = y*] (relative to an appropriate assignment).[5]

Other complications are illustrated by the case of Mrs. Marilyn Frankfurt, former wife of my colleague Harry Frankfurt. When they were married, Marilyn took Harry's last name. When they divorced, she retained it. Later, when she remarried, she retained the surname *Frankfurt* rather than taking her second husband's name or reverting to her maiden name. She now may be (and in fact is) correctly referred to as *Mrs. Marilyn Frankfurt*—though not, of course, as *Mrs. Harry Frankfurt*. This shows that whereas *Mrs.* indicates that a woman is married (or a widow), it doesn't, when prefixed to her full proper name, indicate to whom she is married. As for the phrase *Mrs. Harry Frankfurt*, it is not a name at all, but rather a descriptive phrase, equivalent to *the wife of Harry Frankfurt*. Accordingly, the phrase *Mrs. Frankfurt*, used to designate Marilyn Frankfurt during the time of her marriage to Harry, is ambiguous. On one reading its subconstituent, *Frankfurt*, refers to Marilyn and the phrase is a partially descriptive name. On the other reading, *Frankfurt* refers to Harry, and *Mrs. Frankfurt* is equivalent to a straightforward description—one that used to refer to Marilyn, but now refers to someone else.

A number of other issues of descriptive detail could be raised about these special names, as well as other examples given in (1). It is not always immediately evident what the precise descriptive content of a partially descriptive name is, though often this can be clarified by a careful consideration of cases. Another case in point is provided by examples such as *Fifth Avenue* and *Highway 99*. Consider *Fifth Avenue*. This name semantically encodes the information that its referent is an avenue. But what, if anything, is added by the ordinal number?

Not the information that it is the fifth in a sequence of numbered avenues, nor the information that it lies between Fourth and Sixth avenues. Fifth Avenue in midtown Manhattan lies between Madison Avenue and Sixth Avenue; the avenues (with the exception of Broadway, which runs diagonally) go as follows: First, Second, Third, Lexington, Park, Madison, Fifth, Sixth, Seventh, Eighth, and so on. For this reason I suspect that the semantic content of *Fifth Avenue* is simply that of [*the x*: *Avenue x* & $x = y$] (relative to an assignment of the avenue itself to 'y'). It seems clear that the name does carry further descriptive connotations—for instance, that its referent y is such that if there are avenues x and z (in the same jurisdiction) named *Third Avenue* and *Seventh Avenue*, respectively, then y lies between x and z. But it is hard to imagine anything this complicated being part of the content of what is asserted by normal utterances of sentences containing *Fifth Avenue*. Similar points could be made about *Highway 99*.

Although the examples we have considered up to now show that real questions can be raised about the precise descriptive semantic contents of particular partially descriptive names, these questions do not, in my view, cast doubt on the general analytical framework posited by the partially descriptive theory. There is, however, a final consideration that might, initially at least, seem to do precisely that. Consider the name *World War I*. At first glance, this might seem to be a partially descriptive name that carries the information not only that its referent is a world war—that is, a war of worldwide, or near worldwide, extent—but also that it was the first such war. However, the following example, due to Jonathan McKeown-Green, suggests that this may not be quite right.

6a.   I have often wondered whether there were any world wars before World War I. I think that there were. I think that the Thirty Years War and the Napoleonic War are good candidates.

If *World War I*, as used in (6a), were a partially descriptive name equivalent to [*the x*: (*World War x* & $\forall z$ ((*World War z* & *z/x*) $\supset z$ *Occurred-after x*) & $x = y$)] (relative to the appropriate assignment to 'y'), then the discourse would be incoherent no matter whether the description were assigned narrow or wide scope with respect to *wondered whether*. Since the discourse is not incoherent, this suggests that

World War I, as it is used in (6a), does not have this analysis. But what, then, is its analysis?

One might think that (6a) simply illustrates the general point that ordinal numbering doesn't get into the semantic content of partially descriptive names (just as it doesn't get into the semantic content of *Fifth Avenue*), even though it often contributes to the descriptive connotations carried by a name.[6] On this view, what (6a) shows is that the content of *World War I*, as it is used in that discourse, is the content given by [*the x*: (*World War x* & $x = y$)] (relative to an appropriate assignment to 'y'). But I doubt that this is really the lesson of (6a). The discourses in (6b–e) are parallel to (6a), and seem to indicate that we are dealing here with a much more general point.

6b. I have often wondered whether World War I was really a world war. I am inclined to think that it wasn't. It seems to me that it was little more than a European conflict.

6c. I have often wondered whether World War I was really a war at all. I suspect that most of what we have been told about it consists of exaggerations and falsehoods. I believe that really it was little more than a skirmish.

6d. I have often wondered whether the Millstone River is really a river. It seems to me that it is nothing more than a tiny creek.

6e. I have often wondered whether Professor McDuff is really a professor. I suspect that he has been lying about his background, and is not a professor at all.

These examples seem to indicate that virtually any aspect of the descriptive content of what seems to be a partially descriptive name can be called into question in a manner analogous to that of the discourse of (6a).

One possible reaction to this point would be to conclude that there aren't really any partially descriptive names at all, in the sense of expressions the semantic contents of which accord with the theory outlined above. Instead, it might be maintained, expressions of the sort illustrated in (1) are all to be understood as ordinary proper names, the semantic contents of which are simply their referents. On this view, the descriptive pieces of information associated with such names are mere connotations that give rise to pragmatic implicatures in particular cases that can be withdrawn or removed, at the discretion of the speaker.

Such a reaction would, in my view, be extreme. Certainly it is not warranted by the examples in (6). Whatever is going on with these examples also occurs with uncontroversially descriptive expressions, as is illustrated by (7).

7. I have often wondered whether the Iranian diplomat we met last month was a diplomat at all. The more I have thought about it, the more I have been convinced that his story makes no sense. He was no diplomat. I doubt that that he was even Iranian.

As in the case of (6), there are contexts in which this discourse would make coherent sense. This is true, despite the fact that *the Iranian diplomat we met last month* is clearly a descriptive phrase. Two further points are worth noting. First, if the semantic contents of descriptions include the descriptive properties contributed by their constituents, then no appeal to the different possible scopes of this description with respect to *wondered whether* will, by itself, render (7) semantically coherent. Second, even if one thinks that, in addition to their usual readings, descriptions have a second, semantically referential, reading in which their semantic contents are the objects they uniquely denote, this still will not be enough to make the discourse in (7) semantically coherent. (For suppose the speaker is right in his doubts. Then, since there was no Iranian diplomat that the speaker met last month, the description won't denote anyone. Hence it won't have any semantic content, on the semantically referential reading. But then the sentences in the discourse will, on the speaker's own view, fail to semantically express truths.) Since none of this shows that *the Iranian diplomat we met last month* isn't a genuine semantically descriptive phrase, the discourses in (6) don't show that the partially descriptive names they contain don't have semantic contents that are partially descriptive.

The most natural account of what is going on in (7) is pragmatic. On this account, the speaker conveys his doubts about a particular individual, and his belief, of that individual, that he wasn't a diplomat. The speaker uses the description *the Iranian diplomat we met last month* to draw attention to a particular individual, and to convey, and perhaps even assert, something about him—even though the speaker believes that the description does not literally apply to the individual in question. On this account, the speaker's primary intention in using the sequence of sentences in (7) is to convey information quite different from the semantic content carried by those sentences in the context. Since he is able to do this, the coherence of the discourse does not require us to revise the normal semantic analysis of the sentences uttered. Once this is seen, a similar point might be made about the discourses in (6). Thus, the coherence of what the speaker communicates in those discourses does not show that the partially descriptive analysis of the names that occur there is semantically incorrect.[7]

Nevertheless, I suspect that this isn't the whole story either, and that more is going on in at least some of the discourses of type (6). These discourses indicate that speakers doubt that one or more of the descriptive properties associated with a putative partially descriptive name really apply to its referent. There are two different sorts of responses that speakers may have to such doubts. They may either take those doubts to be grounds for withdrawing the name in the future, or they may decide to continue to use the name without its offending descriptive content.

Consider, for example, (6d). If speakers come to be convinced that the Millstone River is really too small to count as a river, and yet they continue to use the name to refer to it in most ordinary contexts, then they may be understood to be using it as an ordinary, nondescriptive name, with mere descriptive connotations. If, on the other hand, they withdraw the original name, *the Millstone River*, and replace it with *the Millstone Creek*, then this is evidence that they are treating both the original name and the new name as partially descriptive. In principle either option is possible, though with certain examples one course of action seems more natural than the other. For example, in the case of (6e), if McDuff is proven to be a fraud, then it would be quite natural for speakers to refuse to refer to him as *Professor McDuff* anymore. Similarly, if Hoboken, New Jersey, were to secede from New Jersey and be annexed by New York State, presumably the name *Hoboken New Jersey* would cease to be used to refer to that little city on the Hudson. These considerations support the idea that although some phrases may have the form of partially descriptive names while really being semantically nondescriptive, other phrases are genuine partially descriptive names. Still others may be ambiguous between the two.

Rigidity and the Limits of the Partially Descriptive Theory

At the end of chapter 2, I pointed out that partially descriptive names with semantic contents that include contingent properties of their referents are not, strictly speaking, rigid designators. This point is illustrated by the examples *Princeton University* and *Hoboken New Jersey*, which may be taken to be equivalent to [*the x*: (*University x & x = y*)] and [*the x*: (*Located-In x, New Jersey*)], respectively (relative to assignments of the referents of the names to 'y'). According to the partially descriptive theory, these names refer to the same individual in every world in which they designate anything at all. However, in some worlds in which their actual referents exist, they fail to designate either those referents or anything else.

I argued that this result was defensible, and could be squared with intuition by appealing to scope distinctions in modal sentences containing these names. For example, if we stipulate that w is a world in which Princeton is founded as a college and never becomes a university, it seems correct to say that the proposition expressed by (8) is true, when evaluated at w, even though there is a reading of (9a) in which it is also true, and equivalent to (9b), where the description is explicitly given wide scope.

8. There is no such institution as Princeton University.
9a. In w Princeton University exists, but is only a college (and so is not a university).
9b. The institution which is Princeton University is such that in w it exists but is only a college (and so is not a university).

Similarly, if w is a world in which in which the boundaries of New York and New Jersey are different from what they actually are, so that Hoboken and the surrounding area are part of New York State, then it seems intuitively correct to say that the proposition expressed by (10) is true, when evaluated at w, even though there is a reading of (11a) in which it is also true, and equivalent to (11b), where the description is explicitly given wide scope.

10. There is no such city (place) as Hoboken New Jersey.

11a. In w, Hoboken New Jersey exists, but is located in New York (rather than New Jersey).

11b. The city Hoboken New Jersey is such that in w it exists, but is located in New York (rather than New Jersey).

These examples illustrate the kind of justification that must be given if an expression is to be analyzed as a partially descriptive name with a semantic content that includes a contingent property of its referent. Since such names are not, strictly speaking, rigid designators, intuitive support must be found for the claim that some sentences containing them really do have readings that display modal profiles characteristic of nonrigid terms (of a certain restricted type); in addition, readings of some sentences that might seem to suggest full-fledged rigidity must be accommodated by other means—for instance, by appeal to wide scope. This justificatory burden severely limits the range of the partially descriptive theory. Although this burden can often be met when the names to be analyzed are, like those in (1), syntactically complex expressions made up of words that have independent semantic significance, the burden is much more difficult to meet when the names to be analyzed don't have linguistically significant structure. For names of this latter sort,—such as *Aristotle* or *Kripke*—intuitive judgments supporting their rigidity tend to be strong, and extremely difficult to explain away.

One unusual name which may be an exception to this general rule is *Superman*, as used in the fiction. Speaking from within the context of the fiction, one may plausibly maintain that the man Superman could have existed in a world w in which no one had super powers (because of altered circumstances on both Earth and the planet Krypton). But could one similarly maintain that in w, Superman does not exist, that no existing person is Superman, or that there is no such person as Superman? Only if there is a natural sense in which one could correctly maintain these things can *Superman* be analyzed as a partially descriptive name. In my opinion there is a natural sense in which these things, as well as the following sentence, are true: *Since the individual who is actually Superman could have existed without having super powers, he could have existed without being Superman.* Thus, it seems to me that *Superman* (as used in the fiction) is partially descriptive. However, I admit that the intuitive judgements in this case are somewhat elusive, and to that extent the conclusion that the name is partially descriptive must remain tentative.

When one looks at other cases, it is difficult to find clear examples of names that are both partially descriptive and without significant linguistic structure. More precisely, one is hard pressed to find other examples in which the putative descriptive content of a (structureless) name includes something more than that expressed by some general and innocuous sortal—such as *person* or *sentient being* (both of which express essential properties of anything that has them).Two of the best potential candidates for being such names are *Hesperus* and *Phosphorus*.

It is not unreasonable to think that in acquiring these two names for Venus, one learns that *Phosphorus* is associated with its appearance in the morning sky and *Hesperus* is associated with its appearance in the evening sky. A case could be made that a speaker who doesn't know this—either because the speaker has mixed up which description goes with which name, or because the speaker is unaware of any descriptions conventionally associated with the names—simply doesn't understand the terms. If this is right, if it is necessary to associate the right description with the right name in order to be counted as a competent user of the terms, then one would expect the content of the descriptions to be included in the propositions conveyed, and perhaps even asserted, in arbitrary contexts by competent users of sentences containing the names. And if that is so, then the conception of semantic content sketched in chapter 3 will tell us that the semantic contents of *Hesperus* and *Phosphorus* are different. Because of this, it might well seem that they are partially descriptive names.

However, the intuition that these names are rigid designators poses a problem for this thought. Consider a possible world w in which Venus and the Earth have orbits different from the ones they actually have. Because of this, Venus is not visible from Earth in either the morning or the evening. Is w a world in which (12a) is true?

12a. Hesperus is a planet.

12b. [the x: x is a heavenly body & x = y & x is visible in the evening sky] (x is a planet).

Is w a world in which Hesperus is a planet, or in which Hesperus even exists? If the proposition that Hesperus is a planet is the proposition expressed by (12b) (relative to an assignment of Venus to 'y'), then (12a) is not true in the imagined world, since in that world Venus is not visible in the evening. If this seems like the right result, if it seems correct that in w there is no such planet as Hesperus (and hence it is not the case that Hesperus is a planet), then *Hesperus* may well be a partially descriptive name. However, it seems doubtful to me that this is correct. Intuitively, it seems natural to think that the proposition that Hesperus exists, and is a planet, would continue to be true even if it were not the case that Hesperus was seen in the evening. But if that is right, then presumably *Hesperus* is rigid, and our preliminary characterization of it as partially descriptive is wrong.

Perhaps, it will be suggested, we should introduce a rigidification operator into the descriptions associated with special names such as *Hesperus*. On this proposal, the semantic content of (12a) is something like the proposition expressed by (12c) (in our own present context, relative to an assignment of Venus to 'y')—that is, the proposition that the heavenly body, Venus, which is actually visible in the evening sky, is a planet.

(12c.) [the x: x is a heavenly body & x = y & actually x is visible in the evening sky] (x is a planet).

Since this proposition is true at a possible world in which Venus exists and is a planet, but is not visible in the evening, the proposal accords with what seem to be our normal intuitions about the modal truth conditions of (12a). However it does not accord with our intuitions regarding the range of cases in which it is possible to believe that Hesperus is a planet.

This is shown by the argument given in the section "The Analysis of Names as Rigidified Descriptions" of chapter 2. To believe (12c)— that the heavenly body, Venus, which is actually visible in the evening, is a planet—one must believe something of the actual world. Since this is not required to believe the proposition expressed by (12a), the proposition expressed by (12a) cannot be the proposition expressed by (12c) (in our own present context, relative to an assignment of Venus to 'y'). The crucial point is that many agents in merely possible worlds believe that Hesperus is a planet, even though they do not have any corresponding beliefs about the actual world (i.e., about the world I refer to here and now in using *actually*), and so do not believe the proposition expressed by (12c) in my present context (relative to an assignment of Venus to 'y').Given the assumption that sentences that express the same propositions are substitutable in ascriptions of the form *x believes (the proposition) that S*, we may conclude that (12a) does not express the proposition expressed by (12c) (relative to the relevant context and assignment). Thus, one cannot save the view that *Hesperus* is a partially descriptive name by rigidifying the relevant description.

This means that we have no choice but to directly confront the intuitions supporting the claim that *Hesperus* is a rigid designator. Since I take these intuitions seriously, I am inclined to think that *Hesperus* is not a partially descriptive name after all. This leaves two main possible alternatives. The first is that *Hesperus* is an ordinary name the semantic content of which is simply its referent (or its referent plus the content of some very general sortal). On this alternative, the property of being visible in the evening sky is a bit of information that is, as a matter of fact, commonly associated with the name by those (mostly philosophers of language) who use it. Because of this, assertive utterances of sentences like (12a) often convey the information expressed by (12b). It may even be that sometimes this information is part of what is asserted by such utterances. However, on this view it is not necessary to associate the property of being visible in the evening sky with the name in order to be a competent user of it, and there are perfectly proper uses of (12a) in which (12b) is not asserted. These uses support the rigidity intuitions.

The second possibility is that *Hesperus* is a partially descriptive name the semantic content of which includes the property of being visible in the evening sky, but we have not yet given a correct theoretical account of what partially descriptive names are. On this view, the partially descriptive theory that I have defended up to now must be replaced by the following theory.

An Alternative Theory of Partially Descriptive Names

The semantic content of a partially descriptive name is the pair consisting of its referent, o, plus a descriptive property D-hood, associated with n by speakers. The proposition expressed by a sentence *n is F* is <<D-hood, o>, F-hood>. This proposition is true at an arbitrary possible world w iff o has the property F-hood at w (whether or not o has D-hood in w). However, to believe this proposition is to attribute to o the property of having both D-hood and F-hood.[8]

According to this theory, the proposition semantically expressed by (12a) has the same truth conditions, and hence the same modal profile, as the singular, Russellian proposition that Venus is a planet. However, in order to believe the proposition semantically expressed by (12a), one must, in effect, believe the proposition expressed by (12b) (relative to an assignment of Venus to 'y'), and hence one must believe of Venus that it is both a planet and a heavenly body visible in the evening sky.

Although this may initially seem to be an attractive view, it gives rise to counterintuitive consequences that ultimately undermine its credibility. These consequences may be illustrated by considering a possible world w in which Venus is visible in the morning sky but not in the evening sky. In w, something else is visible then. Astronomy is not very advanced in w, and agents incorrectly believe that the planet they see in the morning—Venus—is also what they see in the evening. They sometimes express this view by pointing at Venus in the morning and saying, "That is a planet that is visible in the evening sky (in such and such a place) as well as in the morning sky." In light of this, agents in this world believe of Venus that it is seen in the evening sky, among other things.

Next consider the truth value of (13) with respect to such a world, where Ralph is one of the agents just described (and the alleged descriptive content of *Hesperus* is given small scope).

13. Ralph believes that Hesperus is a planet.

According to the alternative theory of partially descriptive names, both (13) and the proposition that Ralph is said to believe—that expressed by (12a)—are true.

12a. Hesperus is a planet.

However, in order for this to be so, Ralph must believe something false—namely, that Venus is visible in the evening sky. In effect, the alternative theory of partially descriptive names tells us that the claim that Ralph believes something false is a necessary consequence of (12a), (13), and (14), all of which are true at the world in question.[9]

14.   Venus is not visible in the evening sky.

Thus, the alternative theory of partially descriptive names tells us that in certain situations, belief in a false proposition is a conceptual precondition for believing certain true propositions. This is counterintuitive.[10]

Moreover, it is only one of several, related counterintuitive results. For example, if the alternative theory of partially descriptive names were correct, and *Hesperus* were such a name, then it would be hard to explain what would be wrong with sincerely and assertively uttering

15.   Hesperus is a planet but I don't believe that Hesperus is a planet

in a possible circumstance in which Venus was not visible in the evening sky, and the speaker knew this.[11]

Another problem is posed by apparently innocuous T-sentences such as (16).

16.   The (proposition semantically expressed by the) English sentence *Hesperus is a planet* is true iff Hesperus is a planet.

Consider a possible world in which the semantics of English is just as it is in the actual world, but Venus is not visible in the evening sky. If the alternative theory of partially descriptive names were correct, and if *Hesperus* were such a name, then it would seem that for an agent to believe (16) would, in effect, be for the agent to believe the proposition expressed by (17) (relative to an assignment of Venus to 'y').[12]

17.   The (proposition semantically expressed by the) English sentence *Hesperus is a planet* is true iff [the x: x is a heavenly body & x = y & x is visible in the evening sky] (x is a planet).

Since, according to the alternative theory of partially descriptive names, the proposition expressed by (17) (relative to an assignment of Venus to 'y') is false at the world in question, a competent speaker who knew the facts about Venus, and was not in any way linguistically ignorant or confused, would not believe the proposition expressed by (17). Thus, such a speaker would not believe the proposition expressed by (16). Rather, the speaker should be willing to sincerely, assertively utter (18).

18. I do not believe that the (proposition semantically expressed by the) English sentence *Hesperus is a planet* is true iff Hesperus is a planet.

Intuitively, however, it is highly doubtful that a competent speaker in such a situation would fail to believe (16), or be willing to assertively utter (18).

All of these counterintuitive results are the product of a theoretical anomaly at the heart of the alternative theory of partially descriptive names. According to the theory, descriptive information introduced into the proposition semantically expressed by (12a) substantially affects what it is to believe or assert that proposition, while at the same time being completely irrelevant to its truth conditions.[13] Without some principled explanation of why this should be so, the postulation of propositions containing such special descriptive information appears to be nothing more than an ad hoc attempt to reconcile conflicting claims about sentences containing names like *Hesperus* and *Phosphorus*. The fundamental conflict is between intuitions that these names are rigid designators, one the one hand, and the claim that their semantic contents attribute contingent properties to their referents, on the other. In my view, the rigidity intuitions should prevail; hence, claims about the enriched semantic contents of sentences containing these names must be given up.

The central claims that led the alternative theory of partially descriptive names to the counterintuitive results illustrated by (12)–(18) are the following:

C1. Understanding the name *Hesperus* requires associating it with the property of being visible in the evening sky (or of being actually visible in the evening sky).

C2. Because of this, the information that Venus is visible (or actually visible) in the evening sky is included in the information conveyed by assertive utterances of (12a) in all normal contexts involving speaker/hearers who understand the expressions.

C3. In addition, this information is part of what is asserted by assertive utterances of the sentence in such contexts.

C4. Because the information that Venus is visible (or actually visible) in the evening sky is part of what is asserted and conveyed by assertive utterances of (12a) in all normal contexts involving speaker/hearers who understand the expressions, it is reasonable to suppose that this information is part of the semantic content of the sentence, and hence is part of the proposition it semantically expresses.

C5. Sentence (12a) semantically expresses a proposition that is true at a world in which Venus is a planet but is not visible in the evening. Hence the proposition semantically expressed by the sentence is not the proposition expressed by (12b) (relative to an assignment of Venus to 'y').

C6. Since the proposition semantically expressed by (12a) includes the information that Venus is visible (or actually visible) in the evening sky, one who believes that proposition must also believe that Venus is visible (or actually visible) in the evening sky.

C7. The proposition semantically expressed by (12a) is such that agents in various merely possible worlds may believe it without having any corresponding belief about the actual world.

C1–C4 entail that the proposition semantically expressed by (12a) includes descriptive information about the visibility of Venus in the evening. C5 and C6 specify that this descriptive information is constitutive of the content of one's belief in that proposition, even though this information does not impose a condition on the truth of that proposition at a world. C7 assures us that the proposition semantically expressed by (12a) is not the proposition expressed by (12c) (relative to an assignment of Venus to 'y').

Since these seven claims jointly lead to unacceptable results, one or more of them must be incorrect. C5, which expresses the rigidity of the name *Hesperus*, is probably not at fault. Nor is C7, which is supported by the arguments in chapter 2. Since C6 would be acceptable if C4 were, the problem seems to be located at C4 and earlier. In my view, the most plausible alternative is to reject C1, and thereby C2–C4 as well. Instead of holding that understanding the name *Hesperus* requires associating it with the property of being visible in the evening sky, one may note that, as a matter of fact, this property is often associated with it by speakers and, because of this, the information that Hesperus (i.e., Venus) is visible in the evening is often, but not always, conveyed (and sometimes may even be part of what is asserted) by utterances of sentences containing the name. All of this is compatible with the original theory of partially descriptive names, provided that *Hesperus* and *Phosphorus* are not partially descriptive.

There are two further variations on this view that are also compatible with the original theory of partially descriptive names (provided that *Hesperus* and *Phosphorus* are not partially descriptive). These variations involve accepting C1 and C2 while rejecting C3 and C4. On one of the variations, sentences such as (12a), containing the name *Hesperus*, conventionally implicate the information that Hesperus (i.e., Venus) is visible in the evening sky. On the other variation, this descriptive information is used to semantically fix the referent of *Hesperus*. On either variation, this information is not always part of what is asserted by utterances of such sentences, and it is not included in the contents of the objects of belief and assertion reported by the propositions semantically expressed by ascriptions such as *Ralph believed (asserted) that Hesperus is a planet.*[14]

According to each of these alternatives, *Hesperus* and *Phosphorus* do not contribute contingent properties of their referents to the propositions semantically expressed by sentences containing them. Rather, they contribute their referents alone (or their referents plus essential properties expressed by some very general sortals). Thus, unlike the linguistically complex examples mentioned in (1), the names *Hesperus* and *Phosphorus* are not partially descriptive.

To sum up, the conception of semantic content of names for which I have argued is one for which the following theses hold:

(i) The semantic contents of the vast majority of linguistically simple proper names are their referents alone (or their referents plus the properties expressed by some very general sortals associated with the names).

(ii) Nevertheless, the semantic contents of some proper names include properties of their referents in the manner specified by the original theory of partially descriptive names. In many cases these properties are contingent properties of the referents of the names.

(iii) The linguistically complex names mentioned in (1) are partially descriptive in this sense, though the linguistically simple names *Hesperus* and *Phosphorus* are not.

(iv) No names conform to the alternative theory of partially descriptive names.

The Problem Posed by Propositional Attitude Ascriptions

Propositional Attitude Ascriptions

In chapter 3 I argued that the semantic contents of most linguistically simple proper names are their referents. In chapter 4 this result was extended to the semantic contents of indexicals with respect to contexts of utterance, whereas in chapter 5 a special class of partially descriptive names was singled out as an exception to the general identification of the semantic content of a name or indexical with its referent. The central conclusions in each of these chapters rested in part on observations about what competent speakers assert by uttering sentences containing names and indexicals in different contexts. In formulating these observations, I implicitly adopted a relational account of assertion—that is, I assumed that in each case of assertion there is someone, the agent, that does the asserting and something, the object of assertion, that is asserted. I use the term *proposition* to designate the kinds of things that are objects of assertion (and other propositional attitudes) and bearers of truth-value. Assertion itself is a relation holding between agents and propositions. However, it is a mediated relation. An agent asserts a proposition p by doing something or employing some content-bearing representation that is associated with p. The most familiar cases are those in which the agent asserts a proposition by assertively uttering a sentence. I have maintained that normally the semantic content of the sentence uttered, relative to the context of utterance, is one of the propositions asserted by an agent's assertive utterance.

It is now time to consider assertion ascriptions—that is, sentences used to report the assertions of agents. Examples of such ascriptions are given in (1).

1a.   Edward asserted the proposition that Martin denied.

1b.   Edward asserted the proposition that the earth is round.
1c.   Edward asserted that the earth is round.

Sentence (1a), in which *asserted* is flanked by two noun phrases, suggests that *assert* is a two-place predicate, and that a sentence of the form (2) is true just in case its subject expression designates an agent that bears the assertion relation to the entity designated by its direct object—that is, by the noun phrase immediately following the verb.

2.   NP assert NP

This analysis also applies to (1b), which is true iff the referent of the name 'Edward' asserted the proposition designated by the phrase *the proposition that the earth is round.* On the assumption that this proposition is also designated by the clause *that the earth is round,* we can extend the analysis to (1c), which is treated as semantically equivalent to (1b).

Precisely analogous points can be made for a wide variety of other propositional attitude ascriptions—for example, those in (3).

3a.   Edward believed (denied, refuted, proved, established) the proposition that Tony asserted.
3b.   Edward believed (denied, refuted, proved, established) the proposition that the earth is round.
3c.   Edward believed (denied, refuted, proved, established) that the earth is round.

Finally, there is a class of propositional attitude verbs that are very closely related to those in (1) and (3), except that they do not occur with ordinary noun-phrase objects, but instead take only sentential clauses.[1]

4a.   *Edward says (thinks, means, hopes, expects) the proposition that Martin denies.
4b.   *Edward says (thinks, means, hopes, expects) the proposition that the earth is round.
4c.   Edward says (thinks, means, hopes, expects) that the earth is round.

In what follows, I will take the analysis of attitude ascriptions of the sort illustrated by (4c) to be the same as the analysis of the attitude ascriptions illustrated by (1c) and (3c).

The semantically determined truth conditions of all attitude ascriptions of this form are given by (5).

5. (The proposition semantically expressed by) *t v's that s* is true with respect to a context c, world w, and assignment f of objects to variables, iff in w, the referent of t (with respect to c, w, and f) bears the relation expressed by the attitude verb v (with respect to c) to the proposition designated by the clause *that s* (with respect to c and f).

Although (5) is well motivated, certain important questions regarding it have so far been left open. One of these involves the identity of the proposition designated by a clause, *that s*, with respect to a context.[2] What proposition is designated by clauses of this sort?[3]

The discussion in chapters 3 and 4 might seem to suggest a variety of possibilities. There I argued that an assertive utterance of a sentence s (containing names or indexicals) by an agent in a context c often results in the assertion not only of the semantic content of s with respect to c, but also of other, sometimes stronger, propositions as well. Suppose now that a person wants to report one or more of the assertions made by an agent in such a situation. In many cases one can do this by using the same sentence that the agent assertively uttered. That is, in cases in which an agent asserts a proposition by assertively uttering s in a context c, one can report that assertion by assertively uttering *A said/asserted that s* in a related context c'. Let us suppose that we have a case of this sort in which the agent asserted both the proposition p that is the semantic content of s with respect to c, and some stronger proposition q as well. Let us suppose further that the semantic content of s in the original context c is the same as the semantic content of s in reporting context c'. Then, it would seem that the reporter's use of *that s* in c' might be taken either as designating p or as designating q. In other words, a person assertively uttering the attitude ascription might use the *that*-clause either to pick out the semantic content of s in the reporting context, or to pick out a different proposition q. Depending on which of these is selected, the reporter will be taken as claiming either that the agent asserted p or that the agent asserted q.

The possibility envisioned can be made more concrete by considering a relatively clear and straightforward example of an extrasemantic assertion made by a mildly metaphorical use of language, followed by an accurate report of that assertion using essentially the same metaphorical language.

God's Fountain Pen

Professor McX, a notorious windbag and know-it-all, is declaiming on the issues of the day to a group of graduate students at a departmental reception. Having rudely brushed aside attempts by some of the students to express differing opinions, McX is finally interrupted by one of them, Ms. Y, who puts him in his place by remarking, *"You may not like my saying this, Professor, but you aren't God's fountain pen, you know."* McX walks away in a huff. The students in the group are amazed by Ms. Y's audacity. Later, one of them, Mr. Z, reports the incident to a third party, saying, *"You know how McX can go on and on about his pet ideas? Well, he was doing his usual number, pontificating nonstop and not letting anyone else get a word in edgewise, when Ms. Y told him to his face that he wasn't God's fountain pen."*

In this example, the proposition, p, semantically expressed by the sentence, *you are not God's fountain pen*, uttered by Ms. Y, is the proposition that McX is not a certain type of writing instrument used by God. Although p is literally true, its truth is so obvious and uninformative that it is clear to everyone that p cannot be the primary proposition that Ms. Y intended to assert. Rather, what Ms. Y was trying to say, and what she was taken to say by all the conversation's participants, is something the content of which is approximated by the proposition, q, that McX isn't the authority that he takes himself to be. This proposition, or something like it, is asserted by Ms. Y, even though it is not the semantic content of any sentence she uttered. Moreover, when Mr. Z reports her assertion, he uses a sentence, *he wasn't God's fountain pen* (referring to McX), that has essentially the same semantic content in his context that the sentence used by Ms. Y had in her context, and that carries roughly the same extrasemantic implications that hers did.

Thus, just as Ms. Y was able to use a sentence s to assert a proposition distinct from the proposition semantically expressed by s, so Mr. Z is able to report her assertion of that proposition, using a sentence with essentially the same semantic content as s.

Moreover, there is good reason for Mr. Z to have chosen to report Ms. Y's assertion in the way that he did. As I pointed out in chapter 3, when an agent's assertive utterance of a sentence s results in an assertion of more than the proposition semantically expressed by s (in the context), the precise content of this extrasemantic assertion is often to some degree indeterminate.[4] In these cases it is determinate that the agent asserts more than the proposition semantically expressed by the sentence uttered, but it is indeterminate precisely which further propositions are asserted. When this is so, someone who wants to use an assertion ascription to report the extrasemantic assertion of an agent may be well advised to choose a complement clause for the verb of saying that gives rise to the same indeterminacy as the sentence originally used by the agent. This is what Mr. Z does in our example when he selects a sentence that has essentially the same semantic content in the reporting context that the sentence uttered by Ms. Y had in the original context, and that gives rise to roughly the same extrasemantic indeterminacy that hers did.

Putting aside complications introduced by indeterminacy, we may put the general point illustrated by this example by saying that the speaker's referent of *that s* in a reporting context c depends on which proposition (or propositions) the speaker associates with s in c—roughly, by what the speaker means by s in c.[5] However, the speaker's referent of a term is not always the same as its semantic referent—that is, the designation determined by the semantic rules of the language (together with the context).[6] Since (5) is concerned with the semantically determined truth conditions of attitude ascriptions—that is, with the truth conditions of the propositions semantically expressed by such ascriptions—we need an account of the semantic referents of *that*-clauses with respect to contexts. Two candidates for giving such an account are (6a) and (6b).[7]

 6a.   The proposition (semantically) designated by a clause *that s* with respect to a context c (and assignment f of values to variables free in s) is the proposition that is the semantic content of s with respect to c (and f).

6b.   The proposition (semantically) designated by a clause *that s*
with respect to a context c (and assignment f) is the proposition that the agent of c uses s to express (relative to f)—roughly what the agent means by s in c (relative to f).

The difference between these two is that (6b) treats *that*-clauses as
inherently indexical (even when no indexicals occur in the clause),
whereas (6a) does not.

This difference has consequences for the analysis of propositional
attitude ascriptions. When the propositional attitude verb is *assert*, the
combination of (5) and (6a) yields (7a), whereas the combination of
(5) and (6b) yields (7b).

7a.   (The proposition semantically expressed by) *t asserts that s*
is true with respect to a context c, world w, and assignment
f of objects to variables, iff in w, the referent of t (with respect to c, w, and f) asserts the proposition that is the semantic content of s (with respect to c and f).

7b.   (The proposition semantically expressed by) *t asserts that s*
is true with respect to a context c, world w, and assignment
f of objects to variables, iff in w, the referent of t (with respect to c, w, and f) asserts the proposition that the agent of
c uses s to express (relative to f)—roughly what the agent
means by s in c (relative to f).

First consider (7a). The case we have in mind is one in which an
agent, A, assertively utters s in c, thereby asserting both the semantic
content, p, of s in c, and a stronger proposition q. Next a reporter, R,
wants to report A's assertion. R assertively utters

8.   A asserted that s

in a context c' in which the semantic content of s is also p. According
to (7a) the proposition semantically expressed by (8) in c' is true iff A
asserted p. On this account the fact that A also asserted q is irrelevant
to evaluation of the semantic content of (8) in c'. Nevertheless, it may
be relevant to the evaluation of the totality of what R asserted in c'.
That is, just as I have argued that A asserted q in addition to the proposition semantically expressed by s in c, so it might be argued that R

asserted that A asserted q, in addition to the proposition semantically expressed by (8) in c'. On this account, assertion ascriptions of the form (8) may be used to assert different propositions in different contexts even if their semantic contents do not change from context to context—just as simple sentences can.

The analysis given by (6b) and (7b) leads to a different description of the case. According to this analysis, if c' is a context in which R wants to use (8) to report A's assertion of q, then q is the semantic referent of *that s* in c', and the proposition semantically expressed by (8) in c' is true iff A asserted q. In a different context c#, in which R wants to report A's assertion of p, p is the semantic referent of *that s*, and the proposition semantically expressed by (8) in c# is true iff A asserted p. On this analysis, the fact that (8) may be used to assert different propositions in different contexts is seen as a consequence of its having different semantic contents in different contexts.

There are, I believe, reasons to be suspicious of this analysis. One of these involves examples like (9).

9a. The English sentence 'the earth is round' means that the earth is round.

9b. The English sentence 'the earth is round' is true iff it is true that the earth is round.

9c. The English sentence 'the earth is round' semantically expresses the proposition that the earth is round.

These examples are trivially true. In particular, there are no possible contexts of utterance in which the English sentence 'the earth is round' retains its actual meaning in which the propositions (semantically) expressed by (9a, b, c) are false.[8] The reason for this is that the clause *that the earth is round* present in these examples semantically designates with respect to any context the proposition semantically expressed by 'the earth is round' relative to that context. This strongly suggests that the rule for determining the semantic referents of *that*-clauses is (6a) rather than (6b).

By itself this doesn't falsify (7b). It is possible to maintain (7b) while denying (6b), provided one also denies that the semantic content of an assertion ascription (8) with respect to a context c is a function of the semantic content of its constituents—the subject expression, the

verb, and the *that*-clause—with respect to c. This position is by no
means incoherent. However, it does face serious problems of its own.
For example, consider again the assertion ascriptions in (1).

1a. Edward asserted the proposition that Martin denied.
1b. Edward asserted the proposition that the earth is round.
1c. Edward asserted that the earth is round.

In the ascription (1a) the verb *assert* is followed by a noun phrase that
describes the object of assertion without containing any constituent that
expresses that proposition. There is, I think, no plausible alternative to
taking the semantically determined truth conditions of examples like
these to be given by (10).[9]

10. (The proposition semantically expressed by) *t asserts d* is
    true with respect to a context c, world w, and assignment f
    of objects to variables, iff in w, the referent of t (with respect
    to c, w, and f) asserts that which is (semantically) designated
    by d (with respect to c and f).

But now, this rule applies directly to (1b). In light of our discussion of
(9), we take the proposition semantically designated by the noun phrase
the proposition that the earth is round (as well as by the *that*-clause
itself) to be the proposition semantically expressed by the sentence 'the
earth is round,' rather than any other proposition q that the speaker
may have in mind. If this is right, then (7a+) rather than (7b+) gives
the correct account of the semantically determined truth conditions of
assertion ascriptions of the form (1b).

7a+. (The proposition semantically expressed by) *t asserts the
     proposition that s* is true with respect to a context c, world
     w, and assignment f of objects to variables, iff in w, the
     referent of t (with respect to c, w, and f) asserts the proposi-
     tion that is the semantic content of s (with respect to c and
     f).
7b+. (The proposition semantically expressed by) *t asserts the
     proposition that s* is true with respect to a context c, world
     w, and assignment f of objects to variables, iff in w, the
     referent of t (with respect to c, w, and f) asserts the proposi-

tion that the agent of c uses s to express (relative to f)—
roughly what the agent means by s in c (relative to f).

Surely, we don't want fundamentally different analyses for pairs like
(1b) and (1c). Thus (7a) must be correct for (1c), and for assertion
ascriptions of the form (8) in general. In fact, the single rule (10) can
be applied to all ascriptions of the sort illustrated in (1), provided that
we recognize *that*-clauses as singular terms designating propositions.

The falsity of (7b) and (7b+) is further illustrated by the following
logically valid argument.

11a.   Edward asserted the proposition semantically expressed by
       the English sentence *Peter Hempel lived in Princeton.*
11b.   The proposition semantically expressed by the English sen-
       tence *Peter Hempel lived in Princeton* is the proposition that
       Peter Hempel lived in Princeton.
11c.   Edward asserted the proposition that Peter Hempel lived in
       Princeton.
11d.   Edward asserted that Peter Hempel lived in Princeton.

Since this argument is logically valid, there is no context of utterance
c in which the propositions semantically expressed by (11a) and (11b)
are true, but the proposition semantically expressed by (11c) or (11d)
is false. Let c be a context in which (11a) is true. Since (11b) is true
in all contexts in which English words retain their standard meanings,
we may also take it to be true in c. But then the propositions semantically expressed by (11c) and (11d) must also be true in c—even if the
speaker in c wishes to use these ascriptions to (falsely) report that Edward asserted a proposition q stronger than the proposition semantically
expressed by *Peter Hempel lived in Princeton.* If (7b+) and (7b) gave
the semantically determined truth conditions of (11c) and (11d), respectively, then the proposition semantically expressed by (11c) or (11d)
could be false in such a context, even when the propositions semantically expressed by (11a) and (11b) were true. Since this is impossible,
(7b) and (7b+) do not give the correct account of the semantically
determined truth conditions of assertion ascriptions.

There are, then, reasons to believe that (the proposition semantically expressed by) an assertion ascription *t asserts* (*the proposition*)

that s is true (in a context) iff the referent of t asserts the proposition semantically expressed by s (in the context). There is also reason to generalize this treatment of assertion ascriptions to all the propositional attitude verbs we have considered. This leads to (12), which is a sharpening of the account of the semantically determined truth conditions of propositional attitude ascriptions given by (5).

12. (The proposition semantically expressed by) *t v's that s* is true with respect to a context c, world w, and assignment f of objects to variables, iff in w, the referent of t (with respect to c, w, and f) bears the relation expressed by attitude verb v (with respect to c) to the proposition semantically expressed by s (with respect to c and f).

With this analysis in place, we are now ready to address the problem posed by propositional attitude ascriptions for the account of the semantic content of names and indexicals given in chapters 3 and 4.

Direct Reference and Substitutivity in Attitude Ascriptions

I have argued that both indexicals and the vast majority of linguistically simple proper names are directly referential—that is, if t is such a term, then the semantic content of t with respect to a context c is the referent of t with respect to c.[10] It follows from this that if t_1 and t_2 are two such terms, and the referent of t_1 in context c_1 is the same as the referent of t_2 in context c_2, then the semantic contents of the two terms are the same in their respective contexts. When this view of names and indexicals is combined with the account of propositional attitude ascriptions given in (12), plus a standard, compositional treatment of the semantic contents of sentences occurring as complement clauses in such ascriptions, we get the result that substitution of coreferential names or indexicals in attitude ascriptions must preserve truth-value.

It is often taken to be obvious that this claim about substitution cannot be correct, which in turn is standardly taken to show that names and indexicals cannot be directly referential. For example, it has frequently been maintained that (13b) and (14b) are false, even though they result from substituting one coreferential name for another in (13a) and (14a), which are true.[11]

$B_L \langle x = x \rangle$

13a. Lois Lane believes that Clark Kent is Clark Kent.

F? 13b. Lois Lane believes that Superman is Clark Kent. $B_L \langle x = y \rangle$

14a. The ancients believed that the Evening Star was visible only in the evening. $B_A \langle x \neq y \rangle$

F? 14b. The ancients believed that the Morning Star was visible only in the evening. $B_A \langle x = y \rangle$

Thus, it is often concluded, the semantic content of a name cannot be its referent.

On the basis of our discussion thus far, it should be clear that this reasoning is too hasty. We have seen that, quite independently of the semantics of attitude ascriptions, there is good reason to believe that some names are partially descriptive. In addition to this, there is at least some reason to think that the names *the Evening Star*, *the Morning Star*, and *Superman* might be among them. If, in fact, these names are partially descriptive, then their semantic contents are not their referents. However, we have also seen that these names are unusual, and that the overwhelming majority of linguistically simple, ordinary proper names cannot be understood on the model of the special case of partially descriptive names. Thus, even if it is a fact that substitution of these particular names in (13) and (14) results in pairs of sentences that semantically express propositions with different truth-values, this tells us nothing about the semantic contents of ordinary, linguistically simple names (and indexicals).

However, the underlying problem is not so easily dealt with, since it seems to reoccur with ordinary, simple names as well. For example, the names *Carl Hempel* and *Peter Hempel*, discussed in chapter 3, as well as the names *Ruth Barcan* and *Ruth Marcus*, are simple, ordinary, and not partially descriptive. Since these pairs are coreferential, it follows, on my account, that they have the same semantic content. But then the semantic account of attitude ascriptions given by (12), plus a compositional treatment of the semantic contents of the complement clauses of these ascriptions, yield the result that the semantically determined truth conditions of (15a) and (16a) are the same as those of (15b) and (16b), respectively.

$B_E \langle x = x \rangle$

15a. Edward believes that Ruth Barcan is Ruth Barcan.

15b. Edward believes that Ruth Barcan is Ruth Marcus.

$B_E \langle x = y \rangle$

16a. Edward believed that Peter Hempel lived on Lake Lane in Princeton.

$B_E \langle (\exists x L x) \, L \, a \rangle$

16b. Edward believed that Carl Hempel lived on Lake Lane in Princeton.

$B_E \langle [(\exists x L x) L a] \wedge a = b \rangle$

Thus, the semantic theses I have adopted lead to the result that neither the propositions semantically expressed by (15a) and (15b), nor those expressed by (16a) and (16b), can differ in truth-value. But this is apt to seem counterintuitive, since, if asked, many competent speakers of English (including those who are competent users of the names *Ruth Barcan*, *Ruth Marcus*, *Peter Hempel*, and *Carl Hempel*) will report that it is possible for (15a) and (16a) to be true, even when (15b) and (16b) are not.

The conflict between this intuitive response to examples like (15) and (16) and the semantic theses I have adopted is not to be taken lightly. On the one hand, the intuitions are persistent and widespread. On the other hand, the semantic theses I have adopted are highly motivated; it is not at all easy to see how they could be wrong, or what modified theses could be put in their place. In order to resolve this dilemma, we will have to look very carefully at the sources of our intuitions about examples like (15) and (16), and to review the arguments given for our central semantic claims.

In this chapter and the next I will concentrate on the latter task. I begin by pointing out a gap in the argument given in chapter 3 for the conclusions (i) that the semantic content of the names *Carl Hempel* and *Peter Hempel* is the man they both refer to, and (ii) that the semantic contents of (17a) and (17b) are the same.

17a. Peter Hempel lived on Lake Lane in Princeton.
17b. Carl Hempel lived on Lake Lane in Princeton.

In giving that argument, I noted that there are contexts of utterance in which the conversational participants associate different descriptive properties, the properties expressed by F and G, with the two names. Because of this, different propositions may be asserted and conveyed by assertive utterances of (17a) and (17b) in these contexts. In these contexts, an assertive utterance of (17a) may result in the assertion of the proposition expressed by *[The x: x is F and x = y] lived on Lake Lane in Princeton* (relative to an assignment of Mr. Hempel to 'y'), whereas an assertive utterance of (17b) may result in the assertion of the proposition expressed by [*The x: x is G and x = y*] *lived on Lake Lane in Princeton* (relative to a similar assignment). Since the properties expressed by F and G are different, the propositions asserted may also be different.

Nevertheless, I argued that the semantic contents of (17a) and (17b) do not include the properties expressed by F or G. The reason they don't, is that the semantic content of a sentence s is something that is asserted and conveyed by assertive utterances of s in all normal contexts in which s is used with its literal meaning by competent speakers and hearers who understand it. Since it is not a condition of being a competent user of the name *Peter Hempel* that one associate it with the property expressed by F, and it is not a condition of being a competent user of the name *Carl Hempel* that one associate it with the property expressed by G, there will be normal contexts involving competent speakers and hearers in which what is asserted and conveyed by assertive utterances of (17a) and (17b) doesn't involve the properties expressed by F or G at all. Hence, neither of these properties is a constituent of the semantic contents of (17a) or (17b); and, of course, they are not constituents of the semantic contents of the names either. Since the same can be said for any pair of different descriptive properties that speakers might associate with the names, the semantic contents of the names do not include such properties, and the semantic contents of (17a) and (17b) are descriptively identical.[12]

That is not all. If one asks of (17a), and also of (17b), "What is asserted and conveyed by assertive utterances of it in all normal contexts in which competent speakers and hearers who understand it, use it with its literal meaning?," one gets the same answer in both cases. Assertive utterances of these sentences always involve asserting of Mr. Hempel that he lived on Lake Lane in Princeton. In all these cases the same property is predicated of the same individual. At a minimum this shows that the semantic contents of (17a) and (17b) are propositions such that to assert them is to say of the same man that he has the same property.

Since the semantic contents of the two sentences involve exactly the same properties predicated of exactly the same things, they represent the world as being exactly the same way. For this reason, one is hard pressed to find any difference between the semantic contents of the two sentences, or between the semantic contents of the two names.

It was on this basis that I postulated that the semantic content of both sentences is the singular, Russellian proposition consisting of Mr. Hempel together with the property of having lived on Lake Lane in Princeton, and that the semantic content of both names is their common referent.[13]

The last step in this argument may be seen as implicitly based on a principle about the identity of propositions. An elementary version of this principle, involving simple propositions that predicate a property or relation of one or more objects, is given by (18).

18. If p and q are simple propositions in which precisely the same properties are predicated of precisely the same things, then p = q.

The idea behind (18) is that all there is to propositions is the way they represent things as being. Since the propositions semantically expressed by (17a) and (17b) both represent the same man as having the same property, and don't differ in the way in which they represent anything else as being, the proposition semantically expressed by (17a) and the proposition semantically expressed by (17b) are one and the same.

This view of propositions, recently defended by Michael Thau, is, I think, very plausible.[14] However, it is not beyond question. For example, if propositions include nonrepresentational constituents—constituents that are neither objects of which properties are predicated nor properties that are predicated of any object (nor truth functions nor anything else contributing to the truth conditions of propositions)—then two propositions may represent things in the world as being exactly the same way and yet not be identical. Of course, this abstract possibility will not seem realistic unless one can give some reasonable specification of what these nonrepresentational constituents of propositions might be. It does no good to posit some mysterious "one knows not what" and then try to use it to solve a difficult philosophical problem. However, in this case there are intelligible candidates for nonrepresentative constituents of propositions. The proposition semantically expressed by a sentence *Fn* might be taken to include as constituents not only the referent of n and the property expressed by F, but also the expressions n and F. In other words, the proposition semantically expressed by a sentence of this sort might be taken to be an amalgam of the sentence itself together with the singular, Russellian proposition that represents the referent of n as being a certain way.

Although this view is incompatible with principle (18), it is consistent with the main points made in chapter 3. For example, it might be maintained that the proposition asserted and conveyed by assertive utterances of (17a) in all normal contexts involving competent speakers and hearers who understand the sentence is the amalgam of sentence (17a) together with the singular, Russellian content consisting of Mr. Hempel and the property of having lived on Lake Lane in Princeton. A similar point might be made about (17b), in which case we would get the result that the semantic contents of the two sentences—the propositions they semantically express—are different, even though their representational content is the same. Moreover, on a relational treatment of propositional attitude ascriptions, this will mean that the semantic contents of

16a. Edward believed that Peter Hempel lived on Lake Lane in Princeton

16b. Edward believed that Carl Hempel lived on Lake Lane in Princeton

will be different. The former will characterize the belief relation as holding between Edward and one linguistically enhanced proposition, whereas the latter will characterize the belief relation as holding between Edward and a different linguistically enhanced proposition. Since the two propositions are different, we no longer get the conclusion that it is impossible for these two belief ascriptions to differ in truth-value. In this way it may seem as if the problem involving substitution of coreferential names in belief ascriptions can be made to disappear.

I believe that this (dis)appearance is an illusion. To show this, in chapter 7 I will examine two of the most well-developed versions of the strategy of taking propositional attitude ascriptions as reporting relations between agents and linguistically enhanced propositions (objects of belief, assertion, etc.). I will argue that these attempts to provide a semantic account of attitude ascriptions fail for principled reasons. Once this is done, I will turn in chapter 8 to an entirely different approach. There I will present my own view, which attempts to reconcile a Millian account of meaning with (pseudo) Fregean intuitions about how the truth-value of what is asserted may be affected by the substitution of coreferential names. On the view I will develop, (17a) and (17b) semantically express the same singular, Russellian proposition, and (16a) and (16b) have the same semantically determined truth conditions, even though assertive utterances of (16a) and (16b) in certain contexts may result in the assertion of propositions with different truth-values.

The Case Against Linguistically
Enhanced Propositions

At the end of the previous chapter, I sketched a strategy for analyzing propositional attitude ascriptions of the form *x v's that S* that treats them as expressing relations between an agent, on the one hand, and what one might call "a linguistically enhanced proposition," on the other. The idea is that the linguistically enhanced proposition expressed by S is an amalgam of the semantic contents of the expressions occurring in it—such as the objects corresponding to names and indexicals, and the properties and relations corresponding to predicates—together with something much more fine-grained: either the linguistic expressions of S themselves, or internal mental representations associated with one's use of those expressions. The resulting picture is one in which a pair of attitude ascriptions

    1a. x v's that . . . a. . . .   *where a=b*
    1b. x v's that . . . b. . . .

that differ by containing two different symbols, a and b, will express relations to different linguistically enhanced propositions. As a result, the analysis will not be committed to the claim that the truth-value of such an ascription is always preserved by substitution of coreferential names, or indeed by substitution of anything else. In this chapter, I will comment on two of the most promising and well worked-out variants of this idea that exist in the literature.

Interpreted Logical Forms

The first analysis to be considered is given by Richard Larson and Peter Ludlow in their paper "Interpreted Logical Forms."[1] According to Larson and Ludlow, propositional attitude ascriptions report relations between agents and what they call "interpreted logical forms." An interpreted logical form for a sentence S is a syntactic representation of S, in particular a phrase marker the terminal nodes of which are the individual words in S paired with n-tuples of objects (their "semantic values"). The nonterminal nodes of the phrase marker are associated with values related to the semantic values of their daughter nodes.

A pictorial representation of the interpreted logical form associated by Larson and Ludlow's semantic theory with the sentence (2a) is given by (2b).

2a.   John speaks Spanish.
2b.

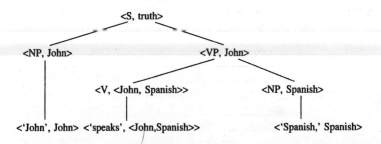

The proposed semantic theory works in the following way: We are given as input to the theory grammatically analyzed sentences of the object language—in effect, sentences with explicit syntactic representations of their hierarchical organization into constituents and subconstituents. The semantic theory is a Davidson-style theory of the material truth conditions of grammatically analyzed sentences.

Rough examples of the rules used to interpret (2a) are given in (3).

3a.   A sentence of the form [$_S$ NP VP] is true iff there is an object x which is a semantic value of both NP and VP.

3b.   x is a semantic value of [$_{NP}$ 'John'] iff x = John.

3c.   x is a semantic value of [$_{NP}$ 'Spanish'] iff x = Spanish.

3d.   x is a semantic value of [$_{VP}$ V NP] iff there is an object y such that <x,y> is a semantic value of V and y is a semantic value of NP.

3e.   <x,y> is a semantic value of [$_V$ 'speaks'] iff x speaks y.

These rules are used to derive the statement of the truth conditions of (2a) given in (4).

 4. The (grammatically analyzed) sentence '[s [NP John] [VP [V speaks] [NP Spanish]]]' is true iff there is an object x such that x = John and there is an object y such that y = Spanish and x speaks y—in effect, iff John speaks Spanish.

To get the interpreted logical form (2b) that is assigned by the theory to sentence (1a), one starts with the uninterpreted logical form (5) which is given by the syntax, and which serves as the input to the semantic theory.

 5.

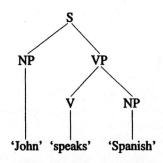

One then attaches a putative semantic value to each of the nodes to get the interpreted logical form.[2] The value one attaches to the S-node is always truth, and the value one attaches to any other node is the unique object which can be proved to be a semantic value of that node from the assumption that the sentence is true, using the semantic rules for the sentence. So, in our example, the rules (3b) and (3c) give us directly that the semantic value of the NP-node dominating 'John' is the man John, and the semantic value of the NP-node dominating 'Spanish' is the Spanish language. From this, together with (3a) and the assumption that the sentence is true, we derive that the man John is a semantic value of the VP-node as well. Combining this with the rule (3d) for verb phrases gives us the ordered pair <John, Spanish> as a semantic value of the V-node dominating 'speaks.' The end result is the interpreted logical form (2b).

According to Larson and Ludlow, such interpreted logical forms are objects of the attitudes. The rules for individual attitude verbs 'assert' and 'believe' are given in (6).

6a. <x,y> is a semantic value of 'asserts' iff x asserts y.
6b. <x,y> is a semantic value of 'believes' iff x believes y.

The rule that tells us that the objects of belief and assertion ascriptions are the interpreted logical forms of their complement clauses is (7).

7. x is a semantic value of [$_{VP}$ V S]—that is, of a verb phrase consisting of a propositional attitude verb followed by a complement clause—iff there is a y such that <x,y> is a semantic value of V and y = the interpreted logical form assigned to S (in accord with the above process).

By putting all of these rules together, one can derive theoretical statements of the truth conditions of propositional attitude ascriptions like (8).

8. Mary asserts/believes that John speaks Spanish.

The theorem of the semantic theory interpreting this sentence will have roughly the form (9), where the dots in (9) are filled in by a description of the interpreted logical form (2b).

9. The (grammatically analyzed) sentence '[$_S$ [$_{NP}$ Mary] [$_{VP}$ [$_V$ asserts/believes] [$_S$ that John speaks Spanish]]]' is true iff Mary asserts / believes. . . . . . (Fill in the dots with a description of (2b.)

If we were to spell out in words the intended content of the theorem of the form (9) that is derivable from the theory, it would be something like (10).

10. The (grammatically analyzed) sentence '[$_S$ [$_{NP}$ Mary] [$_{VP}$ [$_V$ asserts/believes] [$_S$ that John speaks Spanish]]]' is true iff Mary asserts/believes the interpreted phrase marker whose root node is the pair <'S', truth>, which dominates a pair of

nodes <'NP', John> and <'VP', John>, where <'NP', John> dominates <'John', John>, and <'VP', John> dominates a pair of nodes <'V' <John, Spanish>> and <'NP', Spanish>, with the first of these nodes dominating <'speaks', <John, Spanish>> and the second dominating <'Spanish', Spanish>.

When spelled out in full detail, this T-sentence, allegedly interpreting the attitude ascription (8), is quite a mouthful. Certainly no truth theory issuing such theorems is homophonic, a fact noted by Larson and Ludlow, with heroic understatement, in a footnote.

More troubling is the fact that the T-sentences are themselves mysterious, and hard to interpret. At this point it is essential that one not get caught up in technicalities, but rather step back and ask what is going on. The task we are engaged in is to give a semantic theory for propositional attitude ascriptions. According to Larson and Ludlow, this means giving a Davidsonian theory of the truth conditions of those ascriptions. The most crucial aspect of this sort of theory is that it is supposed to issue in theorems of the form

11. S is true (in L) iff. . . .

that interpret the object language sentence S by giving its truth conditions. Suppose, however, that a particular theory of this sort generates theorems of the form (11), in which the clause filling in the dots on the right-hand side of the biconditional expresses a theoretical claim that we have no pretheoretic understanding of, nor any ability to directly test or evaluate. In such a situation the semantic theory cannot be said to have accomplished the fundamental task of giving interpretive truth conditions for object language sentences.

That is precisely the situation that Larson and Ludlow's semantic analysis of attitude ascriptions confronts us with. Suppose that someone walked up to you and assertively uttered, out of the blue, the right-hand side of (10). That is, suppose the person simply said "Mary believes the interpreted phrase marker whose root node is the pair <'S', truth>, which dominates. . . ." Would you understand the person's remark, or know how to determine whether it was true? Surely not. Prior to being convinced of the correctness of some contentious theory, we have no idea what it would mean to say that a person believes one of these unfamiliar objects. Thus, until we are given an explanation of what it might mean to believe or assert what Larson and Ludlow call interpreted logical forms, accompanied by persuasive empirical evidence that we really do believe and assert these things, we won't have any grip on the right-hand sides of T-sentences like (10).

The problem is that Larson and Ludlow provide no such explanation. It is, of course, tempting when reading them to rely on the fortuitous fact that we already understand the attitude ascriptions on the left-hand sides of the T-sentences. Given this understanding, we might be tempted to use the T-sentences to interpret the theoretical claims on their right-hand sides. But this is illegitimate, from the point of view of the overall Davidsonian framework that Larson and Ludlow adopt. The information expressed by the full range of theorems like (10) is supposed to allow someone with no antecedent knowledge of the object-language to interpret, and come to understand, the object-language sentences on the left. It is impossible for the propositions expressed by the T-sentences produced by Larson and Ludlow to play this role if the meanings of the object-language sentences are going to be presupposed, and used to interpret the theoretical claims on the right-hand side.

This problem for Larson and Ludlow arises directly from their commitment to a Davidsonian conception of semantic theories. It is a central feature of the Davidson program that no meanings are assigned to sentences, and no theorems stating what sentences mean are derivable from Davidsonian semantic theories. Because of this, some independent justification is needed to support the claim that a Davidsonian truth theory for a language may play the role of a theory of meaning. The problem for Larson and Ludlow is that obscure and theoretically loaded theorems like (10) cannot play the justificatory role standardly required by Davidsonians in order for their theories of truth conditions to count as theories of meaning.[3]

Although I suspect that this problem may be intractable from the Davidsonian perspective, there is an additional difficulty here that goes beyond the Davidsonian program. Many semantic theories attempt to state the truth conditions of attitude ascriptions in terms of the relations that agents bear to the objects of those attitudes. Different theories characterize these objects differently—for instance, as interpreted logical forms, structured propositions, or sets of possible worlds. In addition, each theory faces the task of explaining what it is to bear the relevant relation to the relevant object of the attitude. It is only by giving such explanations that semantic theories are able to make empirically testable claims about the truth conditions of attitude ascriptions. In the case of Larson and Ludlow, what we need is some set of additional principles that will allow us to derive testable empirical predictions from theorems like (10). Although Larson and Ludlow do not say much about this, the problem they face is illustrative of similar problems faced by a variety of theories.[4] For this reason it is instructive to see what steps can be taken to alleviate the problem in their case.

First, observe that Larson and Ludlow's analysis claims that the ascription (8) is true iff Mary asserts or believes the interpreted logical form (2b). If the theory also told us that the interpreted logical form (2b) were true iff John speaks Spanish, then we could put these two results together to derive the conditionals (12a) and (12b).

12a. If the (grammatically analyzed) sentence '[$_S$ [$_{NP}$ Mary] [$_{VP}$ [$_V$ asserts/believes] [$_S$ that John speaks Spanish]]]' is true, then Mary asserts/believes something that is true iff John speaks Spanish.

12b. If the (grammatically analyzed) sentence '[$_S$ [$_{NP}$ Mary] [$_{VP}$ [$_V$ asserts/believes] [$_S$ that John speaks Spanish]]]' is not true, then there is something that is true iff John speaks Spanish which is such that Mary doesn't assert/believe it.

These results would at least provide some correct and testable information about the truth conditions of the attitude ascription.

As it stands, the theory does not provide an account of the truth conditions of interpreted logical forms like (2b). As a result, it does not allow us to derive (12a, b). However, this could be fixed. The theory does give an account of the truth conditions of what one might call "uninterpreted logical forms" like (5); and this account could in principle be extended to provide a treatment of the truth conditions of so-called interpreted logical forms like (2b). Doing so would allow us to derive informative theorems like (12a, b).

Although this is progress, we are not out of the woods. Since Larson and Ludlow's semantic theory provides only material truth conditions, the information provided by (12a, b) is minimal. In effect, (12a) tells us that if the attitude ascription (8) is true, then there is some p such that Mary asserts/believes p, and p has the same truth value in the actual world as the claim that John speaks Spanish; (12b) tells us that if (8) is not true, then there is some p such that Mary doesn't assert/ believe p and p has the same truth value in the actual world as the claim that John speaks Spanish. Note, in addition to being quite weak, these conditionals cannot be turned into biconditionals. Thus, they do not provide necessary and sufficient truth conditions for the attitude ascription (8), even in the minimal sense standardly demanded of Davidsonian truth theories. Although they do provide some clear, testable information about the truth conditions of (8), this information falls well short of what we need to evaluate theorems like (10).

If the theory could be transformed into one that assigns to sentences and interpreted logical forms truth conditions relative to different possible worlds, then the information provided by the theory would be substantially enhanced. Although this goes well beyond Larson and Ludlow's actual discussion, it seems as if it is the sort of thing that could in principle be done. If it were done, one could generate strengthened versions of (12) along the lines of ($12a_w$) and ($12b_w$).

($12a_w$). If the (grammatically analyzed) sentence '[$_S$ [$_{NP}$ Mary] [$_{VP}$ [$_V$ asserts/believes] [$_S$ that John speaks Spanish]]]' is true with respect to a possible world w, then in w Mary asserts/ believes something that is true with respect to an arbitrary world w* iff in w* John speaks Spanish.

($12b_w$). If the (grammatically analyzed) sentence '[$_S$ [$_{NP}$ Mary] [$_V$ asserts/believes] [$_S$ that John speaks Spanish]]]' is not true with respect to a possible world w, then there is something p that is true with respect to an arbitrary world w* iff in w* John speaks Spanish and, in w Mary does not assert/ believe p.

These theorems are more informative than (12a, b). ($12a_w$) tells us that if the attitude ascription (8) is true, then Mary asserts/believes some claim that is necessarily equivalent to the claim that John speaks Spanish; while $12b_w$) assures us that if (8) is not true, then there is something necessarily equivalent to the claim that John speaks Spanish that Mary does not assert/believe. However, these theorems are still not informative enough, since ($12a_w$) doesn't tell us which of the many claims necessarily equivalent to that claim that John speaks Spanish Mary asserts/believes, when (8) is true; and ($12b_w$) does not tell us which of these claims she fails to assert/believe, when (8) is not true.

Because the information carried by theorems of the sort (12a$_w$) and (12b$_w$) is still incomplete, we need to see if the theory can be made to provide further information that could be used to determine whether or not the original statements like (10) that it makes about the truth conditions of attitude ascriptions are correct. One type of information standardly provided by a semantic theory is information about which object-language sentences follow from which. In the case of propositional attitude ascriptions, the information we want concerns cases in which the truth of one attitude ascription, perhaps together with the truth of other supplementary premises, does, or does not, guarantee the truth of other attitude ascriptions. Indeed, it was precisely in order to deliver certain results of this kind that Larson and Ludlow formulated the theory in the way they did.

Foremost in their minds was the desire to provide a semantics that would block inferences like the one from (13a, b) to (13c).

(13a. Max believes Judy Garland sang "Somewhere over the Rainbow."
13b. Judy Garland = Frances Gumm.
13c. Max believes Frances Gumm sang "Somewhere over the Rainbow."

Their account of why this inference is blocked is as follows: although the truth of (13b) guarantees that the semantic values of the names *Judy Garland* and *Frances Gumm* are the same, and although this semantic value—the woman named by both expressions—is one constituent of the interpreted logical forms that are supposed to be the objects of the beliefs reported by (13a) and (13c), the interpreted logical forms are different in these two cases, because one of them contains the name *Judy Garland* while the other contains the name *Frances Gumm*. Since (13a) reports that Max stands in the belief relation to one object, and (13c) reports that Max stands in the belief relation to a different object, Larson and Ludlow conclude that the truth of (13a, b) does not guarantee the truth of (13c).

However, there is a problem here. The semantic theory tells us that sentence (13a) is true iff Mary believes a certain interpreted logical form, and that (13c) is true iff Mary believes a slightly different interpreted logical form. But nothing in the semantic theory, or in any theory explicitly provided by Larson and Ludlow, tells us whether it is possible for an agent to bear the belief relation to one of these interpreted logical forms without bearing the belief relation to the other interpreted logical form. Moreover, since the whole idea of believing one of these specially constructed objects is a theoretical one, we have no intuitions to consult to settle the matter. In theory, one could combine the Larson and Ludlow semantic account with any one of many different principles governing the belief relationship between agents and interpreted logical forms.

Two such principles are given in (14).

14a. The belief relation is such that whenever two interpreted logical forms differ in any way whatsoever, it is possible for some agent to believe either one without believing the other.

14b. The belief relation is such that whenever two interpreted logical forms agree entirely in their nonlexical constituents and differ only in the lexical material associated with simple singular terms, it is impossible to believe one without believing the other.

If one were to combine our extended version of the Larson and Ludlow semantics with (14a), one would get the conclusion that it is possible for (13a, b) to be true while (13c) is false. On the other hand, if one were to combine the semantics with (14b), one would get the conclusion that it is not possible for (13a, b) to be true while (13c) is false. Since Larson and Ludlow do not explicitly adopt (14a), (14b), or any other comparable principle, their theory makes no predictions about when substitution in attitude ascriptions is truth-preserving.

This is unacceptable. It is also, I think, not their real intent. Although they do not explicitly formulate the needed principle, they often speak as if they take it for granted that any difference in interpreted logical forms arising from substitution of one expression for another in attitude ascriptions gives rise to a possible divergence in truth-values.[5] If this was their intent, then perhaps we should modify their explicit theory by conjoining it with (14a). This has the virtue of giving the theory needed predictive content. Unfortunately, however, many of the predictions turn out to be false.

For example, consider the pair (15a, b).

15a. Mary believes that John speaks Spanish.
15b. Maria cree que Juan habla español.

A Larson and Ludlow-style semantic theory for English will tell us that (15a) is true iff Mary believes the interpreted logical form (2b). A similar-style semantic theory for Spanish will tell us that (15b) is true if Mary believes the interpreted logical form (16).

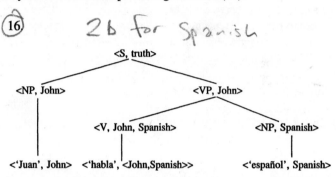

(16) 2b for Spanish

Since (2b) differs lexically from (16), the semantic theories for the two languages together with (14a) predict that it is possible for (15a) and (15b) to differ in truth-value. The same predication is made for every pair of attitude ascriptions in different languages. This prediction is, I take it, clearly false.[6]

Additional instances of what seems to be the same problem are given by the following pairs.

17a. There is a professor x in my department such that Mary believes that x speaks Spanish.
17b. There is a professor y in my department such that Mary believes that y speaks Spanish.
18a. There is a man and there is a woman such that Mary believes that the former loves the latter.
18b. There is a woman and there is a man such that Mary believes the latter loves the former.
19a. Mary believes that you are interesting to talk to (said to me).
19b. Mary believes that I am interesting to talk to (said by me).
20a. Mary believes it will rain in Recife tomorrow (said yesterday).

20b. Yesterday, Mary believed it would rain in Recife today (said today).

21a. Mary believes that Peking is one of the world's largest cities, but she doesn't know its name.

21b. Mary believes that Bejing is one of the world's largest cities, but she doesn't know its name.

In each case, the interpreted logical form which is the alleged object of the (a)-ascription differs linguistically from the interpreted logical form that is the alleged object of the (b)-ascription. Hence the Larson and Ludlow semantics, augmented with (14a), predicts that the two ascriptions may differ in truth-value. But this seems wrong.

Similar problems are posed by (22)–(24).

22a. Mary believes that I/you speak Spanish (said by me).

22b. There is someone such that Mary believes that person speaks Spanish.

23a. Mary believes that thing is heavy (said demonstrating an anvil).

23b. There is something such that Mary believes it is heavy.

24a. Mary believes that Kripke wrote *Naming and Necessity*; moreover, Kripke still lives in Princeton.

24b. There is someone who still lives in Princeton such that Mary believes he wrote *Naming and Necessity*.

In each case, the (b) sentence is a consequence of the (a) sentence. Thus, if the (a) sentence is true, then the (b) sentence must be true. Since the enriched theory consisting of Larson and Ludlow's semantics plus principle (14a) conflicts with this conclusion, the enriched theory is false.

The general lesson here goes far beyond Larson and Ludlow, and cannot be stressed enough. There is a class of celebrated cases, on which philosophers and semanticists have concentrated, in which substitution in attitude ascriptions appears to change truth-value. However, in addition to this there is another large class of uncelebrated cases in which substitution in attitude ascriptions of names, indexicals, or variables which are coreferential (relative to contexts and assignments) seems clearly to preserve truth-value. Both sorts of cases deserve to be taken seriously. The first class of cases might motivate one to adopt the working hypothesis that objects of the attitudes contain linguistic as well as nonlinguistic elements. If one does this, however, one must also account for the second class of cases by formulating clear principles about precisely when and how the linguistic elements incorporated into the objects of the attitudes should be ignored, because they make no difference to the truth-value of attitude ascriptions, and when they should not be ignored, because they do make a difference. Moreover, there is no guarantee in advance of a systematic investigation of this kind that linguistic elements will prove to be needed in the objects of the attitudes at all.

Context-Sensitive Relations to Linguistically Enhanced Propositions

Mark Richard's Theory of Propositional Attitudes

Like Larson and Ludlow, Mark Richard has proposed a semantic analysis of propositional attitude ascriptions that views them as reporting relations between agents and linguistically enhanced propositions.[7] In addition, he seems to have been guided by the general lesson I have drawn from the previous discussion. In fact, his book, *Propositional Attitudes*,[8] and his subsequent paper, "Defective Contexts, Accommodation, and Normalization,"[9] present a theory of this type that is, in my view, the most plausible, well-developed, and sophisticated of any that can be found in the literature today. One can learn a great deal about both the potential and the limitations of this general approach by examining the strengths and weaknesses of Richard's theory.

The general outline of the theory is as follows: Sentences express linguistically enhanced propositions, which are amalgams of structured Russellian propositions with the words of the sentences themselves. Attitude ascriptions report relations to the enhanced propositions expressed by their complement clauses. In addition, belief predicates, as well as predicates expressing other attitudes, are indexical. When I say, in a context C, *Ralph believes that S*, I am reporting that Ralph accepts a linguistically enhanced proposition p that is a **close enough match** to the linguistically enhanced proposition q that is correlated with the sentence S that I use to make the report. What counts as close enough varies from one context of utterance to another. In some contexts, the identity of the words in the enhanced propositions doesn't matter at all;

as long as the Russellian content of the sentence used to report the belief matches the Russellian content of the sentence the agent would use to express his belief, the belief ascription counts as true. In these cases, substitution of expressions with the same Russellian content—including coreferential names or indexicals—preserves truth-value. In other reporting contexts there are restrictions—in addition to sameness of Russellian content—on which words, used in reporting the attitude, can stand in for the agent's words. In such contexts substitution of expressions with the same semantic content is constrained, and may change truth-value.

In order to evaluate Richard's theory of belief ascription, it is necessary to examine its main features more carefully. Five such features are central to the theory. First, sentences express "annotated propositions," which are amalgams of the Russellian propositions corresponding to them plus the words of the sentence themselves. For example, the propositions expressed by (1a) and (2a) are (1b) and (2b).

1a. Peter Hempel is Carl Hempel.
1b. <<'is', the identity relation>, <<'Peter Hempel', Mr. Hempel>, <'Carl Hempel', Mr. Hempel>>>
2a. Carl Hempel is Carl Hempel.
2b. <<'is', the identity relation>, <<'Carl Hempel', Mr. Hempel>, <'Carl Hempel', Mr. Hempel>>>

The constituents of these propositions are called *annotations*. For example, the proposition (1b) contains three annotations—the word 'is' together with its Russellian content, the identity relation; the name 'Peter Hempel' together with its Russellian content, the man Mr. Hempel; and the name 'Carl Hempel' plus its Russellian content, Mr. Hempel again. In general, the annotation corresponding to a linguistic constituent of a sentence is the pair consisting of the expression itself plus its Russellian content. The annotated proposition expressed by a sentence is a structured complex built up out of the annotations of its simple linguistic constituents.

The second main feature of Richard's theory is that belief ascriptions report relations between individuals and annotated propositions. A belief ascription, *x believes that S* reports that the relevant relation holds between the agent and the annotated proposition expressed by the complement sentence, S.[10] This is spelled out in (3).

3. A belief ascription *x believes that S* is true relative to a context of utterance C, possible world w, and assignment A of values to variables iff in w, the individual denoted by x relative to A stands in a certain relation R to the annotated proposition expressed by S relative to C and A.

The third main feature of Richard's theory is that according to it, belief predicates are indexical. The relation R expressed by the predicate *believe* varies from one context of utterance to another.

4. For any context C, the relation R_c expressed by the predicate *believe* in C is one that applies to a pair consisting of an agent A and an annotated proposition p iff A accepts a sentence (or internal mental representation) that expresses in A's context an annotated proposition q that is obtainable from p via some function f, which (a) maps annotations onto annotations with the same Russellian content and (b) satisfies relevant contextual restrictions in C regarding which words can be used in C to represent words used by A to express A's beliefs in A's context.

The fourth main feature of Richard's theory is its introduction of correlation functions. These functions map expressions with the same Russellian contents onto one another, and hence derivatively map annotated propositions onto one another. Since these functions never change the nonlinguistic content of annotations, their effect is simply to map the words of the person ascribing the belief onto the words of the believer. The need for these functions is prompted by the extremely fine-grained conception of propositions that results from Richard's introduction of linguistic material into the objects of belief. This fine-grained conception of propositions is necessary, once descriptivism about ordinary proper names and indexicals has been rejected, in order to block what Richard takes to be the substitutivity problems of Russellianism. However, the resulting propositions are so fine-grained that we now need an account of how an agent can truly be said to believe one of them even though he accepts and perhaps even understands no sentence that expresses it. Functions mapping the words used in ascribing such beliefs onto the words found in annotated propositions explicitly accepted by the agent are used to solve this problem. These functions allow one, when assessing the truth-value of belief ascriptions, to ignore differences in annotated propositions arising from different expressions with the same Russellian content.

But now one must be careful to make provision for correlation functions to be restricted, so they don't do too much. If Richard's theory did not allow contexts of utterance to place restrictions on these functions, then it would assign essentially the same truth conditions to belief ascriptions differing only in the substitution of expressions with the same Russellian content, and thus it would not avoid the most controversial consequences of Russellianism. For this reason, restrictions on correlation functions are crucial to Richard's theory.

These restrictions are the fifth main feature of his theory. I begin with the original and simplest formulation of Richard's idea. Originally, he took a restriction on a correlation function to be a triple, <i, A, S>, consisting of an individual i (representing a potential agent of a belief ascription), an annotation A (representing the content of an expression used in ascribing a belief), and a set S of annotations with the same Russellian content as A. (S contains acceptable candidates for mapping A onto when evaluating beliefs ascribed to i.)

For example, a context C reflecting a conversation in which

5a.   Tom believes that Carl Hempel was a philosopher of science

is regarded as true, while

5b.   Tom believes that Peter Hempel was a philosopher of science

is regarded as false, might contain the restrictions in (6).

6a.   <Tom, <'Carl Hempel', Mr. Hempel>, {<'Carl Hempel', Mr. Hempel>}>
6b.   <Tom, <'Peter Hempel', Mr. Hempel>, {<'Peter Hempel', Mr. Hempel>}>

Restrictions like these work in the following way: An attitude ascription *t believes that S* is true, as taken in a context C, iff there is a correlation function which (i) obeys all restrictions in C relating to the individual i designated by t and (ii) maps the annotated proposition expressed by S in C onto an annotated proposition q associated with a sentence (or internal mental representation) explicitly accepted by i. For a correlation function to obey a restriction <i, A, S> is simply for the function to map the annotation A onto some member of S. In this case, the restrictions in (6) tell us that mappings from expressions used in ascribing beliefs to Tom to expressions used by Tom himself must, in the case of the names 'Peter Hempel' and 'Carl Hempel', be identity mappings. Thus, if Tom would assent to *Carl Hempel was a philosopher of science* but would not assent to *Peter Hempel was a philosopher of science*, then in this context we could not substitute 'Peter Hempel' for 'Carl Hempel' in the belief ascription (5a) without changing truth-value.

That was Richard's original account. However, it soon became clear that the original conception of a restriction on a correlation function needed to be refined to account for the modal profile of certain attitude ascriptions.[11] Consider, for example, a belief ascription of the form (7).

7. The F believes that n is G.

In certain contexts a speaker might assertively utter (7) with the intention of attributing a belief to the unique person who has the property expressed by F, without knowing of any particular individual i that i is the unique person with that property. Intuitively, the proposition semantically expressed by (7) in such a context should be true, with respect to an arbitrary possible world w, iff in w the unique person with property F has the belief in question. When *the F* is a nonrigid designator, this means that the truth-value of (7) at different worlds will depend on the beliefs of different individuals. For Richard, this means that the intentions of speaker-hearers in the original context C must determine restrictions on correlation functions that may involve different individuals at different worlds.

One way to accommodate this requirement would be to modify Richard's original conception of a restriction by specifying that the first member of such a restriction must be a property rather than an individual. In the case in which speaker-hearers have a specific agent in mind, the property may simply be the property of being identical with that individual. In cases in which speaker-hearers have only a general intention about the individual or individuals who have a certain property P, the initial constituent of the restriction arising from this general intention is just P.

On this conception, the individuals relevant to an arbitrary restriction, <P, A, S> at a given world w are those that have the property P at w. The semantics of a belief ascription, *t believes that S*, where t is any name, indexical, variable, or definite description, remain as before. An ascription of this sort is true with respect to a context of utterance C, assignment V of values to variables, and world w iff there is a correlation function f obeying all restrictions relevant to the denotation i of t (with respect to C, V, and w) that maps the annotated proposition expressed by S (with respect to C and V) onto an annotated proposition accepted by i in w. This modified view allows Richard to handle ascriptions like (7).

The end result is a theory the aim of which is to retain the virtues of Russellianism while avoiding its most controversial consequences. The way this is to be achieved is by allowing restrictions on correlation functions to vary from context to context. According to Richard, the intentions of speaker-hearers determine the restrictions that are operative in a context. In some contexts, speaker-hearers are concerned only with the Russellian content of the beliefs reported. In these contexts no restrictions on correlation functions are operative, and substitution of coreferential names, indexicals, and variables (relative to assignments) is essentially free, just as it is on Russellian accounts.[12] However, Richard thinks that in other contexts speaker-hearers have views, which they intend to communicate, about the specific linguistic or mental representations used by agents to express certain Russellian contents, and they require sentences used to report an agent's beliefs to bear certain specific relations to the sentences or mental representations used by the agent. In these contexts, the intentions of speaker-hearers determine substantial restrictions on correlation functions, with the result that substitution of coreferential names and indexicals in sentences ascribing beliefs to an agent may change truth-value.[13] In this way, Richard attempts to account for the many cases that provide intuitive support for Russellianism—in which substitution of coreferential names, indexicals, and variables in attitude ascriptions seems to preserve truth-value—while also accounting for the many cases that seem to cause problems for Russellianism, in which such substitution appears to change truth-value.

The Problem of Using Metalinguistic Surrogates
for Descriptive Information

The first, and I believe most revealing, problem with Richard's theory is that it seems to misidentify the basis of our reluctance to substitute coreferential names and indexicals in many attitude ascriptions. Consider, for example, the pair (8a) and (8b).

8a. The ancient astronomer Hammurabi believed that Phosphorus was not visible in the evening.

8b. The ancient astronomer Hammurabi believed that Hesperus was not visible in the evening.

The reason we are inclined to regard (8a) and (8b) as potentially differing in truth-value is that we would often take the propositions asserted by someone assertively uttering them to differ in descriptive content. In particular, we would often take someone who assertively uttered (8a) to have asserted a proposition from which it follows that Hammurabi believed of a certain celestial body that it was visible in the morning but not the evening, whereas this is not the case with (8b).

Richard's theory, in its present form, does not capture this. The theory treats our inclination to regard assertions of (8a) and (8b) as potentially differing in truth-value as being due to the fact that in certain contexts the truth of the proposition semantically expressed by (8a) does not guarantee the truth of the proposition semantically expressed by (8b). According to the theory, if C is such a context, then C contains a pair of restrictions on correlation functions corresponding to (9a) and (9b).

9a. <the property of being the ancient astronomer Hammurabi, <'Phosphorus', Venus>, S_P>

9b. <the property of being the ancient astronomer Hammurabi, <'Hesperus', Venus>, S_H>

These restrictions differ in that (9a) requires the name 'Phosphorus' used in the attitude ascription (8a) to be mapped onto some word (or mental representation) used by Hammurabi in the set of potential translation targets S_P, whereas (9b) requires the name 'Hesperus' to be mapped onto some word (or mental representation) used by Hammurabi in the set S_H. In order for this difference to be capable of leading to a difference in truth-value between (8a) and (8b), the sets of translation targets S_P and S_H must differ. To make matters simple, let us suppose that P is a name for Venus that was actually used by Hammurabi and that <P, Venus> is the only member of S_P, whereas H is another name for Venus actually used by Hammurabi and <H, Venus> is the only member of S_H. With this understanding of the restrictions, what we learn from an assertive utterance of (8a) in C is that Hammurabi accepted some sentence ... **P** ... of his language that expressed a Russellian content attributing the property of not being visible in the evening to Venus. Since Hammurabi could have done this without accepting the corresponding sentence ... **H** ... of his language, we need not be prepared to accept (8b) in the context, even if we are prepared to accept (8a).

Although this account does block the substitution of 'Hesperus' for 'Phosphorus' in the case imagined, it seems clear that it does not capture what is really going on in typical situations in which we imagine an assertive utterance of (8a) conveying information different from that conveyed by an assertive utterance of (8b). The information derived from Richardian restrictions of the sort just indicated is far too specific and metalinguistic to explain our different reactions to utterances of the two sentences. Most of us don't know which language Hammurabi spoke, let alone which particular words (or mental representations) he used to refer to Venus. Thus, the different information we derive from assertive utterances of (8a) and (8b), and hence the information that is the basis for our reluctance to substitute one name of Venus for another in these ascriptions, is not information involving the identity of the different expressions Hammurabi used.

In addition, there is a related technical problem with Richard's overspecific characterization of restrictions on correlation functions. The crucial elements in these restrictions are the sets of translation targets they contain. For Richard these are simply sets of pairs, each pair consisting of an expression together with a Russellian content. In our example these are the sets S_P and S_H, which are simply {<P, Venus>} and {<H, Venus>}, respectively—where P and H are two different names for Venus that Hammurabi actually used. Given this characterization of the restrictions in C, we can use Richard's theory to evaluate the propositions expressed in C by the ascriptions (8a) and

(8b) not only in the actual world (world of the context), but in arbitrary possible worlds as well. When we do this, however, we get unacceptable results.

In the case we are imagining, the theory tells us that the proposition expressed by (8a) in C is true at an arbitrary world w only if in w Hammurabi accepted some sentence S, such that (i) S contains the expression P, and (ii) the Russellian content of S in Hammurabi's context in w consists of the planet Venus plus the property of not being visible in the evening. But this means that the theory predicts that the proposition expressed by (8a) in C will be false with respect to any world w in which Hammurabi did not use the expression P to refer to Venus (perhaps because he spoke a slightly different language). This will be so even if in w Hammurabi (i) used a new name P* for Venus, (ii) associated the property of being visible in the morning with P*, and (iii) accepted the sentence . . . P* . . . , the Russellian content of which in his context consisted of the planet Venus plus the property of not being visible in the evening. According to Richard's theory, the actual world (i.e., the world of the context) may be a world in which the proposition expressed by (8a) in C is true, whereas w is not such a world, even if the only difference between Hammurabi's epistemic state in the actual world and his epistemic state in w turns out to be that in w he used the linguistic form P* in all and only those cases in which he used the linguistic form P in the actual world. Surely, this is not an accurate account of the truth conditions of the proposition expressed by (8a), or asserted by a speaker who utters (8a), in the sorts of contexts we are apt to imagine when contemplating suspect instances of substitution of coreferential names.

As I have indicated, this problem is related to the observation that normal speakers who use (8a) and (8b) typically have no idea which particular words Hammurabi actually used. Because of this the truth-values of the propositions asserted by utterances of these sentences, when evaluated at arbitrary possible worlds, do not depend on the particular linguistic forms used by Hammurabi to express his beliefs in those worlds. Rather, they depend on the descriptive contents of the beliefs he has there. In the case of (8a) we take the proposition asserted to be true at a world iff Hammurabi believed some proposition at that world from which it follows that a certain celestial body is visible in the morning but not the evening. There is no way to capture this using the kinds of restrictions on correlation functions that are allowed by Richard's theory, as presently stated.[14]

One could, however, modify his notion of a restriction on correlation functions so as to approximate the desired result. In the sort of case that Richard has in mind, the person assertively uttering (8a) assumes that if Hammurabi were to have expressed the reported belief, he would have used some sentence of his language consisting of a phrase expressing the property of not being visible in the evening plus a name or indexical referring to Venus that he associated with the property of being visible in the morning. Presumably, to say that a term t is associated with a property p by a speaker s is to say that s accepts some sentence Ft in which F expresses p. The fact that Hammurabi is required to have associated the name or indexical with this property could then be invoked to ensure that (8a) is true in the context in question only if Hammurabi believed of Venus both that it is visible in the morning and that it is not visible in the evening, by virtue of accepting a pair of sentences expressing these Russellian contents in which the same term is used to refer to Venus in both cases. This, it might be argued, is tantamount to ensuring that (8a) is true in the context only if Hammurabi believed of Venus that it had the property of being visible in the morning but not the evening.

If this reasoning is correct, then there is a way of modifying Richard's conception of a restriction on correlation functions that would allow his semantics to capture the descriptive content of the belief attributed to Hammurabi by utterances of (8a) in the usual sorts of contexts in which substitution of 'Hesperus' for 'Phosphorus' is resisted. The modification involves changing his conception of a restriction on correlation functions so that its third constituent is no longer a set of translation targets, but rather a property that determines such a set, with respect to an arbitrary possible world. With this modified conception in place, we can construct a context for interpreting (8a) and (8b) containing the restrictions (10a) and (10b).[15]

10a. <the property of being the ancient astronomer Hammurabi, <'Phosphorus', Venus>, the property of being a name or indexical that refers to Venus and is associated by Hammurabi with the property of being visible in the morning>

10b. <the property of being the ancient astronomer Hammurabi, <'Hesperus', Venus>, the property of being a name or indexical that refers to Venus and is associated by Hammurabi with the property of being visible in the evening>

One now argues as follows: (i) to know that there is a correlation function satisfying (10a) that makes (8a) true is to know that the ancient astronomer Hammurabi believed of Venus both that it is visible in the morning and that it is not visible in the evening by virtue of accepting a pair of sentences (mental representations) expressing these Russellian contents in which the same term (mental representation) t is used to refer to Venus in both cases; (ii) this is tantamount to knowing that Hammurabi believed of Venus that it is visible in the morning but not the evening; (iii) since it is clear that this is not sufficient for ensuring that there is a correlation function satisfying (10b) that makes (8b) true, one knows that substitution of 'Hesperus' for 'Phosphorus' is not guaranteed to preserve truth in a context that includes restrictions (10a) and (10b). In this way, the descriptive basis for apparent instances of substitution failure in belief ascriptions can be captured by (our extension of) Richard's metalinguistic semantics for these ascriptions.

There are, it seems to me, two main problems with this argument. First, the move from (i) to (ii) is not entirely innocent. It is widely recognized that Kripke's Paderewski case, in which Peter accepts both *Paderewski has musical talent* and *Paderewski does not have musical talent* because he wrongly treats the two occurrences of the name as occurrences of names of different people, shows that it is possible for an agent like Hammurabi to satisfy (i) without satisfying (ii)—if he wrongly treats the two uses of t in (i) as referring to different things.[16] This possibility must somehow be ruled out in advance—by something about the normal use of the ascriptions (8a) and (8b) by ordinary speakers—if anything like the proposed modification of Richard's restrictions is to succeed in capturing the descriptive contents of the beliefs attributed to Hammurabi by (8a) and (8b) in typical contexts in which substitutivity of 'Hesperus' for 'Phosphorus' is resisted.

Second, even if this could be done, the resulting account is apt to seem baroque and indirect. Standard cases in which utterances of belief ascriptions differing only in coreferential names and indexicals seem to result in the assertion of propositions with different truth-values are cases in which beliefs with different descriptive contents are attributed to the agent. In many of these cases, speakers and hearers of such ascriptions have little knowledge of, or interest in, which expressions the agent would use to express his beliefs, If Richard's metalinguistic treatment of the objects of belief and the truth conditions of belief ascriptions can be made to accommodate this observation at all, then it can do so only in a manner that is indirect, complicated, and theoretically contentious. Do ordinary speakers really intend to commit themselves to claims about the languages or internal mental representations used by agents to which they typically ascribe beliefs? Are the descriptive contents of the beliefs that ordinary speakers attribute to agents when assertively uttering ascriptions like (8a) really mediated by complicated assumptions (sufficient to account for Paderewski-type cases) about the expressions or mental representations used by the agent?

These questions raise serious doubts about the strategy of using metalinguistic means to capture speakers' assumptions about descriptive contents. They also provide compelling motivation to look for a more direct way of capturing the descriptive basis for most instances of substitution failure involving the propositions asserted by utterances of attitude ascriptions. Here, I hasten to add, the problem we have been considering goes far beyond examples involving the names *Hesperus* and *Phosphorus*. In chapter 5, I considered the suggestion that sentences containing these names semantically express partially descriptive propositions to which the names contribute both their referents and certain conventionalized descriptive contents. Suppose, for the sake of argument, that I was wrong in rejecting this suggestion. In that case, the proposition that Phosphorus is not visible in the evening would be a proposition that, in effect, attributes to Venus the property of being visible in the morning but not the evening. Failure of substitution in (8a) and (8b) would then be directly attributable to the different descriptive contents of the propositions semantically expressed by the complement clauses of these ascriptions. No metalinguistic detour would be needed.

However, even if all of this were so, the problem would still arise in cases involving ordinary names, which do not carry conventionalized descriptive content. As in the case of (8a) and (8b), so also in the case of (5a) and (5b), it appears that one can find contexts in which an utterance of one of the sentences results in the assertion of a true proposition p, whereas an utterance of the other would result in the assertion of a false proposition q.

5a. Tom believes that Carl Hempel was a philosopher of science.
5b. Tom believes that Peter Hempel was a philosopher of science.

The reason for this difference seems to be that p and q differ in the descriptive contents of the beliefs involving Mr. Hempel that they attribute to Tom. In this case the descriptive difference is not attributable to a difference in the propositions semantically expressed by the complement clauses of the ascriptions. The challenge is to explain how this can be without invoking questionable metalinguistic detours of the sort that I have raised doubts about in my discussion of Richard.

This will be my task in chapter 8. There I will argue that (5a) and (5b) semantically express the same proposition (as do (8a) and (8b)), but that in certain contexts, utterances of them result in the assertion of propositions with different truth-values. If this is right, then the lesson to be learned from familiar examples of substitution failure is that we need a clearer understanding than we have had up to now of the difference between the proposition semantically expressed by a sentence, as used in a given context, and the proposition or propositions asserted by an utterance of the sentence in that context.

In this chapter I have raised doubts about two metalinguistic theories of belief ascriptions, and have tried to motivate the search for a positive, nonmetalinguistic alternative. Readers who wish to move directly to the development of that positive view are encouraged to turn to chapter 8. Those who are interested in examining further difficulties in Richard's view in some detail may proceed to the following appendix.

Appendix: Further Difficulties with Richard's Metalinguistic Approach

Too Many Semantic Options

I have argued that most cases in which we feel resistance to substitution of coreferential names or indexicals in belief ascriptions are those in which assertive utterances of the relevant ascriptions would naturally be taken to attribute descriptively different belief contents to the agent in question. I have also indicated that Richard's metalinguistic semantics of belief ascriptions provides him with a strategy, albeit circuitous and contentious, for attempting to accommodate this observation. However, the strategy has another defect, in addition to those already mentioned. It makes a range of semantic contents available for certain kinds of belief ascriptions that these sentences never in fact carry, thus raising an explanatory question to which the theory provides no ready answer.

Consider, for example, the belief ascriptions (11a) and (11b).

11a.   Frank and Kathy each believe that Phosphorous is a planet.
11b.   Frank and Kathy each believe that Carl Hempel was a professor at Princeton.

Intuitively, it seems that we can imagine contexts in which an assertive utterance of (11a) would attribute to both Frank and Kathy belief in the singular proposition that ascribes to Venus the property of being a planet that is visible in the morning. Similarly, we can imagine contexts in which an assertive utterance of (11b) would attribute to them both belief in the singular proposition that ascribes to Mr. Hempel the property of being a famous philosopher who was a professor at Princeton. Moreover, the contexts in question are those in which it appears that substitution of 'Hesperus' for 'Phosphorus' and 'Peter Hempel' for 'Carl Hempel' would change the propositions asserted, and perhaps even their truth-values.

I have described the metalinguistic strategy available to Richard for incorporating approximately this information into the semantic contents of (11a) and (11b) in the contexts in question. However, I now want to point out that the semantic machinery provided by his theory also makes room for the assignment of quite different semantic contents to these sentences in other, seemingly possible contexts. We begin by noting that a sentence *A and B each believe that S* should be true in a context C iff the sentence *For each x: such that x = A or x = B, x believes that S* is true in C. Next we observe that the latter sentence is true in C iff *x believes that S* is true in C with respect to an assignment of the referent, a, of A to the variable 'x,' and *x believes that S* is also true in C with respect to an assignment of the referent, b, of B to the variable 'x'. According to Richard's theory, this will be the case iff there is a correlation function satisfying all restrictions in C involving a that maps S onto a sentence S_a accepted by a (with the same Russellian content in a's context that S has in C), and there is another correlation function satisfying all restrictions in the context involving b which maps S onto a sentence S$_b$, accepted by b (with the same Russellian content in b's context that S has in C). Finally, we note that it is common for Richard's theory to allow a context to contain different restrictions for different individuals.[17] Moreover, there is nothing to prevent restrictions involving different individuals a and b to require correlation functions to map the same sentence S onto quite different sentences S$_a$ and S$_b$.

In particular, there is nothing to prevent the context C for an utterance of (11a) from containing restrictions requiring the sentence *t is a planet* accepted by Frank to contain a name t for Venus that he associates with the property of being visible in the morning while requiring the sentence *t* is a planet* accepted by Kathy to contain a name t* for Venus that she associates with the property of being visible in the evening. Given such a context C, the Richardian semantics just outlined will predict that the proposition semantically expressed by (11a) in C is true iff Frank believes of Venus that it is a planet and that it is visible in the morning, while Kathy believes of Venus that it is a planet and that it is visible in the evening. However, this is problematic, since (11a) is never interpreted in this way by speakers of English. An analogous point holds for (11b).

Anyone adopting Richard's theory is faced with the problem of explaining why this is so. Here, it should be noted that such a problem need not arise for alternative approaches. For example, imagine a theory that maintains that sometimes speakers who assertively utter an attitude ascription *NP believes that S* in a context C use S to stand for a proposition other than its semantic content in C. For example, in some contexts a speaker might use the complement clause in an ascription of the form (12)

12. NP believes that Carl Hempel was a professor at Princeton

to stand for the proposition that the philosopher Carl Hempel was a professor at Princeton, despite the fact that the information that Mr. Hempel was a philosopher is not part of the semantic content of the complement clause. Once the complement clause has been associated with this descriptively enriched proposition, an assertive utterance of the sentence results in an assertion that attributes belief in that proposition to each individual referred to or quantified over by the subject expression. Thus, on this theory, there is no possibility that (12) could be interpreted as attributing different descriptive beliefs about Mr. Hempel to different agents in the range of the plural or quantified noun phrase subject.

No similar explanation of the lack of such an interpretation can be given by Richard. Moreover, he cannot simply rule out as illegitimate contexts containing restrictions involving different individuals a and b that require correlation functions to map the same sentence S, used in a belief ascription, onto quite different sentences S_a and S_b, accepted by a and b, respectively. In fact, contexts of this sort are routinely required by his theory. For example, consider (13).

13. Most of the ancients believed that Hesperus wasn't Phosphorus.

Richard holds that this belief ascription has a natural interpretation in which it is true, and in which substitution of 'Hesperus' for 'Phosphorus' would change truth-value. In order for this to be so, the context must contain restrictions on what counts as acceptable mappings of the names 'Hesperus' and 'Phosphorus' onto terms used by the ancients. In point of fact, the ancients spoke a variety of different languages, containing a wide range of different terms referring to Venus. Thus, what is required by Richard's theory is that the context for (13) should contain for each relevant ancient, i, restrictions on correlation functions requiring them to map the names 'Hesperus' and 'Phosphorus' onto different sets of terms for Venus used by i. Since, for each name, the sets of translation targets for it differ from individual ancient to individual ancient, and since these sets are often disjoint, the context has to be one in which restrictions involving different individuals require correlation functions to map the same sentence S, used in the belief report, onto different target sentences used by different agents.[18]

In essence, Richard's theory tells us that a belief ascription, *All (most/many/some) . . . F's believe that S* is true (in a context C) iff all (most/many/some . . .) of the individuals in the extension of F accept some annotated proposition that is similar to the annotated proposition expressed by S (in C)—where what counts as similar may vary for different members of the extension of F. Although the mechanism Richard uses to characterize these different similarity relations is metalinguistic, it is essentially a technical artifice which, to the extent that it is plausible at all, may be used to attribute to agents beliefs with descriptive contents that go beyond the Russellian content of the sentence S used to ascribe the belief. Given these two features of the theory, one would naturally expect it to accommodate contexts in which an ascription like (11a), or (11b), attributes radically different descriptive beliefs to the pair of individuals given by its compound subject. If contexts like this could routinely be found, in which belief ascriptions with compound or quantified subjects were clearly given such interpretations, then this would constitute further confirmation of Richard's theory. It appears, however, that such contexts cannot be found. In the absence of any natural and independently motivated explanation of this within Richard's framework, the fact that belief ascriptions with compound or quantified subjects typically cannot be given interpretations in which they attribute radically different descriptive beliefs to the individuals provided by the subject constitutes evidence against the theory.

Contextual Restrictions vs. Extensional, World-Indexed Restrictions

Up to now I have characterized restrictions on correlation functions as items present in the context of utterance that are applied directly to correlation functions in evaluating the truth or falsity of attitude ascriptions. In so doing, I have followed the main lines of Richard's discussion in *Propositional Attitudes*. I have, however, suggested two modifications of his original treatment: (i) whereas Richard originally took individual agents (of attitudes) to be the first members of contextual restrictions on correlation functions, I suggested that we would do better to take properties that determine such agents as occupying that position; (ii) whereas Richard took sets of translation targets to be the third members of restrictions, I suggested that we would do better to take properties that determine such sets to play that role.

There were two reasons for these suggestions. First, conversational participants in a context in which *The F believes that n is G* is assertively uttered often have little or no idea whom *the F* denotes, as well as little knowledge of, or interest in, which particular expressions that individual would use to express the belief in question. To the extent that conversational participants have such intentions on the matter, often their intention is that whoever turns out to denoted by *the F* be someone who associates certain descriptive content D with the expression corresponding to n used by the agent to express the belief. This can be captured by letting the first constituent of the correlation restriction arising from their intentions be the property P_F expressed by F and the third constituent be the property of being an expression that is associated with D by the individual who uniquely possesses P_F (or the property of being a pair consisting of such an expression plus its Russellian content).

The second reason for suggesting this change in Richard's original conception of a correlation function involved the modal profile of ascriptions like *The F believes that n is G*. Where **the** *F* is nonrigid, different agents are relevant to the truth value of the ascription at different worlds. Similarly, since these agents may use different expressions to express the relevant belief in different worlds, what is important is usually not the linguistic identity of the expressions themselves, but the descriptive information associated with the expressions by the agents in those worlds. These facts can be accommodated if the first constituents of restrictions present in a context are properties that may pick out different agents in different worlds, and the third constituents of such restrictions are properties that pick out different expressions (or different pairs consisting of such expression plus its Russellian content) in different worlds, depending on which expressions are associated with certain descriptive information by the relevant agents at those worlds.

However, not all attitude ascriptions can be handled this easily. For example, consider ascriptions with quantified subjects, like *All (most/many/some . . .) F's believe that n is G*. Let p be the proposition semantically expressed by one of these ascriptions in a context of utterance C. To evaluate p at an arbitrary possible world w, something in C must determine a set of extensional, world-indexed restrictions on correlation functions of the sort given in W.

W. $\langle i_1, \langle n, o \rangle$, the set of expressions $\langle m, o \rangle$ such that o is the Russellian content of m in i_1's context (in w), and i_1 associates m with the descriptive content D (in w)>

   $\langle i_2, \langle n, o \rangle$, the set of expressions $\langle m, o \rangle$ such that o is the Russellian content of m in i_2's context (in w), and i_2 associates m with the descriptive content D (in w)>

In order for the proposition p expressed by *All (most/many/some . . .)* *F's believe that n is G* in C to be true with respect to w, all (most/ many/some) of the individuals i such that i is in the extension of F at w must accept some linguistically enhanced proposition q obtainable from the linguistically enhanced proposition expressed by *n is G* in C by a correlation function that satisfies all the extensional, world-indexed restrictions on i in W. To ensure that correlation functions are properly restricted no matter which of the F's turn out to be the relevant believers, it would seem that typically W must contain an extensional, world-indexed restriction for each i in the extension of F in w.

This characterization of truth conditions requires a clear conception of how contexts of utterance determine different sets of extensional, world-indexed restrictions in different worlds. One might imagine, on the basis of our discussion of earlier examples, that the determination in question involves the following two steps:

(i) The intentions of speaker-hearers in the context determine an (intensional) restriction $\langle P_F, \langle n, o \rangle, P_S \rangle$ that is present in the context, where the property P_F expressed by F determines the extension of F at each world, and the property P_S determines different sets of translation targets for different worlds (one set for each world).

(ii) For any world w, the extensional, world-indexed restrictions determined by $\langle P_F, \langle n, o \rangle, P_S \rangle$ will be the set of those restrictions $\langle i, \langle n, o \rangle, S \rangle$ such that i has P_F in w, and S is the set of translation targets determined by P_S in w.

However, a moment's reflection is all that is required to see that when ascriptions like by *All (most/many/some . . .)* *F's believe that n is G* are involved, this won't do. The sets of translation targets given in the extensional, world-indexed restrictions in W vary with the first constituents of those restrictions—that is, they vary from one member of the extension of F at w to the next. Moreover, in many cases this must be so, if the Richardian truth conditions assigned to attitude ascriptions relative to contexts and worlds are to approximate our intuitive grasp of the truth conditions of the propositions asserted by uttering such ascriptions. However, there is no way to get this result as long as the (intensional) restrictions on correlation functions present in the context of utterance are triples the first and third constituents of which are independently specified properties of individuals and translation targets respectively, as in (i), and the extensional, world-indexed restrictions that arise from these (intensional) restrictions do so in the manner specified in (ii).

Since Richard has not explicitly addressed the problem, it is not clear precisely what to do at this point. One possibility that can be used in a substantial range of cases involving assertive utterances of ascriptions like *by All (most/many/some . . .) F's believe that n is G* is given by (i') and (ii').

(i')　The intentions of speaker-hearers in the context determine an (intensional) restriction $\langle P_F, \langle n, o \rangle, P_D \rangle$ that is present in the context, where the property P_F expressed by F determines the extension of F at each world, and P_D is a descriptive property associated with n in the context.

(ii')　For any world w, the extensional, world-indexed restrictions determined by $\langle P_F, \langle n, o \rangle, P_D \rangle$ will be the set of those restrictions $\langle i, \langle n, o \rangle, S \rangle$ such that i has P_F in w, and S is the set of translation targets $\langle m, o \rangle$ such that o is the Russellian content of m in i's context in w and m is associated with P_D by i in w.

This, or something very much like it, seems to be the most reasonable way to handle quantified belief ascriptions of this sort in the Richardian framework.

Nevertheless, there are worries concerning this account. First, we have complicated the system. Whereas initially we talked only of one kind of restriction on correlation functions, now we have two—(intensional) restrictions present in contexts that arise from the intentions of speaker/hearers and the extensional, world-indexed restrictions that are determined by them with respect to different worlds. The need to account for attitude ascriptions with quantified subjects makes this sort of complication essentially unavoidable within the Richardian framework. Second, although I have illustrated intensional restrictions, extensional world-indexed restrictions, and the way in which the former may determine the latter, nothing I have said should be taken to indicate that the account is now complete, and that other kinds of intensional restrictions, extensional world-indexed restrictions, or determination relations between them will not be needed. The extent to which additional complications may be necessary remains an open question. In my mind this increasing complication of Richard's framework, while not amounting to a refutation by itself, does strengthen the motivation to look for a simpler treatment of the variation one finds in the information carried by assertive utterances of attitude ascriptions in different contexts. Third, nothing said in this section removes the problem of too many semantic options allowed by the theory that was illustrated by the sentences in (11) above. Finally, the need to generate extensional, world-indexed restrictions for each individual in the extension of F when evaluating ascriptions like by *All* (*most/many/some . . .*) *F's believe that n is G* makes the already serious problem of conflicting restrictions that we will discuss in the next section even worse, and more widespread, than it would otherwise be. It is to this that we now turn.

The Problem of Conflicting Restrictions

We now turn to a different problem concerning multiple restrictions in a single context: the problem of conflicting restrictions.[19] We have seen that Richard's treatment of substitutivity puzzles involving belief ascriptions depends crucially on such restrictions. According to the theory, the semantic content of a belief ascription in a context C depends on the restrictions on correlation functions present in C. It is a central feature of the theory that belief ascriptions differing only in the substitution of coreferential names and indexicals may be assigned substantially different semantic contents in C, provided that C contains substantially different restrictions involving acceptable translation targets for those names and indexicals in the language (or system of mental representations) of the agent.

But how do restrictions on correlation functions arise in a context of utterance? Surely, they are not primitive elements, entirely unrelated to other aspects of the context. Rather, Richard sees them as arising from the beliefs, intentions, and expectations of speakers and hearers. The idea, in simplest form, is that when speakers report an agent's belief by assertively uttering *t believes that S*, they (and their audience) have some idea of how the words in S relate to the words that the agent would use to express that very belief. The speaker intends the words in S to be understood by the audience not only as expressing the same Russellian content as the words used by the agent, but also as bearing some further, more restrictive, relation to the agent's words.

Thus, for Richard, substitutivity puzzles involving propositional attitude ascriptions are to be resolved by appealing to restrictions on correlation functions, which in turn arise from other propositional attitudes—beliefs, intentions, and expectations—held by conversational participants. But this raises a potential difficulty. Might it not turn out that the same sorts of puzzles about the attitudes that motivate Richard's theory in the first place also arise for the propositional attitudes underlying the restrictions on correlation functions that are invoked by the theory to solve those puzzles? If so, then might not Richard's theory be subject to the same sorts of problems that it is designed to solve?

Here it is instructive to compare Richard's theory with orthodox Russellianism. Substitution puzzles in attitude ascriptions arise from two main aspects of the Russellian theory. First, propositions—the objects of the attitudes—are supposed to be the contents of both sentences and mental states (such as belief). Second, the factors determining the contents of these sentences, and mental states, are not entirely internal to the agent. As a result, the agent may not be in a position to recognize when two of his sentences or mental states have the same content. For example, the Russellian contents of two sentences, or mental states, may be identical because they correspond to the same external objects, without the agent being in a position to recognize this.

Now consider Richard's theory. According to Richard, the content of a belief ascription depends on the restrictions on correlation functions present in the context. Moreover, Richard's restrictions are supposed to arise from the intentional states of individuals in the context—in particular, from beliefs and intentions about which of the words referring to a specific object may be used to represent words used by a specific agent. However, which specific agents are subject to a given Richardian restriction (as well as which specific words used by the agent count as translation targets determined by the restriction) are often not determined solely by the beliefs and intentions of the conversational participants, or by any other facts entirely internal to them. Because of this it is possible for the same agent to be subject to different Richardian restrictions without conversational participants in the context being in any position to recognize this. When this happens, Richard's theory assigns semantic contents to belief ascriptions that differ radically from what the conversational participants take them to be. This gives rise to counterintuitive results on a par with the counterintuitive results that the theory was designed to avoid.

The problem may be illustrated by imagining a context C in which a pair of belief ascriptions, (14a) and (14b), are uttered.

14a. The F believes that t is A.
14b. The G believes that t is B.

To bring out the problem we make two assumptions about C:[20] (i) the speaker in C intends to convey with (14a) the information that the F—whoever that individual may be—accepts some sentence, t_1 is A, with the appropriate Russellian content, while associating t_1 with the property P_1 (and so believes of the referent, o, of t that it has the property of instantiating both P_1 and the property expressed by A); (ii) the speaker in C intends to convey with (14b) the information that the G—whoever that may turn out to be—accepts some sentence, t_2 is B, with the appropriate Russellian content, while associating t_2 with the property P_2 (and so believes of o that it has the property of instantiating both P_2 and the property expressed by B).[21] In our modified version of Richard's system these assumptions would normally be expressed by including the (intensional) restrictions on correlation functions (15a) and (15b) in the context.

15a. <the property of being the unique individual who is F, <t, o>, the property P_1>
15b. <the property of being the unique individual who is G, <t, o>, the property P_2>

Next, we evaluate the propositions expressed by (14a) and (14b) in C with respect to an arbitrary possible world w (which may be either the world of the context or some other world). Suppose that in w (a) the F is the G; (b) n_1 and n_2 are different names for o; (c) n_1 is the only term for o that the F associates with P_1, and n_2 is the only term for o that the G associates with P_2. We can now generate a conflict between what we intuitively understand about this example and what Richard's theory tells us about it.

Intuitively, it seems perfectly possible for the propositions asserted by utterances of (14a) and (14b) to be true with respect to w. Suppose, for example, that in w the individual who is both the F and the G accepts the sentences n_1 is A and n_2 is B, with the appropriate Russellian contents, but does not accept the sentences n_2 is A and n_1 is B. In such a case the information conveyed by utterances of the pair of ascriptions (14a) and (14b) is entirely correct—including the claim that there is some expression t_1 referring to o such that the F both associates it with P_1 and accepts some sentence *t_1 is A* with the appropriate Russellian content (and so believes of o that it has the property of instantiating both P_1 and the property expressed by A), and also the claim that there is an expression t_2 referring to o such that the G both associates it with P_2 and accepts some sentence *t_2 is B*, with the appropriate Russellian content (and so believes of o that it has the property of instantiating both P_2 and the property expressed by B). In such a case it seems obvious that (14a) and (14b) are used to assert propositions that are true with respect to w.

However, they are not true according to Richard's theory as it has been stated. For Richard an attitude ascription, **α *believes that S***, as used in a context C, is true with respect to a world w only if there is a correlation function f satisfying **every** extensional, world-indexed restriction for w (determined by the intensional restrictions in C) that involves the referent i of α (with respect to C and w), and f maps S onto a sentence accepted by i in w. But in this case there can be no such function, since the restrictions (15a) and (15b) conflict with respect to w. Their first constituents—the property of being the unique individual who is F and the property of being the unique individual who is G, respectively—determine the same person in w. Their second constituents identify the term t with the same Russellian content. Their third constituents—the properties P_1 and P_2, respectively,—are associated by the agent with different expressions, and so determine disjoint sets of translation targets $\{n_1\}$ and $\{n_2\}$ for t in w.[22] Thus, the (intensional) restrictions (15a) and (15b) in C determine conflicting extensional, world-indexed restrictions for w—namely, (15a*) and (15b*).[23]

15a*. $<i, <t, o>, \{n_1\}>$
15b*. $<i, <t, o>, \{n_2\}>$

Since no function can map t only onto n_1 and also map it only onto n_2, Richard's theory, as presently stated, predicts that there can be no attitude ascription containing t the subject of which refers in w to the individual who is both F and G, that is true with respect to C and w. Surely, this is incorrect.

It is worth noting that this problem can be made to recur in many different guises. Suppose, for example, that we substitute

14c. Some G's believe that t is B

for (14b) in a context C' in which (i) the speaker intends to convey with (14a) the information that the F—whoever that individual may be—accepts some sentence, t_1 *is A*, with the appropriate Russellian content, while associating t_1 with the property P_1 (and so believes of o that it has the property of instantiating both P_1 and the property expressed by A); and (ii) the speaker intends to convey with (14c) the information that at least two G's— whoever they may turn out to be— are such that each accepts some sentence, t_2 *is B*, with the appropriate Russellian content, while associating t_2 with the property P_2 (and so each believes of o that it has the property of instantiating both P_2 and the property expressed by B). Since, presumably, the (intensional) restriction in C' governing (14c) will not identify any particular G's, it must be thought of as generating extensional, world-indexed restrictions for **each** member of the extension of G at a given world w. This will have the effect of generating the conflicting restrictions (15a*) and (15b*) for any world w in which the thing that is uniquely F is one of perhaps many G's (whether or not the thing that is uniquely F turns out to be crucial to determining the truth of (14c) relative to C' and w). As a result, Richard's theory as presently stated wrongly characterizes (14a), along with all other ascriptions, α *believes that . . . t . . .* , in which the denotation of α with respect to C' and w is the thing that is uniquely F in w, as untrue with respect to C' and w.

Richard acknowledges the version of this problem involving (14a) and (14b) in his paper "Defective Contexts, Accommodation, and Normalization,"[24] where he proposes a way of modifying and extending his original account of how restrictions on correlation functions arise from the beliefs and intentions of conversational participants, and of what is required in order for a belief ascription to be true with respect to an arbitrary context. His strategy is to break up the original problem of conflicting restrictions into two subcases—one in which the conversational participants in a context in which (14a) and (14b) are used mistakenly presuppose that the F is not the G, and one in which the conversational participants do not make this assumption.

In the first case, in which the conversational participants wrongly think that the F and the G are different people, Richard claims that speakers' intentions regarding which words may serve as acceptable translations of those used by the agents of the attitudes give rise to restrictions (15a) and (15b). These restrictions conflict with respect to a world w in which the F is the G and the terms for o associated by that individual with the properties P_1 and P_2 are different, since in w the restrictions require mapping the same term t onto different (and in our example disjoint) sets of translation targets when reporting the beliefs of one and the same agent. In our example this is reflected by the fact that the extensional restrictions indexed to the world w include both (15a*) and (15b*), which are jointly unsatisfiable. Richard calls contexts containing restrictions that conflict with respect to the world of the context "defective," and he modifies his theory of what it means for an attitude ascription to be true in a context in order to take account of the special case of defective contexts.[25] The idea is roughly that given in (16).[26]

16. An attitude ascription α *believes that S* is true with respect to a defective context C iff for every way of rendering C nondefective (by eliminating just enough extensional restrictions indexed to the world C_w of C to remove the conflict among these restrictions) the ascription comes out true (in C_w). An ascription α *believes that S* is false with respect to a defective context C iff for every way of rendering C nondefective (by eliminating just enough restrictions to eliminate the conflict) the ascription comes out false (in C_w). Otherwise, the ascription is not true and not false with respect to C.

This proposal can be applied to our example involving the ascriptions (14a) and (14b). Here we stipulate that the world w described above is the world of the context, and we imagine a case in which the speaker, and other conversational participants, (wrongly) assume that the F and the G are different people. In this sort of case, Richard admits that the context will contain the (intensional) restrictions (15a) and (15b), which determine the conflicting extensional, world-indexed restrictions (15a*) and (15b*), and so will be defective. It can be rendered nondefective either by eliminating (15a*) while leaving (15b*) in place, or by eliminating (15b*) while leaving (15a*) in place. On the first alternative, Richard's semantic treatment of truth and falsity in nondefective contexts characterizes (14a) as false and (14b) as true. On the second alternative, it characterizes (14b) as false and (14a) as true. Thus, according to (16) the ascriptions (14a) and (14b) are not true and not false in the original context C, in which speakers and hearers wrongly assume that the F and the G are different people.[27]

This, it seems to me, is still the wrong result. In my original description of the example, I did not specify whether the speaker and hearers assume that the F and the G are different people. The reason I didn't is that it doesn't matter whether or not they assume this. In either case the information intended to be conveyed by assertive utterances of (14a) and (14b) is entirely correct. Thus, these examples should be characterized as true. The fact that Richard's modified proposal characterizes them as not true, in those cases in which the conversational participants happen to have wrongly assumed that the F and the G are different people, shows that his theory remains incorrect on this point.

Next we turn to Richard's second subcase—one in which the conversational participants do not assume that the F and the G are different people, but rather make no assumption about this one way or the other. All other facts about the beliefs and intentions of conversational participants in the context, and about the epistemic state of the individual who is the F and the G, remain as originally described. These facts about the context are repeated in (17).

17. C is a context with the following characteristics: (i) the speaker in C intends to convey with (14a) the information that the F—whoever that individual may be—accepts some sentence, t_1 *is* A, with the appropriate Russellian content, while associating t_1 with the property P_1 (and so believes of o that it has the property of instantiating both P_1 and the property expressed by A); (ii) the speaker in C intends to convey with (14b) the information that the G—whoever that may turn out to be—accepts some sentence, t_2 *is* B, with the appropriate Russellian content, while associating t_2 with the property P_2 (and so believes of o that it has the property of instantiating both P_2 and the property expressed by B); (iii) speakers and hearers in C do not presuppose that the F is not the G; (iv) the world of the context is such that in it (a) the

F is the G, (b) n_1 and n_2 are different names for o, (c) n_1 is the only term for o that the individual who is the F and the G associates with P_1, and n_2 is the only term for o that that individual associates with P_2, and (d) the individual who is both the F and the G accepts the sentences *n_1 is A* and *n_2 is B*, with the appropriate Russellian contents, but does not accept the sentences *n_2 is A* and *n_1 is B*.

This, I have argued, is a context in which the propositions asserted by utterances of (14a) and (14b) should be characterized as true.

Richard has proposed a way of accommodating this point. He does so by modifying his account of the way in which restrictions in a context arise from the beliefs and intentions of conversational participants about which words used in reporting the beliefs of agents may be taken as representing the words used by the agents themselves. Think again about the conversational participants in C. As Richard sees it, they intend the term t, when used to refer to o in ascriptions of belief to the F, to be taken as a contextually acceptable translation of words (or mental representations) that the F both uses to refer to o and associates with the property P_1. This intention gives rise to the (intensional) restriction (15a) in C. In addition, they intend the term t, when used to refer to o in ascriptions of belief to the G, to be taken as a contextually acceptable translation of words (or mental representations) that the G both uses to refer to o and associates with the property P_2. This gives rise to the presence in C of the (intensional) restriction (15b). In addition, we may suppose that the conversational participants make no assumption about whether or not the F is the G. In such a case, Richard claims, the context will contain an (intensional) restriction (15c) that results from merging (15a) and (15b).

15c.   <the property of being the unique individual who is F and the unique individual who is G, <t, o>, {the property P_1, the property P_2}>

Next we consider the extensional, world-indexed restrictions determined by the (intensional) restrictions (15a), (15b), and (15c). Let C_w be the world of the context C. If the F and the G were different individuals in C_w, then the first constituent of (15c) would not pick out any individual in C_w, and (15c) would not give rise to any extensional re-

striction indexed to that world; whereas (15a) and (15b) would give rise
to extensional restrictions involving different individuals. However, in
our example, the F and the G are the same individual in C_w. Because
of this, Richard maintains, (15a) and (15b) are superceded by (15c) in
the sense that former determine no extensional restrictions indexed to
C_w, whereas the latter determines an extensional, world-indexed restriction requiring t to be mapped into the union of the set of translation
targets determined by (15a) and the set of translation targets determined
by (15b).[28] Thus, the extensional restrictions indexed to C_w will not
include (15a*) or (15b*), but instead will include (15c*).

15a*.　$<i, <t, o>, \{n_1\}>$
15b*.　$<i, <t, o>, \{n_2\}>$
15c*.　$<i, <t, o>, \{x \mid x \in \{n_1\} \text{ or } x \in \{n_2\}\}>$

The idea here is that if one leaves it open that the F might turn out to
be the G, and if the F really does turn out to be the G, then one should
grant that any acceptable translation of the G's words is an acceptable
translation of the F's words, and vice versa.[29]

Richard's claim is that when a context C is coherent (not defective), an attitude ascription, *α believes that S*, is true in C iff there is
some correlation function f such that (i) f satisfies all the extensional
restrictions indexed to the world C_w of C involving the referent, a, of
α with respect to C and C_w, and (ii) f maps S onto some sentence
accepted by a in C_w, with the same Russellian content that S has in C.
Where C is the particular context we have described, the ascriptions
(14a) and (14b) are evaluated as true in C. This is so, since in the world
of C there is a correlation function f that obeys (15c*) by virtue of
mapping t onto n_1 that satisfies the truth conditions for (14a), and there
is a different correlation function g that obeys (15c*) by virtue of mapping t onto n_2 that satisfies the truth conditions for (14b). Hence, Richard is able to assign these ascriptions the truth-values they intuitively
demand in this context.[30]

Nevertheless, I don't think that Richard's modification provides an
adequate treatment of this example. In the case at hand, the speaker
intends the utterance of (14a) to convey the information that the F
believes of o that it has the property of instantiating both P_1 and the
property expressed by A, and the speaker intends the utterance of (14b)
to convey the information that the G believes of o that it has the prop-

erty of instantiating both P_2 and the property expressed by B. In fact, it is highly plausible to suppose that the speaker in this context has asserted propositions which have (18a) and (18b) as trivial consequences.

18a.   The F believes that something that has P_1 is A.
18b.   The G believes that something that has P_2 is B.

Even though these are precisely the kinds of facts that Richard routinely takes it to be the job of a semantic theory to capture, and although they are on a par with the facts that his semantic theory was designed to explain, nothing in his modified account accommodates them. The most that might be said is that his proposal predicts that the speaker has conveyed and asserted propositions about o from which (19a) and (19b) trivially follow.

19a.   Either there is an individual i who is the F and the G, and i believes that something that either has P_1 or has P_2 is A, or the F isn't the G, and the F believes that something that is P_1 is A.
19b.   Either there is an individual i who is the F and the G, and i believes that something that either has P_1 or has P_2 is B, or the G isn't the F, and the G believes that something that is P_2 is B.

But this falls well short of the mark. It might be possible to get the speaker to admit that (19a) and (19b) are convoluted consequences of what he has asserted. But if this is so, it is only because (18a) and (18b) are. Richard's theory cannot account for this.

The problem with Richard's modification can also be seen from a slightly different angle. We consider a context C′, just like the context C described in (17) except for the final point (ivd). Whereas in the world C_w of context C, the individual who is both the F and the G accepts the sentences n_1 *is A* and n_2 *is B*, with the appropriate Russellian contents, but does not accept the sentences n_2 *is A* and n_1 *is B*, in the world $C′_w$ of context C′, the individual who is both the F and the G accepts the sentences n_2 *is A* and n_1 *is B*, with the appropriate Russellian contents, but does not accept the sentences n_1 *is A* and n_2 *is B* (though this is, of course, unknown to the speaker). Intuitively, the world C'_w is one in which the ascriptions in (20) are true, whereas those in (18) are not.

20a.   The F believes that something that has P_2 is A.
20b.   The G believes that something that has P_1 is B.

Despite the fact that the speaker in C' might vigorously reject (20a, b), and intend his assertive utterances of (14a) and (14b) to convey and assert propositions from which the false (18a, b) trivially follow, Richard's modified semantics characterizes the propositions expressed by (14a) and (14b) in C' as true in C'_w. This should count against a theory designed to capture anti-Russellian intuitions.

But that isn't the worst of it. The worst problem for Richard's treatment of these examples concerns the modal profile of (the propositions semantically expressed by) attitude ascriptions in these contexts. Consider, in particular, the truth-values at arbitrary possible worlds assigned by Richard's account to (the propositions semantically expressed by) the ascriptions (14a) and (14b), with respect to the context C'. Let w be a merely possible world just like the world C'_w of the context C', just discussed, except that the individual i who is both the F and the G in C'_w is not the G in w. (The property of being G is some relatively trivial extrinsic property that i has in C'_w but lacks in w.) In all other respects the two worlds are as much alike as possible. In particular i is the F in w, i accepts and rejects the same sentences in w (with the same Russellian contents) as i does in C'_w, and i's brain states in w are molecule for molecule identical with his brain states in C'_w. Intuitively i is in the same epistemic state in w as he is in C'_w. Since i is the F in both worlds, one would expect (the proposition expressed by) the ascription (14a), as used in context C', to have the same truth-values in both worlds.

On Richard's account (as reconstructed here) this turns out not to be so. On this account, an ascription α *believes that S* is true with respect to a context C and arbitrary world w iff there is a correlation function f satisfying all of the extensional, world-indexed restrictions determined by C with respect to w that involve the referent i of α (with respect to C and w), and f maps the annotated proposition expressed by S in C onto an annotated proposition explicitly accepted by i in w. The crucial notion here is that of the world-indexed restrictions determined by C with respect to an arbitrary world w. Although Richard does not give an explicit definition of this notion, he does define it for the special case in which w is the world of the context. Moreover, it seems apparent how to extend that definition to the general case. (See note 30.) When this is done, it turns out that the extensional, world-indexed restrictions determined by a context with respect to one world may differ significantly from those determined by the context with respect to other worlds.

In the case of our context C', the extensional, world-indexed restriction it determines with respect to the world C'_w of the context is (15c*). (C' does not determine any world-indexed restrictions with respect to C'_w corresponding to (15a) and (15b).)

15c*. $<i, <t, o>, \{x \mid x \in \{n_1\}$ or $x \in \{n_2\}\}>$

Because of this, Richard's account characterizes (the proposition expressed by) (14a) in context C' as true (in C'_w). However, (15c*) is not included among the extensional, world-indexed restrictions determined by C' with respect to the possible world w. Instead, the restrictions determined by C' with respect to w are (15a*) and (15b**)—where u is the individual who is the unique G in w. (Again see note 30.)

15a*. $<i, <t, o>, \{n_1\}>$
15b**. $<u, <t, o>, \{n_2\}>$

Because the relevant restriction for the evaluation in w of (the proposition expressed by) (14a), with respect to C', is (15a*) rather than (15c*), Richard's theory characterizes it as false in w—despite the fact that the F is in the same epistemic state in w as in C'_w.

Surely, this cannot be right. Pretending for a moment that we are now speaking in context C', Richard's theory tells us that the proposition that the F believes that t is A is true in the world of the context but false in w, even though the same individual i is the F in both worlds, and all facts about i's mental representations, the sentences i accepts and rejects, their Russellian contents, and all intrinsic facts about i's brain states are the same in both worlds. This, it seems to me, is obviously wrong. The ascription (14a) has no reading in which the proposition it semantically expresses in context C' is true with respect to the world of the context, but false with respect to w. Richard's theory, which began with the laudable attempt to capture both Russellian and anti-Russellian intuitions about attitude ascriptions, fails in this case to do either. Instead, the reading assigned by Richard is a hybrid that doesn't correspond to any genuine linguistic intuitions about (14a).[31]

Semantics and Communication

Although I have argued that the problem of conflicting restrictions remains a fundamental defect with Richard's theory, it should be recognized that the modifications he proposed to deal with it were designed with a legitimate insight clearly in mind. Richard tells us that he wanted his semantics for attitude ascriptions to validate the principle that arguments of the form (21) are logically valid, in the sense that for any possible context C, the proposition semantically expressed by (21c) with respect to C is true (in the world of C) if the propositions semantically expressed by (21a) and (21b) with respect to C are also true (in the world of C).

21a. α believes that S
21b. $\alpha = \beta$
21c. β believes that S

It seems clear that (21) is valid in this sense, and hence that Richard was right to try to preserve the principle. In order to achieve this, within the framework of his semantic theory of attitude ascriptions, he had little choice but to insist that in order for an ascription of the form (21a) to be true with respect to a context, there must be a correlation function of a certain sort satisfying all restrictions in the context that turn out to involve the referent of α, whoever that individual turns out to be. Because of this, the problem of conflicting restrictions was bound to arise for Richard, and his means of dealing with it were, of necessity, limited to the sort of responses that he actually proposes. The fact that these responses are inadequate, while arguments of the form (21) are indeed logically valid, suggests that his semantic treatment of attitude ascriptions is wrong in some fundamental way.

I believe that the source of the problem lies in the attempt to include within the semantics of attitude ascriptions information that is not properly semantic, but rather is a part of the way these ascriptions are used in communication. In setting up the problem, I constructed a context in which a speaker assertively uttering (14a) wishes to convey the information that the F holds a belief—that a certain object that has P_1 is A—the descriptive content of which goes beyond that contained in the (Russellian) proposition semantically expressed by the complement clause in (14a). In fact, I imagined that conveying this information was the primary intention of the speaker, and hence I was willing to characterize the speaker as asserting that the F holds this belief. Corresponding points were made about (14b).

In making these points I was following Richard's typical treatment of cases in which we feel resistance to substituting coreferential names or indexicals in the complement clauses of attitude ascriptions. These are cases in which a speaker who assertively utters *α believes that S* wishes to attribute to the referent of α belief in a proposition the descriptive content of which goes beyond the (Russellian) semantic content of S in the context. Richard takes these to be cases in which the speaker not only conveys the information that the agent holds this stronger descriptive belief, but also asserts that the agent does so. Since substitution in S of one coreferential name or indexical for another does not change Russellian semantic content, but may change the stronger descriptive belief attributed to the agent, Richard implicitly concludes that such substitution may change what propositions are asserted by utterances of the relevant sentences in the context.

So far so good. However, we still have not said anything about the semantic contents of these attitude ascriptions in the relevant contexts. At this point we encounter an unspoken assumption that underlies much of the work in descriptive semantics of natural language. The question at issue involves the relationship between the semantic content of a sentence S in a context—the proposition semantically expressed by S in the context—on the one hand, and the proposition, or propositions, asserted by an assertive utterance of S in the context. The implicit assumption about the relationship between these two that guides much work in natural language semantics is roughly that expressed by (22).

22. Special cases such as those involving irony, sarcasm, or metaphor aside, if p is the proposition asserted by an assertive utterance of a sentence S in a context C, or (if more than one proposition is asserted by the utterance) p is the proposition that it is the speaker's primary intention to assert, and so is the most salient of the propositions asserted by the utterance,

then p is the proposition semantically expressed by S in C, and thus is the semantic content of S in C.

If this assumption is correct, then typical cases in which we feel resistance to substituting coreferential names or indexicals in the complement clauses of attitude ascriptions are those in which the semantic content of the ascription *α believes that S* in the context C is a proposition that attributes to the referent of α belief in a proposition the descriptive content of which goes beyond the Russellian content of S in C. In particular, if (22) is correct, then the semantic contents of the ascriptions (14a) and (14b) in the problematic contexts indicated above are propositions that attribute to the F, and the G, belief in propositions the descriptive content of which exceeds that of the Russellian contents of the complement clauses of (14a) and (14b). In Richard's system the extra descriptive content in these cases is contributed by the restrictions on correlation functions in the relevant contexts, which are incorporated into the particular belief relations expressed by the belief predicate in those contexts. The problem, as we have seen, is that the semantic results obtained in this way are incorrect.

My suggestion is that the source of this problem is not to be found in the semantic details of Richard's system, but in his implicit adherence to something approximating (22). The contexts I constructed were ones in which the propositions that speakers were primarily interested in using (14a) and (14b) to assert attribute beliefs the contents of which exceed the Russellian contents of their complement clauses. However, the fact that these propositions are asserted by utterances of (14a) and (14b) in C does not show that they are the semantic contents of (or the propositions semantically expressed by) (14a) and (14b) in C. If (22) is false, then it may be that the semantic contents of these sentences in C attribute beliefs in the Russellian propositions semantically expressed by their complement clauses, even though the (primary) propositions asserted by utterances of the sentences in C go beyond this.

Moreover, there is independent reason to believe that (22) is false. In chapter 3, we saw that simple sentences like

23.   Carl Hempel lived in Princeton

are often used by speakers to assert propositions—such as the proposition that the philosopher Carl Hempel lived in Princeton—the descriptive content of which exceeds that of the proposition semantically expressed by the sentence in the context. If something similar occurs with attitude ascriptions like

    24.   Ralph believes that Carl Hempel lived in Princeton

then substitution of 'Peter Hempel' for 'Carl Hempel' may change the truth-value of the (primary) proposition asserted by the speaker without changing the proposition semantically expressed by the sentence (in the context). This possibility will be discussed in more detail in chapter 8.

    For the moment, we may use the distinction between the proposition semantically expressed by an attitude ascription in a context, on the one hand, and the (primary) proposition asserted by an utterance of the ascription in the context, on the other, to illuminate our discussion of (14a) and (14b). Consider the following versions of (14a) and (14b) (in which 'Paderewski' is the name common to the content clauses, and the predicates in the content clauses are the same)

    25a.   The F believes that Paderewski was born in Warsaw.
    25b.   The G believes that Paderewski was born in Warsaw.

As before, we imagine the world of the context to be one in which the F is the G, though the speaker and his audience do not know this. In addition, the speaker and his audience use the name 'Paderewski' to refer to the famous Polish statesman and musician, realizing that the famous statesman and the musician by that name are one and the same man. However, the speaker and his audience also know that many people do not realize that the statesman named 'Paderewski' is the same man as the musician named 'Paderewski'. All of this is straightforward. The unusual feature of this context is that the speaker and his audience believe that the F (whoever that person may be) is a music lover who knows about Paderewski's musical accomplishments; but the speaker and his audience are completely unaware of whether or not the F knows anything about Paderewski's life in politics. Correspondingly, both speaker and audience think that the G (whoever that individual may be) knows about Paderewski's political career, without having any idea whether the G knows that Paderewski had anything to do with music.

In such a context the speaker's assertive utterance of (25a) might result in the assertion of the proposition expressed by (26a), while the speaker's assertive utterance of the negation of (25b) might result in the assertion of the proposition expressed by (26b).

26a. The F believes that the musician Paderewski was born in Warsaw.
26b. The G doesn't believe that the politician Paderewski was born in Warsaw.

In such a context, both of these propositions might be true, even though the F is the G and the two ascriptions concern the same man, Paderewski.[32]

It should be noted that this result does not cast any doubt on the logical validity of arguments of the form in (21). In particular, it casts no doubt on the argument from (25a) plus the premise

25c. The F is the G

to the conclusion (25b). The context, C, in question is one in which the propositions semantically expressed in C by (25a), (25c), and (25b) all are true. Moreover there is no context in which (25b) semantically expresses a false proposition, whereas (25a) and (25c) semantically express true propositions. To say the same thing in another way, there is no context in which the negation of (25b) semantically expresses a true proposition, while (25a) and (25c) also semantically express true propositions. This is so despite the fact that in C the primary assertions made by the speaker's utterances of (25a) and the negation of (25b) may both be true, while (25c) is also true. In short, the logical validity of an argument consisting of a sequence of sentences is not a matter of the relationship between the (primary) assertions made by those sentences in different contexts; instead, it is a matter of the relationship between the propositions semantically expressed by those sentences across the full range of contexts.[33]

Iterated Attitudes, Double Indexicality, and Relativized Truth

Richard notes that his account of belief and other attitude ascriptions requires the introduction of a new kind of indexicality into semantic theory that is not required by other constructions. Standardly, it is sentences that are said to be context-sensitive, in the sense that they contain expressions the interpretation of which is provided by elements in the context—such as the time, place, agent, and world of the context. When a sentence is placed in a context, it determines a proposition, which may be then evaluated for truth or falsity at different possible worlds. This conception of indexicality is standardly invoked in giving the semantics of sentences containing indexicals like 'now', 'here', 'I', 'you', 'actually' and so on.

According to Richard, 'believe', 'say', 'assert' and other propositional attitude verbs are also indexical. However, as he recognizes, his metalinguistic conception of their meanings makes it impossible for them to conform to the standard conception of indexicality. There are two reasons for this, both of which involve iterated attitude ascriptions.

The first of these is illustrated by Richard's example (27).

27.   John said that Ham thinks that Hes is hot.

Suppose I assertively utter (27) in a context C shortly after John assertively uttered (28) in a related context C'.

28.   Ham thinks that Hes is hot.

A Richardian account of the semantics of 'say' would hold, roughly, that (27) is true relative to C iff the sentence, (28), that John assertively uttered (a) is mapped onto itself by a correlation function satisfying the restrictions in C, and (b) the nonlinguistic component of the annotated proposition expressed by (28) in C is the same as the nonlinguistic component of the annotated proposition expressed by (28) in C'. ((a) and (b) together require the annotated propositions expressed by (28) in the two contexts to be identical.) In addition, suppose for the sake of argument two things that we have taken as axiomatic for Richard until now—namely, that (c) the nonlinguistic components of the annotated proposition expressed by a sentence in a context are the Russellian contents of the semantically significant constituents of the sentence in the context, and that (d) the Russellian content of 'believe' or 'think' with respect to a context is a relation between agents and annotated propositions that incorporates the restrictions present in the context.

The problem posed by examples like (27) lies in the combination of (b), (c), and (d).

From the assumptions (a)–(d) it follows that on Richard's view (27) is true in C only if (28) has the same Russellian content in C and C′, which in turn requires the attitude verb 'thinks' to have the same Russellian content in both contexts. However, there is no reason to believe that this will generally be so. Suppose, for example, that one of the two contexts contains a restriction R that the other lacks. To make the case more graphic, imagine that R concerns an expression that does not occur in (28), or an individual other than Ham—either of which may be relevant to other ascriptions made in the context. If this is so, then according to Richard's theory, the Russellian content of 'think' in C will not be the same as its content in C′. In fact, the relations between agents and annotated propositions expressed by 'think' in these two contexts may be extensionally different, since one of them will incorporate restrictions on agents other than Ham, or annotated propositions that contain words that don't occur in (28). Although, intuitively, this should be irrelevant to the truth of (27) in C, on the version of Richard's account encompassing (a)–(d) it prevents (27) from being true in C.

Richard realizes that this is unacceptable. His solution, which seems to be dictated by the basic features of his account, is to replace assumption (c) with the following principle.

29. The nonlinguistic components of the annotated proposition expressed by a sentence S in a context C are the Russellian contents in C of the (semantically significant) expressions occurring S, except for any propositional attitude verbs occurring in S; such verbs contribute their meanings—that is, functions from contexts to Russellian contents—to the annotated proposition expressed by S in C.

In other words, Richard makes propositional attitude verbs special exceptions to an otherwise conceptually unified treatment of indexicality. Once this is done, the fact that in our example Richard's theory is forced to assign 'thinks' different Russellian contents in C and C′ does not prevent (28) from expressing the same annotated proposition in the two contexts, and so does not prevent Richard's analysis of (27) from characterizing it as being true with respect to C.

The second reason Richard gives for treating the indexicality of propositional attitude verbs as exceptional is illustrated by pairs of attitude ascriptions from different languages that are translations of one another. For example, consider (30) and its German translation (31).

30.   John believes that Hans believes that Cologne is dirty.
31.   John glaubt, dass Hans glaubt, dass Koln schmutzig ist.

Richard says the following about this pair.

Consider, for example, uses of [30] and its German translation [31], where each of the speakers is trying to get across that John's belief is held under a sentence in which 'Koln' is used to refer to the relevant city. Such uses ought typically to have the same truth conditions. Now, in a case such as this, the English is used with the restriction 'Cologne' → 'Koln.' The difference in restrictions results in different [Russellian] contents for 'believes' and 'glaubt.' If we use the verbs' contents to construct RAMs [i.e., linguistically enhanced propositions] for the t-clauses to name, the results would be RAMs [linguistically enhanced propositions] that differed not just in vocabulary items, but in the semantic values paired with these. And this can be expected to result in an assignment of different truth conditions to the original sentences. Using the verbs' meanings instead of their contents allows agreement in truth conditions.[34]

Richard's concern about this example reflects essentially the same issue illustrated by (27) and (28). Let C be the context envisioned for (30) and C' be the context envisioned for (31). According to Richard's theory, (30) is true in C only if John accepts some sentence S the Russellian content which in his context is the same as the Russellian content of (32) in C.

32.   Hans believes that Cologne is dirty.

Similarly, for Richard (31) is true in C' only if John accepts some sentence S' the Russellian content of which in his context matches the Russellian content of (33) in C'.

33.   Hans glaubt dass Koln schmutzig ist.

However, since C contains a restriction on the English word 'Cologne' that is not present in C', on Richard's account the Russellian content of 'believe' in C will not match the Russellian content of 'glaubt' in C', even though the two words have the same meaning.

Thus, if Richard were to allow propositional attitude verbs to contribute their Russellian contents to the annotated propositions expressed in different contexts by sentences containing them, then he would have to acknowledge that the nonlinguistic components of the proposition expressed by (32) in C differ from their counterparts in the annotated proposition expressed by (33) in C'. This in turn would mean that the truth conditions of (30) in C would not be the same as the truth conditions of (31) in C', despite the fact that the two sentences are synonymous. For example, if John has never heard the word 'Cologne,' then it is unlikely that the Russellian content of his belief predicate will match the Russellian content of 'believes' in C, with the result that (30) may be characterized as false on the grounds that there is no sentence that John accepts the content of which in his context is the same as the content of (32) in C. Since this would not be enough to falsify (31), the ascriptions (30) and (31) would be characterized as having different truth conditions in their respective contexts.

Again, Richard rightly regards this as unacceptable. As with (27) and (28), his solution to the problem is to make propositional attitude verbs exceptions to the standard treatment of indexical expressions in the manner expressed by (29). Unlike other indexicals, which contribute their Russellian contents in a context to the propositions expressed by sentences containing them, propositional attitude verbs are said to contribute their (indexical) meanings to the propositions expressed by sentences containing them. The upshot of this is that **propositions** expressed by sentences containing propositional attitude verbs become indexical in the way in which **sentences** containing ordinary indexicals are. Just as the sentence *I am hungry* cannot be evaluated for truth or falsity at an arbitrary possible world until it has been set in a context that provides a referent for 'I,' so the proposition expressed by an attitude ascription cannot be evaluated at an arbitrary possible world until a context has been specified which, when applied to the meaning of the attitude verb, provides a Russellian relation between agents and objects of the attitude. In effect, indexicality is piled on top of indexicality. For Richard, we have indexicality at two levels.

There are several reasons to doubt the correctness of this account. First, the original difficulty—with (27) and (28)—does not seem to reflect any genuine linguistic puzzle; rather, it seems to be simply an artifact of Richard's semantic machinery. The linguistic facts are straightforward: if my utterance of (27) in C is intended to report John's primary assertion in C′, then I must use the complement clause of (28)—that is, *Hes is hot*—to pick out a proposition that John picks out by uttering (28) in C′. Perhaps in assertively uttering (28) John intends the complement clause to pick out a proposition stronger than the Russellian proposition semantically expressed by *Hes is hot*. For example, his primary intention may be to pick out the proposition that the planet Hes, seen in the evening, is hot. If so, then John may have succeeded in asserting that Ham thinks that the planet Hes, seen in the evening, is hot. In order to report this in C, I must use the complement clause in (28) in the same way. If I do, then there is no need, in interpreting and evaluating my assertion, to be concerned about how other beliefs involving different agents or different words would be reported. Irrelevant considerations like these are brought into the picture only by Richard's metalinguistic semantic strategy for indirectly capturing facts about the descriptive contents of beliefs attributed to agents by the assertions made by speakers in different situations. The difficulties caused by these irrelevant considerations do not require some technical solution; in a correct theory, they wouldn't arise in the first place.

Second, Richard's proposed solution to the problem complicates an otherwise conceptually unified conception of indexicality. The fact that he is forced to carve out a special exception for the semantics of propositional attitude verbs suggests that there is something wrong with his semantic account.

Third, the relativization to contexts of the truth of objects of belief and assertion required by Richard's solution is problematic. Consider again Richard's example (27).

27.   John said that Ham thinks that Hes is hot.

Let C be a context in which I assertively utter (27), some time after John assertively uttered its complement sentence, (28). Suppose that C contains a restriction relevant to propositional attitude ascriptions the agent of which is John requiring that the word *Hes*, referring to Venus, be mapped onto some term that John associates with the property of being a heavenly body visible in the evening sky. Suppose further that the world of C is such that in it John uses the name *Hes* to refer to Venus, and associates it with the property of being a heavenly body visible in the evening. Then, on Richard's account, my utterance of (27) should be true in C. However, knowing this provides us with very little information about the mental state Ham must be in, in order to have the belief that John attributed to him.

To ask for such information is to ask for an informative specification of the truth conditions of the proposition, or propositions, that John asserted. Sentence (27) reports John as having asserted a certain proposition—the proposition that Ham thinks that Hes is hot. Let us call this proposition 'p'. Although (27) explicitly reports that John asserted p, it doesn't claim that p is the only proposition he asserted (at the time). It may be that in asserting p, John was implicitly asserting other, related propositions as well. If so, then in order to determine what mental state John attributed to Ham, we need to specify the truth conditions not only of p, but also of any other propositions that were asserted by John in virtue of asserting p. With this in mind, let us add to my assertive utterance of (27) in C an assertive utterance of (34).

34. The proposition p, that John asserted, is true, as are all other propositions that John asserted in virtue of asserting p.

Since, for Richard, the truth of propositions is relativized to contexts, my assertive utterance of (34) in C claims that p is true in C, and that any other relevant propositions asserted by John are also true in C. Since p and the other asserted propositions are propositional attitude ascriptions, the characterization of Ham's mental state by the combination of (27) and (34) in C depends on the restrictions in C governing translations from my words onto Ham's. Suppose, for the sake of argument, that when I ascribe propositional attitudes to Ham, I require my word 'Hes' to be mapped onto some term t of his language with which he associates the property of being a heavenly body visible in the evening sky. Then we may take it that the truth of (27) and (34) in C ensures that Ham accepts some sentence that attributes to Venus the property of being a heavenly body that is both visible in the evening and hot.[35] In light of this we may conclude that Ham was characterized by John not only as believing that Hes is hot, but also as believing that some heavenly body that is visible in the evening is hot. In effect, in my context C, I report John as having said that Ham believes that Hes is hot and, in so doing, as having said that Ham believes that some heavenly body that is visible in the evening is hot.

This result is potentially troubling. Note that the answer just given to the question "How was Ham's mental state characterized by John?" depended crucially on how I translate my words onto Ham's, and not at all on how John translates his words onto Ham's. For all that has been said, the context C' in which John assertively uttered (28) may be one in which John does not require that his word 'Hes' be mapped onto a term that Ham associates with the property of being a heavenly body visible in the evening. Instead, John's context C' may be one in which there are no restrictions (beyond sameness of reference) limiting appropriate translations of John's word 'Hes' onto terms used by Ham, or it might be one in which John's word 'Hes' must be mapped onto a term that Ham associates with some quite different property—such as the property of being a heavenly body visible in the morning. If C' contains no restrictions on 'Hes,' then in assertively uttering (28) John was saying something that is true in his context, provided only that Ham believed the singular proposition that predicates the property of being hot of Venus. If C' contains a restriction requiring 'Hes' to be mapped onto the property of being a heavenly body seen in the morning, then in assertively uttering (28) John was saying something that is true in his context only if Ham believed that a certain heavenly body that is visible in the morning is hot.

Thus, it should be clear that on Richard's account it may turn out that both (27) and (34) are true, when assertively uttered in context C, even though the sentence John assertively uttered expressed something false in his context. Similarly, it is possible for the proposition expressed by (28), and all other propositions John asserted by virtue of assertively uttering (28), to be true in his context, while (27) is true in C, even though (28) is false in C. These results are strongly counterintuitive. One might object, on Richard's behalf, that results like these are just what one should expect if one relativizes the truth or falsity of the propositions expressed by attitude ascriptions to contexts of utterance. Perhaps so. But if so, then the conclusion to be drawn is that such a relativization is intuitively incorrect.

Finally, it should be noted that if knowledge is understood in the usual way as something like true, justified belief, then on Richard's account it ought to be possible for a person x to know a true (annotated) proposition p, even if the (annotated) proposition q that x explicitly accepts, and that p is used to represent in the context of the knowledge report, is false in x's context. Richard realizes this, and complicates the semantics of *know* in order to avoid it. His suggestion is given in (35).[36]

> 35. An attitude ascription *x knows that S* is true relative to a context C, world w, and assignment A of values to variables iff (i) the annotated proposition p expressed by S relative to C and A is true with respect to C, w, and A; and (ii) there is a correlation function f satisfying the restrictions in C involving the individual i that is the value of 'x' with respect to A such that f(p) = q and (a) q is one of the annotated propositions accepted by i in w, and (b) q is true with respect to C*, w—where C* is the context with i as agent determined by facts about x in w.

In this formulation, clause (iib) rules out the possibility of knowing something in virtue of accepting something false in one's own context. However, (35) does not rule out the possibility that one can fail to know p, even though one believes p, one's justification for one's belief is complete and airtight, and one accepts only those things that are true in one's context. Under Richard's proposal this will happen when the knowledge report is set in a context C in which the subject is counted as believing a proposition p that is false in C by virtue of explicitly accepting a related proposition q that is true in the subject's context and that the subject has the strongest possible justification for accepting. This, too, seems counterintuitive.

In sum, Richard's metalinguistic strategy for capturing the apparent, extra-Russellian content of the assertions made by utterances of attitude ascriptions carries with it a host of problematic consequences for the treatment of iterated attitude ascriptions, truth, indexicality, and knowledge ascriptions. In my view these are not so much genuine problems that the theory fails to solve as pseudo problems created by the theory itself. If this is right, then what is needed is not a further refinement of Richard's basic idea, but a new approach.

8

Millian Meaning and
Pseudo-Fregean Attitudes

In chapter 3, I presented an account of the meaning, or semantic content, of nonindexical sentences. The account recognizes that despite being nonindexical, such sentences are routinely used by speakers to assert and convey different information in different contexts of utterance. Nevertheless, if s is such a sentence, typically there is some common core of information that is asserted and conveyed by utterances of s across different contexts. The meaning of an unambiguous, noncontext-sensitive sentence s—the proposition p that it semantically expresses—is this common information; that is, it is information that would be asserted and conveyed by an assertive utterance of s in any context in which s is used with its literal meaning by competent speakers who understand it (provided that s is used nonmetaphorically, nonironically, nonsarcastically, and without any conversational implicature defeating the presumption that the speaker intends to be committed to p).

When this view was applied to simple sentences containing ordinary, linguistically simple proper names, we reached the result that the proposition semantically expressed by a sentence *Fn* containing such a name is the singular, Russellian proposition <o, F-hood> that predicates the property expressed by F of the referent of n. As we saw, this view has the consequence that the (a) sentences in (1) and (2) mean the same (semantically express the same propositions) as the corresponding (b) sentences, even though in many contexts speakers would mean something different by them, in the sense that they would use them to assert and convey different information.

1a. Peter Hempel lived on Lake Lane in Princeton.
1b. Carl Hempel lived on Lake Lane in Princeton.

2a. Carl Hempel was Carl Hempel.
2b. Peter Hempel was Carl Hempel.

On this view, the meaning of an ordinary, linguistically simple proper name—in the sense of that which it contributes to the propositions semantically expressed by sentences containing it—is its referent, and the crucial facts that one must know about proper names in order both to understand them and to use them in the ordinary way are those given in (3).

3a. If n is a name, then assertively uttering a sentence ... n ... involves saying of the referent of n that it is so and so (where "so and so" expresses the property expressed by λx (... x ...).

3b. One can become a competent user of a name not only by being presented with its referent, but also by picking up the name from other competent users, and intending to use it to refer to whatever they do. _Chain of Communication_

This account of meaning and semantic content was extended to ambiguous and context-sensitive sentences in chapter 4. In chapter 5 an exception to this general treatment of names was carved out for partially descriptive names. In chapter 6 a puzzle about propositional attitude ascriptions was presented. On the one hand, the semantic views developed in chapters 3 and 4, together with a small number of plausible and apparently well-motivated auxiliary assumptions, lead to the conclusion that substitution of coreferential names or indexicals in the complements of attitude ascriptions cannot change semantic content or (semantically determined) truth-value. On the other hand, it seems obvious that sometimes such substitution leads to different propositions being asserted by utterances of such ascriptions, and even to the assertion of propositions with different truth-values. Examples of this are provided by (4) and (5).

4a. Edward believed that Peter Hempel lived on Lake Lane in Princeton.
4b. Edward believed that Carl Hempel lived on Lake Lane in Princeton.

5a.   Edward believed that Carl Hempel was Carl Hempel.
5b.   Edward believed that Peter Hempel was Carl Hempel.

How, if the (a) sentences mean the same as the (b) sentences, and hence semantically express the same propositions, could the assertions made by normal utterances of these sentences differ in truth-value? That was our puzzle.

In chapter 7 I discussed one version of a popular strategy for resolving this puzzle—namely, denying that propositional attitude ascriptions report relations between agents and Russellian singular propositions semantically expressed by their complement clauses. The idea was to replace Russellian singular propositions as objects of the attitudes with some more finely grained conception of the semantic contents of the complements of attitude ascriptions. The traditional version of this strategy was to take the semantic content of a particular use of name (or indexical) in a context to be given by descriptions that the speaker associates with it. However, as we saw in chapter 2, there is little hope of defending this approach against the host of objections that have been brought against it. With semantic descriptivism put to rest, the brightest prospects for the fine-grained approach seemed to lie with the introduction into propositional contents of linguistic or mental representations, in addition to Russellian objects and properties. However, in chapter 7 I argued that the difficulties inherent in this approach are crippling. Because of this, we need to find another line of attack.

This brings me to the final, and I believe most promising, strategy for solving our puzzle. In what follows, I will argue that the propositions semantically expressed by attitude ascriptions really do report relations to the Russellian propositions expressed by their complement clauses, and hence that pairs of ascriptions like (4a, b) and (5a, b), which differ only in the substitution of linguistically simple, coreferential names, really are semantically equivalent. I will also explain how ascriptions that are equivalent in this way may nevertheless be used by speakers to assert propositions with different truth-values. In constructing this account it is important is to show how naturally it emerges when the line of reasoning about semantic content that was applied in chapter 3 to simple sentences containing names is applied directly to propositional attitude ascriptions themselves. I will begin by developing this simple picture, after which I will consider various complications.

The Semantic Content of Attitude Ascriptions

In chapter 3 I argued that if n is a name that refers to an object o, then assertively uttering a sentence ... *n* ... involves saying of o that it is so and so (where "so and so" expresses the property expressed by λx (... *x* ...).[1] To say this of o is to predicate the property expressed by λx (... *x* ...) of o, and thereby to assert the singular, Russellian proposition expressed by (6) relative to an assignment of o to the variable 'y'.

6. λx (... x ...) y

For all intents and purposes, this amounts to the same thing as asserting the singular, Russellian proposition expressed by

7. ... x ...

relative to an assignment of o as the value of 'x'. A speaker who assertively utters ... *n* ... may, of course, assert more than this, but in standard cases he asserts at least this.

Applying this idea to the attitude ascription (4a), we get the result that a competent speaker who assertively utters (4a) in a normal context predicates the property expressed by

8. λx (Edward believed that x lived on Lake Lane in Princeton)

of the man Mr. Hempel, and thereby asserts the singular, Russellian proposition expressed by (9), relative to an assignment of Mr. Hempel as value of 'y'.

9. λx (Edward believed that x lived on Lake Lane in Princeton) y

This amounts to essentially the same thing as asserting the proposition expressed by (10) relative to an assignment of Mr. Hempel to 'x'.

10. Edward believes that x lived on Lake Lane in Princeton.

We next appeal to the assumptions in (11).

11a. The proposition expressed by *Edward believed that x lived on Lake Lane in Princeton*, relative to an assignment of Mr. Hempel as value of 'x', is the proposition that Edward believed p, where p is the proposition expressed by *x lived on Lake Lane in Princeton*, relative to an assignment of Mr. Hempel to 'x'.

11b. The proposition expressed by *x lived on Lake Lane in Princeton*, relative to an assignment of Mr. Hempel to 'x', is the singular, Russellian proposition consisting of Mr. Hempel and the property of having lived on Lake Lane in Princeton.[2]

It follows that a speaker who assertively utters (4a) asserts that Edward believed the singular, Russellian proposition about Mr. Hempel that predicates of him the property of having lived on Lake Lane in Princeton. In certain normal contexts, the speaker may assert more than this, but the speaker always asserts at least this. Similarly for assertive utterances of other attitude ascriptions.[3] In general, we may put this result as follows:

12. If n is a linguistically simple proper name that refers to an object o, and i is a competent speaker who assertively utters an attitude ascription, α *believes/asserts/etc. that.... n....* in a context C, using it with its literal meaning (nonmetaphorically, nonironically, nonsarcastically, and without a defeating conversational implicature), then i asserts that the agent (the individual designated by α) believes/asserts/etc. p— where p is the singular, Russellian proposition expressed in C by the clause.... *x*... with respect to an assignment of the referent of n to 'x'.

This principle has important consequences for our view of the semantic content of attitude ascriptions. In chapter 3, I argued for a certain principled conception of the semantic content of a sentence—that is, of the proposition it semantically expresses. The account formulated there was applied to unambiguous, noncontext-sensitive sentences. If propositional attitude constructions—*x believes that S, x asserts that*

S, etc.—are unambiguous and noncontext-sensitive, then that account can be applied directly to them. In hypothesizing that these constructions are unambiguous and noncontext-sensitive, I am not denying that the subjects or objects of propositional attitude verbs may themselves contain indexicals. Of course they may. What I am supposing is that the attitude verbs themselves are neither ambiguous or context sensitive, and also that attitude ascriptions containing them are context sensitive only to the extent that their subjects or content clauses are.[4]

I believe that this view of propositional attitude constructions is plausible, and I will accept it as a provisional hypothesis. In the end, whether this hypothesis stands or falls will depend on whether it can be incorporated into a plausible account of the attitudes. We have already seen one indirect argument in its favor when we chronicled the difficulties with Richard's view of attitude constructions as inherently indexical. In what follows, I will attempt to construct a more satisfactory, nonindexical, account of these constructions. To the extent that I am successful, the provisional hypothesis will be supported.

The account of semantic content developed in chapter 3 is summarized in (13).

13. A proposition p is semantically expressed by (is the semantic content of) an unambiguous, noncontext-sensitive sentence s iff (i) p is included in the information a competent speaker would assert and intend to convey by an assertive utterance of s in any context in which s is used with its literal meaning by conversational participants who understand s, provided that (a) s is not used metaphorically, ironically, or sarcastically in C, and (b) the presumption that the speaker intends to commit himself or herself to p is not defeated by a conversational implicature to the contrary; and (ii) for any other proposition q satisfying (i) the fact that p satisfies (i) explains why q does as well, and not vice versa.

The reasoning behind (12) shows that if s is an attitude ascription, *α believes/asserts/etc. that . . . n . . .* , and p is the proposition that i believes/asserts/etc. r (where i is the individual designated by α, and r is the singular, Russellian proposition expressed by . . . *x* . . . relative to an assignment of the referent of n to 'x'), then the pair s,p satisfies (i) of (13).

In addition, two further observations are in order. First, in certain contexts speakers and hearers may associate descriptive information D with n, with the result that in these contexts assertive utterances of the attitude ascription attribute to the agent of the attitude belief in (or the assertion of) the proposition expressed by ... *the x: Dx & x – n* .... However, there is no substantial descriptive content associated with n that remains constant across all contexts in which the ascription is used with its normal meaning. Thus, (i) of (13) will not be satisfied by the pair consisting of the attitude ascription s and a proposition p* that includes substantial descriptive information associated with n. As a result, the semantic content of the attitude ascription will not include any such descriptive information. Second, when p is the proposition that attributes belief or assertion of the singular Russellian proposition r, expressed by ... *x.* . relative to an assignment of the referent of n to 'x', it seems plausible that (ii) of (13) is also satisfied. Thus, if the account of semantic content given by (13) is correct, then a Russellian account of the semantic content of attitude ascriptions should be accepted.

The Assertions Made by Utterances of Attitude Ascriptions: An Example

It is now time to consider in more detail the relationship between the semantic content of an attitude ascription and the proposition, or propositions, it is used to assert in a context. The first point to note is the most basic: sometimes a speaker who assertively utters an attitude ascription such as *Mary said/asserted/believed that S* asserts that Mary said/asserted/believed p, even though (i) p is not the proposition that is semantically expressed by S in the speaker's context, and (ii) the proposition that Mary said/asserted/believed p is not the semantic content of the ascription in the context.

A simple illustration of this point comes from the special case in which a sentence is used metaphorically. For example, just as the sentences in (14) can be used metaphorically to assert propositions different from, but related to, those that constitute their literal meanings or semantic contents (in the context of utterance), so the ascriptions in (15) can be used to report the assertions made, and beliefs expressed, in such cases. (Think of example sentences in (14) being used metaphorically by Mary in a context to make assertions the contents of which are approximated by the material in parentheses; the examples in (15) are then used to make assertions that report those beliefs and assertions.)

14a. That boy is a little devil. (That boy is a mischievous trouble-maker.)

14b. Bill Clinton's numerous felonies and abuse of the presidency make Richard Nixon look like a choirboy. (Bill Clinton's numerous felonies and abuse of the presidency make Richard Nixon look innocent by comparison.)

14c. Over the next few years the fire that once burned so brightly within us slowly flickered and died. (Over the next few years the passion we felt slowly dissipated and faded away.)

15a. Mary thinks that he (that boy) is a little devil. (Mary thinks that he is a mischievous troublemaker.)

15b. Mary believes that Bill Clinton's numerous felonies and abuse of the presidency make Richard Nixon look like a choirboy. (Mary believes that Bill Clinton's numerous felonies and abuse of the presidency make Richard Nixon look innocent by comparison.)

15c. Mary said that over the next few years the fire that once burned so brightly within them slowly flickered and died. (Mary said that over the next few years the passion they felt slowly dissipated and faded away.)

In these cases, we may think of the complement clauses in (15) as being used metaphorically, even though the clauses are not assertively uttered on their own, but merely contribute to the assertions made by utterances of the larger sentences. Because of this metaphorical use, utterances of the ascriptions in (15) result in assertions that are different from, though related to, the propositions they semantically express (in the relevant contexts). Moreover, the assertions that are made report the agent, Mary, as bearing an attitude toward a proposition different from, but related to, the proposition semantically expressed by the complement clause. Attitude ascriptions that have this feature due to the metaphorical use of their complement clauses are common in ordinary speech. However, cases involving the metaphorical use of language by no means exhaust this phenomenon. Many quite ordinary, nonmetaphorical uses of attitude ascriptions have precisely the features found in (15). It is time to look into the question of how this can be so.[6]

Let us begin with a simple example. In the previous section I indicated that an attitude ascription ***Harry believes that Peter Hempel is F*** can be used to assert different things in different contexts. The one thing that is asserted across all normal contexts is the proposition that ascribes to Harry belief in the singular proposition that predicates the property expressed by F of Mr. Hempel. This is the semantic content of the belief ascription, and it is the same as the semantic content of ***Harry believes that Carl Hempel is F***. However, and this is crucial, there are contexts in which the two sentences would be used to assert different things.

For instance, consider a case in which Tom, Dick, and Harry are friends. They all know Mr. Hempel by sight, they all call him 'Peter Hempel', and they are all ignorant of his brilliant career as a philosopher. However, they have heard the name 'Carl Hempel', and they know that there was a philosopher by that name who wrote on scientific explanation. Suppose that Harry reads an obituary and forms a belief that he expresses to Tom by assertively uttering, *Carl Hempel died last week*, taking it for granted that Tom will realize that he is talking about the philosopher Carl Hempel, whom they have heard about. In so doing, Harry asserts a proposition the content of which is approximated by (16).

16.   The philosopher Carl Hempel died last week.

Later, Tom reports Harry's belief to Dick by assertively uttering (17).

17.   Harry believes that Carl Hempel died last week.

In making this report Tom is thinking about Mr. Hempel in a way that he knows is shared by Dick and Harry—roughly, as *the x: (x is a philosopher & x = Carl Hempel)*. Because of this, what Tom is trying to convey is the fact that Harry believes that the philosopher Carl Hempel died last week. Since his audience, Dick, can be expected to recognize this, in assertively uttering (17) Tom conveys, and even asserts, a proposition the content of which is approximated by (18), which attributes belief in the proposition (16) to Harry.

18. Harry believes that the philosopher Carl Hempel died last week.

Since Harry does believe this proposition, Tom has conveyed and asserted something true, and nothing false.

Now consider the sentence (19).

19. Harry believes that Peter Hempel died last week.

Tom did not assertively utter this sentence in the context, because he did not take it to be true. Suppose, however, he were to utter it assertively. In using the name *Peter Hempel*, he would be thinking about Mr. Hempel in a way that he knows is shared by Dick and Harry. We may suppose that this way of thinking of Mr. Hempel involves attributing to him something like the property of being an elderly, white-haired gentleman of their acquaintance. Because Tom knows that he, Dick, and Harry all take the association of this property with the name *Peter Hempel* (and the man Mr. Hempel) for granted, Tom would assertively utter (19) only if he wanted to convey to Dick that Harry believes a proposition the content of which is approximated by (20).

20. The elderly white-haired gentleman of our acquaintance, Peter Hempel, died last week.

In fact, we may presume that this is the primary information Tom would want to convey by his utterance of (19). In light of this, we may take it that Tom would assertively utter (19) only if he intended to convey and assert something like the proposition expressed by (21).

21. Harry believes that the elderly white-haired gentleman of our acquaintance, Peter Hempel, died last week.

Finally, let us suppose that Harry really does not believe this. Under this assumption, if Tom were to assertively utter (19), he would convey, and even assert, something false. (He would, of course, also assert something true—namely, that Harry believes of Mr. Hempel that he died last week. However, in the context imagined, this is of secondary importance, and would be overshadowed by the falsity of Tom's primary assertion.)

What we have is a context of utterance in which a speaker who assertively utters (19) would convey, and even assert, something false, whereas a corresponding assertive utterance (17) by the same speaker would assert and convey something true, and nothing false. This, I suggest, is the source of many speakers' intuitions that substitution of ordinary, coreferential proper names in attitude ascriptions can change truth-value. Such substitution **can** change truth-value, in the sense just outlined. However, this is compatible with the claim that the two sentences have the same semantic content, and hence that the proposition semantically expressed by one is true iff the proposition semantically expressed by the other is true.

If this is right, then there is a sense in which both Millians (i.e., contemporary Russellians) and Fregeans have contributed something correct to the account of names and attitude ascriptions. Millians are right in insisting that the semantic contents of most linguistically simple names are just their referents, and that, because of this, substitution of two such coreferential names in attitude ascriptions does not change the proposition semantically expressed by, or the semantically determined truth conditions of, the ascriptions. Fregeans are right in maintaining that such substitution can affect the truth-value of what is asserted by normal assertive utterances of the ascriptions. These two insights are compatible because what is asserted by the utterance of a given ascription often consists of more than simply the proposition semantically expressed by that ascription.

One way of looking at the situation is as follows. What one learns when one comes to understand attitude ascriptions is that a speaker who assertively utters *x asserted/believed that S* says of the pair consisting of the agent of the ascription and the proposition the speaker is using *that S* to refer to that the former asserted/believed the latter. Moreover, it is understood that the proposition the speaker is using the *that*-clause to refer to normally includes, but is not necessarily limited to, all the information in the semantic content of S, relative to the context. In some contexts the proposition the speaker has in mind will simply be the semantic content of the sentence in the context. However, in other contexts it may be a proposition in which extra descriptive information evident to the conversational participants has been added.

On this picture, the common content that is asserted and conveyed by assertive utterances of (19) across contexts is simply that Harry believed the Russellian singular proposition that predicates the property of having died last week to Mr. Hempel. This is the semantic content of the ascription. It is also the content of (17). Hence contemporary versions of Millianism/Russellianism are true semantic doctrines. On the other hand, there are particular contexts of utterance in which assertive utterances of these two sentences would convey substantially different propositions, due to the different information associated with the names *Peter Hempel* and *Carl Hempel* by conversational participants. In some contexts these different propositions would even be asserted by speakers uttering the ascriptions. Since what is asserted by utterances of (17) and (19) in these contexts is substantially different, it is possible for one to be true and the other false. This is the genuine insight about how attitude ascriptions are used in communication that Fregeans have wrongly tried to build into their semantics.[7]

At this stage, it should be noted that in using (17) and (19) to illustrate this picture, I have simplified matters somewhat by making it seem more or less fully determinate what extra propositions would be asserted by utterances of these ascriptions in the relevant context, over and above the proposition they both semantically express. It is important to realize that this feature of the case is inessential to the central points I have tried to establish. As we saw in chapter 3 (in the discussion of examples (8)–(10)), in many situations it may be determinate that a speaker who assertively utters a sentence s in a context C asserts more than the proposition p that is the semantic content of s in C, without it being determinate precisely which further proposition, or propositions, q_i from a relatively restricted range of propositions q_1, ..., q_n, is, or are, asserted. In the case of Harry's original assertive utterance of *Carl Hempel died last week*, this means that although it may be determinate that he asserted one or more of a restricted range of propositions including those in (I-16), it may be to some extent indeterminate which one, or ones, he asserted.

I-16a.   The philosopher Carl Hempel died last week.
I-16b.   The philosopher of science Carl Hempel died last week.
I-16c.   The writer on scientific explanation Carl Hempel died last week.

Corresponding to this, in the case of Tom's assertive utterance of (17), *Harry believes that Carl Hempel died last week*, it may be determinate that he asserted one or more of a restricted range of propositions including those in (I-18), without it being determinate precisely which.

I-18a.   Harry believes that the philosopher Carl Hempel died last week.

I-18b.   Harry believes that the philosopher of science Carl Hempel died last week.

I-18c.   Harry believes that the writer on scientific explanation Carl Hempel died last week.

Finally, in the case of (19), *Harry believes that Peter Hempel died last week*, it may be determinate that an assertive utterance of that sentence in the context would result in the assertion of one or more of a restricted range of propositions including those in (I-21), without it being fully determinate which one, or ones.

I-21a.   Harry believes that the elderly white-haired gentleman of our acquaintance, Peter Hempel, died last week.

I-21b.   Harry believes that the elderly white-haired gentleman Peter Hempel, whom we have seen at the café, died last week.

I-21c.   Harry believes that the elderly gentleman Peter Hempel, whom we have seen at the café, died last week.

I-21d.   Harry believes that the white-haired gentleman, Peter Hempel, of our acquaintance died last week.

I-21e.   Harry believes that Peter Hempel, whom we have seen at the café, died last week.

All of this is fully in keeping with the general picture I have presented. Even with the indeterminacy just indicated, it remains determinate that in our example, assertive utterances of the attitude ascriptions (17) and (19) by Tom would result in different assertions, over and above the assertion of the proposition that is the semantic content of both. In addition, since the claims in (I-18) are uniformly true, whereas those in (I-21) are uniformly false, it is determinate that assertive utterances of the two ascriptions would result in assertions with different truth-values. Hence, even when we take the indeterminacy of what is asserted into account, it remains true that substitution of linguistically simple coreferential names in attitude ascriptions may result in a change of truth-values in the assertions made using those ascriptions, without changing the propositions they semantically express. With this in mind, I will put aside further consideration of indeterminacy from here on out, in order to simplify the discussion.[8]

How Contextually Salient Information Contributes to the Assertions Made by Utterances of Attitude Ascriptions

In the previous example Tom's assertive utterance to Dick of the attitude ascription (17) resulted in an assertion the content of which is approximated by (18), whereas his assertive utterance of (19) would have resulted in an assertion the content of which is approximated by (21).

17. Harry believes that Carl Hempel died last week.
18. Harry believes that the philosopher Carl Hempel died last week.
19. Harry believes that Peter Hempel died last week.
21. Harry believes that the elderly white-haired gentleman of our acquaintance, Peter Hempel, died last week.

In both cases, salient common background information in the context contributed to the assertions made by utterances of the attitude ascriptions. We need to understand how this occurs.

At first glance, there seem to be two significant factors at work. First, the speaker (Tom) and his audience (Dick) share a set of common associations with the names *Carl Hempel* and *Peter Hempel*. In the case of the name *Carl Hempel*, each takes it to be obvious, salient, and relevant that sentence (22) expresses a truth; each takes it to be clear that the other recognizes this; each knows that each takes it to be clear that the other recognizes this; and so on.

22. Carl Hempel was a philosopher.

A similar point holds regarding the name *Peter Hempel* and sentence (23).

23. Peter Hempel is an elderly white-haired gentleman of our acquaintance

Because of this, the complement sentence, *Carl Hempel died last week,* of the attitude ascription (17) is such that if it were assertively uttered in this context, the result would be an assertion the content of which is approximated by (16).

16. The philosopher Carl Hempel died last week—that is, [the x: (x is a philosopher & x = Carl Hempel)] (x died last week).

Similarly, the complement sentence, *Peter Hempel died last week,* of the attitude ascription (19) is such that if it were assertively uttered in this context, the result would be an assertion the content of which is approximated by (20).

20. The elderly white-haired gentleman of our acquaintance, Peter Hempel, died last week—that is, [the x: (x is an elderly white-haired gentleman of our acquaintance & x = Peter Hempel)] (x died last week).

Of course, the complement sentences of the attitude ascriptions (17) and (19) are not assertively uttered in this context. However, they are used by the speaker to pick out a proposition. It is plausible, as a first approximation, to think that the proposition a speaker uses the complement clause of an attitude ascription to pick out is one that the speaker would assert in the context if he were to assertively utter the clause. What we have seen is that the propositions expressed by (16) and (20) satisfy this condition in our example.

There is a second factor at work in determining the proposition asserted by an assertive utterance of an attitude ascription in a context. In our example, the speaker (Tom) and the audience (Dick) each take it to be obvious, salient, and relevant that sentences (24) and (25)

$$B_H[x:(Px \wedge x=C)]$$

24. Harry believes that Carl Hempel was a philosopher.
25. Harry believes that Peter Hempel is an elderly white-haired gentleman of our acquaintance.

$$B_H[x:(Ex \wedge x=P)]$$

express truths; each knows this about the other; each knows that each knows this about the other; and so on. One reason for this is that Tom, Dick, and Harry are friends who associate essentially the same descriptive information with the names *Carl Hempel* and *Peter Hempel,* and who know this about each other. As a result, Tom and Dick are in a position to take it to for granted that Harry accepts sentences (22) and (23), and hence that the ascriptions (24) and (25) express truths.

Because of this it is obvious to both the speaker and his audience that acceptance of (17) in the context will carry with it acceptance of (26), and acceptance of (19) in the context will carry with it acceptance of (27).

26. Harry believes that Carl Hempel was a philosopher and Carl Hempel died last week. $B_H(P_C \wedge D_C)$

27. Harry believes that Peter Hempel was an elderly white-haired gentleman of our acquaintance and Peter Hempel died last week. $B_H(E_P \wedge D_P)$

In light of this, it is reasonable to take assertive utterances of (17) and (19) in this context to convey, and even to result in the assertion of, the propositions expressed by (26) and (27), respectively. Moreover, in the context in question, it is a short step from acceptance of (26) and (27) to acceptance of (28) and (29).

28. Harry believes that the philosopher Carl Hempel died last week. $B_H [x: (P_x \wedge x = C)(D_x)]$

29. Harry believes that the elderly white-haired gentleman of our acquaintance, Peter Hempel, died last week.
$B_H [x: (E_x \wedge x = P)(D_x)]$

Thus, there is reason to believe that assertive utterances of (17) and (19) in this context also result in the assertion of the propositions expressed by (28) and (29).

The difference between (26) and (27), on the one hand, and (28) and (29), on the other, is subtle, but worth noting. In illustrating this difference let us focus on the relationship between (26) and (28). The ascription (26) characterizes Harry as believing the conjunctive proposition expressed by (30), while the ascription (28) characterizes Harry as believing the proposition expressed by (31).

30. Carl Hempel was a philosopher and Carl Hempel died last week. $P_C \wedge D_C$

31. The philosopher Carl Hempel died last week—that is, [the x: x is a philosopher & x = Carl Hempel] (x died last week))

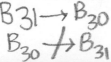
$B_{31} \rightarrow B_{30}$
$B_{30} \nrightarrow B_{31}$

We may take it that anyone who believes proposition (31) believes proposition (30). However, in certain unusual circumstances it is possible to believe proposition (30) without believing proposition (31). This will happen if the agent believes proposition (30) by virtue of accepting some sentence *α was a philosopher and β has died*, in which α and β are different names or indexicals both of which refer to Mr. Hempel, even though the agent doesn't know that they refer to the same person. In such a case it is possible for an agent to believe the conjunctive proposition (semantically) expressed by both (30) and the sentence the agent accepts, without believing that any philosopher died last week.

However, in the context involving Tom and Dick's discussion of Harry's beliefs, this possibility is remote. In this context the speaker, Tom, has excellent reason to think that Harry believes the proposition expressed by (31), since he was present when Harry used the sentence *Carl Hempel died last week* to convey and assert that proposition. In addition, Tom's audience, Dick, has no reason to be suspicious of the move from (26)—which he judges to be obviously acceptable if (17) is—to (28). The natural inclination of most speaker/hearers in most contexts would be to grant this sort inference without further reflection, and we may take it that Dick is no exception.

Moreover, even if Dick were to think more about the particular facts in this case, he would find nothing to undermine his confidence in the inference. He already knows that Harry accepts the sentence *Carl Hempel was a philosopher*. What is more, he has no reason to think that Harry has had any personal contact with the person they all refer to with the name *Carl Hempel*. Remember, Tom, Dick, and Harry do not take *Carl Hempel is Peter Hempel* to be true. Because of this, Dick has no reason to take seriously the possibility that Harry might fail to believe the proposition expressed by (31) while nevertheless believing the proposition expressed by (30)—solely by virtue of accepting some sentence *α was a philosopher and β has died*, in which α and β are different names or indexicals both of which refer to Mr. Hempel, even though Harry doesn't know that they do.

The upshot of this is that both the speaker, Tom, and the hearer, Dick, have good grounds to believe that if the speaker's utterance of (17) is true, then (28) is also true, and hence that Harry believes the proposition expressed by (31).[9] Moreover, Tom knows that Dick will ascribe this belief to Harry if he accepts Tom's utterance, and Dick realizes that Tom knows this about him. In light of this, it is natural for both speaker and hearer to take Tom's utterance of (17) to convey the proposition expressed by (28), and even to constitute an assertion of it. Similarly, both would take his utterance of (19) to constitute an assertion of the proposition expressed by (29).

To sum up, the simple example of Tom, Dick, and Harry conforms to a certain general view about the propositions conveyed and asserted by assertive utterances of attitude ascriptions containing ordinary proper names—propositions conveyed and asserted beyond those semantically expressed by the sentence uttered. Principle (32) is a first approximation of that general view; principle (33) is an instance of (32) covering the special type of case we have been discussing—namely, attitude ascriptions containing proper names that are associated with certain descriptive information by speakers and hearers in the context.

32. An assertive utterance in a context C of a propositional attitude ascription, *α believes that S*, results in the assertion of a proposition that ascribes belief in p to the referent of α if

    (i) the common background information shared by speakers and hearers in C is such that an assertive utterance of S in C would result in an assertion of p; and

    (ii) the common background information shared by speakers and hearers in C is such that, given it, conversational participants in C will readily assume that if the speaker's assertive utterance is true in the context, then the referent of α believes p; moreover, each knows this about the other.

33. An assertive utterance in a context C of a propositional attitude ascription, *α believes that Fn*, containing an ordinary proper name n, results in the assertion of the proposition (semantically) expressed by *α believes that F[the x: (Dx & x = n)]* in C if

    (i) it is part of the common background information shared by speakers and hearers in C that the name n is associated by them with the description *the x: (Dx & x = n)*, and as a result of this, an assertive utterance of *Fn* in C would result in an assertion of the proposition (semantically) expressed by *F[the x: (Dx & x = n)]* in C; and

    (ii) the common background information shared by speakers and hearers in C is such that given it, conversational participants in C will readily assume that if the speaker's assertive utterance is true in the context, then the proposition (semantically) expressed by **α believes that F[the x: (Dx & = n)]** is true; moreover, each knows this about the other.

Complications

Our example involving Tom, Dick, and Harry was particularly simple in that all three shared substantially the same information about Mr. Hempel, they all associated the same descriptions with the names *Carl Hempel* and *Peter Hempel*, and they all knew this about one another. Thus, when Tom was reporting Harry's beliefs about Mr. Hempel to Dick, it was easy for Dick to identify what propositions Tom was using the complement clauses of his attitude ascriptions to stand for, and it was plausible to see Tom as attributing belief in those propositions to Harry. Not all cases are this straightforward. I will illustrate this by considering two variations on this simple case.

First consider a case like our simple example except that the agent, Harry, of the attitude ascriptions is not a close acquaintance of Tom or Dick. In this example Tom and Dick have the same information about Mr. Hempel, and associate the same descriptions with the two names for him, as in the original scenario. However, they do not know very much about Harry's knowledge of Mr. Hempel, and they do not know which descriptions he would associate with the names *Carl Hempel* and *Peter Hempel.* They do know who Harry is, however; and one day, when standing in line at the bookstore-café Tom overhears Harry say the following words to a companion. "*Do you remember the elderly white-haired gentleman, Peter Hempel, whom we have often seen here having Sunday brunch? You know how we haven't seen him for quite some time? Well, I just heard that he died last week.*" Later, Tom reports Harry's remark to Dick by assertively uttering (19). He says, "*I overheard Harry talking to a friend the other day. Apparently he used to see Peter Hempel at the bookstore-café having Sunday brunch. Harry said that he hadn't seen him for some time. In fact, Harry believes that Peter Hempel died last week.*" Our question is "What has Tom said that Harry believes?"

One proposition that Tom has asserted that Harry believes is the singular, Russellian proposition that says of Mr. Hempel that he died last week. Of course, Tom may also have asserted that Harry believes more than this. If so, however, Tom has not asserted that Harry believes the proposition expressed by (20) in this context—even though his assertive utterance of (19) in the original scenario did characterize Harry as believing this proposition.

20. The elderly white-haired gentleman of our acquaintance, Peter Hempel, died last week—that is, [the x: (x is an elderly white-haired gentleman of our acquaintance & x = Peter Hempel)] (x died last week).

The reason that Tom's assertive utterance of (19) in the present context does not result in the assertion that Harry believes p, where p is the proposition expressed by (20), is that clause (ii) in (32), as well as (ii) in (33), are not satisfied. In the present case, neither Tom nor Dick has any reason to believe that Harry knows about their acquaintance with Mr. Hempel. Hence, neither Tom nor Dick takes it for granted that if Tom's assertive utterance expresses a truth, then Harry must believe the proposition expressed by (20). Therefore, Tom's assertive utterance of (19) in this context does not result in the assertion of the proposition semantically expressed by (29) in this context.

29. Harry believes that the elderly white-haired gentleman of our acquaintance, Peter Hempel, died last week.

However, there is good reason to think that it does result in the assertion of the closely related proposition (34), which attributes to Harry belief in proposition (35).

34. Harry believes that the elderly white-haired gentleman Peter Hempel died last week.

35. The elderly white-haired gentleman Peter Hempel died last week—that is, [the x: (x is an elderly white-haired gentleman & x = Peter Hempel)] (x died last week).

To see this, first consider clause (i) of (33). We know that it is part of the salient and relevant common background information shared by the speaker, Tom, and his audience, Dick, that the name *Peter Hempel* is associated with the description *the x: (x is an elderly white-haired gen-*

tleman of our acquaintance & *x = Peter Hempel*), and as a result of this an assertive utterance of *Peter Hempel died last week* would result in an assertion of the proposition (semantically) expressed by (20) in the context. From this it trivially follows that it is part of the salient and relevant common background information shared by the speaker, Tom, and his audience, Dick, that the name *Peter Hempel* is also associated with the related description *the x*: (*x is an elderly white-haired gentleman* & *x = Peter Hempel*), and as a result of this an assertive utterance of *Peter Hempel died last week* in the context would result in an assertion of proposition (35). Thus, clause (i) of (33) is satisfied when the proposition in question is the proposition expressed by (35).

There is reason to think that clause (ii) is also satisfied. Recall that Tom's report to Dick included the information that Harry had regularly seen Mr. Hempel at the bookstore-café. From this it is reasonable for Dick to conclude that Harry believed Mr. Hempel to be an elderly white-haired gentleman—since one could see this about Mr. Hempel just by looking. (Tom already knew that Harry believed this, since he heard Harry describe Mr. Hempel in those words.) Since it is clear from Tom's story that Harry was expressing his beliefs about the man he had seen at the café, Tom and Dick may safely assume that if Tom's assertive utterance of (19)—*Harry believes that Peter Hempel died last week*—is true in the context, then Harry believes the proposition expressed by (35), and hence (34) must be true. Since both clauses of (33) are satisfied, Tom's assertive utterance of (19) in this context results in the assertion of (34).

When this example is compared with the original simple case, we see how the same attitude ascription can be used to make different assertions in different contexts. Moreover, we see how what a speaker means by the complement clause of an attitude ascription depends both on the common background information shared by conversational participants and on the cognitive perspective that the agent of the attitude ascription can be presumed to have. In cases in which the agent's presumed perspective does not include all the salient information available to the conversational participants, there can be differences between the propositions that would be asserted by assertive utterances of the complement sentence in the context, on the one hand, and the beliefs that the complement sentence is used to ascribe.

Next consider an example from chapter 3.

The Party

The scene is the Princeton philosophy department's party held at the beginning of the academic year to introduce new people to one another, and to regular members of the Princeton community. Among the guests is Peter Hempel. At a certain point Paul Benacerraf gestures in Mr. Hempel's direction and asks one of our new graduate students, Mary, "Have you been introduced to Peter Hempel?" Mary says that she hasn't, and the following conversation ensues:

> Mary: "Who is Peter Hempel?"
> Paul: "Peter Hempel is Carl Hempel."
> Mary: "You mean the famous philosopher of science?"
> Paul: "Yes."
> Mary: "Why do you call him 'Peter' instead of 'Carl'?"
> Paul: "His friends and colleagues call him that."

In this example, we may suppose that Paul's primary intention in assertively uttering (36) is to assert and convey the information expressed by (37).

36. Peter Hempel is Carl Hempel
37. The man standing over there, Peter Hempel, is the famous philosopher of science Carl Hempel.

Paul is able to do this because he has good reason to assume (i) that Mary has in the past encountered the name *Carl Hempel* and has come to associate it with the property of being a famous philosopher of science, and (ii) that Mary can tell whom Paul is gesturing at, and can see that Peter Hempel is a man standing over there. In addition, Paul knows that Mary can work out that he must be assuming something like this. Hence, it is reasonable to take him as asserting and conveying something like (37).[10]

Later, two other members of the faculty, Gil and John, are talking, and Gil reports, on the basis of a conversation he has had with Mary, that she has just learned that Peter Hempel is Carl Hempel. That is, he assertively utters (38).

38. Mary has just learned that Peter Hempel is Carl Hempel.

On this basis John takes him to have asserted that Mary has just come to have certain beliefs. What beliefs has Gil asserted she has just come to have?

Here we face a difficulty. Gil and John have long known that the complement sentence, (36), of the attitude ascription, (38), expresses a truth. Moreover, each has known that the other knows this. As a result, neither Gil nor John would assertively utter (36) to the other in most normal situations. Thus, clause (i) of principle (32), as well as clause (i) of (33), seem irrelevant in this case. In addition, since Gil and John both know that the two names are coreferential, there is no extensional sentence containing one that they would accept without accepting the corresponding sentence containing the other. For all intents and purposes one may take this to mean that Gil associates the two names with the same descriptions, and John does, too. But then, it may seem to be a challenge to determine what Gil means by his assertive utterance of (38).

Often it is a challenge for the hearer to determine what the speaker means by an assertive utterance of an attitude ascription such as this. In the case at hand, John's task as a hearer is to come up with the interpretation that makes most sense of Gil's remark. In doing so he relies on two salient facts that both he and Gil take to be part of the common background information assumed in the context.

Fact 1   *What Mary likely knows:*

People who have read Mr. Hempel's philosophical work, or who are familiar with others' discussions of his work, have encountered the name *Carl Hempel*, and are likely to associate it with the property of being a famous philosopher of science. Since Mary is an incoming graduate student in the philosophy of science program, she probably falls in that category.

Fact 2   *What Mary likely does not know:*

Mr. Hempel is known to his friends and colleagues, including those at the party, as *Peter Hempel*. Since Mary is new on the scene, she probably didn't know this.

Given these facts, John forms the hypothesis that the most likely interpretation of Gil's utterance is that it was based on his discovery that someone at the party had told Mary something like "Peter Hempel is Carl Hempel" in a context in which it led her to believe something like the proposition (39).

> 39. Our colleague here at the party, known to us as 'Peter Hempel', is the famous philosopher of science, Carl Hempel.

On this basis, John concludes that Gil's utterance was intended to convey the information that Mary has just come to believe (39). Moreover, Gil anticipated and intended that John would come to this conclusion. Because of this, his assertive utterance of (38) resulted in the assertion of the proposition expressed by (40).

> 40. Mary has just learned that our colleague here at the party, known to us as 'Peter Hempel', is the famous philosopher of science Carl Hempel.

There are several lessons to be drawn from this example. First, clause (i) of principle (32) and clause (i) of (33) should not be considered hard-and-fast criteria for determining what proposition a speaker is using the complement clause of an attitude ascription to pick out. Rather, they are heuristic principles that are often highly useful in interpreting a speaker's remarks, but sometimes play no significant role. Second, the task of determining what someone who has uttered an attitude ascription has attempted to assert and convey is often a matter of interpretation that is both open-ended and highly sensitive to salient information that is part of the set of shared common background assumptions present in the context at the time of the utterance. Third, what is asserted and conveyed by utterances of attitude ascriptions often goes well beyond the semantic contents of those ascriptions, and can be expected to vary significantly from one context to another.

Communication, Competence, and Error

In chapter 3, I argued that simple (unambiguous, noncontext-sensitive) sentences are used to assert and convey different information in different contexts, and that the semantic content of a sentence is information that it would be used to assert and convey in all normal contexts involving speakers and hearers who understand it. I have now extended this account to attitude ascriptions containing such simple sentences as complement clauses. In the case of a simple sentence, **Fn**, containing an ordinary, linguistically simple proper name n that refers to an object, o, I argued that its meaning, or semantic content, is the singular, Russellian proposition, (41), that ascribes the property expressed by F to o.

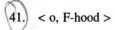

(41.)   < o, F-hood >

Similarly, the semantic content of an attitude ascription, **α believes that Fn**, is a proposition that attributes to the referent of α belief in proposition (41). It is a consequence of this view that since *Carl Hempel* and *Peter Hempel* are ordinary, linguistically simple proper names that refer to the same man, the sentences (42a) and (42b) mean the same thing (have the same semantic content), and the attitude ascriptions (43a) and (43b) semantically express propositions with the same truth conditions, and so cannot differ in semantically determined truth-value.

42a.   Carl Hempel lived on Lake Lane in Princeton.
42b.   Peter Hempel lived on Lake Lane in Princeton.
43a.   Mary believes that Carl Hempel lived on Lake Lane in Princeton.
43b.   Mary believes that Peter Hempel lived on Lake Lane in Princeton.

In chapter 3 I noted that the first of these consequences—that (42a) and (42b) mean the same thing—conflicts with the intuitive judgments of many competent speakers. However, I argued that this does not constitute compelling evidence against the theory, since those intuitive judgments are based on a confusion of what a sentence means—that is, information that would be asserted and conveyed by assertive utterances of it in all normal contexts—with what speakers use it to assert and convey in particular contexts. When speakers say that (42a) and (42b) mean different things, what they are really telling us is that competent speakers may use them to assert and convey different information, which is true. Moreover, the fact that speakers are prone to confuse the semantic content of a sentence, its meaning in the language, with what a speaker uses it to assert in a particular context just shows that being a competent speaker requires neither having a theoretical understanding of what semantic content is, nor the systematic ability to recognize when two sentences that one understands have the same semantic content.

The same points hold regarding (43a) and (43b), plus the additional fact that substitution of one coreferential name for another in an attitude ascription may seem to have the capacity to change truth-values in attitude ascriptions in ways that are not possible in many simple sentences. When asked whether it is possible for one member of the pair (43a)/(43b) to be true while the other is false, many competent speakers—including those who know that *Carl Hempel* and *Peter Hempel* are different names for the same man—would answer that, of course, this is possible. And in a certain sense it is. As we have seen, there are contexts in which assertive utterances of these sentences would result in assertions that attribute different beliefs to Mary. Since Mary may have one of these beliefs without having the other, it is possible for assertive utterances of (43a) and (43b) to result in assertions with different truth-values. To this extent familiar intuitions about the possible difference in truth-value of these ascriptions are perfectly correct. What is not correct is the idea that they show that the propositions semantically expressed by the two sentences (their semantic contents) can differ in truth-value. As before, the reason this may not be evident to ordinary speakers is that being a competent speaker does not require having a clear conception of what semantic content is. So long as speakers are good at recognizing what information is asserted and conveyed by sentences in different contexts of utterance, they may be competent users of the language, even if they are not able in various cases to correctly describe the semantic content of a sentence they understand, or to recognize when two such sentences have the same semantic content.

At this point, however, the theory I advocate runs into a potential difficulty. It follows from the theory that an assertive utterance of an attitude ascription in a particular context will often result in the assertion of several propositions. In itself this is no problem, and generally conversational participants are at least implicitly aware of the different assertions made. However, there is a special class of cases in which the theory I have outlined characterizes an assertive utterance of an attitude ascription as resulting in the assertion of several propositions, only some of which are recognized as asserted by members of the conversation.

A case in point is Gil's assertive utterance of (38) at the philosophy department newcomers' party.

(38.) Mary has just learned that Peter Hempel is Carl Hempel.

I argued that certain common assumptions shared by the speaker, Gil, and his audience, John, are responsible for the fact that his assertive utterance resulted in the assertion of the proposition expressed by (40).

40.   Mary has just learned that our colleague here at the party, known to us as 'Peter Hempel,' is the famous philosopher of science Carl Hempel.

In the case in question, it seems clear the Gil's primary intention in using (38) was to assert and convey the information given in (40)—or something like it. Moreover, since in the context John did interpret his remark in this way, his intention was fulfilled. So far, so good. What the theory says about this seems to fit the facts, as the conversational participants understand them.

However, the theory makes a further claim that may seem more problematic. According to the theory, if n is an ordinary proper name that refers to an object o, then one of the propositions asserted by an assertive utterance of a sentence, ... n ... , is the singular, Russellian proposition expressed by ... v ... relative to an assignment of the object o to the variable v. (This proposition may be seen as predicating the property expressed by λv (... v ...) of the object o.) Applying this rule twice to (38), appealing to the coreferentiality of the two names, and simplifying, we get the result (i).

(i)   One of the propositions asserted by Gil's utterance of (38) was the proposition expressed by (44) relative to an assignment of the man Mr. Hempel to the variables 'x' and 'y'.

44.   Mary just learned that x is y.

Since, on my view, variables are directly referential, if 'x' and 'y' are assigned the same object as value, then one can be substituted for the other without affecting what proposition is expressed. This gives us (ii).

No. Different propositions, same semantic value.

(ii)   One of the propositions asserted by Gil's utterance of (38) was the proposition expressed by (45) relative to an assignment of the man Mr. Hempel to the variable 'x'.

45. Mary just learned that x is x   *No.*

Could be, but not expressed, with no change

Next, I assume that *just learned* can be treated as an attitude verb, and that the truth conditions of ascriptions containing it conform to the following condition: **α just learned that S** is true only if the referent i *semantic value.* of α now believes the proposition expressed by S, but until a very recently i did not believe that proposition. This gives us (iii).

(iii). One of the propositions asserted by Gil's utterance of (38) was a proposition that is true only if Mary now believes the proposition expressed by *x is x* relative to an assignment of Mr. Hempel to the variable 'x', but until very recently Mary did not believe that proposition.

Finally, I take the proposition expressed by *x is x*, relative to an assignment of Mr. Hempel as value of 'x', to be the trivial proposition that says of the pair consisting of Mr. Hempel and himself that the first is identical with the second. This proposition is believed by anyone who believes of Mr. Hempel that he is him. Since we may presume that Mary believed this long before she first heard the name *Peter Hempel* at the newcomers' party, we have results (iv) and (v).

(iv)   One of the propositions asserted by Gil's utterance of (38) was a proposition that is true only if Mary now believes of Mr. Hempel that he is him, but until very recently Mary did not believe this.

(v)   One of the propositions asserted by Gil's utterance of (38) was false.

What makes this conclusion problematic is that although the theory I have outlined is committed to it, the participants in the conversation would almost certainly not recognize the assertion in question, and probably would deny it if asked. If asked to evaluate what Gil asserted, they would, I think, be inclined to characterize it as true, on the grounds that what he said had roughly the content of (40). I doubt very much that it would ordinarily occur to them that in addition to asserting this, Gil also asserted something that falsely attributed to Mary a long-standing ignorance of a certain triviality. Thus, either the theory I have outlined is incorrect, or in cases like these ordinary speakers and hearers are not aware of all of the assertions made by assertive utterances of attitude ascriptions.

Although I don't take this challenge to the theory lightly, I regard the latter alternative as the correct one. One of the most important reasons for this is that the main elements of the theory generating results (iv) and (v) are well supported in the overwhelming majority of cases by facts that would be recognized to be obviously correct by competent speakers. For example, a speaker, s, who assertively utters an attitude ascription,

46.   Ralph knows/believes/hopes/expects . . . that Fn,

which contains an ordinary, linguistically simple proper name n referring to an object o, would standardly be recognized to have said of o that Ralph knows/believes/hopes/expects . . . that he/she/it is F—as is evidenced by our typical readiness to use (47a) to report s's remark, and to take (47b) to be an obvious consequence of (47a) (plus the assumption that there is such a thing as n).

47a.   s said that Ralph v's that Fn.
47b.   There is an x such that x = n & s said that Ralph v's that Fx.

This suggests that the general rule R applies across the board to the full range of sentences, including propositional attitude ascriptions.

R.   A speaker who assertively utters a sentence . . . n . . . containing a name n that refers to an object o asserts a singular, Russellian proposition that, in effect, predicates the property expressed by λx (. . . x. . . .) of o.

Other main elements of the theory used in drawing the seemingly problematic conclusions about Gil's remark include the assumption that variables are devices of direct reference and the assumption that the proposition expressed by x is x relative to an assignment of Mr. Hempel as value of 'x' is a triviality that anyone who knows anything about Mr. Hempel can be expected to believe. These assumptions are also well supported by an overwhelming body of obvious facts. Finally, I assumed that *just learned* can be treated as an ordinary attitude verb that expresses a relation between agents and propositions—in particular a relation in which the agent does not believe a certain proposition at an earlier time, but later comes to believe it. Conceivably one might quarrel with the account of this particular relation. However, it seems doubtful that this can be the main source of trouble, since similarly problematic results could be gotten by considering assertive utterances of (48).

48. Before coming to the party, Mary didn't know/believe that Peter Hempel was Carl Hempel.

I believe the best explanation of why ordinary speakers are inclined not to recognize some of the assertions predicted by the theory I have outlined involves two main factors. First, in cases like Gil's assertive utterance of (38), conversational participants focus on the speaker's primary intention of asserting (40) and obvious consequences of (40); this focus renders his false subsidiary assertion unimportant to them. Second, the subsidiary assertion arises not from extra information the speaker is explicitly trying to convey, but from the interaction of a number of general rules governing his use of language. Although competent speakers typically intend to act in accordance with whatever general rules are relevant to the sentences they use, sometimes these rules have consequences that they have not fully worked out. Because of this, speakers are sometimes committed to, and may even have to be regarded as having asserted, certain things that they are not fully, or explicitly, aware of. That, I suspect, is what is going on in our example. The rules governing the use of names and attitude ascriptions have consequences for Gil's assertive utterance of (38) which neither the speaker nor his audience has worked out. Moreover, these consequences do not come into focus because of the attention paid to what he primarily intends to assert.

One indication that this explanation is correct is that, with help, initially incredulous speakers can often be brought to appreciate the strength of the claim that they have missed certain surprising consequences of remarks like Gil's. For example, suppose that shortly after his assertive utterance of (38) we were to ask, *"Is there some man such that Gil asserted that Mary has just learned that he is Carl Hempel?"* I think that if Gil and his audience were confronted with this question, they would be inclined to agree with the following answer: *"Yes, there is a man, Peter Hempel (standing right over there), such that Gil asserted that Mary just learned that he is Carl Hempel."* In this way, conversational participants could be brought to recognize the truth of (49).

(49) $\exists x$ (x = Peter Hempel & Gil asserted that Mary just learned that x = Carl Hempel)

Next we might ask, *"But isn't it true that Mary has known for a long time that Carl Hempel is Carl Hempel?"* Surely, the answer to this would be *"Yes."* We might follow this up with *"Isn't it therefore also true that there is a certain man, Carl Hempel, such that Mary has long believed that he is Carl Hempel?"* Here again, I think that if ordinary speakers and hearers were to reflect on the matter, they would be inclined to agree that Carl Hempel is such that Mary has long believed that he is Carl Hempel. In this way they could be brought to recognize the truth of (50).

(50) $\exists x$ (x = Carl Hempel & Mary has long believed that x = Carl Hempel)

Finally, we remind them of the truth of (51).

$y = x$

51. Peter Hempel is Carl Hempel.

But surely, we would point out, (52) is a logical consequence of (49)–(51); therefore since they are true, it is true as well.

(52) $\exists x$ [x = Peter Hempel & x = Carl Hempel & (Gil asserted that Mary just learned that x = Carl Hempel) & (Mary has long believed that x = Carl Hempel)]

This means that there is a certain man such that Gil asserted that Mary just learned that he is Carl Hempel even though, in fact, Mary has long believed that he is Carl Hempel. But then, since Gil asserted that Mary has just learned that so and so, when in fact Mary has long believed (and even known) that so and so, it follows that at least one thing that *No.* Gil asserted is false.

That is the argument. In my opinion, if it is presented carefully and explicitly, even ordinary speakers who are initially inclined to deny its conclusion might very well be brought to appreciate its strength. The reason for this is that the individual steps in the argument are licensed by linguistic rules that really do govern the linguistic constructions in question. As a result, when one makes the argument explicit, the individual steps are recognized to be compelling and the conclusion may come to be recognized as true. Moreover, the theory I advocate offers an explanation of why it is that the conclusion, though true, is one that ordinary speakers do not initially recognize in ordinary conversation. They do not recognize it because (i) they focus on the primary assertion made by Gil's assertive utterance—namely, the assertion of the true proposition (40)—and (ii) this focus makes it conversationally unimportant for them to work out the implications of the general linguistic rules governing names and attitude ascriptions that lead to Gil's false subsidiary assertion in this case.

I think this explanation is plausible. Moreover, I take its plausibility to be linked to the plausibility of the theory as a whole. I am willing to attribute a certain limited degree of ignorance and error to ordinary competent speakers because such ignorance and error can be made understandable, because the ignorance and error in question are not very important conversationally, because the general rules that give rise to the results we have investigated are well supported in the great majority of cases, and because we all feel the intuitive force of these rules. In light of this it seems reasonable to take the claims made by the theory I advocate to be correct.

Identity Sentences and the Necessary A Posteriori

In chapter 1, I cited Kripke's well-known thesis, T4, from *Naming and Necessity*.[11]

> T4. Identity sentences involving different, coreferential names are not only true, but necessary. Nevertheless, often such identities are not knowable a priori; rather, they are known only a posteriori.

Since we have now recognized two different classes of names—ordinary, linguistically simple proper names like *Carl Hempel*, and partially descriptive names like *New York City*—we may consider two different versions of this thesis.

> T4a. Identity sentences involving different, but coreferential, ordinary, linguistically simple names are not only true, but necessary. Nevertheless, often such identities are not knowable a priori; rather, they are known only a posteriori.
>
> T4b. Identity sentences involving different, coreferential names, at least one of which is partially descriptive, are not only true, but necessary. Nevertheless, often such identities are not knowable a priori; rather, they are known only a posteriori

We begin with a discussion of T4a. This thesis has been widely accepted, and there is much to be said for it. Nevertheless, I argued that, when combined with other leading doctrines of *Naming and Necessity*, it leads to a puzzle. The problem, in a nutshell, is this: Kripke's arguments against descriptivist analyses of (linguistically simple) proper names, and natural extensions of those arguments, lead to the conclusion that the semantic content of such a name is never the same as that of any description. From here it seems to be a reasonable step to suppose that these names don't have descriptive senses, or descriptive semantic contents, at all. Moreover, if names don't have descriptive semantic contents, then it would seem that their only semantic contents are their referents. But from this it follows that coreferential names have the same semantic content. If we add a plausible principle of compositionality, we get the result that sentences differing only in the substitution of one such name for another must semantically express the same proposition. However, this conclusion seems to play havoc with T4a. For on this reasoning, if a and b are proper names, and the sentence $a = b$ is true, then it semantically expresses the same proposition as the sentence $a = a$. But then, since the latter proposition is surely knowable a priori, so is the former. How, in light of this, is it possible to retain T4a?

We are now in a position to resolve this puzzle. T4a should not be retained. Rather, it should be replaced by a set of more precise theses that carefully distinguish among identity sentences, the propositions they semantically express, and the propositions they are primarily used to assert. One such thesis is T5.[12]

 T5. Identity sentences involving different but coreferential, ordinary, linguistically simple names semantically express propositions that are not only true, but also both necessary and knowable a priori. Nevertheless, the primary assertions made by utterances of such identity sentences are often neither necessary nor knowable a priori.

An example of this thesis discussed above is the sentence (36) and Paul's assertive utterance of it to Mary with the primary intention of asserting proposition (37).

36. Peter Hempel is Carl Hempel

37. The man standing over there, Peter Hempel, is the famous philosopher of science Carl Hempel.

Although the proposition semantically expressed by (36) is both necessary and knowable a priori, the proposition it is primarily used to assert in this context is contingent and knowable only a posteriori.

Thesis T6 is a companion to T5 that explicitly concerns propositional attitude ascriptions.

 T6. If a and b are different but coreferential, ordinary, linguistically simple names, the proposition semantically expressed by an attitude ascription, *α believes (knows, etc.) that a = b*, reports that the agent believes, knows, etc., a proposition that is necessary and knowable a priori. However, often the propositions that are the primary assertions made by utterances of such ascriptions report that the agent believes, knows, etc., a proposition that is contingent and knowable only a posteriori.

An instance of T6 discussed above is the sentence (38) and Gil's assertive utterance of it with the primary intention of asserting proposition (40).

38. Mary has just learned that Peter Hempel is Carl Hempel.

40. Mary has just learned that our colleague here at the party, known to us as 'Peter Hempel', is the famous philosopher of science Carl Hempel.

If the theory I have outlined is correct, then what was right about Kripke's thesis T4a, involving identity sentences containing ordinary, linguistically simple proper names, is captured by the combination of T5 and T6. To the extent that T4a was not viewed in essentially this way, it should be regarded as incorrect. This is not, of course, to cast doubt on Kripke's thesis that many necessary propositions—including many necessary truths (semantically) expressed by sentences containing ordinary proper names—are knowable only a posteriori. That thesis is both true and important. However, identity sentences involving coreferential, ordinary, linguistically simple proper names are not genuine instances of it.

Finally, a word should be said about T4b, which concerns identity sentences containing one or more partially descriptive names. Suppose that n and m are coreferential, partially descriptive names semantically associated with the descriptive properties expressed by N and M, respectively. Then, according to the view developed in chapter 5, n and m are semantically equivalent to *the x*: $Nx \, \& \, x = y$ and *the z*: $Mz \, \& \, z = y$ (relative to an assignment of the referent of n and m to 'y'), respectively. Thus the proposition semantically expressed by (53a) is the proposition expressed by (53b), relative to an assignment of the referent of n and m to 'y'.

53a. $n = m$
53b.   [the x: $Nx \, \& \, x = y$] = [the z: $Mz \, \& \, z = y$]

Since the properties associated with partially descriptive names are standardly not a priori knowable of the objects that are their referents, the propositions expressed by identity sentences like (53a) are standardly knowable only a posteriori. In many cases, however, these properties are also not essential properties of their referents either, in which case the identity sentences are clearly contingent, as well as a posteriori. Thus, T4b is false.

However, there are also cases in which the relevant properties are, arguably at least, essential properties of the referents of the partially descriptive names. For example, it seems plausible to think that the

Trivial?

property of being a mountain is an essential property of Mt. Everest, that the property of being an avenue is an essential property of Sixth Avenue (in Manhattan), and the property of being a city is an essential property of New York City. Let us further assume that *Mt. Everest, New York City,* and *Sixth Avenue* are partially descriptive names and that *Gaurisanker* and *Gotham* are linguistically simple proper names that are coreferential with the first two, respectively, while *The Avenue of the Americas* is a partially descriptive name that is coreferential with the third. We may then take it that the propositions expressed by (54) have the contents indicated in (55) (relative to assignments of the appropriate referents to the variable 'y').

54a. Gaurisanker = Mt. Everest
54b. Gotham = New York City
54c. The Avenue of the Americas = Sixth Avenue
55a. $g = [\text{the } x: (\text{Mountain } x \ \& \ x = y)]$
55b. $gm = [\text{the } x: (\text{City } x \ \& \ x = y)]$
55c. $[\text{the } x: (\text{Avenue } x \ \& \ x = y)] = [\text{the } z: (\text{Avenue } z \ \& \ z = y)]$

Are these examples of the necessary a posteriori? To know the truth of the proposition (54a)/(55a), one must know, of a particular object, Mt. Everest, that it is a mountain. To know the truth of the proposition (54b)/(55b), one must know, of another object, New York City, that it is a city. To know the truth of (54c)/(55c), one must know, of a third object, that it is an avenue. Since one can't know a priori of any object that it is a mountain, or that it is a city, or that it is an avenue, the propositions (54a)/(55a), (54b)/(55b), and (54c)/(55c) are a posteriori. But are they necessary? Not quite. For example, consider a world w in which Mt. Everest does not exist. Even if *Gaurisanker* continues to refer to Mt. Everest with respect to w, and even if the range of the quantifier *the* in (55a), when evaluated at w, is taken to include objects that do not exist with respect to w, the quantifier phrase *the x: (Mountain x & x = y)* will be nondenoting with respect to w (relative to an assignment of Mt. Everest to 'y')—assuming that the property of being a mountain is such that nothing can have it at a world unless it exists at that world. Thus the proposition (54a)/(55a) is not true with respect to w, and so is not necessary. Analogous reasoning leads to the conclusion that, strictly speaking, (54b)/(55b) and (54c)/(55c) are not necessary either.

It is, of course, easy enough to find closely related propositions that are necessary. For example, the propositions in (56) are all necessary truths (when the descriptive phrases corresponding to the partially descriptive names in these sentences are given small scope relative to the conditional construction).[13]

56a. If Mt. Everest exists, then Gaurisanker = Mt. Everest
56b. If New York City exists, then Gotham = New York City
56c. If Sixth Avenue and the Avenue of the Americans exist, then the Avenue of the Americas = Sixth Avenue

However, these propositions are also knowable a priori. Thus, identity sentences involving names—whether they be linguistically simple or partially descriptive—do not provide examples of the necessary a posteriori (or the contingent a priori).[14]

What Is It for a General Term to Be a Rigid Designator?

Extending the Semantic Doctrines about Names to Natural Kind Terms: The Problem

In chapter 1, I identified the two most important pieces of unfinished semantic business left to us by *Naming and Necessity*. The first of these was to answer the question "What are the semantic contents of proper names?" Although Kripke succeeded in demonstrating that linguistically simple proper names are standardly rigid designators, and although extensions of his arguments can be used to show that the semantic contents of most such names are not identical with those of any description,[1] he did not provide a positive doctrine that identifies what the semantic contents of these names are. This in turn led to a dilemma involving the propositions semantically expressed by sentences that differ only in the substitution of coreferential names of this type. On the one hand, one might accept what many have taken to be a datum—namely, that even when two sentences differ only in this way, typically it is possible to assert and believe the proposition semantically expressed by one of them without asserting or believing the proposition semantically expressed by the other. However, if one takes this position, one must provide some positive account of the different semantic contents of linguistically simple, coreferential proper names—a task that, I have argued, is all but hopeless when one puts aside the special category of what I have called *partially descriptive names*. On the other hand, one might reject the alleged datum, and insist that when two sentences differ only in the substitution of one linguistically simple coreferential name for another, they semantically express the same proposition. The challenge for this approach is to explain how speakers nevertheless succeed in using such sentences to convey different information, to assert different propositions, to express different beliefs, and to attribute different beliefs (as well as other propositional attitudes) to various agents.

In the preceding chapters I have tried to answer this challenge and, in so doing, to resolve our dilemma about the semantic content of proper names. I have argued that, on a proper conception of semantic content, there is a principled distinction between the vast majority of ordinary, linguistically simple proper names, the semantic contents of which are simply their referents, and the special, but still quite extensive, category of partially descriptive names, which are often syntactically complex expressions, and which have semantic contents that include both their referents and certain descriptive information conventionally associated with them by speakers. In the former case, substitution of one member of a pair of ordinary coreferential proper names for another does not change the proposition semantically expressed—even though it may change the proposition asserted, believed, or attributed to others as one of their assertions or beliefs. In the latter case—involving partially descriptive names—even the proposition semantically expressed may change. If this account is correct, then we have completed the first main semantic task left to us by *Naming and Necessity*.

We now turn to the second main piece of unfinished business arising out of Kripke's discussion—namely, that of specifying how the semantic model developed for proper names should be extended to a wider class of terms. In *Naming and Necessity*, Kripke propounded a set of interconnected theses relating meaning, reference, metaphysical modalities, and epistemological notions like a priori and a posteriori knowledge. His strategy was to begin by articulating a theory covering the simplest case, proper names, and then to extend the theory to the more complex and philosophically significant case of natural kind terms. We now have a reasonably good conception of what the theory should look like for proper names. However, the extension of this theory to other classes of expressions, including natural kind terms of different grammatical categories, is more problematic, and was never fully developed by Kripke. As a result, this important aspect of the theory remains incompletely developed and poorly understood. My task in this chapter and the next will be to expose some of the gaps in Kripke's discussion of natural kind terms, and to investigate the theoretical resources available for closing them.

I begin by repeating the central theses about proper names defended in the first two lectures of *Naming and Necessity*. (Recall that T4, though defended by Kripke, cannot be maintained when ordinary proper names are involved, but rather must be replaced by theses T5 and T6, discussed at the end of chapter 8.)

Theses about Proper Names

T1. Proper names are nondescriptional: (i) they are not synonymous with descriptions or clusters of descriptions associated with them by speakers; (ii) the referent of a name with respect to an arbitrary world w is not determined semantically via the satisfaction of any description or descriptive condition at w; instead, (iii) the referent of a name is initially fixed at the actual world and, once fixed, is stipulated to remain the same with respect to all other worlds.[2]

T2. The referent of a proper name is initially fixed in one or the other of two ways—by an ostensive baptism, or by a stipulation that it is to be whatever satisfies a certain description. Later, when the name is passed from speaker to speaker, the way in which the reference was initially fixed usually doesn't matter. Typically, speakers farther down the historical chain use the name to refer to the initial referent whether or not they associate properties with the name that (uniquely) apply to it.

T3. Proper names are rigid designators—that is, a proper name that designates an object o does so with respect to all worlds in which o exists, and never designates anything else.

T4. Identity sentences involving different names (or other rigid designators) are necessary if true. Nevertheless, often such identities are knowable only a posteriori.

In lecture 3, Kripke defends similar theses for natural kind terms. For example, he argues that natural kind terms such as *gold*, *tiger*, *cat*, *water*, *heat*, and *light* are not synonymous with clusters of descriptions standardly associated with them by speakers. As in the case of proper names, two ways are given by which the reference of a term may be fixed. One way involves direct presentation of samples of the putative kind, together with the stipulation that the term is to be understood as applying to all and only instances of the unique natural kind (of a certain sort) of which nearly all members of the sample are instances. The other way of fixing reference involves the use of a description that picks out the kind, or members of the kind, by some, usually contingent, properties. Later, when the kind term is passed from speaker to speaker, the way in which the reference was initially fixed normally doesn't matter—just as with proper names.[3] As a result, speakers further down the chain may use the term to apply to instances of the given kind, whether or not the descriptive properties they associate with the term really pick out members of that kind.

In addition, scientific investigation may lead to the discovery of properties that are necessary and sufficient for membership in the kind. These properties are expressed in "theoretical identity sentences" that are necessary but a posteriori. Examples of such sentences specifically discussed in *Naming and Necessity* are the following:

> *Water is H_2O (126–129), Flashes of lightning are flashes of electricity (132), Light is a stream of photons (129–130), Gold is the element with atomic number 79 (123–125), Cats are animals (122–123), Whales are mammals (138), Heat is the motion of molecules (99–100).*

The parallels between Kripke's treatment of proper names and his discussion of natural kind terms are evident. However, special complications arise in the discussion of natural kind terms. Among the most important of these are questions about rigidity, and about the modal properties of certain sentences. As in the case of proper names, natural kind terms are said to be rigid, and the putative rigidity of these terms is used to support the corollary that theoretical identity sentences involving them are necessary, if true. For example, in discussing theoretical identifications involving natural kind terms, Kripke says, *"Theoretical identities, according to the conception I advocate, are generally identities involving two **rigid** designators and **therefore** are examples of the necessary aposteriori."*[4] Another example occurs in the discussion of the mind/body identity theory, where Kripke maintains that *pain* and *c-fiber stimulation* are rigid designators, and adds *"So it seems that the identity theorist is in some trouble, for*, **since we have two rigid designators, the identity statement in question is necessary."**[5]

Again, this carries the implication that any identity statement involving rigid designators will be necessary, if true.

However, there is a difficulty here that has not been widely appreciated. Kripke gives no separate definition of what it means to say that a natural kind term is rigid; nor does he provide distinct arguments to show that they are rigid. This is a problem because his explicit definition of rigidity tells us only what it is for a singular term to be rigid. If all natural kind terms were just ordinary singular terms, each purporting to designate a single object, then this definition could be applied directly to them, without qualification. However, as Kripke recognizes, natural kind terms fall into a variety of syntactic and semantic categories.

For example, he says, "*According to the view I advocate, then, terms for natural kinds are much closer to proper names than is ordinarily supposed. The old term 'common name' is thus quite appropriate for predicates marking out species or natural kinds, such as 'cow' or 'tiger'. My considerations apply also, however, to certain mass terms for natural kinds, such as 'gold', 'water' and the like.*"[6] A little later, summing up his views, Kripke adds, "*. . . my argument implicitly concludes that certain general terms, those for natural kinds, have a greater kinship with proper names than is generally realized. This conclusion holds for certain for various species names, whether they are count nouns, such as 'cat', 'tiger', 'chunk of gold', or mass terms such as 'gold', 'water', 'iron pyrites'. It also applies to certain terms for natural phenomena, such as 'heat', 'light', 'sound', 'lightning', and, presumably, suitably elaborated, to corresponding adjectives— 'hot' 'loud', 'red'.*"[7]

It appears from these passages that Kripke intends his general theses about natural kind terms—including, presumably, the claim that they are rigid—to apply, at least in some form, to terms of various syntactic and semantic categories. This raises obvious questions, among them "What is it for a predicate to be a rigid designator?" and "Are natural kind predicates, like *cow, tiger, animal, chunk of gold*, and *flash of lightning*, rigid?" "What is it for a sentence containing a pair of natural kind predicates to count as a theoretical identity sentence?" "Are such sentences necessary if true?"

Before attacking these questions, I want to say a brief word about the need to take them seriously. Much of the philosophical literature on natural kind terms treats them simply as names for kinds. This idea is superficially plausible for mass terms like *water*, which are grammatically singular. The grammatical singularity of the term *water* leads some philosophers to assume that the term must be semantically singular, too—that is, that it must designate a single thing. The two most natural choices for such a referent are the mereological sum of all bits of water or the abstract type, instances of which are concrete quantities of water. With this model fixed in mind, many philosophers tend to think that, somehow, the same must be true for other natural kind terms, too, even if they are not mass terms. This leads to the mistaken idea that there is no problem making sense of the notion of rigidity for natural kind terms because they are simply names, not predicates. Moreover, the thought continues, identity sentences involving such terms are of the form $a = b$, so they don't present any problem either.

I believe this view to be mistaken for a variety of reasons. First, it has no plausibility as an analysis of all natural kind terms. Whatever its initial plausibility may be in the case of mass terms such as *water*, there is no natural way to extend it to all the terms that Kripke intends to be encompassed by his theses. As we have seen, Kripke includes among the natural kind terms to which his analysis applies count nouns, such as *human*, *tiger*, and *mammal*, as well as adjectives such as *loud* and *hot*. Surely, there is no plausibility in treating all these as singular terms. Thus, there is no way to avoid genuine questions that arise about the application of Kripke's theses to at least some expressions that are not singular terms.

Second, if one focuses on the count nouns, there are good reasons to think that they standardly function as predicates. Like other predicates they combine with quantifiers to form complex quantifier phrases such as *all animals*, *most mammals*, and *a few tigers*, whereas ordinary names do not do this. In addition, they occur naturally in predicative position—for instance, we say *the creatures in the next room are mammals*, and *Fido and Fee Fee are dogs*, where *are mammals* and *are dogs* clearly function as predicates. It is true that if one wished, one could paraphrase these predicates by such phrases as *is an instance of the kind mammal* and *is an instance of the kind dog*, which contain kind-designating nominals. But it is far from obvious that the nominal form is conceptually fundamental, and in many cases a plausible argument could be given that it is the predicative form that has priority. Often, we learn what it means to say that a is an instance of the kind, or property, P* by being told, or figuring out, that necessarily a is an instance of P* iff a is P, where the latter, *a is P*, is something we already understand and take as basic. For example, *Jim's shirt is red* is necessarily equivalent to *Jim's shirt is an instance of the color red*, and *that object is circular* is necessarily equivalent to *that object is an instance of circularity*; but it is the predicative form, *is red* and *is circular*, that is basic, and the nominal form, *the color red* and *circularity*, that is derivative. To the extent that we understand what the color red or circularity is at all, it is because we already understand what it is for something to be red or to be circular, and we are told that there is a necessary connection between x's being red or circular, and x's being an instance of redness or circularity. A similar argument might be made regarding the abstract kind dog or mammal. To the extent that we understand these abstract kinds, it is because we already understand what it is for individuals to be dogs or mammals, and we take the kinds to be what any possible individual must be an instance of in order to be a dog or a mammal. If this is right, then the nominal use of these natural kind terms is understood in terms of the predicative use, and not vice versa.

Third, when we turn to mass nouns, there are similar reasons to analyze them as functioning primarily as predicates. Like count nouns, they occur naturally in predicative position—as in *That stuff is water/gold/snow*. Like count nouns, and other predicates, mass nouns combine with quantifiers to form complex quantifier phrases—for example, *some water, all gold, the snow, much lead*. Finally, mass nouns have bare, unmodified occurrences that parallel the bare, unmodified use of plural count nouns, which are standardly taken to be predicates. For example, just as the sentences in A are equivalent to those in B, so the sentences in C are equivalent to those in D.

A1. Men are mortal.
A2. Children are not allowed to purchase firearms.
A3. Beavers build dams. (generic)
B1. All men are mortal
B2. No children are allowed to purchase firearms
B3. Generally, or characteristically, if something is a beaver, then it builds dams. (generic)
C1. Gold is malleable.
C2. Water isn't found on the moon.
C3. Snow is white. (generic)

D1. All gold is malleable.
D2. No water is found on the moon.
D3. Generally, or characteristically, if something is snow, then it is white (generic)

For all these reasons, it is natural to take the primary use of mass nouns to be one in which they function as predicates.[8]

Once this is seen, we can explain why mass nouns have initially appeared to many to be singular terms. The reason for this is that they are grammatically singular—for instance, we say *gold is malleable*, not *golds are malleable*. Because of this many have assumed that mass terms must be semantically singular—that is, that they must purport to refer to single things. But there is a different explanation for their grammatical singularity. They are singular because, being mass terms, they obey the following rough and ready generalizations:

(i) The parts of something that is P are themselves P.
(ii) If x is something that can be exhaustively divided into parts all of which are P, then x is P.

Let us take *water* as an example. Because it obeys these principles, it makes no sense to ask *how many instances of water are in the bathtub*. If *water* were grammatically plural, so that we said things like *there are lots of waters in the bathtub*, instead of *there is lots of water* in the bathtub, then it would sound natural to ask *How many waters are in the bathtub*? This nonsensical locution is avoided by the grammatical singularity of the term. If this is right, then the grammatical similarity of mass terms can be given a natural explanation without assuming that these are semantically singular terms.[9]

The lesson of all of this is that the natural kind terms with which Kripke is concerned include many expressions that function primarily as predicates, rather than as names. Because of this, there is a serious question of how his central semantic theses about proper names are to be understood when they are applied to the broader class of natural kind terms. Since the concept of a rigid designator is defined by Kripke only for singular terms, we need to address the questions mentioned above: "What is it for a natural kind predicate to be rigid?" and "Are the natural kind predicates that Kripke talks about rigid?" In addition, since Kripke seems to intend his doctrine that identity sentences involving rigid designators are necessary if true, to apply to sentences in which the rigid designators are natural kind predicates, we need to ask "What is it for a sentence containing a pair of natural kind predicates to count as a theoretical identity sentence?" and "Are such sentences necessary if true?"

There are two natural strategies for answering these questions.

Strategy 1. Define a concept of rigidity for predicates that is a natural extension of the concept that has been defined for singular terms. Then determine whether natural kind predicates are rigid in this sense, and whether so-called theoretical identities involving them are necessary if true.

Strategy 2. Relate each predicate to a corresponding singular term. Characterize the predicate as rigid iff its associated singular term is rigid. Then determine whether these singular terms are rigid. If they are, then true identity sentences involving them, as well as corresponding theoretical identification sentences containing the original predicates, will be necessary.

I will begin with strategy 1. One advantage of this is that we may (temporarily) sidestep the problem of having to locate the corresponding singular term for each natural kind predicate. For some of these predicates the choice of an appropriate singular term seems reasonably straightforward—for instance, *is red/the color red*, *is a tiger/the species tiger*, *is a primate/the order primate*, and *is water/the substance water*. However, in other cases it is less obvious. What, for example, are the singular terms associated with the natural kind predicates *is an electron* or *is a star*? It might be suggested that for any predicate P, we can always fall back on the singular term *the kind P* or *the property of being (a) P*. But if these are the singular terms to be appealed to in defining the rigidity of predicates, it is not clear that rigidity will distinguish natural kind predicates from ordinary descriptive predicates such as *is a bachelor*. In any case, this is a problem that need not concern us if strategy 1 can be made to work. Another advantage of beginning with strategy 1 is that, in the case of many natural kind predicates, we seem to understand the predicate prior to understanding any associated singular term, which suggests that it should be possible to state the semantic properties of these predicates independently, without having to derive them from the semantic properties of related singular terms, which are often psychologically and linguistically more complex. For these reasons, strategy 1 will be my preferred method for examining Kripke's doctrines about the rigidity of natural kind predicates and the modal status of theoretical identification sentences containing them. We will turn to strategy 2 only if we are unable to give a reasonable account of these doctrines in any other way.

Strategy 1

Let us begin with the definitional question. What is it for a predicate to be a rigid designator? In the case of a singular term, t, the object designated by t with respect to a world is the extension of t at that world, and the claim that t is rigid entails that it has the same extension at every world in which it has an extension at all. In the case of a predicate, P, the extension of P at a world is the set of objects that P applies to with respect to the world. One idea for characterizing a notion of rigidity for predicates parallel to the notion of rigidity for singular terms would be to stipulate that P is rigid only if P has the same extension at any world in which it has a non-null extension. However, a moment's reflection is all that is needed to show that this won't do. Consider, for example, the predicate *animal*. Its extension at a world is the set of all things that are animals at that world. But if the notion of a predicate's being a rigid designator is to have genuine theoretical significance, then the claim that a predicate is rigid must not entail that it has the same extension at every world in which it has a non-null extension. For if rigidity for predicates were defined in that way, then the mere fact that there could have been animals other than those there actually are, or the mere fact that some animals that actually exist could have failed to exist while others remained, would be sufficient to show that the predicate *animal* is not rigid. Since the same point could be made for virtually every predicate of contingently existing objects, rigidity for predicates shouldn't be seen as requiring sameness of extension at different worlds.

Nor will it do to say that a predicate is rigid iff there is a unique property which it stands for that determines its extension at each possible world. There is, it could be argued, such a property in the case of natural kind predicates like *cow* and *animal*—namely, the property of being a cow and the property of being an animal. However, the same could be said for any predicate; for any predicate F, and any world w, the extension of F with respect to w is the set of things that have, in w, property expressed by **being an F**. But there is no point in defining a notion of rigidity for predicates according to which all predicates turn out, trivially, to be rigid.

There is, however, an obvious alternative definition which does not have this consequence, and which is a natural extension of Kripke's definition of rigidity for singular terms. The idea is that a predicate is rigid iff it is an essentialist predicate, where the latter is characterized as follows:[10]

$$EP \leftrightarrow \forall w \, \forall o \, \left[(P(o))_w \longrightarrow P(o)_{w_1 \ldots w_2 \ldots w_n} \right]$$

EP. A predicate P is essentialist iff for all possible worlds w and objects o, if P applies to o with respect to w, then P applies to o in all worlds in which o exists.

Two other ways of expressing the same idea are the following:

$$EP \leftrightarrow \left[\Box \, \forall x \left[Px \rightarrow ((\neg \exists x) \neg Px) \right] \right]$$

EPa. A predicate P (of English) is essentialist iff **Necessarily any individual that is (was) P could not have existed without being P** expresses a truth.

EPb. A predicate P is essentialist iff the property it expresses is an essential property of anything that has it.

$$EP \leftrightarrow \forall x \left(P_{ep}x \rightarrow \Box Px \right)$$

The parallels between this interpretation of rigidity for predicates and the corresponding theses for rigid singular terms are obvious. For example, the linguistic test for the essentiality/rigidity of English predicates provided by EPa is similar to Kripke's test, TRS, for singular terms.

TRS. A singular term t (of English) is a rigid designator of an object iff **The individual that is (was) t could not have existed without being t (and no one other than that individual could have been t)** expresses a truth.[11]

According to this test the name *Aristotle* is rigid since necessarily the individual who was Aristotle could not have existed without being Aristotle (and no one else could have been Aristotle), whereas the definite description *the teacher of Alexander* is not rigid. Similarly, the predicate *is an animal* is (arguably) essentialist, and therefore, on this interpretation, is rigid, since necessarily anything that is an animal could not have existed without being an animal; by contrast, *is a philosopher* is not essentialist/rigid.

There are three things to be said in favor of this interpretation of what it means for a predicate to be rigid. First, it is a natural generalization of the notion of rigidity defined for singular terms. Second, if this is what is meant by rigidity, then although many predicates are not rigid, it is plausible to suppose that most of the natural kind predicates discussed by Kripke are rigid—for example, it is plausible to suppose that anything that is a tiger is essentially a tiger, that anything that is a chunk of gold is essentially a chunk of gold, and so on. Third, there is ample textual support indicating that Kripke believed many natural kind predicates to be rigid (i e., essentialist) in the sense defined, and there are even some suggestive passages in which he seems to link the rigidity of predicates with their essentiality.

A case in point occurs on pages 148–149 of *Naming and Necessity*, where Kripke discusses a version of the mind/body identity theory. In the discussion he sets up a comparison between the identification of heat with molecular motion and the identification of pain with the stimulation of C-fibers. He says that both "identify two types of phenomena." The question then arises as to whether theoretical identification sentences are necessary or contingent in the two cases. About the first case he says, "*We have seen above that since 'heat' and 'molecular motion' are both rigid designators, the identification of the phenomena they name is necessary.*" Here the fact that 'heat' may be taken to be an abstract singular term suggests that Kripke may be thinking of the relevant identity sentence as some version of 'Heat = the motion of molecules,' in which two singular terms flank the identity predicate.

The corresponding point is less clear when he turns to pain and the stimulation of C-fibers. The passage continues as follows:

> *What about 'pain' and 'C-fiber stimulation'? It should be clear from the previous discussion that 'pain' is a rigid designator of the type, or phenomenon, it designates:* **if something is a pain it is essentially so,** *and it seems absurd to suppose that pain could have been some phenomenon other than the one it is. The same holds for the term 'C-fiber stimulation', provided that 'C-fibers' is a rigid designator, as I will suppose here. . . .*

Thus the identity of pain with the stimulation of C-fibers, if true, must be necessary. (148–149; emphasis added)

The part of the passage that I have emphasized in boldface says, in effect, that 'pain' (or 'is a pain') is an essentialist predicate. Moreover, this is said as an explanation or elaboration of the claim that 'pain' is a rigid designator. Thus we have here some suggestive textual support for interpreting the notion of a rigid predicate as an essentialist predicate. However, the passage as a whole is ambiguous. In particular, in the part of the sentence just after the material emphasized in bold-face, Kripke seems to be using 'pain' not as a predicate but as an abstract singular term that names a certain kind of thing (on analogy with 'heat'), and saying that the kind pain could not have been another kind. (When he turns to 'C-fibers,' he switches to the plural, which seems to rule out regarding it as a singular term, and supports thinking of it as a predicate.)

When one looks at the passage as a whole, it is hard to avoid feeling tempted to run two things together: (i) the rigidity of 'pain' when used as an abstract singular term for a certain abstract kind of thing and (ii) the essentiality of 'pain' when used as a predicate of individual pains. One may get the impression from the passage that these are the same thing, or at any rate that they inevitably go together. This, of course, is not so in the general case, as is illustrated by the fact that 'red' may be used either as a rigid, abstract singular term referring to a color, or as a nonessentialist predicate of individual red things. It is also important to resist the temptation to run together the claim that the predicate 'pain' (like the predicate 'red') is associated with a single kind that determines its extension with respect to all worlds—that is, the predicate "designates" the same kind with respect to all worlds—with the claim that if the predicate applies to something in one world, it does so in all worlds in which the thing exists.

In light of this, one cannot derive from the passage a clear, unequivocal interpretation of what Kripke means when he calls a natural kind predicate 'rigid.'[12] Nevertheless, he certainly flirts with the idea that rigid predicates are essentialist. In addition, as we saw above, the definition of a rigid predicate as an essentialist predicate is a natural extension of the definition of rigidity for singular terms. Moreover, this interpretation of rigidity for predicates nicely fits the observation that most of the natural kind predicates Kripke discusses are essentialist, whereas many nonnatural kind predicates are not.

In light of all this, a reasonable case could be made that Kripke's text should be understood as implicitly committed to the characterization of a predicate as rigid iff it is essentialist. Understood in this way, the doctrine that natural kind predicates are rigid tacitly presupposes a substantive metaphysical claim about kinds—namely, that if K is a natural kind, then it is a necessary property of K that anything that is an instance of K is essentially an instance of it. For many kinds this assumption is plausible, and could reasonably be used to ground the claim that many natural kind predicates are rigid in the sense indicated. Let us, therefore, temporarily accept this as a provisional interpretation of what it means for a natural kind predicate to be rigid.

With this interpretation in mind, we next turn to the doctrine that identity sentences involving rigid designators are necessary if true. When the rigid designators are singular terms, and the relevant true identity sentences are of the form (1a),

1a. $\alpha = \beta$

then either those identity statements themselves, or the slightly weaker variants of them of the form

1b. α exists $\supset \alpha = \beta$,

must be necessary. In this kind of case, there is no room for doubt. If (1a) is true, and the terms are rigid, then the necessity of (1b) is an obvious consequence of the definition of rigidity for singular terms.

However, when natural kind predicates are involved, the question of what sort of sentence is to count as an identity sentence is more complicated. At various points throughout the second half of lecture 3, Kripke discusses a class of sentences involving natural kind terms that he calls "theoretical identifications." The initial examples of these sentences, given on page 116, are as follows:

Examples of Theoretical Identifications

2.   Light is a stream of photons.

3.   Water is H_2O.
4.   Lightning is an electrical discharge.
5.   Gold is the (an) element with the atomic number 79.

It is worth noting that at least some of these sentences, for example (2) and (4), do not appear to be sentences in which a pair of singular terms flanks the identity predicate.

Later in the lecture, Kripke considers other sentences that he seems to place in the same category as the original examples (2)–(5). One such sentence is (6).[13]

6.   Cats are animals.

Clearly, this is not a sentence the logical form of which is given by (1a). Rather, it is constructed using a pair of predicates; for our purposes it may be represented by (7).

7. $\forall x$ (x is a cat $\supset$ x is an animal)

Although it doesn't contain the identity predicate, (7) might still be counted as an identity sentence (broadly construed) on the grounds that it identifies each cat with some animal. In general, English sentences of the form

8a.   (All) A's are B's, An A is a B (on one of its uses)

and

8b.   All and only A's are B's, Something is an A iff it is B (on one use)

may naturally be counted as sentences that identify A's with B's, even though they are routinely represented by formulas of the form (9), which do not contain the identity sign.

9a. $\forall x$ (Ax $\supset$ Bx)
9b. $\forall x$ (Ax $\leftrightarrow$ Bx)

Next consider (4), from Kripke's original list of theoretical identifications. Here, the expression *is an electrical discharge* seems to function as a predicate, just as the expression *is a cat* functions as a predicate in the sentence *Felix is a cat*. Thus (4) is not the sort of identity or identification sentence in which a pair of singular terms flanks the identity predicate. Rather, it says that any individual instance of lightning is an electrical discharge, in which case it is to be understood on the model of (9a). Kripke seems, implicitly, to recognize this on page 132 of *Naming and Necessity*, where, after having discussed the necessary, yet a posteriori, character of theoretical identifications like *Heat is molecular motion*, he adds the following comment: "*Similarly for many other such identifications, say, that lightning is electricity. Flashes of lightning are flashes of electricity. Lightning is an electrical discharge.*" The point I want to emphasize is that his example *Flashes of lightning are flashes of electricity* clearly is on a par with *Cats are animals*, and should be analyzed along the lines of (9a). Once this is recognized, one might analyze the other variants of (4), and also of (2), as being of this form as well.[14]

The general point here is that theoretical identification sentences need not involve singular terms, or the identity predicate, but instead may have the form of universally quantified conditionals or biconditionals. This point is further illustrated by the following passage from *Naming and Necessity*.

> . . . it turns out that **a material object is (pure) gold if and only if the only element contained therein is that with atomic number 79.** Here, the 'if and only if' can be taken to be <u>strict</u> (necessary). In general, science attempts, by investigating basic structural traits, to find the nature, and thus the essence (in the philosophical sense) of the kind. The case of natural phenomena is similar; such theoretical identifications as 'heat is molecular motion' are <u>necessary</u>, though not <u>apriori</u>. The type of property identity used in science seems to be associated with necessity, not with apriloricity, or analyticity: **For all bodies x and y, x is hotter than y if and only if x has a higher mean molecular kinetic energy than y.** Here the coextensiveness of the predicates is <u>necessary</u>, but not <u>a priori</u>.[15]

In this passage, Kripke gives two examples of necessary, a posteriori, theoretical identification sentences that have the form of universally quantified biconditionals. Moreover, he seems to suggest that the doubly quantified biconditional (10b) may be an analysis of the identity (10a).

10a. Heat is molecular motion.

10b.   For all bodies x and y, x is hotter than y if and only if x
has a higher mean molecular kinetic energy than y.

In light of all this, it seems clear that Kripke's claims about theoretical identity sentences involving natural kind terms should be seen as
encompassing cases in which the terms are predicates, and the identity
sentences are represented as universally quantified conditionals or biconditionals. Thus, when he announces, "*theoretical identities, according to the conception I advocate, are generally identities involving two
rigid designators and therefore are examples of the necessary aposteriori*,"[16] there is reason to interpret him as articulating a doctrine that
applies to the types of theoretical identity sentences we have been considering.

If our provisional interpretation of what it is for the predicates in
such sentences to be rigid is correct, then the content of the doctrine is
clear. When the rigid designators are predicates, and the identities are
of the form (9a) or (9b), the doctrine holds that (11c) follows from
(11a) and (11b).[17]

11a. $\forall x\ (Ax \supset Bx)$ is true/$\forall x\ (Ax \leftrightarrow Bx)$ is true
11b.   The predicates 'A' and 'B' are rigid designators—that is,
for all possible worlds w and objects o, if the predicate applies to o in w, then it applies to o in all worlds in which o
exists.
11c. $\forall x\ (Ax \supset Bx)$ is necessary/$\forall x\ (Ax \leftrightarrow Bx)$ is necessary–that
is, $\Box\forall x\ (Ax \supset Bx)$ is true/$\Box\forall x\ (Ax \leftrightarrow Bx)$ is true

However, now that we have a clear interpretation of the doctrine,
the problem with it is obvious. In talking of predicates, let us restrict
ourselves throughout to what is surely the standard case—namely,
those that apply to an object at a world only if the object exists at the
world. Further, let us take the range of the universal quantifier at a
world to be the domain of objects existing at that world. Given these
assumptions, what follows from (11a) and (11b) is not (11c), but
(11d).[18]

11d. $\forall x\ \Box\ (Ax \supset Bx)$ is true/$\forall x\ \Box\ (Ax \leftrightarrow Bx)$ is true

The truth at the actual world of the universally quantified biconditional mentioned in (11a) tells us that every actually existing thing is

either both an A and a B, or neither an A nor a B. The rigidity/essentiality of the predicates guarantees that any object that is both A and B in the actual world must be both an A and a B in every world in which it exists; likewise, anything that exists in the actual world while being neither an A nor a B cannot be an A or a B in any world. Therefore, the statements mentioned in (11d) are true. However, nothing in (11a) and (11b), together with our other assumptions, rules out the possibility of a world w in which some object that doesn't exist in the actual world exists, and is an A in w without being a B in w. Hence the rigidity/essentiality of the predicates in theoretical identity sentences of the forms mentioned in (11a) does not guarantee that those sentences are necessary, if true.

The point can be illustrated using the following, slightly artificial, example. Consider the natural kind predicate *primate* and the related species terms *human*, *ape*, *monkey*, and *lemur*. Each of these is a genuine natural kind predicate, and it is plausible to suppose that each is essentialist/rigid in the sense we have defined. Next consider the compound predicate

12. λx (x is a human or x is an ape or x is a monkey or x is a lemur).

Since each of the species predicates is essentialist / rigid, it follows that the compound predicate (12) is too. Let us further suppose that the theoretical identity sentence (13) is true.

13. $\forall y$ [y is a primate $\leftrightarrow \lambda x$ (x is a human or x is an ape or x is a monkey or x is a lemur) y]

Then,

14. $\forall y \ \Box$ [y is a primate $\leftrightarrow \lambda x$ (x is a human or x is an ape or x is a monkey or x is a lemur) y]

is obviously true since each actually existing primate is both essentially a primate, and essentially a human, ape, monkey, or lemur (and vice versa). Nevertheless, there may very well be a world in which a species of primates evolves that is not found in the actual world. The domain of such a world would contain individuals that do not exist in the actual world—individuals that are primates in that world without belonging to any of the four species that make up primates in this world. Thus, the theoretical identity sentence (13) is true, involves only essentialist/ rigid designators, but is not necessary. In short, on this interpretation of what it is for a predicate to be rigid, and of what counts as a theoretical identity sentence involving such predicates, it is false that theoretical identity sentences involving rigid natural kind predicates must be necessary if true.

There are two ways of viewing this result. On one view, our interpretation of a rigid predicate as an essentialist predicate is accurate, but Kripke's doctrine that theoretical identity sentences involving rigid designators are necessary if true fails in some cases in which the terms involved are predicates. On the alternative view, the failure of this doctrine is evidence that we don't have an accurate interpretation of what Kripke meant when calling a natural kind predicate "rigid." After all, the failure is pretty obvious, and it is hard to see how he would have failed to notice it if he had meant to identify rigid predicates with essentialist predicates. Further support for this view comes from the observation that not all of the natural kind predicates Kripke mentions are essentialist. For example, the two-place predicate *hotter than*, occurring in the theoretical identity (10b) above, is regarded as a natural kind predicate, even though the relation it expresses may apply to a pair of objects in one world without applying to that pair in every world in which the objects exist. Thus, it would seem that we still don't have an unproblematic answer to the question of what it means for a predicate to be rigid.

Strategy 2

I don't know of any more promising way of interpreting the notion of rigidity for predicates that doesn't make the rigidity of a predicate entirely derivative from the notion of the rigidity of some corresponding singular term. Consequently, it is time to explore our second strategy for dealing with the issue. Abstractly, the idea is this: We start with a predicate P, and we find an associated singular term t—something like *the kind P*, *the property P*, *the substance P*, or *the species P*—for which (15) is both necessary and a priori.

15. $\forall x$ (x is P iff x is an instance of t—for instance, the kind P, the property P, the substance P, the species P)

We then define the rigidity of a predicate P in terms of the rigidity of its associated singular term.

16. A predicate P is rigid iff its associated singular term t designates the same thing—such as the same kind, property, substance, or species—in all worlds in which that thing exists (and t never designates anything else).

It will follow that if P and Q are rigid predicates, and t_P and t_Q are the relevant singular terms associated with them, then the sentence

17. $t_P = t_Q$

will be necessary, if true. Of course, it won't follow that if P and Q are rigid, then

18. For all x, x is P iff x is Q

is necessary, if true (since P and Q might be both rigid and coextensive without standing for the same kind). However, it will follow that if (17) is true, then (18) is necessary.

This is one way in which one might try to make sense of the notion of a rigid predicate, and to relate that notion to claims about the modal status of theoretical identification sentences containing such predicates or their related singular terms. However, it is not clear that it is a theoretically interesting, or successful, strategy; nor is it clear that it provides a reasonable interpretation of Kripke's use of the notion of rigidity when talking about natural kind terms, including natural kind predicates. One thing to be said against the interpretation is that it would appear to have the consequence that a great many predicates will come out rigid on this interpretation. For example, if the singular terms corresponding to the predicates *is a philosopher*, *is a bachelor*, and *is a yellow metal* are *the property of being a philosopher*, *the property of being a bachelor*, and *the property of being a yellow metal*, respectively, then even these ordinary descriptive predicates will be classified as rigid, since their corresponding singular terms are. This is problematic, since Kripke wanted to distinguish natural kind predicates like *is gold* and *is a tiger* from ordinary descriptive predicates such as these. If a notion of rigidity for predicates is to play a role in making this distinction, then it cannot be one characterized by (15) and (16).

In fact, the problem is worse. It is not even clear that the approach based on (15) and (16) can coherently distinguish between rigid and nonrigid predicates at all. For example, consider (19) as an attempt to provide a clear case of a nonrigid predicate.[19]

19.   Her eyes are the color of a cloudless sky at noon.

In this sentence the phrase *are the color of a cloudless sky at noon* seems to be functioning as a predicate that applies to objects just in case they are instances of whatever color a cloudless sky at noon is an instance of. Is this predicate rigid or not? On the definition of rigidity we are considering, this is a question about a singular term associated with the predicate. But which singular term? Two candidates suggest themselves.

C1.   The color that cloudless skies at noon are instances of
C2.   the property of being the same in color as a cloudless sky at noon

Let the predicate *is the color of a cloudless sky at noon* replace *is P* in (15). Then (15) will turn out to be both necessary and a priori no matter whether we select C1 or C2 as the singular term t corresponding to the predicate. So both qualify as acceptable candidates for determining whether the predicate is to be classified as rigid or not. However, this is problematic. Since C2 is rigid and C1 is not, it makes a difference which of these terms we choose. Using C2 in (16) gives the result that the predicate is rigid, whereas using C1 gives the result that it is not rigid. Surely, however, the predicate can't be both rigid and nonrigid.[20] The problem here is due to the fact that in formulating the definition of the rigidity of a predicate in terms of the rigidity of a corresponding singular term, we didn't specify a procedure which, given an arbitrary predicate, would provide us with a unique singular term. To make this strategy work, we have to say something about this.

One natural thought is to revise the definition of rigidity for predicates as follows:

20. A predicate P is nonrigid iff there is some nonrigid singular term t such that $\forall x$ *is P iff x is an instance of t* is a necessary, a priori truth knowable by all competent speakers. A predicate is rigid iff it is not nonrigid.

The idea behind this proposal is that the predicate *is (or are) the color of a cloudless sky at noon* should come out nonrigid, while many other predicates, including natural kind predicates, should count as rigid. However, as Kit Fine has pointed out, this idea turns out to be incorrect.[21] On the definition just given, all predicates turn out to be nonrigid. For example, consider the predicate *cow* and the complex singular term *the y*: (*y = the property of being a brown cow, if all cows are brown & if not all cows are brown, then y = the property of being a cow*). This is nonrigid. In some worlds it picks out the property of being a brown cow, and in other worlds it picks out the property of being a cow. In addition, the criterion based on (15) is satisfied in this case, since the relevant instance of it, namely (21), is both necessary and a priori.

21. $\forall x$ (x is a cow iff x is an instance of the y: (y = the property of being a brown cow, if all cows are brown & if not all cows are brown, then y = the property of being a cow)

Since this result generalizes, all predicates will be characterized by (20) as nonrigid. Consequently, the definition is inadequate.

It won't help to replace (20) with definition (22).

22. A predicate P is rigid iff there is some rigid singular term t such that $\forall x$ *is P iff x is an instance of t* is a necessary, a priori truth knowable by all competent speakers. A predicate is nonrigid iff it is not rigid

Since for any predicate P, the singular term *the property of being P* is always rigid, (22) has the unwanted consequence that all predicates are rigid. It is not clear that any other version of strategy 2 will be any more successful in defining a notion of rigidity for predicates.

Conclusion

In the end, we are left with no adequate answer to the question of what it means for a predicate to be a rigid designator. The reason for this, I suggest, is that in *Naming and Necessity*, Kripke simply did not have a clear conception of what it would mean to characterize anything other than a singular term as rigid. It is clear that he was impressed by the semantic similarities between proper names and natural kind terms of many different grammatical and semantic categories, including natural kind predicates. He appears to have sometimes used the term 'rigid', in a rather loose and imprecise way, to indicate, without precisely specifying, the similarities these predicates bear to proper names.[22] In itself, this is not terribly worrying. However, since different similarities are suggested by different strands of Kripke's discussion, it can give rise to problems. In particular, one may be encouraged to think that the notion of rigidity for predicates must satisfy each of the following demands: (i) it must be a natural extension of the notion of rigidity that has been defined for singular terms; (ii) it must have the consequence that nearly all natural kind predicates are rigid, whereas many other predicates are nonrigid; and (iii) it must play a role in explaining the necessity of true "theoretical identification sentences" of the form (9) containing rigid predicates that is analogous to the role played by the notion of a rigid singular term in explaining the necessity of true identity sentences of the form (1). If what I have been arguing is correct, then there is no reason to think that any notion of rigidity for predicates is capable of satisfying all of these demands.

In order to avoid confusion, it may be advisable to reserve the terminology of rigidity exclusively for singular terms.[23] When discussing related notions for other classes of expressions—for example, the notion of an essentialist predicate—we may simply make the definitions precise and note whatever parallels there may be with the concept of rigidity for singular terms, without attempting to discuss them all under a single heading. However, whatever terminological decision is made, an interesting substantive question remains. Is there any semantic property of natural kind predicates that is importantly similar to a corresponding property of proper names, and that can be used to explain why, in the case of many "theoretical identification sentences" involving such predicates, we can be confident that they are necessary if true? In the next chapter I will try to show that there is.

What Do Natural Kind Predicates Have in Common with Proper Names?

Nondescriptionality and Reference-Fixing

In chapter 9, I argued that the attempt to use the notion of rigidity to characterize the semantic similarities between natural kind predicates and proper names was unsuccessful. Thus, we need to look to other semantic properties of names that may be shared by natural kind predicates, and that may play an important role in explicating the modal properties of sentences containing such predicates. In retrospect, this demotion of the status of rigidity in Kripke's overall semantic picture should not be surprising. Even in the case of proper names, it can be argued that their rigidity is the result of other, more fundamental, semantic properties that they possess. More specifically, the doctrine that names are rigid designators may be viewed as a corollary of the more central thesis that they are nondescriptional, together with an account of how their reference is fixed in the actual world. Since names are nondescriptional, the referent of a name at a world is not semantically determined by the satisfaction of any descriptive condition at that world; thus, there is no semantic mechanism by which the reference of a name might change from world to world. Instead, the referent of the name is initially fixed at the actual world (for example by a historical chain of use or by a reference-fixing description), and, once fixed, there is no provision for it to vary from world to world.

This point may have been obscured for some by the fact that the progression of Kripke's argument is just the reverse. First he uses the observation that names are rigid to undermine descriptive analyses of the semantic contents of proper names. Then he presents his more general semantic picture. It is only after this picture is in place that we can see the nondescriptionality of names as explaining the fact that they are rigid. This suggests that the important parallel between names and natural kind predicates may be their nondescriptionality, and the way in which their reference is fixed.

In chapter 9, I quoted passages from *Naming and Necessity* which indicate that Kripke intended his analysis of the parallels between proper names and natural kind terms to apply to kind terms of several grammatical categories, including those that function as predicates. It is striking that, although he sometimes mentioned rigidity as being included among the parallels between names and natural kind terms, it is nondescriptionality that occupies center stage in the discussion immediately following one of the passages in which he recognizes the grammatical diversity of natural kind terms to which his analysis applies.

> . . . *my argument implicitly concludes that certain general terms, those for natural kinds, have a greater kinship with proper names than is generally realized. This conclusion holds for certain for various species names, whether they are count nouns, such as 'cat', 'tiger', 'chunk of gold', or mass terms such as 'gold', 'water', 'iron pyrites'. It also applies to certain terms for natural phenomena, such as 'heat', 'light', 'sound', 'lightning', and, presumably, suitably elaborated, to corresponding adjectives—'hot' 'loud', 'red'.*
>
> *Mill, as I have recalled, held that although some 'singular names', the definite descriptions, have both denotation and connotation, others, the genuine proper names, had denotation but not connotation. Mill further maintained that 'general names', or general terms, had connotation. Such terms as 'cow' or 'human' are* **defined by the conjunction of certain properties which pick out their extension**—*a human being, for example, is a rational animal with certain physical characteristics. The hoary tradition of definition by* genus *and* differentia *is of a piece with such a conception. If Kant did, indeed, suppose that 'gold' could be* defined *as 'yellow metal', it may well be this tradition which led him to the definition. . . .*
>
> *The modern logical tradition, as represented by Frege and Russell, disputed Mill on the issue of singular names, but endorsed him on that of general names. Thus* all *terms, both singular and general, have a 'connotation' or Fregean sense. More recent theorists have followed Frege and Russell, modifying their views only by replacing the notion of a sense as given by a particular conjunction of properties with that of a sense as given by a 'cluster' of properties, only* enough *of which need apply. The present view, directly reversing Frege and Russell, (more or less)* endorses *Mill's view of* singular *terms, but* disputes *his view of* general *terms.*[1]

This passage occurs in the third lecture of *Naming and Necessity*, where Kripke says he is "recapitulating" his main theses about natural kind terms before going on to a discussion of the mind-body identity thesis. This recapitulation involves the point just made about the nondescriptionality of natural kind terms (of various grammatical categories), plus his account of how the reference of these terms is fixed. The important parallels between proper names and natural kind terms that Kripke emphasizes here involve the nondescriptionality of such terms, and the ways in which their reference is fixed. These parallels hold the key to understanding a number of his observations about the modal status of theoretical identification sentences containing natural kind predicates. If we can get clear about what precisely these parallels involve, we may be able to explain the necessity of at least some of these theoretical identification sentences without bringing in any notion of rigidity for predicates at all.

To begin with nondescriptionality, it is evident that for Kripke the extensions of natural kind terms at different possible states of the world—whether they be predicates or abstract singular terms—are not determined by whatever descriptive properties, if any, are associated with them by speakers. It is true, of course, that speakers often associate natural kind terms with descriptive properties that they use to identify particular instances of the kinds. However, these properties typically fail to provide necessary and sufficient conditions for something to be a member of a kind (at a world), and sometimes the properties associated with such a term are not even true of actual instances of the kind (as when speakers think of a whale as a kind of fish). Just as someone can successfully use a proper name to refer to an object without associating the name with descriptive properties that uniquely apply to its referent, so a speaker can successfully use a natural kind predicate to say something about members of a kind, even if he lacks the ability to accurately describe either the kind itself or its instances. All of this goes to show (i) that natural kind predicates are not synonymous with descriptive predicates that speakers associate with them, and (ii) that the extension of a natural kind predicate at a world is not semantically determined to be the set of objects that satisfy, at that world, the descriptive characteristics we (actual-world) speakers associate with the predicate.

Next, we turn to Kripke's positive account of how the extension of a natural kind predicate at an arbitrary world is semantically determined. According to that account, the predicate is first associated by speakers with a kind—either ostensively or via a description. In the ostensive case speakers directly associate the predicate with a certain sample of individuals, which they presume to be instances of a single natural kind of a given type (e.g., a single substance or a single species). In the descriptive case, speakers employ a description that picks out a unique kind, often by appeal to contingent properties of the kind, or its instances. Once the kind k has been determined, either ostensively or descriptively, it is understood that for any world w the extension of the predicate at w is to be the set of instances of k at w.[2]

The Modal Status of Theoretical Identity Sentences Involving Simple Natural Kind Predicates

With this in mind, let us return to the question of whether theoretical identity sentences involving natural kind predicates are necessary if true. The statements in question are examples of the form (1a, b), which are analyzed along the lines of (2a, b).

1a. All A's are B's, An A is a B (on one of its uses)
1b. All and only A's are B's, Something is an A iff it is a B (on one of its uses)
2a. $\forall x (Ax \supset Bx)$
2b. $\forall x (Ax \leftrightarrow Bx)$

To begin, I will restrict attention to those sentences of this form in which the predicates A and B are different, semantically simple, natural kind predicates (typically single words). In addition, it will be convenient, initially, to further restrict the case by assuming that the reference of at least one of the predicates—let us say predicate A—is fixed ostensively. That is, we assume that the reference of A is fixed by stipulating that it is to apply to all and only instances of the unique natural kind of a certain type T (e.g., substance or species) of which nearly all elements of the sample used in introducing it are instances. Unlike A, the predicate B is not required to be an ostensive natural kind term; rather, we allow its extension to be fixed either ostensively or by description. However, we do require that A and B be predicates that designate kinds of the same type T—for instance, both may be substance terms, both may be species terms, or both may be of some other category.

When A and B are related in this way, it may turn out that the relationship between their extensions is not evident to competent speakers, but is discoverable only by empirical investigation. Let us suppose that this is the case, and that, as the result of some empirical investigation, it has now been discovered that every object in the extension of A is also in the extension of B. This discovery establishes that sentence (1a) is true. What needs to be shown is how this apparently modest empirical result, combined with the semantic character of the predicates, suffices to guarantee that they designate the same natural kind, and hence to guarantee that (1b) is also true, and that both (1a) and (1b) are necessary.

To show this, we reason as follows: (i) From the assumption that the ostensive natural kind predicate A has successfully been introduced, it follows that there is a unique natural kind k_A (of a certain type T) of which nearly all members of the sample associated with A are instances, and A applies (at a world) to all and only instances of k_A (at the world). (ii) From the assumption that the natural kind predicate B has successfully been introduced, it follows that there is a natural kind k_B which is such that B applies (at a world) to all and only members of k_B (at the world). (iii) By hypothesis, the two predicates designate kinds of the same type T; thus both k_A and k_B are species, or both are substances, or both are kinds of some other category. (iv) If the theoretical identity sentence (1a) is true, then (since nearly all objects in the A-sample are A's) nearly all of the objects in the A-sample are B's, and hence they are instances of kind k_B as well as kind k_A. (v) Since the A-sample determines a single kind (of the given type T—species, substance, etc.), of which nearly all members of the sample are instances, it follows that kind k_A = kind k_B. (vi) But this means that in addition to (1a), (1b) must also be true. (vii) Moreover, both must be necessary, since from steps (i), (ii), and (v) it follows that for all worlds w the extension of A at w = the set of instances of k_A at w = the set of instances of k_B at w = the extension of B at w. (viii) In short, if A and B are natural kind predicates of the sorts indicated, then a theoretical identity sentence (1b) involving those predicates is necessary, if the corresponding sentence (1a) is true.

This provides us with the paradigm (3).

3a. $\forall x \, (Ax \supset Bx)$ is true
3b.   A and B are simple natural kind predicates of the same type T (e.g., both species predicates, both substance predicates, etc.). Moreover, A "designates" the unique natural kind (of type T) instantiated by nearly all members of its associated sample. Where k_A and k_B are the kinds associated with ("designated by") A and B, respectively, the extensions of A and B at a world w are the sets of individuals that are members of k_A and k_B, respectively.
3c.   Therefore, $\forall x \, (Ax \supset Bx)$ and $\forall x \, (Ax \leftrightarrow Bx)$ are necessary truths.

Although this argument may initially seem surprising, it is easy to see why it works. On Kripke's account, the linguistic mechanism that fixes the extension of an ostensive natural kind predicate guarantees that if it has successfully been introduced, then there can be only one natural kind, of the specified type T, of which most members of the sample are instances. Thus, when A is ostensive, and the predicate B is related to A in the appropriate way, finding out that everything in the extension of A is in the extension of B is tantamount to finding out that the kind associated with A is identical with the kind associated with B. This powerful conclusion does not come from nowhere. Rather, it comes from the fact that the semantic presuppositions associated with the introduction of natural kind predicates make very substantial nonlinguistic claims—including the claim that the individuals in the sample associated with the ostensive predicate A are members of a single natural kind of a given type, and the claim that the predicates A and B designate kinds of the same type.

For this reason one should be cautious in taking the argument as showing how easy it is to learn that certain identification sentences are necessary. One might just as well take the argument to show how hard it is to discover that certain nonmodal sentences of the form (2a) and (2b) are true. To show that the extension of A is included in the extension of B, where the predicates are understood to have been successfully introduced in the manner intended, one must show that the kinds associated with them are identical. In some cases we can make an even stronger point. It should be noted that the argument underlying (3) did **not** assume that an individual cannot be a member of two kinds of a given type. However, for some types of kinds (e.g., substances or species) that assumption may not be unreasonable (at least in the case of certain substances or species). Suppose that this extra assumption is added to the argument for some specific choice of the two predicates, and that the assumption is correct. In this case, the only further bit of empirical information that is needed to show that the kind associated with A is identical with the kind associated with B, and hence that *All and only A's are B's* is a necessary truth, is the information that *at least one* individual in the extension of A is in the extension of B. It is striking that such a strong conclusion can be drawn from such a meager empirical result.

This special case is an instance of the paradigm (3').

3'a. $\exists x \, (Ax \, \& \, Bx)$ is true

3'b. A and B are simple natural kind predicates of the same type T (e.g., both species predicates, both substance predicates, etc.). Moreover, A "designates" the unique natural kind (of type T) instantiated by nearly all members of its associated sample. Where k_A and k_B are the kinds associated with ("designated by") A and B, respectively, the extensions of A and B at a world w are the sets of individuals that are members of k_A and k_B, respectively.

3'c. An individual cannot be a member of two different kinds of type T (e.g., two species, two substances, etc.)

3'd. Therefore, $\forall x \, (Ax \supset Bx)$ and $\forall x \, (Ax \leftrightarrow Bx)$ are necessary truths.

The fact that the conclusion (3'd) can be validly drawn on the basis of the seemingly slender empirical discovery (3'a) plus the special auxiliary assumption (3'c) illustrates how much in the way of presupposed empirical content is built into Kripke's account of the ostensive introduction of natural kind terms summarized by (3b).

In addition, the argument underlying (3) can be extended to a wider range of cases. For example, the paradigm illustrated by (3) will continue to hold in cases in which A has its extension fixed by a description, rather than being ostensively introduced by appeal to a certain sample, provided that it is built into the description that there can be at most one natural kind of the specified type T of which all members of the extension of A are instances. For example, the extension of

A might be fixed by the description *the unique kind k of type T such that some instances of k cause such and such effects*. If A is understood in this way, and B purports to designate a kind of type T, then (3) will continue to hold. In all of these cases, the truth of a theoretical identity sentence involving simple natural kind predicates, together with claims about the semantic character of these predicates, guarantees the necessity of the associated identity sentences.

Extending the Account to a Wider Class of Theoretical Identity Sentences

In saying that theoretical identity sentences that fit paradigm (3) are guaranteed by the semantic presuppositions associated with their predicates to be necessary if true, I am not claiming that the necessity involved is merely conventional. Nor am I claiming that the proposition expressed by such a theoretical identity sentence is necessary because of conventional facts about our words. On the contrary, I reject any such claims.[3] Rather, in saying that certain theoretical identity sentences are linguistically guaranteed to be necessary if true, I am simply saying that the claim that they are necessary follows from the claim that they are true together with straightforward claims about the semantics of the expressions that make them up. It is an interesting question how many theoretical identity sentences involving natural kind predicates fall into this category. .

I should say at the outset that I don't think that all theoretical identity sentences involving natural kind terms, of the sort discussed by Kripke, have this character. For example, the sentence *all whales are mammals* is not, in my opinion, linguistically guaranteed to be necessary if true. Rather, the claim that it is necessary follows from the claim that it is true, the semantic claim that the predicates *whale* and *mammal* designate two natural kinds k_w and k_m, plus the independent metaphysical claim that it is an essential property of the kind k_w that any instance of it is an instance of k_m. In my opinion, many theoretical identity sentences involving natural kind predicates are like the sentence *all whales are mammals* in this respect; they are necessary, but their necessity is not a consequence simply of their semantics together with their truth. If this is right, then there are two classes of necessary theoretical identification sentences involving natural kind predicates— those that are linguistically guaranteed to be necessary if true, and those that are not. Our next task is to explore how extensive the first of these classes is.

So far, we have restricted paradigm (3) to universally quantified conditionals and biconditionals involving semantically simple natural kind predicates A and B. However, we also know that Kripke was willing to characterize a wider class of theoretical identity sentences, including those like (4) and (5), as being necessary if true.

4. For all bodies x and y, x is hotter than y iff x has a higher mean molecular kinetic energy than y.
5. For all x, x is a drop of water iff x is a drop of a substance molecules of which contain two hydrogen atoms and one oxygen atom.

Example (5) is an identity sentence of the form (2h) in which one of the predicates, *is a drop of water*, may, for present purposes, be taken to be a simple natural kind predicate, whereas the other predicate is a semantically compound expression that is necessarily coextensive with the kind designated by that simple predicate.[4] Because this compound expression is not semantically simple, (5) is not an instance of paradigm (3). Thus, even though (5) is an example that is widely agreed to be both necessary and a posteriori, nothing we have said up to now shows that its necessity can be derived from its truth together with linguistic claims about the working of language.

But why should the complexity of one of the predicates in (5) make a difference? Shouldn't we be able to apply the reasoning behind (3) directly to (5), despite the fact that the predicate B is a semantically complex phrase? The restriction in (3) that B should be semantically simple seems inessential. Surely, it might be maintained, it is enough that the predicate designate a natural kind. And doesn't the predicate *is a drop of a substance molecules of which contain two hydrogen atoms and one oxygen atom* do that?

Anyone who is tempted by this reasoning would be well advised to compare (5) with (6).

6. For all x, x is a drop of water iff x is a drop of the substance instances of which fall from the sky in rain and fill the lakes and rivers.

This example is, we may assume, true but contingent. Thus, the reasoning in (3) cannot apply to it. But why not? The predicate on the right-hand side of the biconditional contains a singular definite description that nonrigidly designates a certain substance. In this world, that substance is water; in other worlds a completely different substance may be designated. Since the substance designated by this description at an arbitrary world is the kind (of the relevant type T) that determines the extension of the compound predicate at the world, different kinds (of type T) determine the extension of the predicate at different worlds. As a result, the reasoning behind paradigm (3) fails at step (ii) and step (vii). Hence (6) is not necessary.

What distinguishes (5) from (6)? Why are we inclined to think that the former is necessary, whereas the latter is not? The answer has to do with what we believe about substances. As Nathan Salmon pointed out years ago, we believe that it is a feature of any genuine substance S that whatever its molecular structure turns out to be, all possible instances of S share that structure (and all possible instances of that structure are instances of S).[5] From this, plus the truth of (5) and the semantics of *water*, it will follow that (5) is necessary.

I believe this is correct as far as it goes. There are, however, further questions that remain unanswered. What exactly are substances, and how do we arrive at our modal intuitions (pretheoretic beliefs) regarding them? As long as we have no account of what sorts of things substances are, the source of our modal intuitions about them will remain mysterious, and our justification for relying on these intuitions may be unclear. Hence, it may be profitable to try to give an explanation of these matters.

Here is a proposed explanation. Since natural kinds are abstract objects capable of having instances, we may identify them with properties of a certain sort. Substances, which constitute a subclass of natural kinds, may then be taken to be properties of a special type. A substance is a property of an individual, or sample of matter, x that specifies how x is constituted out of basic physical constituents of some sort or other. Now imagine that the simple term *water* is introduced with the intention that it is to be a substance term that applies to everything that shares the same physical constitution as the elements in some original sample. On this view, when we introduce the term, we may know neither what the physical constituents of these elements are nor how they are combined. Nevertheless, we intend the predicate to apply (at a world) to all and only those things that share the basic physical constitution (whatever it may turn out to be) exhibited (in the actual world) by all, or nearly all, elements in the sample. We may put this by saying that when we introduce the predicate *is a drop of water*, we in effect stipulate that it is to apply to instances of the substance—that is, the unique physically constitutive kind—that nearly all members of the sample are instances of.

On this idealized model, it may well be that no one knows very much about the nature of this physically constitutive kind when the predicate *is a drop of water* is introduced. For the sake of argument we may even suppose that the predicate is introduced in this way long before the development of chemical theories of complex molecular structure. When these theories are later developed, we acquire new families of concepts to describe these structures, and we come to understand claims about the molecular structures of macroscopic objects as claims about how these objects are constituted out of basic physical constituents. In short, these theories bring with them a class of formulas specifying different possible molecular structures that are understood as determining different possible physically constitutive kinds, or substances, which may or may not have actual instances. After empirical investigation, some of these formulas—for example, *molecules of x contain two hydrogen atoms and one oxygen atom*—may be taken to be candidates for giving the basic physical constitution of standard water samples. Note that if this is right, then the predicates *is a drop of water* and *is a drop of a substance molecules of which contain two hydrogen atoms and one oxygen atom* are both understood as designating physically constitutive kinds, which means that they are understood as designating kinds of the same type. This has the consequence that when it is discovered empirically that water samples have the molecular structure H_2O, this is sufficient to guarantee that the two predicates designate the same kind. Since this kind determines the extension of both predicates at all worlds, it follows, without need of further metaphysical assumptions, that (5) is necessary.

If this account is correct, then (5) is a theoretical identity sentence involving natural kind predicates that is linguistically guaranteed to be necessary if true. The same explanation might be given for related examples, such as

7. Chunks of gold are chunks of an element the atomic number of which is 79.

What about other natural kind predicates which are not substance terms? One familiar sort of case involves what might be called *explanatory kinds*, where these are thought of as properties the possession of which causally explain certain observed characteristics. Kripke's discussion of heat and molecular motion seems to fall in this category.

To see how this is supposed to go, imagine that the abstract singular term *heat* is introduced by an ostensive definition stipulating that it is to designate the unique kind of physical state or process present in a certain class of samples that causes certain effects—including certain sensations in us. Imagine the further stipulation that the related predicate, *is hotter than*, is to apply to pairs in which the relevant physical state or process in one object is more pronounced than the relevant physical state or process in the other object. When the kinetic theory is formulated as a hypothesis to be tested, it will be antecedently understood that a relational predicate characterizing different levels of mean molecular kinetic energy is a candidate for specifying the natural kind designated by the predicate *is hotter than*. Once it is discovered that certain facts about kinetic energy causally explain certain effects, including certain of our sensations, it will follow that the kind designated by *is hotter than* just is the kind having-a-higher-mean-molecular-kinetic-energy-than, and Kripke's example (4) will be characterized as not only true but necessary.

This derivation of the necessity of (4) is slightly different from the paradigm illustrated by (3). When an explanatory kind is involved, the derivation is as follows: (i) A simple natural kind term E is introduced with the stipulation that it applies in any possible world to all and only instances of the property (or kind) possession of which (causally) explains certain phenomena (in the actual world). (ii) It is then discovered scientifically that the property (kind) of being such and such (causally) explains the phenomena. (iii) From this it follows that the kind E just is the property (kind) of being such and such. (iv) This is sufficient to establish the necessity of the claim that says that an individual, or a pair, is E iff it is such and such.[6]

Refining the Model

The above account of the linguistic grounding of the necessity of certain theoretical identification sentences involving natural kind predicates is, I think, worth taking seriously. The virtue of the account is that it tries to say something about what natural kinds are that explains the otherwise mysterious modal intuitions that underlie our confidence in the necessity of examples like (4) and (5). Nevertheless, there are two serious problems raised by this account that must be faced.

The first problem involves the relationship between a semantically compound predicate like *is a drop of a substance molecules of which contain two hydrogen atoms and one oxygen atom* and the natural kind water which, on the account sketched above, it "designates." On that account, the natural kind water is a property: the property of being a substance molecules of which contain two hydrogen atoms and one oxygen atom. This sounds very much as if the property of being water is the property of being a substance molecules of which contain two hydrogen atoms and one oxygen atom. But surely, one is inclined to think, the property of being water is the meaning or semantic content of the term *water*. So it would seem I am committed to the idea that the meaning or semantic content of the predicate *is a drop of water* is the property of being a drop of a substance molecules of which contain two hydrogen atoms and one oxygen atom. But now we are in trouble, since if that property is the meaning of any predicate, then presumably it is the meaning of the predicate *is a drop of a substance molecules of which contain two hydrogen atoms and one oxygen atom*. Thus we have arrived at the conclusion that the two predicates in (5) have the same meaning. That can't be correct. If it were, then the proposition expressed by (5) would be the same as the proposition expressed by (8), and hence (5) would be a priori rather than a posteriori.

8.   For all x, x is a drop of water iff x is a drop of water.

Since, I presume, this is unacceptable, something has gone wrong.

Let us call this "the meaning problem." The second problem with the account developed so far—"the depth problem"—is posed by the fact that a natural kind can often be characterized "at different levels," with different degrees of specificity. For example, on the account I have suggested, the substance water is the property that specifies the physical constitution of a certain sample of stuff. However, in general there is no such thing as the (unique) property that specifies the physical constitution of a sample. In the case of water, I have used the property of having a certain molecular structure to specify the physical constitution of the relevant stuff. Presumably, however, that very molecular structure could be characterized in terms of its constitution at the atomic and subatomic levels. Thus we might in principle have a certain range of predicates—one specifying the constitution of water at the molecular level, one at the atomic level, another at a subatomic level, and so on. These predicates could all be used to formulate true, universally quantified biconditionals specifying the physical constitution of water. Since each predicate expresses a property that has an equal claim to being identical with the kind water, each of these quantified biconditionals has an equal claim to being linguistically guaranteed to be necessary if true. However, if, as I have been assuming, properties are the meanings of predicates, then the properties expressed by these different predicates must themselves be different. Thus, one cannot identify the kind water with all of them. Nor does there seem to be any reason to identify it with any one of them. Rather, the kind should be something that is equally determined by them all.

These two problems, the meaning problem and the depth problem, point in the same direction. They suggest that natural kinds should not be identified with properties after all—where properties are the sorts of things that are the meanings of arbitrary predicates. Instead of taking natural kinds to be properties, I propose that we identify them with intensions—that is, functions from worlds to extensions. On this view, the meanings of many predicates are properties. These properties determine the intensions of the predicates, and are constituents of the propositions expressed by sentences containing the predicates. As before, substances are a subtype of natural kinds; they are intensions determined by properties that specify how individuals, or samples of matter, are constituted out of basic physical constituents at whatever level. The reasoning behind paradigm (3) can then be invoked to show that the kind (i.e., intension) water is identical with the kind (intension) substance molecules of which contain two hydrogen atoms and one oxygen atom, even though the two predicates do not express the same properties. In this way the necessity of (5) can be maintained while recognizing that the proposition expressed by (5) is not the same as the proposition expressed by (8). Thus, the fact that (8) is knowable a priori does not show that (5) is.

If, in addition, the intension I_w of *water*—that is, the function from possible worlds to instances of water in those worlds—is such that one cannot know of I_w, except by empirical investigation, that x is an instance of I_w at a world w iff in w molecules of x contain two hydrogen atoms and one oxygen atom, then (5) is not knowable a priori. Since intensions are abstract objects of a rather unusual kind, it is not transparent just what such *de re* knowledge of them consists in. Still, it seems plausible to suppose that just as knowing that the F is G is not in general enough to know of the object o that is denoted by the description that o is G, so knowing that x is a drop of a substance molecules of which contain two hydrogen atoms and one oxygen atom is not enough to know of the intension I_w (i.e., the kind water) determined by the compound predicate that x is an instance of I_w. If this is right, then (5) is both necessary and a posteriori.

An important part of this account is the explanation of why the two predicates in (5) do not express the same properties. Here, I suggest that we adopt a position in our treatment of simple natural kind predicates that may be called "Extended Millianism." According to simple Millianism the meaning (semantic content) of a proper name is its referent; thus coreferential names have the same meaning (semantic content), and identity sentences involving coreferential proper names semantically express propositions that are necessary and a priori, rather than a posteriori—though, as we have seen, such sentences are standardly used in different contexts to assert a variety of a posteriori truths as well. According to Extended Millianism the meaning (semantic content) of a simple natural kind predicate is the natural kind it designates; as a result, simple natural kind predicates that designate the same natural kind—such as *groundhog* and *woodchuck*—mean the same thing (have the same semantic content). This has the immediate consequence that the theoretical identity sentence

9.   All and only woodchucks are groundhogs,

which fits paradigm (3), and hence is linguistically determined to be necessary if true, semantically expresses the same proposition as

10.   All and only woodchucks are woodchucks,

and hence is *a priori* rather than *a posteriori*. (As in the case of proper names, this is compatible with the fact that assertive utterances of (9) in different contexts would standardly convey, and even result in the assertion of, a posteriori propositions that would not be conveyed or asserted by corresponding utterances of (10).)

Things change when we consider compound expressions. Just as, in the case of singular noun phrases, definite descriptions have meanings that are not identical with the objects they designate, but rather are properties in virtue of which the descriptions designate what they do, so a semantically compound natural kind predicate, such as *is a drop of a substance molecules of which contain two hydrogen atoms and one oxygen atom*, has a meaning that is not identical with the natural kind (i.e., intension) it designates, but rather is a property that determines that intension. On this picture, simple natural kind predicates are analogous to proper names, and compound descriptive predicates are analogous to singular definite descriptions. Because of this it is possible for at least some sentences that may be represented as having the form (2b)

2b. $\forall x\, (Ax \leftrightarrow Bx)$

to be both a posteriori and linguistically guaranteed to be necessary if true—where one of the predicates is a simple natural kind predicate, and the other is a compound descriptive phrase.

Questions and Complications

An Alternative Solution to the Meaning Problem

In my discussion of the meaning problem, I pointed out that natural kinds cannot be identified with properties, if properties are taken to be the meanings of both simple and complex predicates. My solution was to identify natural kinds with intensions, which I claimed could be taken to be the meanings of simple natural kind predicates, even though they do not determine, but are merely determined by, the meanings of (i.e., properties expressed by) the semantically complex predicates with which they are associated. This is not the only potential solution to the meaning problem. In particular, an alternative account arises from certain semantic theses adopted independently by Jeff King and Mark

Richard in their work on the traditional "paradox of analysis" and related issues.[7]

According to King and Richard, the simple predicate *is a brother* expresses the same property as the syntactically complex predicate *is a male sibling*. However, their meanings—that is, that which they contribute to propositions semantically expressed by sentences containing them—are different. Whereas the meaning of *is a brother* is just the property it expresses, the meaning of *is a male sibling* includes in addition the properties of being male and being a sibling, which are the semantic contents of its syntactic constituents, *male* and *sibling*. One way of thinking of this is to take the meaning of the complex predicate, *is a male sibling*, to be a hierarchically structured tree the root node of which is the property it expresses (i.e., the property of being a male sibling, which is, of course, the property of being a brother), and the daughter nodes of which are the properties being male and being a sibling.[8] This alleged difference in meaning between the two predicates is used to distinguish the trivial proposition semantically expressed by (11b) from the allegedly nontrivial proposition semantically expressed by (11a).

11a. Someone is a brother iff he is a male sibling.
11b. Someone is a brother iff he is a brother.

Both King and Richard maintain that it is possible to believe the proposition semantically expressed by (11b) without believing the proposition semantically expressed by (11a).

Applying these ideas to the meaning problem for natural kind predicates, one might easily arrive at the following view. Natural kinds are properties, and simple natural kind predicates express properties that are identical with the properties expressed by certain complex predicates. However, the contribution made by a complex predicate to propositions semantically expressed by sentences containing it includes more than the property it expresses. For example, the simple predicate *is a drop of water* expresses the very same property as the property expressed by the compound predicate *is a drop of a substance molecules of which contain two hydrogen atoms and one oxygen atom*. However, this property is the only contribution made by *is a drop of water* to propositions semantically expressed by sentences containing it, whereas the compound predicate phrase contributes not only this property to propositions but also the semantic contents of each of its constituent parts. Because of this, the proposition semantically expressed by (5) can be distinguished from the trivial proposition semantically expressed by (8).

5. For all x, x is a drop of water iff x is a drop of a substance molecules of which contain two hydrogen atoms and one oxygen atom.
8. For all x, x is a drop of water iff x is a drop of water.

In light of this, it might be argued that it is possible to believe the latter proposition without believing the former.

Although I am somewhat skeptical that the relationship between (5) and (8) should be likened to that between (11a) and (11b), I will not attempt to evaluate this version of the King-Richard view here. In particular, I leave it open whether or not this alternative account provides a reasonable basis for arguing that (5) is a posteriori, as well as for solving what I have called "the depth problem." What does seem reasonable to me is that either some version of my original solution, or some version of the King-Richard view, will prove acceptable. If this is right, then we are not far from having a workable semantic model of natural kind predicates.

When Semantic Presuppositions Fail

On Kripke's model of natural kind terms, the ostensive introduction of such expressions typically involves strong empirical presuppositions—that the elements in the sample are instances of a kind of a certain sort (e.g., a certain substance or species), and that they are instances of only one kind of that sort. Often there is no way of knowing for certain, at the time the expression is introduced, that these presuppositions are fulfilled. This raises the possibility that in some cases speakers might introduce a term and use it for a substantial period of time before discovering that the presuppositions associated with it are false. What should we say about such a case?

One might maintain that since the presuppositions associated with introduction of the expression are false, one must conclude that it never acquired a meaning. If so, then the term must be judged to have been meaningless throughout the period in which speakers took themselves to understand it. However, such a judgment seems harsh. We may presume that during the period in question, speakers used sentences containing the term to convey lots of information. Perhaps, at least partially in virtue of this, the term did acquire a meaning after all—only one somewhat different from the meaning originally intended.

There are several possibilities to consider. The simplest case is one in which the elements in the original sample make up two kinds of the intended type rather than one. Suppose, for example, we introduced the term *jade* ostensively by appealing to a sample that, unknown to us, contained instances of two different substances rather than one. Later, when this is discovered, the natural thing to say is that we have found out that there are two kinds of jade. Instead of designating a single substance that determines its extension, *jade* designates a pair of substances, and its extension at a world is everything that is an instance of either. This seems to be more or less how the term *jade* actually functions in English.[9]

A different kind of case is one in which the elements in the sample make up a single kind, but not one of the type originally intended. One way in which this could come about involves mistakenly taking a collection of animals to be made up of members of a single species, when in fact the animals are members of different species of the same family. For example, one might find oneself in this situation if one had observed mountain lions, bobcats, cheetahs, and panthers, wrongly taken them to belong to a single species, and introduced a natural kind predicate with the intention that it should apply to all and only members of that species. Since there is no one species in such a case, the semantic presuppositions associated with the introduction of the predicate are not, strictly speaking, fulfilled. Nevertheless, it seems reasonable to suppose that the predicate might pick out a natural kind of a higher level—the cat family, for example.

A different and more extreme case of presupposition failure occurs if the elements in the sample do not constitute a single natural kind of any type, nor any small number of kinds, but rather share nothing significant in common beyond the obvious observational properties that lead people to believe, wrongly, that they are instances of the same natural kind. Imagine, for example, a situation like the one actually associated with the introduction of the term *water*, except for the fact that the elements in the sample are not instances of a single substance, but rather exhibit a wide variety of different chemical compositions. In this case, the elements in the sample are quantities of liquid that are colorless, odorless, and thirst-quenching. These sample elements include liquid that falls from the sky as rain, as well as liquid that makes up lakes and rivers. However, despite manifesting obvious observational similarities, the elements in the sample are instances of a heterogeneous collection of substances.

On the model of natural kind terms that I have drawn from Kripke, the semantic presuppositions associated with *water* fail so completely in this case that it is reasonable to think that no natural kind term has been introduced. Perhaps we should say that the term fails to acquire any meaning. However, it also seems possible that the term may have acquired a meaning involving the observational properties with which it is associated. If so, then in the sort of situation imagined, *water* ends up applying, in any possible world, to all and only quantities of any colorless, odorless, thirst-quenching liquid that falls from the sky and fills lakes and rivers, no matter what substance, or substances, those quantities are instances of.

But would *water* mean the same as *colorless, odorless, thirst-quenching liquid that falls from the sky and fills lakes and rivers*, in such a situation? Not, I think, if in the imagined scenario the community's use of the term *water* was just like the actual use of *water* before the discovery of its molecular structure. One can (and could) satisfy our actual standards for understanding the term without knowing that *water* applies to a colorless, odorless, thirst-quenching liquid that falls from the sky and fills the lakes and rivers. Similarly, someone who understands the term may use a sentence like *the glass is full of water* to assert and convey information, without asserting and conveying the information that the glass is full of a colorless, odorless, thirst-quenching liquid that falls from the sky and fills lakes and rivers. On the account of semantic content developed in chapter 3, this means that the proposition that the glass is full of such a liquid is not a part of the semantic content of that sentence—as the sentence is used by us in the actual world. The same is true in our imagined scenario, if in that scenario the use of *water* is the same as it actually is for us, save for the fact that in the imagined scenario the sample to which it is routinely applied is made up of observationally similar liquids that are instances of a heterogeneous collection of substances.

If this is right, then it is hard to say what the meaning of *water* is in the imagined scenario. One possibility is that in such a situation it really has no semantic content, though ordinary speakers often succeed in using it to convey different, but overlapping, pieces of information in different situations. A second possibility is that in such a situation *water* stands for a nonnatural kind that has the same extension in all possible worlds as that determined by the property being a colorless, odorless, thirst-quenching liquid that falls from the sky and fills lakes and rivers, even though *water* does not semantically express this, or any other, descriptive property. A third possibility is that *water* does express the same property as *colorless, odorless, thirst-quenching liquid that falls from the sky and fills lakes and rivers*, even though, for King-Richard type reasons, the two expressions are not fully synonymous, and it is possible to believe or assert that something is water without believing or asserting that it is a colorless, odorless, thirst-quenching liquid that falls from the sky and fills the lakes and rivers. A final possibility is that in the imagined scenario *water* really is fully synonymous with some descriptive predicate that determines its extension at arbitrary worlds, but we have so far misidentified it. On this view, the predicate is not *colorless, odorless, thirst-quenching liquid that falls from the sky and fills lakes and rivers*; perhaps, however, it is some more complicated disjunctive predicate defined in terms of notions like being colorless, being odorless, being thirst-quenching, and so on.

I will not attempt here to choose among these different alternatives. It must be recognized, however, that the resolution of this issue is potentially relevant to the account of the actual semantic contents of natural kind terms like *water*—where the semantic presuppositions connected with the introduction of the term are fulfilled. The reason for this is that different accounts of semantic content in cases of presupposition failure may be connected with adjustments in the account of semantic content that has been developed for cases in which the presuppositions are satisfied. Suffice it to say that although these issues remain open-ended, nothing we have seen invalidates the basic picture developed up to now.

The Role of Intention in Determining the Reference of Natural Kind Terms

On the model of natural kind predicates that I have extracted from Kripke, an ostensive introduction of such a predicate is one in which the predicate comes to apply to all instances of the kind, of a certain type, that the great majority of the elements in the sample are instances of. Since elements in the sample are often members of natural kinds of several different types, something about the introduction of the predicate, and the way speakers come to use it, must determine the specific type of kind under which the samples are to be subsumed. In my discussion, I have focused mostly on scenarios in which speakers have intended the term they are introducing to be associated with a kind of a specific type, such as a substance or a species.

In the case of *water* I imagined that the term was introduced with the intention that it should apply to all quantities of stuff that share the same underlying physical constitution with elements in its associated sample. Certainly the term could have been introduced with this explicit intention, and if it were so introduced, then it would have come to have the semantic properties I have described. However, it might also have come to have those properties in some other way. I don't know for a fact that the speakers who introduced the term had any such definite intention in mind. Perhaps they just thought of water as *that kind of stuff*—where the kind in question was dimly understood to involve properties of the elements of the sample that "made them what they are"—without having any explicit idea that the kind in question must involve the physical constitution of elements of the sample out of more basic physical stuff. The thought that physical constitution may play such a role could well have came later.

In addition to speakers' explicit intentions, their dispositions to use a term in certain ways may have helped to determine the type of kind associated with it. For example, even if early speakers who used the term *water* had no explicit ideas about underlying physical structure, nevertheless it may still be true that they would have classified any newly encountered quantity of liquid as being in the extension of the term if they had been shown that it had the same underlying physical composition as the elements in their sample. A related possibility is that these speakers were disposed to classify any quantity of liquid as being in the extension of *water* if it could be shown to have whatever characteristics possession of which by the sample explained its observational qualities. If this was the disposition that was crucial to determining the extension of the term, then recognition of the truth of (5) depended upon learning both that the chemical composition of the sample was H_2O and that this composition explained its observational properties. On this picture, *water* is in the first instance a term for an explanatory kind, and the account of the necessity of (5) should be viewed as parallel to the account of the necessity of (4) given above at the end of the section "Extending the Account to a Wider Class of Theoretical Identity Sentences."

It should be clear from this discussion that there are several possibilities regarding precisely which features of speakers' use of an ostensively introduced natural kind term determine the kind that ends up being semantically associated with it. Although it is necessary (in cases of straightforwardly successful introductions of such terms) that most of the elements in the sample be instances of the kind in question, this is not sufficient, since instances of the sample typically are instances of several natural kinds of different types. Something about speakers' use of the term must, therefore, distinguish among these types. It may be intentions with various contents, or dispositions of various sorts. Nor is there any reason to suppose that there is only one pattern that applies to every case. How, precisely, these factors play out may well vary from term to term.

The Boundaries of Natural Kind Terms

Not all water is chemically the same. Heavy water, or D_2O (deuterium oxide), may also be counted as water—where deuterium is the isotope of hydrogen with atomic weight 2. In addition to counting as a form of water itself, deuterium oxide has been found to occur in small amounts (about 1 part in 6,000) in ordinary water. Moreover, ordinary water also contains even smaller amounts of tritium—where tritium is another isotope of hydrogen, with atomic weight 3. So ordinary water, of the sort we normally encounter, is a mixture of at least three slightly different chemical kinds—even if the water in question is free of impurities like lead, mercury, and so on. Pure water, it seems, is a mixture of H_2O, deuterium oxide, and tritium, with the first being the overwhelmingly dominant part.[10]

This raises a question about the account of the semantics of *water* that I have given. I have suggested that the term might have been introduced with the stipulation that it is to apply to all and only quantities of stuff that have the same physical composition as that of the sample associated with the term. But when do we count two quantities as having the same physical composition? Surely the precise ratio of H_2O, deuterium oxide, and tritium in the two quantities need not be strictly identical. Two quantities of liquid may both count as water, even pure water, despite the fact that the ratios of these ingredients in the two cases differ somewhat—perhaps even substantially. This suggests that the notion *same physical composition* used in fixing the extension of 'water' may be somewhat vague and open-ended. It also suggests that no explicit intentions of past users of the term could have been fully determinate in fixing its extension. Whatever the role of such intentions in fixing reference, some other aspect of the use of the term may well be relevant to determining the (vague) boundaries of its application.

A Puzzle

In this chapter I have been concerned with natural kind predicates like *is a drop of water*, and with theoretical identification sentences like (5) that contain such predicates.

5. For all x, x is a drop of water iff x is a drop of a substance molecules of which contain two hydrogen atoms and one oxygen atom.

However, I have not said anything directly about simpler identification sentences like (12).

12. Water is H_2O.

One difference between (5) and (12) is that the former is concerned only with particular quantities—namely, drops—whereas the latter is not limited in this way. Two possible analyses of (12) suggest themselves. According to the first, *water* and H_2O function as singular terms, *is* expresses the identity relation, and (12) is understood along the lines of (13).

13. The substance water = the substance H_2O.

According to the second possible analysis, *water* and H_2O are mass terms—that is, predicates that apply to all and only quantities (instances) of water and H_2O, respectively—and (12) semantically expresses a proposition along the lines of (14).

14. For all x, if x is a quantity (instance) of water, then x is a quantity (instance) of H_2O.

It follows from what I said in the first part of this chapter that (13) is true. Moreover, if (13) is true, then (14) is also true. However, as Mark Johnston has pointed out, this view leads directly to a puzzle.[11] For, intuitively, just as (12) is true, so, it seems, is (15).

15. Ice is H_2O.

However, if we say that the kind ice is identical with the kind H_2O, then we will be forced to say that (16) and (17) are also true, which is absurd.

16. Water is ice.
17. All quantities (instances) of water are quantities (instances) of ice.

Thus we need to deny that the kind ice is the kind H_2O. But how can we do this while maintaining that the kind water is the kind H_2O? Perhaps this identification must be reconsidered. In order to determine whether this is so, we will have to look more closely at how terms like *water*, *ice*, and *H_2O* actually function. It is to this that we turn in chapter 11.

Natural Kind Predicates, Mass Nouns, and Abstract Singular Terms

As noted in chapter 9, the natural kind terms discussed by Kripke in *Naming and Necessity* include expressions of several different syntactic and semantic categories. In developing the model in chapter 10, I focused on natural kind predicates while ignoring the difference between those, like *cat*, that are count nouns and those, like *water*, that are mass terms. In discussing Kripke's examples involving *water*, I simply substituted the syntactically compound count noun *drop of water* for the mass term *water*, and treated it as if it were simple natural kind predicate. This allowed me to present the semantic model of natural kind predicates in its simplest form while ignoring the complications introduced by mass terms. It is now time to look at those complications and to spell out in more detail how terms like *water* work.

A good place to begin is with the adjective *red*, which bears important similarities to mass nouns like *water*. *Red* is a natural kind term the primary use of which is as a predicate of individual concrete objects, illustrated in (1).

1. Bill's shirt is red.

However, it also has a secondary use in which it functions as a singular term naming the kind—that is, the color—instances of which are individual red things.

2. Red is a color.

In (2) the word *red* functions as an abstract singular term, and the predicate *is a color* expresses a property that is predicated of its referent. To say of a kind that it has this property is, at least in part, to say that predicating the kind of an individual concrete object involves saying of that object that it is colored. The relationship between the two uses of *red* is straightforward. When used as an abstract singular term, it names the kind which is the meaning of the predicate *is red*, and which determines its extension in all possible circumstances.

Next, consider mass nouns such as *water*, *gold*, and *snow*. The most familiar use of these terms is as mass predicates. This use of mass nouns may be illustrated by noting three ways in which they are similar to ordinary count nouns, which standardly function as predicates. First, like count nouns, they can be used in ordinary predicative position.

3a. That is a cat/a man/an animal.
3b. The stuff in the container is water/gold/snow.

Second, like other predicates, mass nouns combine with quantificational expressions to form quantifiers.

4a. some man, every man, the man
4b. many men, all men, few men, the men, twenty men
4c. some water, the snow, all gold, a gallon of water, much snow, a little gold

Some quantificational expressions, like *many* and *few*, combine only with plural count nouns; other quantificational expressions, like *much* and *a little*, occur only with mass nouns (which are grammatically singular); still other quantificational expressions, like *some* and *the*, occur with predicates of all types. Third, mass nouns have bare, unquantified occurrences the interpretations of which parallel those of bare, unquantified plural count nouns (which function as predicates). For example, just as the sentences in (5) are equivalent to those in (6), so the sentences in (7) are equivalent to those in (8).[1]

5a. Men are mortal.
5b. Children are not allowed to purchase firearms.
5c. Beavers build dams. (generic)
6a. All men are mortal.
6b. No children are allowed to purchase firearms.

6c. Generally, or characteristically, if something is a beaver, then
     it builds dams. (generic)

7a. Gold is malleable.

7b. Water isn't found on the moon.

7c. Snow is white. (generic)

8a. All gold is malleable.

8b. No water is found on the moon.

8c. Generally, or characteristically, if something is snow, then it
     is white. (generic)

If this analysis is correct, then *water* is a natural kind term the
primary use of which is as a mass predicate that applies to something
x iff x is some amount or quantity of water (no matter how large or
how small). Here, in speaking of an amount or quantity of water, I do
not mean some abstract measure, such as a pint or a gallon, which
different concrete instances of the kind water may share. Rather, I mean
the instances themselves: the liquid in a particular glass, the puddle on
the bathroom floor, the drop of rain that just fell on my face. All of
these are examples of water—instances to which the predicate *water*
applies. Further examples in which *water* is used as a mass predicate
are (9a) and (9b), which are paraphrased by (10a) and (10b).

9a. Water is H_2O.

9b. The glass contains six ounces of water.

10a. For all x, if x is water, then x is H_2O.

10b. [$\exists$x: x is water and x weighs 6 ounces] the glass contains x.

In (10a), both *water* and H_2O are mass predicates.[2] The former applies
to all and only quantities (i.e., instances) of water, while the latter applies to all and only quantities (instances) of H_2O. Such quantities (instances) include individual molecules consisting of two hydrogen
atoms and one oxygen atom, as well as all aggregates of such molecules—that is, concrete entities of various and sundry types (particular
vapors, liquids, solids, and so on) that are made up of such molecules.
The range of the quantifier in (10a) includes all such instances, and
the sentence expresses a truth iff every instance of water is something
molecules of which consist of two hydrogen atoms and one oxygen
atom.

Like the adjective *red*, the primary use of which is as a predicate of individual objects and the secondary use of which is as a name of the color designated by the predicate, the mass noun *water* also has a secondary use in which it is a singular term naming the kind instances of which constitute the extension of the predicate *water*.One sentence in which *water* is used in this way is (11), which parallels (2) above.

11.   Water is a liquid.

In this sentence, *water* occurs as a singular term standing for a certain kind, and *is a liquid* expresses a higher-order property of that kind. To say that a kind is a liquid is, at least in part, to say that predicating that kind of something involves characterizing it as liquid. Here, *liquid* (as opposed to *a liquid*) is used as a mass predicate applying to any concrete physical stuff in liquid form. Thus, if I say

12.   Your glass contains more liquid than mine

I am saying that the quantity of concrete stuff in liquid form in your glass is greater than the quantity of concrete stuff in liquid form in my glass. On the other hand, if I say

13.   That glass contains a mixture of three liquids

I am saying that the stuff in that glass contains instances of three kinds, each of which has the property of being a liquid.

Sentence (11) has a natural interpretation in which it is true—as do the sentences *Coca-Cola is a beverage, Coffee is a drink*, and so on. This suggests that the mass predicate *water* has a corresponding interpretation in which it stands for a kind each instance of which is something liquid, such as a puddle or a drop. What, then, are we to make of the intuition that (14a) and (14b) are true?

14a.   Ice is frozen water.
14b.   Water vapor is water in gaseous form.

Like *water*, *ice* and *water vapor* are mass predicates. Thus (14a) and (14b) are equivalent to (15a) and (15b).

15a. For all x, if x is ice, then x is frozen water.
15b. For all x, if x is water vapor, then x is water in gaseous form.

Sentence (15a) is true iff all instances of ice are instances of frozen water. In general, if something is frozen F, then it is F—for instance, frozen meat is meat, frozen vegetables are vegetables, frozen milk is milk, and frozen water is water. Thus, (15a) is true only if (16a) is true; similarly for (15b) and (16b).

16a. For all x, if x is ice, then x is water.
16b. For all x, if x is water vapor, then x is water.

But these sentences cannot be true if the mass predicate *water* applies only to quantities of liquid.

Surely, however, there is an interpretation of *water* in which the sentences in (14), (15), and (16) are true. On this interpretation, *water* designates a kind instances of which include solid chunks of ice and clouds of gas, in addition to liquid quantities. In light of this, it would seem that *water*, in both its use as a mass predicate and its use as a name, is ambiguous between an expansive and a restricted interpretation. On the expansive interpretation, it stands for a certain substance k, the extension of which consists of all and only instances of H_2O—including solid blocks of ice as well as liquid and gaseous quantities with that molecular structure.[3] On the restricted interpretation, *water* stands for the property of being a quantity of the kind k in liquid form. Similarly, *ice* and *water vapor* (both of which can be used either as mass predicates or as singular terms) stand for the property of being an instance of the kind k in (frozen) solid form, and the property of being a instance of the kind k in gaseous form, respectively.

It is worth noting that words like *coffee* and *tea* are similarly ambiguous. Both can be used either as mass predicates or as names. In addition, these words have expansive and restricted interpretations. On their restricted interpretations, *Coffee is a drink* and *Tea is a drink* are true, and the associated mass predicates apply only to liquid quantities. On their expansive interpretations, these terms apply to all instances of the kinds coffee and tea, in whatever form.[4]

The Resolution of Johnston's Puzzle

We are now in a position to address Mark Johnston's puzzle, sketched at the end of chapter 10. The simplest and most straightforward version of the puzzle may be put as follows: If the sentences in (17) are true theoretical identity sentences involving natural kind terms, then it would seem that the sentences in (18) and (19) must also be true. After all, identity is symmetric and transitive, isn't it?

   17a.   Water is H_2O.
   17b.   Ice is H_2O.
   17c.   Water vapor is H_2O.
   18a. H_2O is water.
   18b. H_2O is ice.
   18c. H_2O is water vapor.
   19a.   Water is ice.
   19b.   Water is water vapor
   19c.   Ice is water vapor.

But the sentences in (19) are obviously false. Does this show that the sentences in (17) are not true, that they are not necessary, that they are not theoretical identity sentences, or what?

It doesn't show that the sentences in (17) are not true. On the account I have sketched, the primary use of the mass nouns in these examples is as predicates. When these nouns are used in this way, the sentences in (17)–(19) are not of the form $a = b$, but rather are quantified conditionals. Thus, (17)–(19) are interpretable as (17′)–(19′).

   17a′.   For all x, if x is water, then x is H_2O.
   17b′.   For all x, if x is ice, then x is H_2O.
   17c′.   For all x, if x is water vapor, then x is H_2O.
   18a′.   For all x, if x is H_2O, then x is water.
   18b′.   For all x, if x is H_2O, then x is ice.
   18c′.   For all x, if x is H_2O, then x is water vapor.
   19a′.   For all x, if x is water, then x is ice.
   19b′.   For all x, if x is water, then x is water vapor.
   19c′.   For all x, if x is ice, then x is water vapor.

The sentences in (17′), and hence in (17), are true. In addition (18a′), and hence (18a), are true on the expansive interpretation of *water*. However, (18b′) and (18c′), and hence (18b) and (18c), are false. Thus, on this analysis the truth of the sentences in (17) is compatible with the falsity of the sentences in (19).

Although there is no interpretation of *water* in which the sentences in (19) (and (19′)) are true, the sentences in (20) are true, on the expansive interpretation of the predicate *water*.

20a.   All and only water is H_2O.
20a′.   For all x, x is water iff x is H_2O.
20b.   Ice is water.
20b′.   For all x, if x is ice, then x is water.
20c.   Water vapor is water.
20c′.   For all x, if x is water vapor, then x is water.

By contrast, the sentences in (21) are true on the restricted interpretation of predicate *water*.

21a.   No water is ice.
21a′.   No x is such that x is water and x is ice.
21b.   No water is water vapor.
21b′.   No x is such that x is water and x is water vapor.

As I see it, the resolution of Johnston's puzzle about theoretical identification sentences involving natural kind terms depends on three fundamental points: (i) the recognition that natural kind terms such as *water, ice, water vapor,* and *H_2O* function primarily as mass predicates; (ii) the realization that when these terms are used as predicates, the relevant theoretical identification sentences are not of the form $a = b$, but rather are universally quantified conditionals and biconditionals; and (iii) the observation that the predicate *water* has both an expansive and a restricted interpretation. However, this is not all. There are two further factors involved in generating the puzzle that I haven't brought out yet.

The first concerns a difference between the expansive, mass predicate *water*, on the one hand, and the natural kind predicates *ice, water vapor,* and the restricted version of *water*, on the other. If the account developed in chapter 10 is correct, and the expansive version of the

predicate *water* is governed by a stipulation that it is to apply to all
and only instances of the same substance (physically constitutive kind)
as the elements in the sample, then the truth of (17a), together with the
presumption that the predicates *water* and H_2O have been successfully
introduced, guarantee the truth, and even the necessity, of (18a) and
(20a). However, the same cannot be said for the natural kind predicates
ice, *water vapor*, or the restricted version of the predicate *water*. If P
is one of these predicates, the truth of (22a) does not guarantee the
truth, let alone the necessity, of (22b) or (22c).

    22a.   P is H_2O.
    22a'. For all x, if x is P, then x is H_2O.
    22b. H_2O is P.
    22b'. For all x, if x is H_2O, then x is P.
    22c.   All and only P is H_2O.
    22c'. For all x, x is P iff x is H_2O.

In order to resolve Johnston's puzzle, we have to explain why this
is so.

    The explanation is simple. Although *ice*, *water vapor*, and the re-
stricted version of *water* are natural kind predicates, they are not substance predicates—that is, they are not governed by the stipulation that
they are to apply to all and only instances of the unique substance (that
is, physically constitutive kind) of which the elements in their respective samples are instances. Rather, the restricted version of *water* is
governed by the rule that it is to apply to all **liquid** instances of that
substance, *ice* is governed by the rule that it is to apply to all **frozen**
(solid) instances of that substance, and *water vapor* is governed by the
rule that it is to apply to all **gaseous** instances of that substance. Thus,
when the substance in question is found to be H_2O, and instances of
(22a) involving the predicates *ice*, *water vapor*, and the restricted version of *water* are found to be true, the combination of this fact with
the semantics of the predicates does not guarantee the truth of (22b) or
(22c). It does, however, guarantee the necessity of the relevant instances of (22a). Thus, all of the sentences in (17′) are linguistically
guaranteed to be necessary, if true, as is (20a) on the expansive interpretation of *water*.

    It should be noted that these results are compatible with several
different ways of conceptualizing the linguistic properties of the predi-

cates in question. One way of thinking of the matter is to treat the expansive substance term *water* as understood ostensively, and to define the other predicates in terms of it. For example, *ice* might be stipulated to mean *frozen water* and the restricted version of *water* might be stipulated to mean *liquid water*, while the semantically complex *water vapor* may be viewed as deriving its meaning compositionally from the meanings of *water* and *vapor*. A different way of conceptualizing the situation is to treat the restricted version of *water* as governed by the ostensive stipulation that it is to apply to all liquid instances of the substance of which all elements in the relevant sample are instances. The expansive version of *water* can then be defined in terms of it, with the definitions of the predicates *ice* and *water vapor* following in train. It is even possible to treat the expansive version of *water*, the restricted version of *water*, and the predicate *ice* as all understood ostensively, with different but related stipulations. The results we have arrived at regarding theoretical identification sentences involving these predicates does not depend on conceptualizing their semantic properties in one of these ways as opposed to the others.[5]

This brings us to the final factor at work in Johnston's puzzle. On the account I have given, the mass nouns in (17) can be seen as functioning as predicates, and when they are, (17a, b, c) are true, as is (20a) (on the expansive interpretation of *water*). Johnston disputes the claim that these sentences are true, and gives a metaphysical argument to support his position. He agrees that the mass nouns in (17) can be understood as predicates, and that when they are, the sentences in (17) are equivalent to those in (17′). He also says that if the predicate *is H_2O* is taken to mean *is constituted by H_2O*, so that the sentences in (17′) are paraphrases of the sentences in (C-17), then they are true.

C-17a. For all x, if x is water, then x is constituted by (made up of) H_2O.

C-17b. For all x, if x is ice, then x is constituted by (made up) of H_2O.

C-17c. For all x, if x is water vapor, then x is constituted by (made up) of H_2O.

However, he maintains that if the predicate *is H_2O* is understood as applying to something x iff x is an instance of the kind H_2O, and the sentences in (17′) are taken to be equivalent to those in (I-17), then they must be false.[6]

I-17a.   For all x, if x is an instance of the kind water, then x is an instance of the kind H_2O.

I-17b.   For all x, if x is an instance of the kind ice, then x is an instance of the kind H_2O.

I-17c.   For all x, if x is an instance of the kind water vapor, then x is an instance of the kind H_2O.

On the account I have given, mass predicates like *water* and *H_2O* are necessarily equivalent to the phrases *instance of the kind water* and *instance of the kind H_2O* (where the mass nouns in these phrases function as abstract singular terms naming the kinds associated with the predicates). Thus, on my view, the sentences in (17′), and hence in (17), are equivalent to the sentences in (I-17). As a result, Johnston's claim that these sentences are false conflicts with my claim that they are true.

Johnston's claim that the sentences in (I-17) are false, while the sentences in (C-17) are true, is based on arguments of the following sort.

23.   (a) Suppose that x is a chunk of ice. (b) Then it is an instance of the kind ice. (c) It is also made up of (constituted by) a certain quantity (i.e., instance) of H_2O. (d) However, since the H_2O that makes up (constitutes) x would continue to exist even if x were melted, and so ceased to exist, x cannot be identical with the H_2O that makes it up (constitutes it). (e) Nor is x identical with any other quantity (i.e., instance) of H_2O. (f) Since x is not identical with any quantity (instance) of H_2O, x is not an instance of the kind H_2O. (g) Thus (I-17b) is false.

Johnston's argument for the falsity of (I-17c) is similar, with x being a particular vaporous cloud or yellow fog.[7] The argument directed at the version of (I-17a) involving the expansive kind water is only slightly more complicated. Although the structure of the argument (a)–(g) is essentially the same, one of the steps—step (b)—is broken down into a pair of steps. The argument may be put as follows.

24.   (a) Suppose that x is a chunk of ice. (b-i) Then it is an in-
      stance of the kind ice; (b- ii) since all instances of the kind
      ice are instances of the expansive kind water, x is an instance
      of the expansive kind water. (c) In addition, x is made up
      of (constituted by) a certain quantity (instance) of H_2O. (d)
      However, since the H_2O that makes up (constitutes) x would
      continue to exist even if x were melted, and so ceased to
      exist, x cannot be identical with the H_2O that makes it up
      (constitutes it). (e) Nor is x identical with any other quantity
      (instance) of H_2O. (f) Since x is not identical with any quan-
      tity (instance) of H_2O, x is not an instance of the kind H_2O.
      (g) Thus (I-17a) is false, even on the expansive interpretation
      of *water*.

Although Johnston's arguments regarding the sentences in (I-17)
are challenging, I believe they are unpersuasive. My critique will consist of two parts. First, I will show that there are precisely parallel
arguments from equally plausible premises to conclusions that are obviously false. If these parallel arguments are good, then one of Johnston's
premises must be false. As a result, Johnston's arguments cannot be
taken as establishing their conclusions. Having demonstrated this, I will
next try to show exactly where and why the arguments fail.

Consider the following case. Suppose we have a particular chunk
of ice, x. As Johnston is prepared to admit, x is an instance of the kind
ice. Suppose, however, we were to smash x, breaking it into a hundred
separate pieces of ice—without losing any. Although x would no
longer exist, the ice that made it up would continue to exist, in a hundred separate pieces. Thus, Johnston should maintain, x cannot be identical with the ice that made it up. Maintaining the parallel with arguments (23) and (24) leads to the claim that x is not identical with any
other instance of ice either. But then, since something is an instance of
the kind ice only if there is some ice it is identical with, we have a
reductio of the claim that x is an instance of the kind ice.

Precisely analogous arguments could be constructed for the conclusions (i) that particular chunks of wood are not (instances of the
kind) wood, (ii) that particular drops of water are not (instances of the
kind) water, (iii) that particular clouds of water vapor are not (instances
of the kind) water vapor, (iv) that particular sugar cubes are not (instances of the kind) sugar, (v) that particular piles of sand are not (in-

stances of the kind) sand, and so on for virtually all mass nouns applying to concrete entities. The arguments for these conclusions are clearly
incorrect. If M is a mass predicate of concrete individuals, then it is
characteristic for M to have instances i, such that i is entirely made up
of parts that may survive the destruction of i while still being M.[8] Thus,
arguments of the sort just given for the claim that chunks of ice are not
ice after all conflict with a general semantic truth about mass predicates.

Putting the argument about ice in the form of Johnston's original
argument for the falsity of (I-17b), we have (25).

25.   (a) Suppose that x is a chunk of ice. (b) Then it is an instance
      of the kind ice. (c) It can also be divided into a hundred
      pieces of ice that make it up (constitute it). (d) However,
      since this ice that makes up (constitutes) x would continue to
      exist even if x were broken into those 100 pieces, and so
      ceased to exist, x cannot be identical with the ice that makes
      it up (constitutes it). (e) Nor is x identical with any other
      quantity (i.e., instance) of ice. (f) Since x is not identical
      with any quantity (i.e., instance) of ice, it is not (an instance
      of) ice. (g) Thus (b) is false, after all.

I maintain that if Johnston's original argument, (23), for the falsity
of (I-17b) is sound and persuasive, then this argument is, too.[9] But if
this argument is sound, then step (b) of (23) is false, in which case (23)
is unsound. Since if Johnston's original argument, (23), is sound and
persuasive, then it is unsound, we must conclude that it is not sound
and persuasive. The same holds for other versions of Johnston's argument, for example, those for the falsity of (I-17a) and (I-17c).

Now in fact I don't think that the (b) steps in Johnston's arguments
are false. Thus, the arguments must fail somewhere else. We can get a
good idea of where they fail by determining precisely where the obviously incorrect argument, (25), fails. Steps (a)–(c) of (25) are not the
problem; they are clearly correct. Step (d), on the other hand, is equivocal. Part of what it asserts is that pieces 1–100 of ice together form
some instance of the kind ice that completely constitutes x, without
being identical with x, since it can exist in circumstances in which x
does not. This seems to be true. Surely the 100 pieces of ice that exhaustively make up x continue to exist after x is smashed, and therefore

ceases to exist. Presumably, some fusion of these 100 pieces, which itself is ice, may be taken to exist both before and after x is smashed. This instance of the kind ice constitutes x, but is not identical with x, because, unlike x, its survival does not depend on the particular arrangement and attachment, one to another, of those 100 parts.

So far, so good. However, (25d) also speaks of *the ice that makes up x*. It is not entirely clear how this should be understood. If what is being asserted is merely (26a), then there is reason to believe it; however, if it is (26b) that is asserted, then what is asserted is false.

26a. There exists a fusion, y, of parts of x that are themselves ice, such that y both constitutes x and is itself ice; moreover, y is not identical with x, because its survival does not depend on the particular arrangement and attachment of its 100 parts.

26b. There exists one and only one fusion, y, of parts of x that are themselves ice, such that y both constitutes x and is itself ice; moreover, y is not identical with x, because its survival does not depend on the particular arrangement and attachment of its 100 parts.

There are many different ways to divide the original chunk of ice x into parts with numerically different fusions with different survival conditions, all of which completely constitute x while themselves being instances of the kind ice. Thus, if (25d) asserts (26b), then it is false, and the argument fails at this point.[10] On the other hand, if (25b) asserts only (26a), then the argument (25) fails at step (e). The original chunk x is itself (an instance of the kind) ice. Since it is identical with itself, there is some instance of the kind ice with which it is identical. Either way, the argument fails.

Johnston's arguments (23) and (24) suffer from analogous problems. In each case, steps (a) and (b) are correct, as is (c), provided that what is meant by *a certain quantity of H_2O* is simply *a certain instance of H_2O*. As in the case of (25), however, step (d) is equivocal. If what is intended is merely (27a), then there is no objection to it; however, if it is (27b) that is intended, then we have no reason to believe it.

27a. There exists a fusion, y, of parts of x that are (instances of) H_2O, such that y both constitutes x and is itself (an instance of) H_2O; moreover, y is not identical with x, because its survival does not depend on all its H_2O molecules being arranged to form a solid mass.

27b.   There exists one and only one fusion, y, of parts of x that are (instances of) H_2O, such that y both constitutes x and is itself (an instance of) H_2O; moreover, y is not identical with x, because its survival does not depend on all its H_2O molecules being arranged to form a solid mass.

The points about (27) parallel those about (26). As before, there are many different ways to divide the original chunk of ice x into H_2O-parts with numerically different fusions, with different survival conditions, all of which completely constitute x while themselves being instances of the kind H_2O. Thus, if (23d) and (24d) assert (27b), then they are false, and Johnston's arguments fail at this point. On the other hand, if (23d) and (24d) assert only (27a), then we have no reason to accept step (e). On the contrary, the original chunk x meets the stipulation governing the application of the mass predicate H_2O—that is, it is either a molecule made up of two hydrogen atoms and one oxygen atom, or **it is made up of such molecules**. Thus, x is (an instance of the kind) H_2O. Since x is identical with itself, there is some instance of the kind ice with which it is identical. Either way, the argument fails.

Johnston, of course, disagrees. To see why, let us take (23d) and (24d) to assert only (27a). The weight of the arguments then falls on step (e), which he accepts, but which I have argued is unsupported and implausible. In discussing this step, Johnston uses an example different from the one given here. Instead of talking about a chunk of ice that is later melted, preserving the H_2O that constituted it, as in (23), he uses the example of a fog—a certain instance of water vapor—that is later liquefied, preserving the H_2O that constituted it. His argument involving this example parallels (23) and includes the conclusion that the original fog was not itself an instance of H_2O, but rather was merely constituted by H_2O. In discussing step (e) of the argument he says:

No one should want to say that there are here two instances of the kind H_2O which happen to be exactly co-incident at least before the liquefaction—that is, the fog and the quantity of fog which makes it up. Or if they do they should recognize that they are already in the constitution business: on their view, oddly enough, constitution holds among instances of the very *same kind, namely, H_2O. Better to say that the fog is not an extra instance of the kind H_2O.*[11]

The question at issue is whether prior to the liquefaction (in the case of the fog), or the melting (in the case of the ice), there were two instances of H_2O that exactly coincided while differing only in their survival conditions. Johnston brands the view that there were "odd" in that it allows the constitution relation to hold among instances of the same kind. But, as the example on which argument (25) is based shows, there is nothing odd about this. In that case there is an instance y of the kind ice that survives the destruction of a different instance x of ice, whereas prior to the smashing of x into 100 pieces, y constituted x, and exactly coincided with x, without being identical with x. But if there is nothing odd or absurd about this when x and y are both instances of the kind ice, why is there anything odd or absurd in the supposition that they may be so related in cases in which both are instances of the kind H_2O?

Johnston thinks that there is something special about terms for chemical kinds like H_2O. In defending the idea that after the fog liquefies, we still have the same quantity of H_2O, though now in liquid form, he says, "After all, part of the point of talking of a chemical kind like H_2O is to allow that particular quantities of it can first be in one state and then another."[12] This is certainly right; it is an important feature of the kind H_2O that some instances of it can survive change of chemical state. But in order to rule out the possibility that the fog was an instance of H_2O, Johnston needs the claim that all instances of H_2O can survive change of chemical state, and nothing he says shows that they do. Thus, nothing he says rules out the possibility that some instances of H_2O have built-in survival conditions requiring those instances to be in a particular chemical state, whereas others do not.

In fact, Johnston's position seems to be that nothing solid, gaseous, or liquid is ever (an instance of) H_2O (though it may be constituted by H_2O). Thus, he says, "a particular liquid is essentially a liquid, just as a particular fog is essentially a vapor," which suggests that he thinks that any particular gaseous stuff is essentially gaseous, any particular stuff that is liquid is essentially liquid, and any solid object is essentially solid.[13] But then, since he tacitly assumes that every instance of H_2O can survive change in chemical state, he is committed to the view that if something is (an instance of) H_2O, then it is never solid, liquid, or gaseous (at any time). This, it seems to me, makes instances of H_2O unduly mysterious and elusive.[14] This mystery can be avoided by recognizing (i) that some instances of H_2O have survival conditions requiring them to be in a particular chemical state, whereas others do not, and (ii) that both sorts of instances of H_2O can be solid, liquid, or gaseous (at a given time), but only one of these sorts can survive change of chemical state.[15]

All this suggests that Johnston is wrong about the sentences in (I-17); they are true after all, as are the sentences in (17'), with which they are equivalent, and the sentences in (17), when the mass nouns they contain are used as predicates.[16] However, this does not mean that Johnston is wrong about the truth of the sentences in (C-17). Water, ice, and water vapor are made up of (constituted by) H_2O. This is clearly true of ice, water vapor, and the restricted interpretation of *water*—that is, liquid water. Since (i) the mass predicate H_2O is stipulated to apply to x iff x is either a molecule made up of two hydrogen atoms and one oxygen atom, or x is made up of such molecules, and (ii) every instance of ice, water vapor, and liquid water is made up of many molecules of this sort, every instance of these kinds is in the extension of H_2O.

The situation is similar in the case of the expansive interpretation of *water*, except for two further requirements on the truth of (20a)— *For all x, x is water iff x is H_2O*. First, the truth of this sentence requires not just that the expansive kind water includes each instance of water in a solid, liquid, or gaseous form, but also that some instances of the expansive kind water persist through changes in chemical state—since some instances of H_2O clearly do (as when ice is first liquefied and then heated to form a water vapor while the H_2O remains the same). As it turns out, this is not a problem, for we do ordinarily think and talk about water in just this way. Imagine, for example, that we fill a glass with water from the tap, noting that it is liquid. After we freeze it, we may correctly describe the situation as one in which the water that came from the tap is now frozen solid, and has turned to ice. Later, when we melt the ice, we may correctly say that the water that originally came from the tap, and was later frozen solid, is now liquid again. If, as I believe, what we say in this sort of case is true, then some instances of the expansive kind water survive change in chemical state. Since the same sort of thing could be said in cases in which the water from the tap changes to a gaseous form and back, the first (extra) requirement for the truth of (20a) is met.

The second (extra) requirement for the truth of (20a) involves special instances of H_2O—such as individual H_2O molecules, small numbers of such molecules, or widely scattered aggregates of molecules—that may be too small, or too scattered, to count as solid, liquid, or gas. If such instances of H_2O are indeed genuine, then there is a question whether they should also qualify as instances of the expansive kind water. I am inclined to think that they should—as is evidenced by our willingness to characterize such individual molecules as *water molecules*. In such cases, we seem to be saying of individual molecules that they are water, and hence in the extension of the expansive kind water. If this is right, then both of the additional requirements on the truth of (20a) are met.

To sum up, although the sentences in (C-17) may be accepted as true, this is compatible with taking the sentences in (I-17) plus (20a) (on the expansive interpretation of *water*) to be true as well.[17] Saying that liquid water, ice, and water vapor are all made up of (or constituted by) H_2O need not commit one to denying that they are themselves instances of H_2O—provided that one doesn't impose a contentious technical interpretation on *is made up of* and *is constituted by*. Moreover, the theoretical identification statements relating instances of the relevant kinds may naturally be expressed by the sentences in (17′), or by the sentences in (17), when the mass nouns they contain are treated as predicates. These sentences, along with the sentences in (20), on the expansive interpretation of *water*, are true theoretical identity sentences involving natural kind predicates that are mass terms. As such, the semantic model developed in chapter 10 applies to them.[18]

Identity Sentences Involving Singular Term Uses of Mass Nouns

This completes my reconstruction and reformulation of Kripke's model of natural kind predicates. The reconstructed model encompasses mass nouns, count nouns, and adjectives functioning as predicates. Thus, the points made in chapters 9 and 10 should be applicable, in a reasonably straightforward way, to all the natural kind predicates discussed in *Naming and Necessity*. These include predicative uses of the mass nouns *water*, H_2O, *gold*, *iron pyrites*, *heat*, *sound*, *light*, *electromagnetic radiation*, *electricity*, *lightning*, and *pain*; predicative uses of the count nouns *cat*, *animal*, *tiger*, *whale*, *mammal*, *molecule*, and *photon*;

and predicative uses of the adjectives *hot*, *red*, *yellow*, and *loud*. Theoretical identity sentences involving these predicates have the force of universally quantified conditionals or biconditionals. Many are necessary, and some of these are a posteriori. As we have seen, some but not all necessary theoretical identity sentences involving natural kind predicates may be regarded as linguistically guaranteed to be necessary if true in the following sense: the claim that they are necessary is a consequence of the assumption that they are true, together with a description of their semantic properties (including the claim that the natural kind predicates they contain have been successfully introduced in a manner fulfilling the semantic presuppositions governing their introduction). As I indicated in chapter 10, cases in which this is so should be viewed not so much as showing how easy it is to know that certain claims are necessary, but rather as making clear how much is empirically presupposed in the introduction and use of certain natural kind terms.

A final point along these lines involves mass nouns of the sort discussed in this chapter. Although the primary use of these terms is as predicates, they also have a secondary use in which they function as abstract singular terms that name the kinds or properties associated with the predicates. Examples of this are the uses of *water*, *quartz*, and *gold* in (28a–c).

28a.   Water is a liquid.
28b.   Quartz is a crystal.
28c.   Gold is an element.

With this in mind, suppose that A and B are arbitrary mass nouns. Using them as predicates, we can construct theoretical identity sentences of the form (29).

29a.   For all x, x is an A iff x is a B.
29b.   For all x, if x is an A, then x is a B.
29c.   For all x, if x is a B, then x is an A.

However, we can also construct identity sentences using A and B as names of the kinds or properties associated with the predicates in (29). This results in (30).

30. $A = B$

Finally, since mass nouns are grammatically singular, the English sentence

31. A is B

might be taken to be ambiguous between the identity sentences (29b) and (30).

All of this might encourage the following thought: Where A and B are mass nouns, such as *water* and H_2O, Kripke's doctrine that theoretical identity sentences involving rigid natural kind terms are necessary if true can be salvaged, simply by interpreting the relevant English sentences of the form (31) as having the force of (30). For this class of terms, the complications discussed in chapters 9 and 10 can be avoided. In particular we can capture the connection between the semantics of mass terms for natural kinds and the necessity (plus aposterioricity) of corresponding sentences of the form (31), without invoking the semantic model developed in chapter 10. In short, in the special case of natural kind terms that are mass nouns, Kripke's central semantic and philosophical doctrines can be captured without considering predicative uses of such terms.

Although this line of thought is not entirely without merit, it is important to recognize that the sweeping conclusions it arrives at are substantially overstated. For one thing, some of the theoretical identities considered by Kripke involving mass nouns A and B do not require the coextensiveness of the two terms. For instance, Kripke's example

32. Lightning is electricity

is taken to assert that all lightning is electricity, but not that all electricity is lightning. Thus, it can't be analyzed as having the form (30), but rather must be taken to be equivalent to (29b). Other examples of this kind are (17a), on the restricted interpretation of *water*, (17b), and (17c).

17a. Water is H_2O.
17b. Ice is H_2O.
17c. Water vapor is H_2O.

The only interpretation in which these sentences are true is one in which their mass terms function as predicates, and the sentences are equivalent to those in (17′). To explain the connection between the necessity of these sentences and the semantics of the natural kind terms they contain, one needs the semantic model developed in chapter 10. Kripke's doctrine that identity sentences of the form (30) that contain rigid designators are necessary if true is irrelevant.

What about cases in which we do want to identify all and only instances of A with instances of B, as we do when we identify all and only instances of the expansive kind water with instances of H_2O? To fix ideas, let us suppose that *water* is given the expansive interpretation and that (17a) is interpreted as (33).

33.   Water = H_2O

The first thing to note is that the abstract singular terms *water* and H_2O in (33) do not name concrete totalities consisting of all instances of water and H_2O, respectively.[19] Rather, they name kinds or properties associated with the respective predicates. Given this, we face two questions—*Are the meanings of the predicates 'water' and 'H_2O' the same or different?* and *If their meanings are different, do the singular term uses of these expressions name the kinds associated with their predicative uses, or do they name the meanings associated with those uses?*

The import of the first of these questions is clear. If the meanings of the mass predicates *water* and H_2O are the same, then we lose what was supposed to be a prime example of the necessary a posteriori, since, on this alternative, (17a) must be regarded as expressing the same proposition as *Water is water*, and so must be characterized as knowable a priori (both on the analysis in which its terms are predicates and on the analysis in which its terms are names). This is counterintuitive. As I noted in chapter 10, in my opinion the two predicates *water* and H_2O do not mean the same thing. The meaning of *water* is the kind it is associated with, which I am inclined to identify with its intension—a function from possible worlds to its extensions at those worlds (where the extension of *water* at a world is the set of all and only quantities of water at that world). Although this is also the intension of the predicate H_2O, there is reason to think that there is more to the meaning of H_2O than just this. Unlike *water*, the predicate H_2O appears to be semantically complex. It seems to mean roughly the same as the phrase *something molecules of which consist of two hydrogen atoms and one oxygen atom.* If this is right, then the predicates *water* and H_2O have different meanings, and theoretical identification sentences involving them—such as *Water is H_2O* and *H_2O is water*—are examples of the necessary a posteriori.

We now turn to the second question. Do singular term uses of *water* and H_2O name the kinds associated with the predicative uses of these terms, or do they name the meanings associated with those uses? In the case of *water* there is no difference between these alternatives, since the predicate *water* has no meaning apart from the kind which is its intension. Thus, the singular term *water* unambiguously names that kind (intension). In the case of H_2O the situation is different. The meaning of this predicate—roughly, the property of being something molecules of which consist of two hydrogen atoms and one oxygen atom—is distinct from the kind, or intension, determined by that property. As a result, there are two possible choices for the referent of the singular term H_2O. If its referent is the property expressed by the predicate, then the abstract singular terms *water* and H_2O name different things and the identity sentence (33) is false. On this alternative, the only true identity sentences involving these mass nouns are those in which they function as predicates. If, on the other hand, the abstract singular term H_2O refers to the kind (i.e., intension) associated with the corresponding predicate, then the singular terms *water* and H_2O designate the same thing, and (33) is true. Moreover, it would seem reasonable to suppose that these abstract singular terms are rigid designators.[20] Thus, if this last way of construing the relationship between singular term versus predicative uses of these expressions is correct, then Kripke's doctrine of the necessity of identities involving rigid singular terms will apply to (33) and, by extension, to the nonpredicative interpretation of (17a) in which *water* and H_2O are abstract singular terms that both designate the expansive kind water.

Let us suppose that this account of these singular terms is correct. It might be thought that if this is so, then the rigidity of the abstract singular terms in question provides an explanation of the necessity of certain theoretical identity sentences on a par with the explanation of how it is that the semantics of the predicates *water* and H_2O guarantee that (34) is necessary if true.

34.   For all x, x is water iff x is H_2O.

This impression is, however, misleading. The semantic account presented in the last three chapters explains why (34) is, if true, necessary. The important point to notice is that this account is also required to explain the **truth** of theoretical identities of like (33). If such identity sentences are true, then the rigidity of the terms flanking the identity sign will, of course, explain their necessity. But this is secondary; first we need an explanation of how empirical discoveries can establish that (33) is true.

On the account of the reference of mass nouns used as abstract singular terms that we are considering, (33) says that a certain kind (i.e., intension) w_i is identical with a certain kind (i.e., intension) h_i. Since this is a statement about intensions, the claim that it is true is equivalent to the claim that (34) is necessary. Thus, the philosophically interesting question about (33) is (33Q), which is equivalent to the philosophically interesting question (34Q) about (34).

33Q.   Why does the discovery that paradigmatic water samples have the chemical structure H_2O lead us to believe that (33) is true (on the analysis we are considering)?

34Q.   Why does the discovery that that paradigmatic water samples have the chemical structure H_2O lead us to believe that (34) is not only true, but necessary?

The answer to these questions is given by the model of natural kind terms presented in the last three chapters. The crucial points used in answering them are (i) the nondescriptionality of both the predicate and the related abstract singular term *water*; (ii) the explanation of how these expressions may be taken to be governed by an ostensive stipulation to the effect that (a) the predicate is to apply to all and only instances of the substance of which nearly all members of the associated sample are instances, and (b) the abstract singular term is to designate that substance; (iii) the treatment of substances as physically constitutive kinds; and (iv) the understanding of standard chemical predicates as specifying possible kinds of this sort. With these points in place we can answer the questions (33Q) and (34Q) without bringing in the notion of rigidity in any substantial way.

Of course, the abstract singular term *water* is a rigid designator, and this is not entirely without significance. However, even this claim about rigidity is essentially a corollary of the result that both the predicate and the singular term *water* are nondescriptional, and in fact Millian—a fact that plays a role in explaining why (33) and (34) are a posteriori rather than a priori.[21] To sum up, if one wishes, one can, without error, treat the English sentence (17a)—*Water is H_2O*—on the model of (33), in which a pair of abstract singular terms flank the identity sign. However, there is nothing essential about this way of putting things, and the most important issues about sentences like (33) require an explanation that goes beyond the doctrine that identity sentences involving rigid singular terms are necessary, if true.

Notes

Preface

1. Saul Kripke, *Naming and Necessity* (Cambridge: Harvard University Press, 1980). Originally published in D. Davidson and G. Harman, eds., *Semantics of Natural Languages* (Dordrecht: Reidel, 1972), pp. 253–355. Citations will be to the 1980 edition.

2. Salmon develops his view in *Frege's Puzzle* (Cambridge: MIT Press, 1986), as well as in a number of subsequent articles.

3. Hilary Putnam, "The Meaning of Meaning," in K. Gunderson, ed., *Language, Mind and Knowledge*, Minnesota Studies in the Philosophy of Science, no. 7 (Minneapolis: University of Minnesota Press, 1975). Reprinted in *Mind, Language and Reality*, vol. 2 of Putnam's *Philosophical Papers* (Cambridge: Cambridge University Press, 1975).

Chapter 1

1. Boldface italics are used as corner quotes.

2. For a discussion of nondescriptionality, see Nathan Salmon, *Reference and Essence* (Princeton, N.J.: Princeton University Press, 1981), chapter 1.

3. In *Naming and Necessity*, Kripke avoids any talk of propositions, and makes no explicit positive theoretical commitments concerning the semantic contents of sentences containing names, the objects of propositional attitudes such as belief, or the semantics of attitude ascriptions. Nevertheless, it is hard to see how he can avoid the challenge posed by this argument. He repeatedly talks about "statements," "truths," "identity statements," sentences "expressing" necessary truths, contingent truths, a priori truths, a posteriori truths, and so on. Thus, it seems evident that he thinks there are things expressed by sentences that are capable of being known, either a priori or a posteriori, and which may be true or false, either necessarily or contingently. Since this is what propositions are standardly intended to be, much of Kripke's informal discussion can be understood as implicitly involving propositions while avoiding, as far as possible, definite theoretical commitments about what proposi-

tions are and precisely how they figure in the semantics of different linguistic constructions.

4. Kripke, *Naming and Necessity*, pp. 100–105.

5. Kripke, *Naming and Necessity*, pp. 103–104.

6. The idea for filling in the gap in Kripke's argument along roughly these lines was suggested to me by my student Michael Nelson, in a graduate seminar at Princeton jointly offered by David Lewis and me in the spring term of 2000.

7. The sentences mentioned in the principle are restricted to unambiguous sentences that do not contain any indexicals or other context-sensitive expressions. In the discussion that follows, the language from which the sentences are drawn is English when we actual speakers are being considered, and a slight variant of English—in which *Hesperus* and *Phosphorus* may have referents different from those they actually do—when considering agents in Kripke's qualitatively identical possible world.

8. Saul Kripke, "A Puzzle About Belief," in A. Margalit, ed., *Meaning and Use* (Dordrecht: Reidel, 1979), pp. 239–283. Reprinted in Nathan Salmon and Scott Soames, eds., *Propositions and Attitudes* (New York: Oxford University Press, 1988).

9. This argument depends on strong disquotational principles for French and English, together with the apparently innocuous claims (i) that *Pierre croit que Londres est jolie* and *Pierre believes that London is pretty* are translations of one another and (ii) that sentences that are translations of one another cannot differ in truth-value.

10. In such a case, the individual i satisfies $\exists p\ x$ *knows that* (S_1 *expresses p and* S_2 *expresses p*), but i does not satisfy *x knows that* $\exists p$ (S_1 *express p and* S_2 *expresses p*). Note that in the case of Pierre, a similar point holds about reference: $\exists x$ Pierre knows that ('Londres' refers to x and 'London' refers to x), but Pierre does not know that $\exists x$ ('Londres' refers to x and 'London' refers to x). For a discussion of cases like this, see Scott Soames, "Direct Reference, Propositional Attitudes, and Semantic Content," *Philosophical Topics* 15 (1987): 47–87; reprinted in Salmon and Soames, *Propositions and Attitudes*. Further relevant discussion can be found in Stephen Reiber, "Understanding Synonyms Without Knowing That They Are Synonymous," *Analysis* 52 (1992): 224–228.

11. Nathan Salmon, "A Millian Heir Rejects the Wages of *Sinn*," in C. A. Anderson and J. Owens, eds., *Propositional Attitudes: The Role of Content in Logic, Language, and Mind*, (Stanford, Calif.: CSLI, 1990), pp. 215–247, at 220–222.

12. Kripke's official position in "A Puzzle About Belief" regarding the strong disquotational principle, as well as a variety of related issues, is agnostic. The aim of the paper is to show that disquotational principles, sometimes

alone and sometimes together with apparently innocent principles involving translation from one language to another, give rise to puzzling and sometimes clearly unacceptable results. Since Kripke sees these principles as also playing a crucial role in the derivation of parallel counterintuitive results about attitude ascriptions from the Millian doctrine that the meaning (semantic content) of a proper name is its referent, he argues that such results cannot be properly attributed to the Millian doctrine, and should not be held against it. As for the disquotational principles themselves, Kripke admits that they should be regarded as questionable, at least as applied to certain difficult cases. And surely the most questionable of these is strong disquotation, since it gives rise to genuine contradictions. By contrast, weak disquotation (which incorporates only the left-to-right direction of the strong principle) leads not to contradiction but, in the case of Pierre, only to the claim that he has contradictory beliefs which he is not in a position to recognize as contradictory (in virtue of understanding and accepting both *Londres est jolie* and *London is not pretty*).

In light of all this, it would seem to be Kripke's considered view that strong disquotation cannot be assumed to be true, in which case it cannot be used to fill the gap in his argument at the end of lecture 2 of *Naming and Necessity*. What his views were on this matter at the time he gave the lectures is harder to determine. Certainly he then assumed that substitution of coreferential names in attitude ascriptions sometimes failed to preserve truth, even though nine years later, in "A Puzzle About Belief," he thought that no conclusion, positive or negative, could properly be drawn about this.

13. Less problematic examples of the necessary a posteriori are provided by necessary non-identities, such as *Mars is not Hesperus* and *Brian Soames is not Scott Soames*.

14. Kripke, *Naming and Necessity*, p. 139.

15. Kripke, *Naming and Necessity*, p. 140. Emphasis added.

16. Saul Kripke, "Identity and Necessity," in M. Munitz, ed., *Identity and Individuation* (New York: New York University Press, 1971), p. 162 (see also footnote 17). Emphasis added. The discussion in "Identity and Necessity" (and *Naming and Necessity*) is informal, and there is some unclarity about precisely which expressions are being characterized as rigid designators, and precisely which identity statements are being characterized as necessary, if true. In his brief discussion of this issue, Kripke sometimes seems to be using 'pain,' and variants like 'my pain,' as singular terms, designating either an individual pain or the general phenomenon of pain, or even property of being pain. At other times, however, he seems to use 'pain,' 'c-fiber stimulation,' and variants of these as predicates of individual things—in particular, of particular sensations and brain states. It appears that he wishes to characterize all of these expressions as rigid, and all of the relevant identity statements as necessary, if true. At any rate he does not carefully distinguish among them, even though the

form of the relevant "identity statements" will differ, depending on whether singular terms or predicates are involved. Whatever his exact intentions may have been concerning these matters, the passages can easily be read in an expansive way, as assuming that whatever grammatical type may be involved, identity statements involving rigid designators are necessary if true.

17. For purposes of this book, I will take singular terms to include proper names; demonstratives such as 'I' 'you,' and 'today'; individual variables or pronouns functioning as such; and functional expressions such as '2+3.' Although singular definite descriptions are more naturally viewed as quantifier phrases, I sometimes find it convenient to speak of them as if they were singular terms, which they superficially appear to be. In this connection, I will speak of a description designating (or denoting) an object iff the object uniquely satisfies the description. This informal assimilation of singular definite descriptions to the broader class of singular terms is solely a matter of convenience and fidelity to Kripke's text. It should not be taken as inconsistent with an analysis of descriptions as generalized quantifiers, along the same lines as *all F's, some F's, most F's, each F, and at least one F.*

As to the definition of rigidity for singular terms attributed to Kripke above, the passage closest to it is found on page 146 of "Identity and Necessity." There Kripke says that if a term is a rigid designator of an object, "in any possible world where the object in question *does* exist, in any situation where the object *would* exist, we use the designator in question to designate that object. In a situation where the object does not exist, then we should say that the designator has no referent and [or] that the object in question so [though] designated does not exist." The final sentence in this passage seems confused. If "the designator has no referent," how can there be such a thing as the object "so designated"? The sentence would make more sense if *or* were substituted for *and*, and *though* were substituted for *so* (as indicated by the square brackets I have inserted). Kripke himself has suggested that the presence of *and* rather than *or*, and of *so* rather than *though*, in the passage may be the result of a mistranscription of the lecture. (See David Kaplan's report of this matter in "Afterthoughts," in J. Almog, J. Perry, and H. Wettstein, eds., *Themes from Kaplan* [New York: Oxford University Press, 1989], footnote 8). I have no way of determining whether or not there was such a mistranscription. However, it does seem clear that in the original lectures Kripke was not much concerned with the question of whether certain kinds of rigid designators, in particular proper names, designate their referents even in worlds in which the objects don't exist, or whether, like rigid definite descriptions of contingent objects, names fail to designate anything at all in worlds in which the objects they actually designate don't exist. For this reason the best course seems to be to adopt a characterization of rigidity that is neutral on this score. This is what I have attributed to Kripke.

18. Kripke, *Naming and Necessity*, p. 127. Emphasis added.

19. Kripke, *Naming and Necessity*, p. 134.

Chapter 2

1. For further examples of this type, see Kripke's discussion of the *Feynman* and *Einstein* examples in *Naming and Necessity*, pp. 80–82.

2. Kripke discusses examples of this type in *Naming and Necessity*, pp. 83–85. See his discussion of *Godel/Schmidt*, *Peano/Dedekind*, and *Columbus*.

3. Gareth Evans describes such a case in his discussion of the name *Madagascar* in "The Causal Theory of Names," Proceedings of the *Aristotelian Society* supp. vol. 47 (1973): 187–208. For an illuminating discussion of this example and the general phenomena of reference change, see Alan Berger, "A Theory of Reference Transmission and Reference Change," *Midwest Studies in Philosophy* 14 (1989).

4. See Kripke, *Naming and Necessity*, pp. 93–94, and 96–97.

5. This is a slight simplification of Kripke's own characterization of rigidity. According to Kripke, a singular term t rigidly designates an object o iff t designates o in all worlds in which o exists, and never designates anything other than o in any world. Kripke's cautious formulation leaves room both for rigid designators of o that designate o even in worlds in which o does not exist, and for rigid designators of o that fail to designate anything in worlds in which o does not exist. Except where explicitly indicated in the text, the distinction between these two types of rigid designators will not be relevant to our discussion.

6. Perhaps it would have been better if, in the development of "possible world semantics," the word 'world' had been reserved for the existing concrete universe, and the phrase 'possible state of the world' had been used to designate maximally complete properties that the universe could have had. Had this terminology been adopted, we would have spoken of claims being true or false relative to *possible states of the world*, rather than relative to the misleadingly shortened *possible worlds*. Though I won't (consistently) adopt this revisionary terminology in the text, the reader is invited to use it to interpret the standard locutions used there.

7. In order to properly understand the thesis that *Aristotle* is a rigid designator, one must clearly understand how the following two claims are reconciled.

(i) The name *Aristotle* is a rigid designator. Thus, for all possible states of the world w, the name *Aristotle* refers to the same individual—the man Aristotle—in, or at, or with respect to w.

(ii) It is not a necessary truth that Aristotle was named 'Aristotle.' Thus, it could have been the case that the name *Aristotle* did not refer to

Aristotle, which means that there is some world-state w such that
the claim that the name *Aristotle* did not refer to Aristotle is true in,
or at, or with respect to w.

As Kripke would be the first to insist, these claims are both true. At first glance,
this might seem puzzling because they might seem to be inconsistent. In fact,
they are not. What makes (i) and (ii) seem inconsistent is the tendency to
tacitly accept (iii) as something so obvious as to go without saying.

(iii)   The three-place relation _____ *refers to* _____ *in, at, or with respect
to* _____ holds between the name 'Aristotle,' the man Aristotle, and
the world-state w iff it is true in, or at, or with respect to w that the
two-place relation _____ *refers to* _____ holds between 'Aristotle'
and Aristotle—that is, iff the claim that 'Aristotle' refers to Aristotle is true when taken as a description of w.

Although (iii) might at first seem undeniable, it is false. The three-place
relation _____ *refers to* _____ *in, at, or with respect to* _____ holds between a
name n, an object o, and a world-state w iff **n, as used by us here and now
in the actual world, refers to the object o, when our words are taken as
descriptions of w**. Because of this, n may refer to o with respect to w even if
(a) in, at, or with respect to w there is no name n; or (b) in, at, or with respect
to w the name n is not used by speakers to refer to anything; or (c) in, at, or
with respect to w, n is used by speakers to refer to something other than o.
What, if anything, speakers in w use the name n to refer to is irrelevant to
whether n refers to o with respect to w. However, what speakers in w use n to
refer to is crucial to determining which pairs of names and objects the two-
place relation _____ *refers to* _____ applies to with respect to w. **It is true with
respect to w that the name n refers to the object o iff speakers in w use n
to refer to o.** Thus, what (ii) says is that there are world-states w such that the
speakers in those world-states do not use 'Aristotle' to refer to Aristotle. This
is compatible with the claim made by (i)—namely, that the name 'Aristotle,'
as we use it here and now in the actual world-state, refers to the man Aristotle
when our words are taken as descriptions of any world-state whatsoever.

8. This strategy was suggested by Michael Dummett in *Frege: Philosophy
of Language* (New York: Harper & Row, 1973), pp. 110–151. He also defends
a variant of the strategy in chapter 9 and appendix 3 of his *The Interpretation
of Frege's Philosophy* (London: Duckworth, 1981). The initial (1973) variant
of the strategy maintains that the thesis that names are rigid designators is just
the thesis that they take wide scope over modal operators (see in particular pp.
128 and 134). In response to Kripke's criticism in the preface of *Naming and
Necessity*, Dummett (1981) presents a second variant of the view, which acknowledges that rigidity and wide scope are alternative theoretical notions used
by semantic theorists to account for pretheoretic semantic facts and intuitions.

What is common to the two variants is the claim that all genuine pretheoretic semantic facts and intuitions bearing on the dispute can be accommodated by treating names as nonrigid descriptions that take wide scope over modal expressions.

A more recent version of the wide-scope position is given by David Sosa in chapter 3, "Russell and Rigidity," of his dissertation, "Representing Thoughts and Language" (Princeton University, 1996).

9. This strategy is discussed sympathetically by Jason Stanley in section V of his "Names and Rigid Designation," in Bob Hale and Crispin Wright, eds., *A Companion to the Philosophy of Language* (Oxford: Blackwell Press, 1997), pp. 555–585.

10. In discussing the wide-scope analysis, I will employ formal representations in which definite descriptions are restricted quantifiers, the scopes of which, like those of other quantifiers, are the formulas to which they are immediately prefixed.

11. To say that a name is synonymous with a wide-scope description is to say that arbitrary sentences containing the name semantically express the same propositions as corresponding sentences in which the description is substituted for the name and given the appropriate wide scope. This point can also be put in terms of the distinction between "assertive content" and "ingredient sense" drawn by Michael Dummett, in his *Frege: Philosophy of Language*, pp. 446–447, and *The Interpretation of Frege's Philosophy*, pp. 572–573. Roughly speaking, the assertive content of a sentence (in a context of utterance) is the proposition semantically expressed by the sentence (in that context), while the ingredient sense is what the sentence contributes to the assertive contents of larger sentences in which it may be embedded. Dummett claims that there are natural examples in which two sentences, S_1 and S_2, have the same assertive content (express the same proposition) in a context of utterance, but have different ingredient senses because *Operator S_1* and *Operator S_2* have different assertive contents (semantically express different propositions) in the relevant context. Phrased in these terms, when I say that according to the wide-scope analysis, names are synonymous with wide-scope descriptions, I am making a claim about the assertive contents of sentences, not about the ingredient senses of sentences or expressions.

12. Where the names *Hesperus* and *Phosphorus* are (semantically) associated with the codesignative descriptions *the heavenly body seen (at a certain place and season) in the evening* and *the heavenly body seen (at a certain place and season) in the morning*, respectively, descriptivists conclude that the ascriptions *Jones believes that Hesperus is so and so* and *Jones believes that Phosphorus is so and so* may have different truth-values since it is possible to believe that the heavenly body seen (at a certain place and season) in the evening is so and so without believing that the heavenly body seen (at a certain

place and season) in the morning is so and so (and vice versa). However, since the heavenly body seen (at a certain place and season) in the evening is in fact the heavenly body seen (at a certain place and season) in the morning, the modal sentences *necessarily Hesperus is so and so* and *necessarily Phosphorus is so and so* must have the same (actual) truth-value. That is, since the object which, in the actual world, is both the unique heavenly body seen (at a certain place and season) in the evening and the unique heavenly body seen (at a certain place and season) in the morning, either that object is necessarily so and so (in which case both modal sentences are true) or it is not necessarily so and so (in which case both are false).

13. Since descriptions are often capable of taking different scopes over other operators, S(d) will sometimes express different propositions, depending on the scope of the description—when S(x) is nonatomic. In many cases these scope differences will be irrelevant to my purposes. For this reason, I will adopt a further proviso in the discussion that follows: unless otherwise indicated, an occurrence of a description corresponding to a name that is not required to take wide scope over a modal operator in the same sentence will be interpreted as taking the smallest possible scope. This proviso is heuristic, and is adopted to reduce the number of ambiguities we will have to consider in the examples that follow. This reduction will not affect the force of the criticisms to be developed, since in each case the problem will be that the analysis assigns certain interpretations to sentences, or sequences of sentences, that they do not, in fact, have.

14. See Kripke, *Naming and Necessity*, pp. 48–49, and p. 62, note 25. If pressed, one might force nonliteral, or metaphorical, interpretations on these sentences according to which they convey the claims that Aristotle need not have played the Aristotle role (done the salient things we associate with him), and someone other than Aristotle could have played that role (done those things). But these are forced pragmatic interpretations with different contents in different contexts (depending on what features of Aristotle we are attending to), not different propositions semantically expressed by an ambiguous sentence.

15. For an illustrative comparison, see David Kaplan's construal of *Ralph believes that* as a "shifty" operator in section V of "Opacity," in Lewis Edwin Hahn and Paul Arthur Schilpp, eds., *The Philosophy of W. V. Quine* (La Salle Ill.: Open Court, 1986), pp. 229–289.

16. The parenthetical remark indicates that I here make the assumption that the proposition denoted by *the proposition that Fx*, and expressed by *Fx*, with respect to an assignment of o as value of 'x,' is the singular, Russellian proposition that predicates the property expressed by F of o. Other choices are theoretically possible, but this is by far the most natural and straightforward. Although I believe the choice to be correct, and will maintain the assumption throughout, the overall argument against the wide-scope analysis does not crucially depend on it.

17. The argument given in this section applies to several positions in the literature, including the two variations of Dummett's views mentioned in note 8. In the preface to *Naming and Necessity* (1980), Kripke criticized the identification of rigidity with wide scope by Dummett (1973); acknowledged that some intuitions about the truth-values of modal sentences containing names can be accounted for either by treating names as rigid or by treating them as nonrigid, wide-scope descriptions; and argued that we nevertheless have pretheoretic semantic intuitions about the modal profile of (the propositions expressed by) sentences containing names that cannot be accounted for by the wide-scope analysis. In Appendix 3 of *The Interpretation of Frege's Philosophy*, Dummett responds. He admits that according to the wide-scope analysis, names are not rigid (pp. 594–595), and he maintains that the only genuinely pretheoretic semantic intuitions bearing on his dispute with Kripke concern the conditions under which assertive utterances of sentences express truths. Claims about the modal profile of sentences (relative to contexts)—that is, about the truth-value at alternative possible worlds of that which a sentence expresses (in a context)—are decreed not to be directly testable by appeal to pretheoretic intuition, but to be matters of theoretical choice (see, e.g., p. 582). For Dummett this means that we have no pretheoretic intuitions that we can bring directly to bear on the question "Is (that which is expressed by) S true, at all worlds, some worlds, or a certain world w?" Rather, the best we can do is appeal to intuitions that bear on the different, but related, question "Is it the case that *necessarily S*, *possibly S*, *or at world w*, *S* is true?" He asserts that when intuitions are restricted in this way, the wide-scope analysis can explain all of the genuinely pretheoretic semantic intuitions that the rigidity thesis can account for (see pp. 577–579). The argument involving (I) given above indicates that this claim is incorrect, provided that there is a description, *the G*, that gives the content of the name. In that case, the wide-scope analysis will characterize as invalid inferences classified as valid by pretheoretic intuitions (about the conditions under which various sentences express truths) that Dummett presumably deems to be legitimate.

The argument also refutes a different, and more restricted, thesis advocated by Gareth Evans in "Reference and Contingency," *The Monist* 62, no. 2 (April 1979): 161–189, reprinted in his *Collected Papers* (Oxford: Clarendon Press, 1985), pp. 178–213. There Evans is concerned with the special case in which the referent of a name, n, is semantically fixed to be the denotation of a description, *the G*, that is used in a stipulative introduction of the name. Evans argues that in this sort of case (i) and (ii) have the same content—in my terminology, semantically express the same proposition (*Collected Papers*, p. 181).

   i.   If there was a unique G, then the G was G.
   ii. If there was a unique G, then n was G.

Evans notes that there is an obvious objection to this view, which he credits to Kripke. Since the proposition expressed by (i) is necessary and the proposition expressed by (ii) is not, the two sentences cannot express the same proposition (*Collected Papers*, p. 182). Evans responds to this objection as follows: "I agree that sentences containing names embed differently under modal operators than do sentences containing descriptions, but it is perhaps the main point of this paper that the conclusion which Kripke draws from this fact follows only upon a questionable view of the connection between the content of an utterance and its modal properties" (p. 182). Evans then goes on to sketch a semantic theory according to which sentences are assigned both contents (which serve as objects of propositional attitudes) and conditions under which the sentences are true at arbitrary possible worlds (which serve as the arguments for modal operators). It is further maintained that sentences may have the same contents (express the same proposition) even though they are associated with different conditions for being true at arbitrary worlds. Because of this, Evans argues that (i) and (ii) can express the same proposition even though (iii) and (iv), which differ only in the substitution of (ii) for (i), have different truth-values.

   iii.   It is necessarily true that if there was a unique G, then the G was G.
   iv.   It is necessarily true that if there was a unique G, then n was G.

The argument involving (I) given in the text—which is essentially just a reworking of Kripke's original objection to Evans—shows that this is incorrect, assuming, as I do, that *it is necessarily true that S, that S is necessarily true*, and *the proposition that S is necessarily true* are equivalent. Like Dummett, Evans gives an empirically incorrect account of the semantics of English, since his position wrongly characterizes certain intuitively valid arguments as invalid. (There are a number of other important errors and confusions in Evans's discussion, some of which are pointed out in my review of his *Collected Papers*, in *Journal of Philosophy* 86, no. 3 [1989]: 141–156, at 148–150.) It should also be noted that although Kripke's original objection to Evans's claim that (i) and (ii) express the same proposition is correct, his own discussion in *Naming and Necessity* contains the seeds of Evans's confusion on this point. There Kripke seems to suggest that one could know the proposition expressed by (ii) a priori, on the basis of a reference-fixing definition of the name. This was naturally taken by many to indicate that knowing the proposition expressed by (i) and knowing the proposition expressed by (ii) come to pretty much the same thing. From here it seemed a short step to identifying the two propositions. My own view is that (ii) is not knowable a priori. See my review of Evans. See also Keith Donnellan, "The Contingent Apriori and Rigid Designators," in P. A. French, T. E. Uehling, Jr., and H. K. Wettstein, eds., *Contemporary Perspectives in the Philosophy of Language* (Minneapolis: University of Minnesota Press, 1979); and Nathan Salmon, "How to Measure the Standard

Metre," *Proceedings of the Aristotelian Society* new ser. 88 (1987/1988): 193–217.

The argument in the text involving (I) also provides strong support for the rigidity thesis RT, questioned by Stanley in "Names and Rigid Designation," and in his "Rigidity and Content," in Richard Heck, ed., *Language, Thought and Logic: Essays in Honor of Michael Dummett* (Oxford University Press, Oxford, 1997).

> RT. The rigidity of proper names demonstrates that utterances of sentences containing proper names, and utterances of sentences differing from those sentences only in containing nonrigid descriptions in place of proper names, differ in content. [In my terminology: The rigidity of proper names demonstrates that the proposition expressed by a sentence containing a name, relative to a context, differs from the proposition expressed, relative to the same context, by a corresponding sentence in which a nonrigid description is substituted for the name.]

If this principle were false, then for some name and description, we would have (i) and (ii) of the intuitively valid argument (I) characterized as true, while (iii) was characterized as false. Since any semantic theory leading to this result is inadequate, no adequate semantic theory of English falsifies RT.

18. See Michael Dummett, *Frege's Philosophy of Language*, appendix to chapter 5, especially pp. 135–137.

19. Dummett holds (i) that, typically, an ordinary proper name does not have the content of any single description; (ii) that it makes no **intuitive** sense to ask about the modal profile of (the proposition expressed by) a sentence containing a name; and (iii) that our intuitions are restricted to assessing the truth-values of sentences in which names are embedded under modal operators. As will be seen, this position, like the slightly more extreme doctrine presented in the text, provides no effective means of avoiding criticisms of the sort illustrated by (I) above.

20. Premise P1a is best thought of as a premise schema, instances of which are gotten from substituting particular names for 'n' and particular predicates for 'F.' For purposes of the argument, claims (1) and (2) should also be thought of as schemata. Many of the arguments in the text may be understood in this way.

21. As before, the premises and conclusions of this argument are schemata.

22. See, for example, the early views of Dummett, discussed in notes 8 and 17. See also my criticism of Gareth Evans's discussion of so-called E-type pronouns, in my review of his *Collected Papers*, pp. 145–146.

23. As before, it is not essential to the argument that there be a descriptive phrase in English expressing the descriptive sense attributed to the name. However, the argument is more simply presented if we assume that there is such a phrase.

24. I assume here that C involves quantification over objects of assertion—that is, propositions, or, in Dummett's terminology, the assertive contents of sentences (in contexts). The argument could, of course, be restated slightly to bring this out.

P1. Bill asserted the proposition that if n exists, then n is F.
P2. The proposition that if n exists, then n is F, is necessarily true.
C. Bill asserted a proposition that is necessarily true.

I assume that English sentences like C cannot be represented adequately by standard substitutional quantification into sentential position. See Mark Richard, *Propositional Attitudes* (Cambridge: Cambridge University Press, 1990), pp. 75–78, for a brief sketch of some of the problems facing attempts to treat apparent instances of objectual quantification over propositions in English substitutionally.

25. It may be noted that the wide-scope analysis, as I have stated it, does not require the descriptions associated with occurrences of n in P1 to take narrow scope. If both are given wide scope over the propositional attitude verb, then, it could be argued, P1 and P2 may both be true while logically entailing C. Thus the wide-scope analysis allows a reading in which the argument from P1 and P2 to C is sound. However, it also allows a reading of P1 in which both occurrences of n take smallest scope—surely the natural reading according to the analysis. When P1 is read in this way, the argument from P1 and P2 to C is wrongly characterized as invalid; there simply is no semantic interpretation of this sequence of English sentences in which they are understood in this way. Strictly speaking, the wide-scope analysis allows for a number of other readings of P1 as well. In principle, one occurrence of n can take wide scope relative to the propositional attitude verb while the other takes small scope relative to that verb; and when either occurrence takes small scope relative to the attitude verb, it can take wide or narrow scope relative to the conditional operator in the complement clause. Thus the analysis takes P1 to be many ways ambiguous (on all but one of which the argument from P1 and P2 to C is characterized as invalid). Surely the English sentence is not multiply ambiguous in this way (and the argument itself is not invalid on a multitude of different semantic interpretations).

26. Like the argument based on (I) above, this argument also applies to the other positions mentioned in note 17.

27. The point made in note 23 applies here as well.

28. More precisely, the wide-scope analysis requires one of the occurrences of n to take wide scope over the modal operator, while allowing the other occurrence of n to remain within the scope of the attitude verb. As we shall see, according to the analysis, this will produce a reading—surely what, on this analysis, must be regarded as the most natural reading—in which (4) and (5) do not express truisms, but rather are simply false. Since (4) and (5) do not have such readings, the analysis is incorrect. It should also be noted that, as stated, the wide-scope analysis allows additional readings, including one in which both occurrences of n are given wide scope over the modal operator. On this reading (4) and (5) may turn out true, but only if the result of substituting occurrences of any coreferential name for the occurrences of n would also be true. Since one of these is within an attitude construction, the descriptivist can't be happy with the consequence that the only reading allowed by the wide-scope analysis on which (4) and (5) are true is a reading on which substitution of arbitrary coreferential names within attitude constructions is guaranteed to preserve truth-value.

29. As before, I assume objectual quantification over propositions; however, here this assumption is not needed for the argument. For example, consider the following version of 4′, in which objectual quantification over propositions has been replaced by substitutional quantification into sentential position: *(the x: Gx)* $\Box$[*(Bill asserts/believes that* [*(the y: Gy) Fy*] *& Fx)* $\supset$ $\exists S$ [*(Bill asserts/believes that S) & S*]]. This sentence is true iff there is a unique individual o that has the property expressed by G, and for all worlds w, if *Bill asserts/believes that* [*(the y: Gy) Fy*] *& Fx* is true at w, with respect to an assignment of o to 'x,' then $\exists S$ [*(Bill believes that S) & S*] is true at w. Let w be a world in which o has the property that F expresses, in which there is a unique object with the property expressed by G but that object does not have the property expressed by F, and in which Bill asserts the proposition expressed by *the G is F*. Then w is a world at which *Bill asserts/believes that* [*(the y: Gy) Fy*] *& Fx* is true (with respect to an assignment of o to 'x'). However, w may also be a world at which $\exists S$ [*(Bill asserts/believes that S) & S*] is false. Suppose that $\exists S$ *(Bill asserts/believes that S)* is true at w, because the substitution instance *Bill asserts/believes that* [*(the y: Gy) Fy*] is true at w. Still, the sentence *(the y: Gy) Fy* (or even the sentence *Fn*) is false at w. (Note that in the previous sentence the description and name are mentioned rather than used, and so cannot, on pain of quantifying into quotes, be given wide scope over 'is false at w.') Hence, according to the wide-scope analysis even the substitutional version of 4′ is false.

30. I am indebted to Mike Thau for drawing my attention to this point.

31. This characterization assumes that the range of the quantifier *the x: Sx* at a world w consists of all and only the things existing at w. If the quantifier is allowed to range not just over objects that exist at w but also over objects that

are merely possible relative to w, then the description will denote the unique possible object that at w satisfies *Sx*. On this possibilist reading of the quantifier, *the x*: *actually Fx* may denote at w the object o denoted at the actual world by *the x*: *Fx* even if o does not exist at w.

32. David Kaplan, "Bob and Carol and Ted and Alice," in K. J. Hintikka, J. Moravcsik, and P. Suppes, eds., *Approaches to Natural Language* (Dordrecht: Reidel, 1973), appendix X; David Kaplan, "Demonstratives," in *Themes from Kaplan*, section IV; Nathan Salmon, *Reference and Essence* (Princeton, N.J.: Princeton University Press, 1981), pp. 32–40.

33. The argument for this conclusion depends on taking sentences containing definite descriptions to make existence claims, and hence on taking the domain of *(the x: Sx)* relative to a world (or circumstance of evaluation) to be a subset of the set of individuals existing at the world (or circumstance). This assumption is explicit in Salmon, "How to Measure the Standard Metre." It is either not made or ignored in David Kaplan, "Afterthoughts," p. 577. If *(the x: Sx)* is given the possibilist interpretation mentioned in note 31, then the argument does not apply.

34. Donnellan, "The Contingent Apriori and Rigid Designators," pp. 54–55.

35. Donnellan's main point was that since knowledge of the proposition expressed by *if n exists, then n is F* is always *de re* knowledge of the referent of n, knowledge of this proposition cannot be a priori even when n is a name that has been introduced by the stipulation that it is to refer (rigidly) to the unique object, if there is one, that has the property expressed by F.

36. Otherwise put, we believe that the proposition that Aristotle was a philosopher is true with respect to the actual world A_w.

37. Equivalently, we believe that the proposition that Aristotle was a philosopher is true with respect to w.

38. In thinking about this argument, it is worth keeping in mind the view of possible worlds expressed earlier. Recall that possible worlds are not different concrete universes, but maximally complete properties that the universe could have instantiated. With this conception of worlds it is no objection to P1 to observe that individuals who believe, with respect to certain merely possible worlds, that Aristotle was a philosopher, and individuals who believe this, with respect to the actual world, believe something about the same concrete universe. This observation may be true, but it doesn't show that the merely possible believers have beliefs about the actual world, since the actual world is not the concrete universe, but rather the way that the universe is. (The observation is incompatible with the bizarre but widespread alternative view of possible worlds according to which they are different concrete universes. On that conception P1 would still be taken to be true, but the observation would simply be denied.)

39. Even in the unlikely case in which there is an agent in some merely possible world who both believes that Aristotle was a philosopher and has some beliefs about the actual world A_w, there is no reason to suppose that included among his beliefs is the belief that whoever was the greatest student of Plato, teacher of Alexander, founder of formal logic, and so on in A_w was a philosopher. (Remember that in the analysis *the F* is the description that we, in the actual world, associate with the name, not necessarily the description that those in other worlds associate with it.)

40. Whether or not we all employ an indexical actuality operator.

41. Kaplan, "Demonstratives."

42. In stating (7) I ignore complications that would result from adding a temporal dimension and taking truth-values to be determined at time/world pairs rather than simply at worlds.

43. It should be noted that although P1 and P2 speak of *de re* beliefs about the actual world—that is, believing of the actual world that it is so and so—the argument for C1 can be made quite general. The general argument does not, strictly speaking, require the beliefs to be *de re*, nor does it depend on the resolution of questions of fine detail about the semantic content of *actual* or *actually*. In explaining this, I will first indicate roughly what I take that semantic content to be, and why, if I am right, believing the proposition semantically expressed by a sentence containing *actual* or *actually* should be seen as having a *de re* belief about the actual world. Next I will explain how, even on alternative accounts of semantic contents and the relevant beliefs, the argument from P1 and P2 to C1 can be reconstructed.

First, the picture I favor. As I indicated above, I follow the standard practice of analyzing the description, *the actual F*, as *the x*: *actually Fx*. Like *necessarily* and *possibly*, the expression *actually* combines with an open or closed sentence S to form a more complex sentence. Semantically, the extensions of these operators (relative to a context C and arbitrary world w) can be regarded as mapping the propositions (or the intensions determined by those propositions) expressed by their sentential arguments (relative to assignments of values to free variables) onto truth-values. The extension of *necessarily* (relative to C and w) maps a proposition p onto truth iff p is true in all worlds that are possible relative to w; the extension of *possibly* (relative to C and w) maps p onto truth iff p is true in at least one world that is possible relative to w; and the extension of *actually* (relative to C and w) maps p onto truth iff p is true at C_w—the "actual" world given by the context. What of the semantic contents of these expressions—that which they contribute to propositions expressed by sentences containing them? A number of alternatives are conceivable; they differ primarily on what, for our purposes, may be regarded as matters of inessential detail. One particularly convenient and straightforward approach takes the semantic contents of these expressions (relative to contexts) to be higher-order properties of propositions. Thus, the content of *necessarily* is the property of being true in all possible worlds; the content of *possibly* is the property of being true in some possible world; and the content of *actually* (relative to a context C) is the property of being true in C_w. On this conception, the proposition expressed by ***the actual F is G*** relative to a context C is, roughly, the proposition that the unique individual x such that the proposition that x is F is true in C_w is G. Here, the "actual" world, C_w, is a constituent of the property of being true in C_w, which in turn is a constituent of the proposition expressed in C by ***the actual F is G***. Because of this, it is natural to take believing that proposition to involve believing something of, or about, C_w—namely, that the unique individual x such that the proposition that x is F is true in, or according to, it is G. The case is analogous to belief in a proposition that attributes the property of being taller than I to my son Greg. Since I am a constituent of the property of being taller than I, which in turn is a constituent of that proposition, believing that proposition involves believing of a certain individual (me) that Greg is taller than that individual. In both of these cases it is plausible to suppose that believing a proposition containing a certain property involves ***de re*** acquaintance with, and belief about, something that is a constituent of that property.

How much of this picture is needed to establish C1? Not much. In order to establish C1, it is sufficient to observe that it is possible to believe that Aristotle was a philosopher without believing anything about the actual world, whereas it is not possible to believe that the actual F was a philosopher without believing anything about the actual world. As far as the argument is concerned, it does not matter whether the proposition believed—the proposition that the actual F was a philosopher—is about the actual world because it describes it in a certain way, or whether it is about the actual world because it directly involves it without describing it. Surely many agents in merely possible worlds believe that Aristotle was a philosopher even though they have neither any direct epistemic acquaintance with the actual world nor any description that uniquely picks out the actual world from among all worlds. Because of this, the argument could be reconstructed without invoking *de re* belief about the actual world at all.

My reason for appealing to *de re* belief in formulating the argument is that I think of *actually* as an indexical like 'I' and 'now' that introduces a designated constituent of the context directly into propositions expressed by sentences containing it. In the case of the singular term 'I,' this constituent, the agent of the context, is the referent of the term. In the case of the sentential operator *actually*, this constituent, the world of the context, is a constituent of the property that is the semantic content of *actually* in the context. What we have just seen is that the argument would work just as well if the semantic content of *actually* were a property one of the constituents of which was not the actual world itself, but a descriptive sense that uniquely picked out that world from all other worlds. In this connection it is worth noting that we may have a description of the actual world that uniquely picks it out—namely, *the maximally complete property that the universe instantiates*. (Let us here waive issues about how many such maximally complete properties are in fact instantiated by the universe.) However, this description picks out different properties (worlds) with respect to different worlds, and so is nonrigid. Because of this, its sense is not a constituent of the content of *actually* with respect to a context. This adds plausibility to the directly referential (indexical) analysis.

Finally, the argument could be maintained even if we abstracted still further from my view of the semantic content *actually*. On my view, the content of *actually* relative to C is the higher-order property of propositions of being true in C_w. One might object to this that all we know for sure is that the content of *actually* (relative to C) is some property that is necessarily coextensive with this property. For all we know, some properties necessarily coextensive with the property of being true in C_w may contain as a constituent neither C_w nor any descriptive component designating C_w. And, it might be maintained, believing a proposition involving one of these properties need not involve believing a proposition about the actual world at all. To this I make two responses. First, we need some plausible account of how one particular property gets to be the semantic content of *actually* relative to C. The view I favor, according to which the property is determined demonstratively (*the property of being true in this world*), gives such an account. If some other property is proposed as an alternative, then we need some equally compelling story of how it gets determined to be the semantic content of *actually* in C. It is not easy to see how this would go. Second, no matter which property P, necessarily coextensive with the property of being true in C_w, is selected as the semantic content of *actually* relative to C, when we consider agents in other merely possible worlds, it is hard to see how they could be assured to have the epistemic acquaintance with P needed to believe propositions containing it. After all, P is a property that is intimately related to C_w; it is necessarily coextensive with the property of being true in C_w. Surely arbitrary agents in arbitrary worlds, including some who believe that Aristotle was a philosopher, are not routinely acquainted with P, nor with any property necessarily coextensive with the property of being true in C_w. This is all that is needed to establish C1.

44. More precisely, the descriptivist's primary motivation would be lost if he were now to maintain that even though the semantic content of *Aristotle* is the same as *the F in C_w*, this content plays no role in determining the truth conditions of α *believes that Aristotle was G*. Conceivably, the descriptivist could reject the principle that expressions with the same content are always intersubstitutable in attitude constructions by appealing to something in addition to semantic content to block substitution. For example, he might maintain

that an ascription, α *believes that S*, reports a relation between a believer and a thing believed, where the latter is conceived of as a complex consisting of the semantic content of S plus something else. Since on this view the semantic content of S plays a substantial (though partial) role in determining the truth conditions of α *believes that S*, it follows that α *believes that Aristotle was G* is true at a world w only if the referent of α at w bears a substantial epistemic relation to the semantic content: the F in C_w was G. But then, the same considerations that gave us C1 can be invoked to show that, in fact, it is possible to believe that Aristotle was G without bearing the necessary epistemic relation to the content: the F in C_w was G. Hence a version of the original argument, sufficient to falsify the analysis of *Aristotle* has an *actually*-rigidified description, can be constructed without invoking the principle of substitutivity for expressions with the same semantic content in attitude ascriptions. All that is necessary for the argument is that semantic content play some substantial role in the determination of the truth conditions of these ascriptions. Since the descriptivist cannot afford to deny this, he cannot avoid the argument.

45. A related argument, similar in spirit to this one, can be found in G. W. Fitch, "Names and the 'De Re-De Dicto' Distinction," *Philosophical Studies* 39 (1981): 25–34. There Fitch considers the view that a proper name like *Cicero* is synonymous with a description *the x: Fx in this world*, where the demonstrative *this world* is treated as a directly referential term whose content in a context is the possible world of the context. On page 30 he argues that this view is incorrect because it wrongly predicts that speakers in trivially and irrelevantly different possible worlds would express different propositions when they utter *Cicero denounced Catiline*. I would like to thank David Braun for pointing this out to me.

46. For further discussion of operators of this general sort, see John Burgess and Gideon Rosen, *A Subject with No Object* (Oxford: Clarendon Press, 1997), pp. 143–144 (and the references cited there).

47. Thanks to David Lewis for pointing out this possibility.

48. Kaplan, "Demonstratives." See also his "Afterthoughts" for a reconsideration of the viability of the *dthat*-operator.

49. Interesting questions arise about the semantic contents of partially descriptive names that lack referents. The theory stipulates that in order for an object to be the referent of such a name, it must both have the property P_D and be determined by one of the ordinary nondescriptive processes of reference determination—such as standing at the end of the historical chain of transmission involving the name—which governs the reference-fixing of names generally. When these conditions are not jointly satisfied by any object, the name fails to refer. What is the semantic content of a sentence containing the name in such cases? In the case in which the nondescriptive reference-fixing process—such as the historical chain of transmission—does not lead to any object,

the content of **n** *is* **F** is the content of [*The* x: **Dx** & **x** = y] **Fx** absent any assignment of an individual to 'y.' In the case in which the nondescriptive reference-fixing process—such as the historical chain of transmission—does lead to an object o, but o doesn't have the property P_D, the content of the sentence **n** *is* **F** is the content of [*The* x: **Dx** & **x** = y] **Fx** relative to an assignment of o to 'y.' For more on the contents of empty names, see the appendix to chapter 3.

50. I here assume without argument that the description is "possibilist" in the sense that its range at a world (and time) is not restricted to the things existing at that world (and time). This issue will be touched on again in chapter 3.

51. In these examples, descriptions are treated as restricted quantifiers, *exist* is a predicate, and *p* is a logically proper name (a pure Millian tag) for the referent of *Princeton University*.

52. What about the rigidity intuitions expressed by the following dialog?

A: Princeton University gives only undergraduate degrees.
B: That's not true. But it would have been, had Princeton remained a
      college and not become a university.

Here, B's remarks are naturally interpretable in a way that makes them true. In order for them to be true, B's use of *it* must refer to a proposition asserted by A that would have been true had Princeton remained simply a college. If *Princeton University* is a partially descriptive name, then that proposition cannot be the one semantically expressed by the sentence A uttered—since according to the theory the proposition semantically expressed can be true at a world only if Princeton is a university at that world. Suppose, however, that A's assertive utterance resulted in the assertion of more than one proposition. In particular, suppose that when one asserts the proposition expressed by [*The* x: **Dx** & **x** = y] **Fx** relative to an assignment of an individual i to the variable 'y', one is also counted as asserting the singular proposition that i is F. (This idea is developed independently in chapter 3.) Applying this idea to the case at hand, we get the result that A's assertive utterance resulted in the assertion of the bare singular proposition that Princeton gives only undergraduate degrees, as well as the assertion of the descriptively richer proposition that the university, Princeton, gives only undergraduate degrees. The referent of B's use of *it* in the dialog is taken to be the former proposition.

53. It is arguable that in order to understand my name, for example, one must know that it designates a sentient being. Similarly, it might be argued that for most names, competence requires that one must associate some very general sortal with it. If this is so, then some highly attenuated version of the partially descriptive theory may turn out to be true for most names. However,

in order to make this plausible, the descriptions must be made so general as to be essentially innocuous. I will touch on this point again in the next chapter.

Chapter 3

1. This view of the meaning of proper names has been defended in the past by me and several other authors, most notably Nathan Salmon in his book *Frege's Puzzle* (Cambridge: MIT Press, 1986), as well as in a number of subsequent articles. While the argument in this chapter is intended to be broadly compatible with these earlier defenses, it seeks to deepen the motivation for the view and render it more plausible by placing it in a broader perspective that illuminates the relationship between the semantic contents of expressions and sentences, on the one hand, and the assertions made, and information conveyed, by utterances of sentences, on the other.

2. This sentence in the text should be understood as a sentence schema, with 's' a schematic letter. In the rest of the paragraph I revert to using 's' as a metalinguistic variable over sentences.

3. The notion of conventional implicature is due to Paul Grice, "Logic and Conversation," reprinted in his *Studies in the Way of Words* (Cambridge: Harvard University Press, 1989).

4. For more on conversational implicature, see Grice, "Logic and Conversation."

5. Grice, "Logic and Conversation," p. 34.

6. I am grateful to Mike Thau for a discussion that helped me come to this general view. He should not, however, be assumed to endorse my conclusions.

7. In chapter 5, I will consider some important additional cases that do not involve metaphor, irony, or sarcasm, in which the normal presumption that the proposition semantically expressed by a sentence is asserted by an utterance of it is defeated by conversational implicatures to the contrary. See in particular discourses (7) and (8), plus note 7.

8. Ignore the contextually sensitive tense operator in (1). No use will be made of it.

9. Of course certain metalinguistic information is commonly conveyed by assertive utterances of (1)—for example, the information that the individual referred to by the name 'Carl Hempel' lived on Lake Lane in Princeton. But that information isn't part of the semantic content of the sentence, since someone who assertively uttered (1) would not commonly intend to communicate, or assert, any metalinguistic claim.

10. The proposition

A.   that someone lived on Lake Lane in Princeton

may well be asserted and conveyed by assertive utterances of (1) in all normal contexts as well. However, presumably the reason that A is asserted is that the singular proposition that says of Mr. Hempel that he lived on Lake Lane in Princeton is asserted and conveyed in all such contexts. If this is right, then the pair consisting of (1) and proposition A does not satisfy SC1, though the pair consisting of (1) and the singular, Russellian proposition about Mr. Hempel does.

What about the pair consisting of (1) and the proposition B

B.   that Carl Hempel existed?

Arguably, one might make the point about (1) and proposition B that was just made about (1) and A. Certainly B is a trivial consequence of something asserted by utterances of (1) in every normal context; and it may well be that B counts as being asserted in these cases. However, it is important to realize that not every trivial consequence of something asserted is itself asserted. For example, when p is asserted and q is any arbitrary proposition, the disjunction of p and q is a trivial consequence of p, but nevertheless it may fail to be one that was asserted in asserting p. So perhaps (1) and B don't even satisfy C+.

There is, I think, a genuine distinction, marked in our ordinary speech, between those trivial consequences of something asserted that must themselves be regarded as having been asserted (e.g., conjuncts of a conjunction) and those that are not so regarded (e.g., arbitrary disjunctions). Although it would be nice to have an explicit and general theory about this, I have none to offer. Fortunately, for present purposes, this doesn't matter much. The important point is that the semantic content of (1), the proposition it semantically expresses, cannot be one that describes Mr. Hempel in a certain way and asserts that whoever satisfies that description lived on Lake Lane in Princeton. Instead, it is reasonable to take the proposition semantically expressed by (1) to be a singular, Russellian proposition about Mr. Hempel.

11. I here ignore the caveat that it may turn out that the semantic content of (1) should be thought of as predicating some extremely general property to Mr. Hempel, such as the property of being some sort of intelligent being.

12. The situation does not change significantly if the proposition includes some extremely general sortal that is associated with both names.

13. As I have argued, the pair consisting of (3) and the singular proposition that predicates identity of Mr. Hempel and Mr. Hempel satisfies constraint C+. It seems clear that if this is right, then the pair also satisfies SC1. Hence, if SC2 is correct, it seems likely that this singular proposition is the semantic content of (3). However, since I regard SC2 as more of a working hypothesis than an established principle or evident fact, I don't want to put too much weight on this particular route to my conclusion. In the case of (3) it might be argued (i) that the proposition that Mr. Hempel existed is asserted by all normal assertive utterances of (3), and (ii) that the explanation of why it is always

asserted is not that the identity proposition that Mr. Hempel was Mr. Hempel is always asserted. If this is right, then both the pair consisting of (3) and the singular, Russellian identity proposition, and the pair consisting of (3) and the existential proposition, satisfy SC1. But then, since these are different propositions that are not both the semantic content of (3), SC2 will be false.

Now I am not convinced of (i) and (ii), so I am not convinced that this is a genuine counterexample to SC2. (See note 10 for worries relevant to (i).) But whether or not SC2 proves to be correct, the identification of the proposition semantically expressed by (3) with the singular, Russellian identity proposition involving Mr. Hempel and Mr. Hempel seems reasonable, once the more familiar descriptive alternatives have been eliminated—as I take them to have been.

I am indebted to Zsofia Zvolenszky for useful correspondence on this point—raised by her in response to a talk I gave on this material at the New School for Social Research Conference on Methods in Philosophy and the Sciences, New York, December 4, 1999.

14. In thinking about this issue, as well as other themes that I have been developing here, I have benefited from discussions with Michael Thau, who developed some similar ideas independently in his Princeton dissertation.

15. In talking of inference here, I don't mean to suggest any conscious or unconscious process of inferring conclusions from premises one consciously or unconsciously represents to oneself and takes to be true. What happens is that a sentence is uttered in a context in which many things are assumed. As a causal result of this, the hearer typically comes to accept (take for granted) a sequence of sentences, and so to believe the propositions they express. The psychological process by which this happens is not something that can be determined by armchair philosophizing. However, we can construct an idealized model whose inputs and outputs correspond to those of the real psychological process. In the idealized model, rational speaker-hearers extract information from utterances by explicitly representing premises and rationally inferring conclusions from them. When we show that the inputs and outputs of the real psychological process match those of the idealized model, we show that our actual methods for gathering information from utterances make sense, and are rationally justified. The account of Gricean conversational implicatures sketched earlier in this chapter is one part of this larger, overall picture.

16. A brief discussion of these points can be found in section III of Scott Soames, "Peacocke on Explanation in Psychology," *Mind and Language* 1, no. 4 (1986): 372–387.

17. See Saul Kripke (the *furze/gorse* example), in "A Puzzle About Belief," in A. Margalit, ed., *Meaning and Use* (Dordrecht: Reidel, 1979), pp. 239–283, reprinted in Nathan Salmon and Scott Soames, eds., *Propositions and Attitudes* (New York: Oxford University Press, 1988), pp. 102–148, at p. 134; Nathan Salmon (the *ketchup/catsup* example) in "How to Become a

Millian Heir," *Nous* 23 (1989): pp. 211–220, at 216–217, and in "A Millian Heir Rejects the Wages of *Sinn*," in C. A. Anderson and J. Owens, eds., *Propositional Attitudes: The Role of Content in Logic, Language, and Mind* (Stanford, Calif.: CSLI, 1990), pp. 215–247; Stephen Reiber, "Understanding Synonyms Without Knowing That They Are Synonymous," *Analysis* 52 (1992): 224–228; and Scott Soames, "Substitutivity," in J. J. Tomson, ed., *On Being and Saying: Essays for Richard L. Cartwright* (Cambridge: MIT Press, 1986), pp. 99–132, in particular sections III, IV, and IX.

18. Typically this is done either by picking up n from others who used it as a name of o and intending to preserve their reference, or by being independently acquainted with o and intending to use n to refer to o.

19. Some might object that individual proper names are associated with rules that both specify their semantic contents and constitute competence conditions grasp of which explains a speaker's understanding of a name. Examples of such rules are

(i)   For all x, 'Saul Kripke' refers to x iff x is Saul Kripke.
(ii) For all x, 'Carl Hempel' refers to x iff x is Carl Hempel.

I have no objection to the claim that someone y who has mastered the names 'Saul Kripke' and 'Carl Hempel' knows, in some sense, that which is stated by these rules. Typically, however, y's mastery of the names is not explained by y's possession of this knowledge; y does not understand the names **because** y has acquired the knowledge. Rather, we attribute the knowledge expressed by these rules to y because y understands the names, knows what it is for an expression to refer to something, and accepts as trivial all instances of the schema *For all x, 'n' refers to x iff x is n*. For more on this, see Scott Soames, "Semantics and Semantic Competence," in *Philosophical Perspectives* 3 (1989): 575–596.

20. See Paul Grice, "Utterer's Meaning and Intentions," in his *Studies in the Way of Words* (Cambridge: Harvard University Press, 1989), at p. 106.

21. Grice, "Utterer's Meaning and Intentions," pp. 110–111. See also Paul Grice, "Utterer's Meaning, Sentence-Meaning, and Word-Meaning," in his *Studies in the Way of Words* at pp. 123–124.

22. Grice, "Utterer's Meaning and Intentions," p. 106.

23. A similar scenario could be produced, with the same moral, without using an identity sentence. For example, suppose I had left the auditorium just before the two officials entered the room. After their announcement, John, who knows me, might rise and say, "Scott Soames just left," with the intention of conveying the information that the man they were looking for just left. Later, someone reporting the incident to a third party could appropriately say, "Two

university officials interrupted the lecture and announced that they were look-ing for Scott Soames. John said [told them] that the person they were looking for had just left."

24. It may even be that propositional attitude verbs of saying—such as *say* and *tell*—are context-sensitive regarding how closely related the semantic contents (in the reporting context) of their complement sentences must be to (the content of) the sentence the agent assertively uttered. Consider the verb *say*, for example. Roughly speaking, *X says that S* is true relative to a context C iff (i) the referent of X assertively uttered a sentence S* in a context C*, and (ii) the proposition semantically expressed by S in C is something reason-ably intended by X to be a potentially direct, immediate, and relevant inference (on the part of the conversational participants in C*) from S* together with the background assumptions presupposed in C*. Suppose further that what counts as directly, immediately, and relevantly inferable from the speaker's utterance plus background information is something that varies to some extent from con-text to context; in some contexts, when reporting the assertions of others, we allow for a fairly expansive conception of the relevant inference, whereas in other contexts we may be very strict, and refuse to count anything except the semantic content of the sentence uttered as having been asserted.

We may illustrate this view as follows: Suppose I assertively utter a sen-tence S* in a context C* that would support an inference of some sort to the proposition expressed by S in context C. Suppose further that someone were to report my remark in C. Depending on whether the inference (on the part of the conversational participants in C*) from S* to the proposition expressed by S in C counts as direct, immediate, and relevant enough, by the standards for evaluating such inferences operative in C, the ascription *Soames said that S* will, or will not, be counted as true in C. If these standards vary from one context to another—for instance, if the standards for correctly reporting what someone has said when one is testifying in a trial are different from, and stricter than, the standards for correctly reporting what one has said in ordinary, informal contexts—then there may be reporting contexts C and C' such that *Soames said that S* has different truth-values in C and C', even though the proposition reported to have been asserted (the proposition semantically ex-pressed by S) is the same in both contexts, and my remark being reported is also the same. If this view is correct, then there should be cases in which the proposition expressed by *Soames said that S* in C is compatible with the prop-osition expressed by *Soames didn't say that S* in C'. In a case like this, what at first might seem to be a factual dispute turns out to be nothing more than the adoption of different discretionary standards regarding how close a proposi-tion must be to the semantic content of the sentence uttered by the agent in order to count as something the agent said.

25. As I have been doing throughout this discussion, I here use the notion of inference in an idealized sense that does not attribute to agents any explicit,

conscious or unconscious, derivation of conclusions from premises the agents represent to themselves and take to be true. For my purposes, it is enough (i) that the process be one in which the hearer's recognition of the sentence uttered in the context causes the hearer to take the speaker to be committed to certain propositions p, and (ii) that this process could be rationally reconstructed as an inference from a description of the speaker's utterance, together with relevant background assumptions, to conclusions about the propositions the speaker is committed to.

26. This is not to say that my hearers would consciously or unconsciously go through this reasoning in interpreting my remark. Standardly, they would just assume that I was talking about our colleague David Lewis. But they could go through such reasoning if doubt were to arise—thus illustrating the salience and relevance to our conversation of the characterization of David as our colleague.

27. The view that sometimes it is determinate that more is asserted by an utterance of *n is F* than the singular, Russellian proposition expressed by the sentence, that this extra assertive information is descriptive in nature, and that it is nevertheless indeterminate precisely what this extra descriptive information amounts to, parallels a familiar descriptivist view about the meanings of proper names. I pointed out in chapter 2 that many descriptivists hold that proper names have descriptive senses that are not identical to the senses of any definite descriptions in the language. In keeping with this, sometimes the alleged descriptive sense of a proper name is said to correspond not to any single description, but to an open-ended and incompletely specified cluster of descriptions. Those who hold this cluster view ought then to hold that the descriptive content of what is asserted by an utterance of a sentence containing a name is to a corresponding degree open-ended, incompletely specified, and perhaps even incompletely specifiable. What we have seen is that something very much like this latter view of assertive content can be separated from the descriptivist's problematic view about semantic content.

A good early source of what one might call the contextually variable, open-ended, cluster view of assertive content is section 79 of Wittgenstein's *The Philosophical Investigations* (Oxford: Basil Blackwell, 1953). There, Wittgenstein comments on our practice of using a name with different (open-ended) descriptive backing in different contexts, and hence without a "fixed meaning." Many later philosophers have taken these comments to provide the inspiration for the cluster theorist's account of the meaning, or sense, of proper names. However, it is instructive to note that Wittgenstein's comments do not themselves take this form. In section 79 he talks about the open-endedness, and contextual variability, of what **the speaker** means by an utterance of a sentence containing a name, while being rather dismissive, and unconcerned, about how one characterizes the meanings of names themselves. Since what a speaker means on a given occasion is closely related to what the speaker intends to say, or assert, on that occasion, Wittgenstein's comments fit the (open-ended and contextually variable) indeterminacy view expressed above in the text rather well.

28. In stating (i)–(iii), I ignore the question of which necessary consequences of p count as being asserted when p is asserted.

29. This example is taken from Paul Grice, "Logic and Conversation" (1967), reprinted in his *Studies in the Way of Words*, at p. 32.

30. For an example of this see note 27.

31. Note that the relationship between the names *Princeton University* and *Princeton New Jersey* is (partially) analogous to the relationship between the names *Bill Clinton* and *Bill Gates*. In both cases we have two different names for two different individuals. In both cases the names are phrases, the first word of which is itself a name that may be used on its own, in certain situations, to refer to the referent of the entire phrase. This fact no more precludes the phrases *Princeton University* and *Princeton New Jersey* from themselves qualifying as names than it precludes the phrases *Bill Clinton* and *Bill Gates* from qualifying as names.

32. In saying that this can be expected, I mean that the conclusion is a natural, though admittedly not inevitable, one to draw from the observation that part of what it is to understand *Princeton University* is to realize that its referent is a university. In light of this it is natural to take the semantic content of the name as including the property of being a university, and the content of assertions made using the name to involve the predication of that property to the referent. There is, however, a conceivable alternative to this. One might maintain that the property of being a university plays a role only in semantically determining the referent of the name (in the world of the context) while being no part of the semantic content of the name or of the assertions made by utterances of sentences containing it. On this alternative, the property of being a university plays no role in determining the referent of the name at other possible worlds, or the semantic content of propositional attitude ascriptions containing the name. Since I believe that the property does play these roles, I regard this alternative view as incorrect. The status of this alternative, as well as certain similar views, will be touched on again, briefly, at the end of chapter 5.

33. As before, I here assume that the description is "possibilist" in the sense that its range at a world (and time) is not restricted to the things existing at that world (and time). A different alternative would be to treat partially descriptive names as sui generis, rather than as making up a special, highly restricted class of descriptions. The alternative I have in mind would stipulate that the semantic content of a partially descriptive name n of an object o is simply a pair consisting of o plus some property (or set of properties). On this

picture the truth conditions of a simple sentence *n is F*, containing a partially descriptive name n, would match the truth conditions assigned that sentence by the partially descriptive theory as stated in the text. If names were allowed to take different scopes in complex sentences, just as ordinary descriptions are, this isomorphism could be extended to complex sentences as well. Since representations involving descriptions are both familiar and useful, I will continue to use them in the text.

34. In contrasting ordinary linguistically simple proper names with partially descriptive names, I am not assuming that all names, or namelike expressions, must be located in one or the other category. In chapter 5 I do endorse the partially descriptive theory for many names. So I do think that there are at least two distinct kinds of names. However, I make no claim about whether or not there might be other kinds of names as well—such as names the semantic contents of which are simply their referents but which are nevertheless semantically associated with descriptive information, either in the form of reference-fixing descriptions or in the form of conventional implicatures.

35. See, in particular, Nathan Salmon, "Existence," in J. Tomberlin, ed., *Philosophical Perspectives*, vol. 1, *Metaphysics* (Atascadero, Calif.: Ridgeview, 1987), pp. 49–108; Nathan Salmon, "Nonexistence," *Nous* 32 (1998): 277–319; Saul Kripke, *Reference and Existence: The John Locke Lectures for 1973* (unpublished manuscript); Peter van Inwagen, "Creatures of Fiction," *American Philosophical Quarterly* 14 (1977): 299–308; and Peter van Inwagen, "Fiction and Metaphysics," *Philosophy and Literature* 7 (1983): 67–77.

36. The "empty names" I consider in this appendix—that is, names that occur in sentences *n does not exist* that express, or are used to assert, truths—will be nondescriptive, linguistically simple names. Although similar considerations apply to partially descriptive names, these considerations must be combined with the points made in note 49 of chapter 2.

37. My discussion of this thesis draws heavily on the thorough and illuminating defense of it given by Nathan Salmon in "Existence" and "Nonexistence," from which I have learned a great deal. Though the picture I present may differ from Salmon's on some ancillary matters, as well as some secondary matters of emphasis and detail, the leading ideas are due to him.

38. The same points apply to any attempt to introduce a name for an object with which one has no acquaintance by supplying a reference-fixing description. No matter whether the object presently exists or not, such a procedure will fail in cases in which the speaker is not sufficiently acquainted with the object uniquely denoted by the description. This requirement of sufficient acquaintance severely restricts the ability of speakers to introduce genuine names by appealing to arbitrary descriptions. Of course, nothing restricts a speaker's ability to introduce an expression as an abbreviation for a description, or for a rigidified version of it. For more on this, see note 39.

39. Either it should be regarded as having no semantic content at all, in which case sentences containing it will be meaningless, or the linguistic ceremony in which it was introduced should be reinterpreted so that *Newman 1* is taken to be an abbreviation—an abbreviation either of the description used to introduce it or of an *actually* rigidified version of that description. A satisfactory resolution of this issue depends on having a general theory of what is accomplished by attempts to stipulate semantic properties of expressions that fail to achieve what they explicitly aim at. Should these attempts be understood as achieving nothing, or should they be taken to achieve something that only approximates that which they explicitly aimed at? Most likely the latter.

40. Nathan Salmon, "Existence," pp. 49–50, 90–96; also "Nonexistence," pp. 286–291; and David Kaplan, "Bob and Carol and Ted and Alice," in K. J. Hintikka, J. Moravcsik, and P. Suppes, eds., *Approaches to Natural Language* (Dordrecht: Reidel, 1973), pp. 490–518, at pp. 516–517, note 19.

41. Nathan Salmon, "Nonexistence"; and Saul Kripke, *Reference and Existence: The John Locke Lectures for 1973*. In addition, see Peter van Inwagen, "Creatures of Fiction" and "Fiction and Metaphysics."

42. Some fictional characters, such as Pierre in *War and Peace*, are purely fictional—they are merely abstract objects that are portrayed in the fiction as having the properties of real people. Other characters in some fictions, such as Napoleon in *War and Peace*, are real people. As I see it, Napoleon himself—the man who actually ruled France—is a character in the novel, where many properties are predicated of him that he didn't actually have. In addition, some characters are doubly fictional—as when a fiction contains within it what is portrayed as another fiction with its own fictional characters. A delightful example of this sort of intricacy is provided by Max Beerbohm's classic short story "Enoch Soames," in his *Seven Men* (London: Alfred Knopf, 1920). Beerbohm himself appears in the story as a character who, we are later led to believe, has written the very story we are reading. He is a fictional character of the second sort, one who is also a real person. By contrast, his main character, Enoch Soames, is purely fictional. Soames is portrayed as a poor, dour, no-talent philosopher whose dreams of being vindicated by posterity lead him to make a deal with the devil (witnessed by Beerbohm) in which he sells his soul for the privilege of being sent 100 years into the future to visit the reading room of the British Museum, where he will be able to learn what impact his works have had on the world. When there, he discovers, to his horror, that the only reference to him is as a fictional character in a short story by Max Beerbohm. It seems that a few years after Soames's deal with the devil, Beerbohm recounted the story, but did such a poor job of writing that it was taken to be a fiction rather than an account of what really happened. Thus, Enoch Soames ends up being a purely fictional character who is portrayed in

the story by Beerbohm as a real person who is mistaken for a purely fictional character.

43. See section VI of "Nonexistence" for Salmon's argument that it does.

Chapter 4

1. See David Kaplan, "Demonstratives," in J. Almog, J. Perry, and H. Wettstein, eds., *Themes from Kaplan* (New York: Oxford University Press, 1989), at pp. 522, 546.

2. This condition could be modified to include the information provided by an extremely general sortal connected with a use of a name. That is, condition (i) might be reformulated so that it stated that when picking up a name from others, it is necessary and sufficient that one both associate it with the same general sortal that they do, and intend to use it to refer to whatever they do. Such a modification would, of course, require a corresponding reformulation of the crucial premise in our argument—one claiming that it is a necessary and sufficient condition for two uses of a name to have the same semantic content, that the two uses both refer to the same object, and that the two uses be associated by the speakers with the same sortal. However, the descriptive information provided by these very general sortals would be extremely modest. It would not come close to determining a unique referent, and it would not play a significant role in standard cases in which one of two coreferential ordinary proper names is substituted for the other. For these reasons I ignore this complicating factor in the text, and continue to speak as if the referent is all there is to the semantic content of an ordinary name. Strictly speaking, however, I do not rule out the possibility of including the information provided by some very general sortal in the semantic content of such a name (as used on a given occasion).

3. David Kaplan expresses the point by saying that knowing the meaning of indexicals involves knowing the relevant rules determining or constraining their reference in a context, and knowing that they are directly referential.

4. See note 19 of chapter 3.

5. Note also that the observations made in the previous paragraph rule out taking the content of 'I' in C to be partially descriptive, along the lines of the content of *the x: x utters this token of 'I' & x = y* relative to an assignment of the speaker in C to 'y.' Thanks to Jim Pryor for noticing this point.

6. More precisely, this proposition is the only proposition p satisfying both (i) and (ii): (i) p's assertion is guaranteed by applying the semantic conventions associated with the sentence to its utterance in the context, and (ii) for any other proposition q satisfying (i), the fact that p satisfies (i) explains the fact that q does so as well, and not vice versa.

7. In this discussion I am considering only the most obvious and straight-forward kinds of indexical expressions—for instance, terms like *I*, *you*, *he*, *today*, and so on. One class of indexical expressions I have not discussed consists of vague predicates, like *bald* or *red*. I believe that these predicates are both context-sensitive and partially defined. See Scott Soames, *Understanding Truth* (New York and Oxford: Oxford University Press, 1999), chapter 7.

In my view, the context sensitivity of a vague predicate consists in its being associated with a family of very closely related partially defined properties. One of these properties represents a sort of default interpretation of the predicate. Its determinate extension is a subset of the determinate extensions of all the other properties in the family, and similarly for its determinate anti-extension. Objects that are not in either its determinate extension or its determinate anti-extension are objects for which the property is undefined. All the other properties in the family associated with the vague predicate differ from one another only in the inclusion of different objects for which the default property is undefined in their determinate extensions or anti-extensions.

One of the ways in which the account of semantic content offered in the text needs to be extended involves the recognition that the semantic content of a vague predicate in a context is not its referent, but a contextually determined property. As with other examples, the semantic content in a context of a sentence containing such a predicate should be a proposition the assertion of which is determined by the application of the competence conditions associated with the sentence to the context in question.

8. The semantic content of (6) in the context includes the semantic content of 'tomorrow' in the context, which is just a certain day—without any information as to where that day falls in the calendar.

Chapter 5

1. Recall that the description is taken to be "possibilist" in the sense that its range at a world (and time) is not restricted to the things existing at that world (and time). See also notes 49 and 52 of chapter 2, and note 33 of chapter 3.

2. I assume that if someone were now my mother, then that person would now be a mother. I further assume that if someone is now a mother, then that person exists now.

3. Another example of this phenomenon is provided by *My first philosophy teacher is dead*. Although the descriptive phrase *my first philosophy teacher* contains no indication of tense, the occurrence of it in this sentence seems to be understood to be equivalent to *the person who was my first philosophy teacher*.

4. She could, I believe, even be correctly addressed *Miss Ruth Marcus*, though that would be a little unusual, and might be stretching things a bit.

5. Can the widow of the late Mr. Jones be correctly designated both as *Mrs. Jones* (because she was married and is now a widow) and as *Miss Jones* (because she is now unmarried)? I suspect so. But if she can't, then some further adjustment of the contents of these terms is needed.

6. Two related examples that seem somewhat puzzling in this regard are *Queen Elizabeth II* and *Willard R. Soames Jr*. What, if anything, is added to the semantic contents of these names by *II*, in the first case, and *Jr.*, in the second? The most natural suggestion seems to be that *II* indicates that the referent of the name is the second queen (in some succession) to be named 'Elizabeth,' and that *Jr.* indicates that the referent is the son of a father named 'Willard R. Soames.' However, it seems unlikely that this information really is part of the semantic contents of the names. If it were, then modal sentences and propositional attitude ascriptions in which these names occurred in the clauses embedded under the relevant operators would have natural readings in which the metalinguistic information associated with these names would be crucial parts of the modal facts or propositional attitudes reported. However, this does not appear to be the case. The contributions of these names to the contents of such sentences seem to be no more metalinguistic than those of ordinary names.

7. This account, which seems quite plausible, raises an issue about principles C+, SC1, and SC2 of chapter 3 (and reformulated versions of them in chapter 4), however. In chapter 3 I argued that the semantic content of a sentence s is a proposition p that is asserted by assertive utterances of s in "normal" contexts in which it is used with its standard literal meaning by speakers who understand it. I pointed out that reference to "normal" contexts is intended to exclude those in which s is used ironically, sarcastically, or metaphorically, as well as those in which the presumption that the speaker is intending to commit himself or herself to p is defeated by conversational implicatures to the contrary. This exception, built into principle C+, is relevant to the characterization of the discourse in (7).

I have suggested that the speaker uses the first sentence in (7), containing the description, to convey, and even assert, something quite different from the proposition semantically expressed by that sentence. Does the speaker also, perhaps secondarily, assert the proposition that the sentence semantically expresses? If so, then in addition to having asserted something true, the speaker may have asserted something false. However, it seems doubtful that this really is so. And if it is not so, what is the explanation of why the proposition that is semantically expressed is not asserted? The answer, I think, parallels what was said about certain cases of irony and metaphor in chapter 3. A speaker who uses *Sam is a fine friend* ironically, in a case in which it is obvious to everyone that Sam is no friend at all, uses the sentence with its literal meaning. However, the normal presumption that the speaker asserts the proposition semantically expressed by the sentence uttered is defeated by an obvious conversational implicature to the contrary. Given that the speaker is obeying the conversational maxim "Speak the truth," and given further that it is obvious that the proposition that Sam (really) is a fine friend is not true, one naturally takes the speaker not to be asserting this proposition, but rather to be asserting something else. The same point was made about *He thinks he is God's fountain pen*. If the pragmatic explanation I have offered of the discourse in (7) is correct, then the same sort of thing is going on in this case as well. In this way, the discourses in (6) and (7) can be squared with principles C+, SC1, and SC2 of chapter 3.

8. A theory along roughly these lines is suggested in C. McGinn, *The Subjective View: Secondary Qualities and Indexical Thoughts* (New York: Oxford University Press, 1983).

9. We are considering here the truth-values, at the alternative possible word described, of the propositions actually expressed by our present uses of these sentences.

10. Suppose one tried to block this result by revising the final clause of the alternative theory of partially descriptive names so that believing the proposition <<D-hood, o>, F-hood> required one to believe of o that it both "was F" and was widely believed to "be D"—without requiring that one believe o to "be D" oneself. On this modification, the claim that Ralph believes something false would not be a necessary consequence of the propositions (12a), (13), and (14); however, the claim that something false is widely believed would be such a consequence. Since this result is just as bad as the original, modifying the alternative theory of partially descriptive names in this way won't help. Similar points could be made regarding other possible modifications of that theory. I am indebted to Jim Pryor for a discussion of this point.

11. To fill out the case, imagine that though Venus was not seen in the evening sky, it was widely believed to be, and that this belief was reflected in the fact that speakers both took *Hesperus* to be a name of Venus and standardly associated the erroneous description with it. If the alternative theory of partially descriptive names were correct, then a speaker understanding the term, while being aware of the real astronomical facts, would understand (15), grasp the proposition it expresses, and recognize that proposition to be true. Hence he ought to be able to assertively utter (15) perfectly coherently and correctly. Since in fact such an utterance would not be coherent and correct, the claim that *Hesperus* is a name of the sort indicated by the alternative theory is wrong.

12. I here presume that since, according to the alternative theory of partially descriptive names, to believe the proposition expressed by (12a) is, in effect, to believe the proposition expressed by (12b) (relative to an appropriate

assignment); to believe the proposition expressed by some sentence S in which (12a) is a subconstituent (e.g., one side of a biconditional) is, in effect, to believe the proposition expressed by S′, where S′ results from S by substituting an occurrence of (12b) for an occurrence of (12a). The alternative would be to suppose that to believe the proposition expressed by some sentence S in which (12a) is a subconstituent is to believe the proposition expressed by S′, where S′ results from S by substituting an occurrence of 'Venus is a planet' for an occurrence of (12a) (where *Venus* is taken to be a nondescriptive name). However, not only is this alternative unnatural, it also would give rise to anomalies of its own. For example, in a situation in which Venus is not visible in the evening, a fully competent, knowledgeable, and reflective speaker should be willing to say, *I believe that Venus is a planet and I believe that Hesperus is a planet iff Venus is a planet, but I do not believe that Hesperus is a planet, since to do that would be to believe something false.* Intuitively, however, such a speaker would not, and should not, be willing to assert this.

13. According to the alternative theory, the proposition expressed by *Hesperus is a planet* is not the singular proposition that simply attributes the property of being a planet to Venus. Thus, in order to assert the former proposition, it is not enough to assert the latter. Presumably one must do something like utter a sentence containing a proper name the semantic content of which matches that of *Hesperus*. But then, assertion being what it is, the speaker in such a case will standardly give the audience reason to think that he or she believes the proposition asserted, and hence believes that Venus is seen in the evening.

14. If (i) (12a) conventionally implicates that Hesperus (i.e., Venus) is visible in the evening sky, and (ii) the proposition semantically expressed by *Ralph believes (asserts) that S* reports that Ralph bears the belief (assertion) relation to a proposition p that is an amalgam of the proposition semantically expressed by S and the conventional implicatures of S, then the counterintuitive results illustrated by (12)–(18) will be repeated. Moreover, the combination of (i) and (ii) gives rise to a further counterintuitive result—namely, that *Ralph asserted that Hesperus is a planet* may be false in a situation in which Ralph assertively uttered *Hesperus is a planet*, and thereby asserted the proposition it semantically expresses. Since, by (i), the claim that Hesperus is visible in the evening sky is merely conventionally implicated, there must be cases in which it is not part of what is asserted by normal assertive utterances of (12a). Suppose we have such a case with Ralph as agent. Then by (ii), the ascription *Ralph asserted that Hesperus is a planet* will be false because it characterizes him as asserting a proposition that includes the implicature that Hesperus (i.e., Venus) is seen in the evening sky. Since this seems wrong, the conjunction of (i) and (ii) must be rejected. A similar problem arises for the combination of (iii) and (iv): (iii) the property of being visible in the evening is not part of the

content of *Hesperus*, but does play a role in semantically determining its referent; (iv) the proposition semantically expressed by ***Ralph believes (asserts) that S*** reports that Ralph bears the belief (assertion) relation to a proposition p that is an amalgam of the proposition semantically expressed by S and the properties used to semantically fix the referents of the expressions in S.

Chapter 6

1. There are other kinds of attitude verbs as well, but those illustrated by (1), (3), and (4) are the only ones that we will consider. When '*' is prefixed to an example, it indicates that the example is ill-formed.

2. Another question yet to be resolved is whether propositional attitude verbs are themselves indexicals in the sense of expressing different relations between agents and propositions in different contexts. I will return to this question at the end of this chapter.

3. For simplicity, I here leave aside assignments of objects to variables, which are needed in the evaluation of attitude ascriptions only when we have "quantifying-in." The extension to these cases is unproblematic.

4. See the discussion of examples (8)–(10) in chapter 3.

5. This is an extension of the Gricean notion of a speaker meaning something by an utterance of a sentence that was appealed to in earlier chapters.

6. See Saul Kripke, "Speaker Reference and Semantic Reference," in P. A. French, T. E. Uehling, Jr., and H. K. Wettstein, eds., *Contemporary Perspectives in the Philosophy of Language* (Minneapolis: University of Minnesota Press, 1977), pp. 6–27.

7. In stating these principles, and those that follow, I ignore complications in their formulation having to do with indeterminacy of content—especially indeterminacy regarding precisely which proposition from a determinate range of propositions a speaker might be using a sentence to assert, or a clause to designate. In the interest of simplicity, I will maintain this policy in subsequent discussion, except when the issue of indeterminacy is especially relevant and requires explicit consideration.

8. This does not mean that the propositions expressed by (9a, b, c) are necessary truths. If the meaning of 'the earth is round' is not one of its essential properties, there may be worlds in which the propositions actually expressed by (9a, b, c) are false.

9. Sentences like (1a), which have the form *t asserts d*, involve the application of a two-place predicate to a pair of arguments which are themselves ordinary names, indexicals, or descriptions. Once it has been settled that x and y are semantically designated (at the world of the context) by those arguments, taking the sentence to **semantically** express a proposition that may be true (at the world of the context) just in case x bears the assertion relation not to y,

but to some other proposition z that the speaker has in mind, would be like saying that the proposition **semantically** expressed by *Mary kissed the man drinking champagne* is true (at the world of the context) just in case Mary kissed not the person y who really is the unique man in the situation drinking champagne, but rather some other person z whom the speaker happens to have in mind (perhaps because the speaker wrongly thinks that z is drinking champagne). This is a position that just about everyone now agrees is untenable. For relevant literature, see Saul Kripke, "Speaker Reference and Semantic Reference"; Nathan Salmon, "Assertion and Incomplete Definite Descriptions," *Philosophical Studies* 42 (1982): 37–45, and "The Pragmatic Fallacy," *Philosophical Studies* 63 (1991): 83–97; Scott Soames, "Incomplete Definite Descriptions," *Notre Dame Journal of Formal Logic* 27 (1986): 349–375, and "Donnellan's Referential/Attributive Distinction," *Philosophical Studies* 73 (1994): 149–168, especially 153–155.

10. In order to simplify the discussion, I put aside here the possibility that the semantic contents of linguistically simple, ordinary names may include very general sortal properties. As before, I take no final position on whether such properties are included in the semantic contents of names. Fortunately, no such position is required for the discussion of substitutivity. Since the properties in question can be expected to be the same for typical pairs of coreferential names, they do not affect the issues discussed here involving substitutivity in attitude ascriptions.

11. Here again, we are treating (13a) and (13b) as they are understood from within the fiction.

12. As before, I leave open the possibility that both names might be associated with the same very general sortal property—for instance, the property of being a sentient being.

13. In characterizing the singular, Russellian proposition expressed by (17a) and (17b) as consisting only of Mr. Hempel and the property of having lived on Lake Lane in Princeton, I am ignoring potential complications that are irrelevant to our discussion. For example, it might be maintained that the Russellian proposition really involves three objects—Mr. Hempel, Lake Lane, and the town of Princeton—plus a three-place relation predicated of them.

14. Michael Thau, *Consciousness and Cognition* (New York: Oxford University Press, 2002).

Chapter 7

1. Richard Larson and Peter Ludlow, "Interpreted Logical Forms," *Synthese* 95 (1993): 305–356, reprinted in Peter Ludlow, ed., *Readings in the Philosophy of Language* (Cambridge: MIT Press, 1997). Citations will be from the reprinted version.

2. Not necessarily its real semantic value. For example, the sentence may not, in fact, be true, and the pair <John, Spanish> may not really be one of the pairs that 'speaks' applies to.

3. Davidson has made two main attempts to justify the claim that a Davidsonian truth theory for a language may play the role of a theory of meaning. According to the first, knowledge of that which is stated by a Davidsonian theory of truth is claimed to be sufficient in order for an agent to learn, and become a competent speaker of, a language. The idea here is that any theory that tells us everything we need to know in order to understand a language may be counted as specifying all essential facts about meaning, even if it does not generate theorems that explicitly state the meanings of individual sentences. In "Truth and Meaning," *Synthese* 17 (1967): 304–323, and "Radical Interpretation," *Dialectica* 27 (1973): 313–328, Davidson claimed that theories of truth of the sort he advocated satisfy this condition, despite the fact that the T-sentences, *'s' is true in L iff p*, entailed by such theories were **not**, at that time, required to be translational in the sense of pairing the object language sentence s with a metalanguage sentence p that is a translation of it. When this claim was proven to be false in J. A. Foster, "Meaning and Truth Theory," in Gareth Evans and John McDowell, eds., *Truth and Meaning* (Oxford: Oxford University Press, 1976), Davidson offered a different justification for taking his theories of truth to be theories of meaning. See Davidson, "Reply to Foster," in *Truth and Meaning*. According to this second attempt at justification, in order to qualify as a theory of meaning, a theory of truth must entail translational T-sentences that pair object-language sentences mentioned on the left with metalanguage paraphrases used on the right. The idea, roughly put, is that knowing both (i) that which is stated by a theory of truth T, and (ii) that T yields a translational T-sentence for each object-language sentence s, should be sufficient for understanding the language. However, this attempted justification has also been proven to be incorrect. For a detailed discussion of the problems with both attempts, see Scott Soames, "Truth, Meaning, and Understanding," *Philosophical Studies* 65 (1992): 17–35.

For purposes of our discussion of Larson and Ludlow, it is important to note that since the T-sentences they derive for attitude ascriptions are not translational, they cannot appeal to any version of Davidson's second attempt to justify the claim that their truth theories should count as a theories of meaning. More generally, until we are given an independent account of the content of the theoretical metalanguage sentences that appear on the right of the T-sentences for attitude ascriptions, there seems to be no prospect for giving any other justification for the claim that a Davidsonian truth theory for a language incorporating their treatment of attitude ascriptions might qualify as a theory of meaning.

4. For a discussion of how this problem faced by Larson and Ludlow applies to semantic theories of attitude ascriptions that identify objects of the

attitudes with sets of possible worlds, or structured propositions, see Scott Soames, "Truth and Meaning: The Role of Truth in the Semantics of Propositional Attitude Ascriptions," in K. Korta and J. M. Larrazabal, eds., *Proceedings of the Seventh International Colloquium on Cognitive Science* (Dordrecht: Kluwer, forthcoming).

5. For example, on page 1002 of "Interpreted Logical Forms," Ludlow and Larson say the following: "The assumption that ILFs [interpreted logical forms] are composed of linguistic forms and extra-linguistic objects yields straightforward individuation criteria for ILFs. Two ILFs will be distinct whenever they contain distinct forms or distinct objects. This in turn yields straightforward criteria for distinguishing attitude reports. Two attitude reports will be logically nonequivalent whenever their complement clauses are associated with ILFs that differ either in form or content." Note that in saying that attitude ascriptions containing different linguistic forms are logically nonequivalent, they seem to be saying that it is genuinely possible for one to be true when the other is not. They might, of course, argue that logical possibility is one thing and metaphysical possibility is another. However, it is not clear whether or how they would draw the distinction. Moreover, the quoted comment is followed by a long discussion of instances in which they take the smallest differences in linguistic form in two complement clauses to lead to a difference in truth-value in attitude reports.

6. In the final section of their paper (section 7), Larson and Ludlow acknowledge the problems posed by examples like (15a, b), as well as other instances in which belief ascriptions with linguistically different complements would normally be counted as "saying the same thing" or having the same content. However, their explanation of this is inconclusive.

7. The material in this section is based in part on section II of Scott Soames, "Beyond Singular Propositions?" *Canadian Journal of Philosophy* 25, no. 4 (1995): 515–550.

8. Mark Richard, *Propositional Attitudes* (Cambridge: Cambridge University Press, 1990).

9. Mark Richard, "Defective Contexts, Accommodation, and Normalization," *Canadian Journal of Philosophy* 25, no. 4 (1995): 551–570.

10. This is a simplification of Richard's official position. According to the official position, the belief predicate expresses a three-place relation between individuals, annotated propositions, and correlation functions (more on these below). In simple cases, belief ascriptions are evaluated by existentially generalizing on the argument place standing for correlation functions. In such cases, *Ralph believes that S* is true relative to a context C iff there is some correlation function satisfying the restrictions involving Ralph in C which maps the annotated proposition expressed by S in C onto some annotated proposition accepted by Ralph. If all cases were like this, we could simply take the belief

predicate to express a two-place relation between individuals and annotated propositions that is the existential generalization of a three-place relation between individuals, annotated propositions, and correlation functions.

However, Richard wishes to extend his theory to cover extended discourses containing multiple belief ascriptions involving what is understood to be the same agent. For example, in evaluating a discourse, *Ralph believes that n is F. What is more, he also believes that n is G*, Richard wants to have the freedom to assign it either of the following readings: (i) there is a correlation function f satisfying constraints involving Ralph in the context that maps the annotated proposition expressed by *n is F* in the context onto an annotated proposition accepted by Ralph, and there is a correlation function g satisfying constraints involving Ralph in the context that maps the annotated proposition expressed by *n is G* in the context onto an annotated proposition accepted by Ralph; (ii) there is a correlation function f satisfying constraints involving Ralph in the context that maps the annotated proposition expressed by *n is F* in the context onto an annotated proposition accepted by Ralph, and that also maps the annotated proposition expressed by *n is G* in the context onto an annotated proposition accepted by Ralph. The freedom to generate both readings is achieved by analyzing the belief predicate as expressing a three-place relation between individuals, annotated propositions, and correlation functions, and allowing different scope possibilities in discourses for the existential quantifier binding the third argument place (including the possibility that a single such quantifier may bind the final argument place of several different occurrences of attitude predicates in the discourse).

The issues concerning Richard's theory that I will be raising do not directly involve discourses like these. Therefore, I will adopt the simplifying assumption that, for Richard, the belief predicate expresses a relation between individuals and annotated propositions.

11. The problems prompting the needed modification were presented in Soames, "Beyond Singular Propositions?," at pp. 536–538.

12. Strictly speaking, this claim must be qualified slightly to cover a feature of Richard's approach that arises in the special case of belief ascriptions the complement clauses of which contain multiple occurrences of the same term. Regarding such cases, a strictly Russellian approach has both (i) and (ii) as consequences, whereas Richard's approach has (i), but not (ii), as a consequence, when the contexts in question are limited to those in which there are no restrictions on correlation functions.

(i)   Let t be any term (i.e., name, indexical, or variable), let t_1 and t_2 be any pair of distinct terms, and let C be a context (and A an assignment of values to variables) such that the Russellian content of t with respect to C (and A) is the same as the Russellian content of both t_1 and t_2 with respect to C (and A). If *Ralph believes that . . .*

$t \ldots t \ldots$ is true with respect to C (and A), then ***Ralph believes that*** $\ldots t_1 \ldots t_2 \ldots$ must also be true with respect to C (and A). For example, if *Ralph believes that Peter Hempel is Peter Hempel* is true, then *Ralph believes that Peter Hempel is Carl Hempel* must also be true.

(ii) Let t be any term (name, indexical, variable), let t_1 and t_2 be any pair of distinct terms, and let C be a context (and A an assignment of values to variables) such that the Russellian content of t with respect to C (and A) is the same as the Russellian content of both t_1 and t_2 with respect to C (and A). If ***Ralph believes that*** $\ldots t_1 \ldots t_2 \ldots$ is true with respect to C (and A), then ***Ralph believes that*** $\ldots t \ldots t \ldots$ must also be true with respect to C (and A). For example, if *Ralph believes that Peter Hempel is not Carl Hempel* is true, then *Ralph believes that Carl Hempel is not Carl Hempel* must also be true.

The disparity between (i) and (ii) on Richard's approach results from the fact that correlation functions take expression types as arguments. Hence multiple occurrences of a single term t have to be provided with identical counterparts. This means that ***Ralph believes that*** $\ldots t \ldots t \ldots$ will be true only if Ralph accepts some corresponding sentence. $\ldots t^* \ldots t^* \ldots$ which contains multiple occurrences of some term with the same Russellian content as t. By contrast, Ralph's acceptance of such a sentence is sufficient, but not necessary, for the truth of ***Ralph believes that*** $\ldots t \ldots t\# \ldots$, in a context in which there are no constraints on correlation functions (since in such a context the distinct terms t and t# can be mapped onto any term or terms with the right Russellian content).

Since this special feature of Richard's theory is independent of most of the issues discussed in the text of this chapter, I will ignore this complication.

13. There are no restrictions on correlation functions involving variables. Hence any variable in an attitude ascription can always be mapped onto any name or indexical that has the same Russellian content as the variable (with respect to a given assignment).

14. In the simplified example used in the text, the sets S_P and S_H of translation targets each contained only a single word in Hammurabi's actual language (together with its Russellian content). The criticisms just developed do not depend on this. So long as the sets are different, they may be expanded to include as many of the expressions of his actual language as one wishes, while leaving the criticisms intact.

15. For ease of exposition I have formulated these restrictions so that their third coordinates (specifying the translation targets) are properties of expressions rather than properties of pairs of expressions together with their Russellian contents. Nothing of significance depends on this.

16. See Saul Kripke, "A Puzzle About Belief," in A. Margalit, ed., *Meaning and Use* (Dordrecht: Reidel, 1979), pp. 239–283. According to Richard, propositional attitude ascriptions reporting the beliefs Peter would express by utterances containing the name *Paderewski* presuppose that Peter has different mental representations of Paderewski which correspond to his two uses of the name, and which provide different translation targets for uses of the name in belief ascriptions.

17. This is commonplace both on Richard's original conception of a restriction as a triple the first constituent of which is an individual and the last constituent of which is a set of translation targets, and on my suggested modification in which the first constituent of a restriction is a property of individuals and the last constituent is a property of expressions (or expression/content pairs). On Richard's original conception, attitude ascriptions involving plural subjects will standardly be used in contexts with different restrictions for the different subjects (whether or not the sets of translation targets differ from individual to individual). Since on my modification the first constituent of a restriction may be a property that applies to more than one individual, it is conceivable that in some cases a single restriction might be used to constrain the translations from the reporter's words to the words of all the different agents referred to or quantified over by the plural subject of an attitude ascription. However, the situation changes when the third constituent of a restriction is the property of being associated with such and such descriptive content **by such and such an agent**. When this sort of relativization to a particular agent is built into the third constituent of a restriction, contexts in which translational constraints are placed on each of the different subjects of a plural attitude ascription using such restrictions will standardly have to contain different restrictions for the different agents.

18. The fact that the acceptable translation targets differ from individual to individual also rules out another technical alternative for dealing with the problem at hand. In note 10, I mentioned that according to Richard's official position, the belief predicate expresses a three-place relation between individuals, annotated propositions, and correlation functions. In simple cases, belief ascriptions are evaluated by existentially generalizing on the argument place standing for correlation functions. In such cases, *Ralph believes that S* is true relative to a context C iff there is some correlation function satisfying the restrictions involving Ralph in C which maps the annotated proposition expressed by S in C onto some annotated proposition accepted by him. However, in more complex cases different possibilities present themselves concerning the relative scopes of the existential quantifier ranging over correlation functions and other items in the sentence or discourse.

In the case of a quantified sentence like (13) there are two possible scopes for the existential quantifier:

(i) ∃f (Most x: ancients x) x believes, f, that Hesperus isn't Phosphorus
(ii) (Most x: ancients x) ∃f x believes, f, that Hesperus isn't Phosphorus

If, as seems obvious, the sets of translation targets for the name 'Hesperus' corresponding to different individual ancients who speak different languages, and who use different expressions for Venus, are disjoint, then possibility (i) is ruled out since no single function can map 'Hesperus' onto members of disjoint sets. Thus (ii) is what is required by the intended interpretation of (13). This will standardly be the case with belief ascriptions the subjects of which are plural or quantified phrases—including the ascriptions in (11) used to motivate the problem.

19. The problem in this section is spelled out in more detail in Soames, "Beyond Singular Propositions?" A version of the problem is also given in Ted Sider, "Three Problems for Richard's Theory of Belief Ascription," *Canadian Journal of Philosophy* 25(4) (1995): 487–514.

20. In what follows, I use 'F' and 'G' essentially as schematic predicate letters while using 'A' and 'B' as metalinguistic variables over predicates; 't' is used as a metalinguistic variable over singular terms. I hope this does not cause confusion.

21. In this section I will assume for the sake of argument something that is otherwise problematic—namely, that Richard can provide a satisfactory explanation of how it is that an agent's acceptance of both *n is P* and *n is F*, where n refers to o, ensures not only that the agent believes of o both that it has the property expressed by P and that it has the property expressed by F, but also that the agent believes of o that it has the property expressed by the conjunction of P and F. This is Kripke's "Paderewski" problem mentioned earlier. The objection I make in this section is designed to hold even if Richard can solve this problem.

22. Recall that the set of translation targets for t determined by (15a) with respect to a world w is the set of expressions (i) that the individual i who is the unique person who is F in w associates with the property P_1 and (ii) that have o as their Russellian content in i's context in w. A similar point holds for (15b).

23. Here again, in stating these restrictions I take it for granted that the Russellian content of both n_1 and n_2 is the object o.

24. *Canadian Journal of Philosophy* 25, no. 4 (1995): 515–550.

25. For Richard, the restrictions $\langle i, \langle t, o \rangle S_1 \rangle$, $\langle i, \langle t, o \rangle S_2 \rangle$ that make a context defective need not be unsatisfiable in the sense that S_1 and S_2 are disjoint; it is enough that the two sets are different.

26. Ideally, what Richard needs is a notion of a context being "defective" with respect to an arbitrary world w, and also an account of the truth of an attitude ascription with respect to a context C and world w, where C is "defective" with respect to w. A context C could then be characterized as "defective"

simpliciter iff it is defective with respect to the world C_w of C. Richard does not explicitly present this more generalized account.

However, I believe his intentions can be discerned. Suppose, for example, that C is as described in the text, and that the F is the G (in C_w), even though the conversational participants presuppose that the F is not the G. C is therefore "defective" simpliciter. Now consider a merely possible world w in which the F is not the G. I presume that Richard would want to say that C is not defective with respect to w, and that therefore the truth or falsity in w of the propositions expressed by (14a) and (14b) in C do not require any special treatment along the lines of (16). Next consider an analogous case. Let C' be a context just like C, except that in the world C'_w of C' the F is not the G. C' is therefore not a "defective" context, simpliciter. Now consider a merely possible world w in which the F is the G. Presumably C' is "defective" with respect to w. Therefore, I take it that Richard would evaluate the truth or falsity in w of the propositions expressed by (14a) and (14b) in C' by invoking an appropriate generalization of the idea expressed in (16).

27. However, other ascriptions *The F believes that S* may turn out true on Richard's revised account, even in certain cases when S contains the term t. For example, *The F believes that t is Z* will come out true in the context C provided that the individual who is the F (and the G) accepts both n_1 *is Z* and n_2 *is Z* with the appropriate Russellian contents. A similar result can be gotten in the example involving (14a) and (14c). Let us assume that C' is a context in which the conversational participants wrongly assume that the individual who is the F is not one of the G's, and that C' qualifies as "defective" for this reason. In addition to containing the extensional restriction (15a*), C' will also contain (15b*), plus other extensional restrictions identical with (15b*) except for containing some other individual who is G as first member. Since only (15a*) and (15b*) conflict, C' can be rendered nondefective by removing either one. The difference between this example and the one involving (14a) and (14b) is that although (14a) ends up getting characterized by Richard as neither true nor false in both cases, (14c) may be characterized as true, provided that at least two other individuals who are G satisfy the ascription *x believes that t is B* in C.

28. This set of translation targets is the union of (i) the set of names or indexicals that refer to o in i's context in C_w and that i associates in C_w with the property P_1, and (ii) the set of names or indexicals that refer to o in i's context in C_w and that i associates in C_w with the property P_2.

29. Whether or not the same sort of intuitive rationale for merging restrictions could be given in a case in which (14c) is substituted for (14b) seems to me to be problematic. However, I will not pursue the point here.

30. My discussion of this example has been simplified in three significant respects. First, I have not described the general procedure that Richard uses to

get from unmerged restrictions like (15a) and (15b) to merged restrictions like (15c). Second, I have not given the details of how these restrictions lead to extensional, world-indexed restrictions like (15c*). Third, since Richard does not explicitly generalize the notion of the extensional, world-indexed restrictions in a context to the more abstract notion of the extensional, world-indexed restrictions determined by a context with respect to an arbitrary possible world, I have not put forward a fully explicit and general proposal to do this either. I will say a word here about each of these points.

Richard adopts a new terminology in "Defective Contexts, Accommodation, and Normalization." What I have here been calling "(intensional) restrictions on correlation functions"—triples the first constituent of which is a property of believers, the second constituent of which is an expression with its Russellian content, and the third constituent of which is a property that plays a crucial role in determining a class of expressions or mental representations used by believers—Richard now dubs "directions for translation." (Actually, Richard takes the third constituent to be sets of expressions or mental representations. In this note I will at times follow him in this, even though it is clear that properties—which can have different extensions at different worlds—are really what is needed.) These are treated as depending directly on the beliefs and intentions of speakers (and hearers) regarding the sorts of words or representations that the agent of the attitude ascription would use to express the belief in question. For example, a speaker assertively uttering (14a) may do so with the intention of getting across the information that the F—whoever that individual may be—has a belief with the relevant Russellian content which that individual would express using a sentence t_1 *is A*, where t_1 is some term or other (referring to o) that the F associates with the property P_1. The speaker may have a corresponding intention about (14b). If so, then (15a) and (15b) will be "directions of translation" included in the context—no matter whether the F is, or is not, the G in the world of the context. In the special case in which the speaker (and hearers) do not presuppose that the property of being the unique F and the property of being the unique G are disjointly instantiated (in the world of the context), the context will also contain the "merged direction for translation" (15c).

Richard would represent (15a), (15b), and (15c) essentially as follows:

a.   <being uniquely F, <t, o>, S_1>
b.   <being uniquely G, <t, o>, S_2>
c.   <{being uniquely F, being uniquely G}, <t, o>, S_1 U S_2>

In general, the set D of directions for translation present in C includes all those directions like (a) and (b) in our example that are directly determined by the beliefs and intentions about acceptable translations held by the conversational participants in C, plus those "merged" directions—such as (c)—that result from the following closure principles for D. ('P' here stands for individual properties, 'Γ' stands for sets of properties, 'e' stands for expressions, 'e_c' stands for the content of e, 'S' and 'T' stand for sets of translation targets, and 'U' indicates set union.)

> Closure: If $<P, <e, e_c>, S>$ is a member of D, so is $<\{P\}, <e, e_c>, S>$; also, if $<P, <e, e_c>, S>$ and $<\Gamma, <e, e_c>, T>$ are members of D, then so is $<\Gamma \cup \{P\}, <e, e_c>, T \cup S>$, provided that there is no property Q which is a member of Γ, such that conversational participants in C presuppose that P and Q are disjointly instantiated.

Applying this to our sample context for (14a) and (14b), in which it is not presupposed that the F is not the G, we get the result that the set of "directions for translation" present in C includes (a), (b), and (c) above (whether or not the F is the G in the world of C).

Next, we need to get extensional, world-indexed restrictions from the directions of translation. (Richard calls these simply "restrictions.") We begin with the extensional, world-indexed restrictions determined by C with respect to the world C_w of C. These arise as follows: for any individual i existing in C_w, for any pair consisting of an expression e and Russellian content e_c, and for any set S of expressions or mental representations, the extensional, world-indexed restriction

(i) $<i, <e, e_c>, S>$

is in the set of such restrictions determined by C (with respect to C_w) iff there is some direction for translation

(ii) $<\Gamma, <e, e_c>, S>$

present in C, such that (a) in C_w, i instantiates every property in Γ, and (b) there is no other direction of translation

(iii) $<\Gamma', <e, e_c>, S'>$

present in C such that in C_w, i has each property in Γ', and Γ is a proper subset of Γ'. The effect of this is to ensure that merged extensional, world-indexed restrictions replace the unmerged extensional restrictions they correspond to, and that nondefective contexts are those in which for each individual i and pair $<e, e_c>$, there is at most one extensional, world-indexed restriction in it (with respect to the world of the context).

Applying this to our sample contexts for (14a) and (14b), in which it is not presupposed that the F is not the G, we get the result that if C and C* are such contexts, and if in C_w^* the F and the G are different individuals, whereas in C_w the F is the G, then although the directions for translation (a), (b), and

(c) are all present in both C and C*, (I) different extensional, world-indexed restrictions corresponding to (a) and (b) are determined by C* (with respect to C_w^*); while there is no extensional, world-indexed restriction corresponding to (c) that is determined by C* (with respect to C_w^*); and (II) an extensional, world-indexed restriction corresponding to (c) is determined by C (with respect to C_w), while C does not determine extensional, world-indexed restrictions (with respect to C_w) corresponding to (a) and (b).

For Richard, an ascription, α *believes that S*, is true with respect to a nondefective context C (and the world C_w of C) iff there is some correlation function f which maps the annotated proposition associated with S in C onto some annotated proposition Q accepted in C_w by the referent i of α with respect to C (and C_w), and f satisfies all extensional, world-indexed restrictions on i. Given this, one can easily see how to generalize the account so that it provides truth conditions for attitude ascriptions with respect to all pairs of contexts C and worlds w such that C is not defective with respect to w. (For this latter notion, see note 26.) If C and w are such a pair, α *believes that S* is true with respect to C, w iff there is some correlation function f which maps the annotated proposition associated with S in C onto some annotated proposition Q accepted in w by the referent i of α with respect to C and w, and f satisfies all extensional, world-indexed restrictions on i determined by C with respect to w. All that is needed for this to make sense is an appropriate generalization of the previous definition of the extensional, world-indexed restrictions determined by C with respect to the world C_w of C. To get the generalized definition, one needs only to replace all occurrences of 'C_w' (standing for the world of the context) in the earlier definition with occurrences of 'w' (standing for any arbitrary world).

31. All of the problems illustrated by (14a) and (14b) can be re-created in cases in which (14c) is substituted for (14b). In addition, the following anomaly also results: According to Richard's theory (as reconstructed here) there are cases in which the proposition semantically expressed by *Some G's believe that t is B*, and asserted by someone who utters it, is true with respect to a world w in virtue of the fact that a particular individual i who is a G believes a certain proposition that attributes the property B, together with a certain descriptive property D, to the referent of t, while a different individual u (who is also a G) believes a proposition that attributes the property B, together with a different property D*, to o. This happens in cases in which (i) the context for (14a) and (14c) contains a pair of (intensional) restrictions, one of which requires mapping t onto expressions associated with D when evaluating attitude ascriptions the agent of which is a G, and the other of which requires mapping t onto expressions associated with a different property D', when evaluating ascriptions of attitudes to an agent who is the F; (ii) it is not presupposed in C that the F isn't a G; (iii) w is a world in which the individual

i is a G but is not the F, whereas u is both a G and the F; and (iv) D* is the property of instantiating either D or D′ that is associated with translation targets in the restriction that results from merging the restriction in C regarding G's with the restriction regarding the F.

32. Note that the assertions (26a) and (26b) made by assertive utterances of (25a) and the negation of (25b) in this context might jointly be true, even though (i) *The F and the G both believe (the proposition) that Paderewski was born in Warsaw* cannot, in any normal context, be used to assert that the F believes (the proposition) that the musician Paderewski was born in Warsaw and the G believes (the proposition) that the politician Paderewski was born in Warsaw. The ascription (i) can, of course, be used to assert (a) the proposition that the F and the G both believe the singular Russellian proposition that predicates being born in Warsaw to Paderewski; (b) the proposition that the F and the G both believe (the proposition) that the musician Paderewski was born in Warsaw; and (c) the proposition that the F and the G both believe (the proposition) that the politician Paderewski was born in Warsaw.

33. Considerable care must be taken when applying notions like logical validity to arguments consisting of sequences of English sentences. When context sensitivity is involved, the relevant notion of logical validity, as originally formulated and investigated by David Kaplan in "Demonstratives" (in J. Almog, J. Perry, and H. Wettstein, eds., *Themes from Kaplan* [New York: Oxford University Press, 1989]), is that of the (semantically determined) truth of the conclusion in all contexts in which the premises semantically express truths. It is important to recognize that the notion of a context central to this enterprise is a highly abstract one. For one thing, a context in which a sentence S is evaluated need not be one in which S (or any other sentence) is actually uttered (e.g., "I am speaking" is not true in all contexts, and so is not logically valid); it need not be one in which the agent of the context understands S (e.g., "I exist" is true even in contexts in which the agent doesn't know English); and it need not be one in which the agent is attempting to demonstrate anything, even if S contains a demonstrative like the pronoun 'he' (e.g., *No one knows that he is here* may be true in a context even though the agent of the context is not attempting to demonstrate anyone). In this framework, a context is something like an abstract point of view from which sentences can be interpreted by providing parameters (e.g., agents, addresses, locations, times, and so on) required by specific linguistic items.

Related to this is the fact that, in this framework, contexts interpret expression and sentence types. Hence, different occurrences of the same sentence, or of the same expression, always receive the same interpretation in any single context. This means that if the argument consisting of the English sentences (i)–(iii) is evaluated directly for logical validity in this framework, it must be classified as valid.

   i. He is a philosopher.
  ii. He is a billionaire.
 iii. Some philosopher is a billionaire.

Surely, however, it cannot be denied that there are contexts in which a speaker assertively utters (i), using 'he' to refer to me, and assertively utters (ii), using 'he' to refer to Warren Buffett. In such contexts the assertions made by (i) and (ii) may be true even though (iii) is false. The standard way of accommodating this fact in the usual Kaplan-style framework is to evaluate arguments consisting of English sentences for logical validity only after they have been subjected to "analysis." When this is done, the different occurrences of 'he' in (i) and (ii) are replaced by occurrences of different demonstratives—for example, 'he$_1$' and 'he$_2$,' or *dthat (the S)* and *dthat (the B)*. These different demonstratives can then be assigned different referents in the context.

A similar point can be made about the adjective 'tall', which requires a reference class (tall for an A, tall for a B) that is often contextually supplied. Thus, if the argument consisting of the English sentences (iv)–(vi) is directly evaluated for logical validity, it, too, must be classified as valid.

  iv. The F is tall.
   v. The F is the G.
  vi. The G is tall.

As before, however, it cannot be denied that there are contexts in which a speaker uses (iv) to assert that the F is tall for an A while using (vi) to assert that the G is tall for a B. In such contexts the assertion made by (iv) may be true while the assertion made by (vi) is false, even though (v) is true. This can be accommodated within the standard Kaplan-style framework by adding an indexical singular term, r_1, to serve as a complement tó the occurrence of 'tall' in (iv) that provides reference class, while adding a different indexical singular term, r_2, to serve as complement to 'tall' in (vi). When the context assigns different reference classes to r_1 and r_2, (iv) and (v) may be true in the context, even though (vi) is false.

  34. Richard, *Propositional Attitudes*, p. 245.

  35. According to Richard's theory, (27) and (34) are jointly true in C only if there is some term t referring to Hes such that Ham accepts both *Et* and *Ht*, where E expresses the property of being a heavenly body that is visible in the evening and H expresses the property of being hot. This is tantamount to accepting the conjunction of these two sentences, which Richard treats as equivalent to accepting $\lambda x \lfloor Ex \And Hx \rfloor t$. This last step incorporates Richard's response to Kripke-inspired Paderewski-type worries. Although I doubt the correctness of this response, I do not make an issue of it here.

  36. Richard, *Propositional Attitudes*, p. 251.

Chapter 8

1. Here, and in what follows, I will not revisit controversial questions involving so-called empty names. See the appendix to chapter 3 for a discussion.

2. As usual, I ignore consideration of how the semantic content of the predicate phrase *lived on Lake Lane in Princeton* is represented.

3. This reasoning is essentially just an extension to propositional attitude ascriptions of the principles O1 and O2 of chapter 3. The extension may be put as follows: (i) If so and so assertively utters *Edward believed that n is F* in a context C, then I can truly say, *So and so asserted that Edward believed that n is F*; (ii) It follows from this, plus the claim that there is such an individual as n, that: $\exists x$ *(x = n & so and so asserted that Edward believed that x is F)* is true. Thus, so and so asserted that Edward believed the singular, Russellian proposition attributing the property expressed by F to the referent of n.

4. I am also ignoring any context sensitivity that may be introduced by verb tense.

5. With the possible exception of the content of a very general sortal. In what follows, I will ignore this potential complication.

6. Standardly, a sentence that is used metaphorically semantically expresses a proposition that is either obviously false, utterly trivial, or clearly irrelevant to the main purposes of the conversation. Typically this results in a conversational implicature to the effect that the speaker is not intending to assert that proposition, but rather is intending to assert some related proposition. Part of understanding the metaphor often involves finding a good candidate, or some restricted range of good candidates, for this asserted proposition. The examples in (14) and (15) illustrate that this process occurs when the metaphor is contained in the content clause of an attitude ascription in a way that parallels simpler cases in which the complement clauses are used on their own.

The more general phenomenon—in which an attitude ascription, *x v's that S*, is used in a context C to assert a proposition that attributes to the agent an attitude toward some proposition over and above the proposition semantically expressed by S in C—subsumes the metaphorical use of attitude ascriptions, like those in (15), as a special case. In the more general case, there is often no conversational implicature canceling the speaker's assertion of the proposition semantically expressed by the attitude ascription, and requiring one to search for some other asserted proposition to take its place. (Though sometimes nonmetaphorical cases involve this, typically they do not.) Nevertheless, there may be reason to interpret the speaker as asserting some further proposition, in addition to asserting the proposition semantically expressed by the attitude ascription.

7. Some Millians might not be willing to go quite this far. It is, I think, uncontroversial that in some contexts a speaker's primary intention in assertively uttering the ascription (17) would be to convey the information expressed by (18), whereas the speaker's primary intention in assertively uttering (19) would be to convey the information expressed by (21). Thus it should be admitted by all that substitution of coreferential names in attitude ascriptions can change the primary information that speakers intend to convey (and the information imparted to hearers). I believe that in many cases it is correct to take the further step of characterizing these speakers as asserting the information in question. Those Millians who are unwilling to take this further step may nevertheless accept the main thrust of my argument by developing an account of linguistic communication that emphasizes the importance of the information that speakers primarily intend to convey (in those cases in which it diverges from what is asserted).

8. In thinking about the assertive indeterminacy of some attitude ascriptions, it is worth recalling a point first made in chapter 6 about the utility of such indeterminacy in accurately reporting the assertions made, or the beliefs expressed, by an agent whose original utterance was itself assertively indeterminate. In our example, Harry's original utterance of (16), *Carl Hempel died last week*, was assertively indeterminate between (I-16a), (I-16b), and (I-16c). In a case like this, someone who wants to use an attitude ascription to report the extrasemantic content of Harry's assertion can scarcely do better than to choose a complement clause that gives rise to the same indeterminacy in the reporting context that Harry's own sentence did in his context. Thus, in the situation we have imagined, Tom could most naturally and accurately report what Harry said by uttering *Harry said that Carl Hempel died last week*. Similarly, in reporting the beliefs Harry expressed by his utterance of (16), the most natural and accurate way for Tom to report those beliefs is by uttering (17). Here, the assertive indeterminacy in Harry's original utterance is accurately mirrored in the assertive indeterminacy of the attitude ascriptions based on Harry's remark.

9. They do not, of course, have to go through the reasoning I have made explicit. More likely, they just jump to the conclusion. In principle, however, one could go through the reasoning if needed.

10. There may, of course, be a certain amount of indeterminacy regarding precisely which propositions Paul has asserted. Small variations in content may yield different propositions that are equally good, or almost equally good, candidates for being asserted. Since this does not affect the main points under discussion, I continue to put aside issues of indeterminacy in discussing these cases.

11. In this statement of T4 I omit, as irrelevant to our present concerns, any consideration of rigid designators other than proper names.

12. In formulating T5, and also T6, I have tacitly assumed that the semantic content of a linguistically simple proper name is its referent, rather than its referent together with a some very general sortal property. (I have also tacitly assumed that if o is the referent of such a name n, then n refers to o even at worlds in which o does not exist.) On the alternative view, in which the semantic contents of even ordinary linguistically simple names always include such sortals, these names simply constitute a subclass of the partially descriptive names, and the comments in the text about examples (53)–(56) apply to identity sentences involving them, too. Since the most plausible candidates for such sortal properties are typically (i) essential properties of the objects that bear them, (ii) properties that can be possessed by an object only when it exists, and (iii) properties which we know to apply to an object only a posteriori, the discussion of (54)–(56) is most relevant. On this alternative view in which the semantic contents of all (simple) names include very general descriptive sortals, a typical identity sentence $n = m$ involving coreferential names n and m of a contingently existing object o will semantically express a proposition that is both contingent and a posteriori, whereas the *if n and m exist, then n = m* will typically be both necessary and a priori.

13. I am treating these *if, then* statements as material conditionals.

14. One could get an example of an identity sentence involving at least one partially descriptive name that was both necessary and a posteriori if one constructed the partially descriptive name using a property of the referent that (i) was one of its essential properties, (ii) was a property that the referent has even at worlds in which the referent doesn't exist, and (iii) was not knowable a priori of the object. There may be such properties and such names, but if there are, then the examples one can construct of the necessary a posteriori involving identity sentences containing such names are decidedly marginal.

Chapter 9

1. I here ignore trivial descriptions, such as *the x such that x = n*.

2. For a discussion of nondescriptionality, see Nathan Salmon, *Reference and Essence* (Princeton, N.J.: Princeton University Press, 1981), chapter 1.

3. Saul Kripke, *Naming and Necessity* (Cambridge: Harvard University Press, 1980), p. 139.

4. Kripke, *Naming and Necessity*, p. 140. Emphasis added.

5. Kripke, *Naming and Necessity*, p. 162. Emphasis added. See also Kripke's "Identity and Necessity," in M. Munitz, ed., *Identity and Individuation* (New York: New York University Press, 1971), footnote 18. The discussion in "Identity and Necessity" (and *Naming and Necessity*) is informal, and there is some unclarity about precisely which expressions are being characterized as rigid designators, and precisely which statements are being character-

ized as necessary, if true. In his relatively brief discussion of this issue, Kripke sometimes seems to be using 'pain', and certain variants like 'my pain', as singular terms—designating either an individual pain or the general phenomenon of pain, or even the property of being pain. At other times, however, he seems to use 'pain', 'c-fiber stimulation', and variants of these as predicates of individual things—in particular, of particular sensations and brain states. It appears that he wishes to characterize all of these expressions as rigid, and all of the relevant identity statements as necessary, if true. At any rate he does not carefully distinguish among them, even though the form of the relevant "identity statements" will differ depending on whether singular terms or predicates are involved. Whatever his exact intentions may have been on these matters, the passages can easily be read in an expansive way, as assuming that whatever grammatical type may be involved, the corresponding "identity statements" involving rigid designators are necessary, if true.

6. Kripke, *Naming and Necessity*, p. 127. Emphasis added. When one looks at the rest of the paragraph from which this passage is drawn, ones sees that the point Kripke seems to have had most in mind here is that proper names and natural kind terms, of whatever grammatical category—singular term, predicate, count noun, mass term—are all what John Stuart Mill would call "non-connotative." That in turn amounts to the view that they are not defined in terms of a conjunction of properties or a cluster of properties. The view that Kripke is combating is one that holds that speakers associate a certain cluster of properties with a given name or a given natural kind term, that this cluster of properties both gives the meaning and determines the extension of the term, and that the claim that the thing has the properties, or that instances of the kind have them, is something that is both necessary and known a priori by speakers. Against this, Kripke claims that in the case of natural kind terms of whatever grammatical category, (i) speakers often have an impoverished set of properties associated with the term, (ii) that these properties do not in general either give the meaning or determine the extension of the term, (iii) that speakers do not know a priori that instances of the kind have these properties, and (iv) that the claim that instances of the kind have these properties is typically not necessary. In short, Kripke contends that proper names and natural kind terms of whatever grammatical category are nondescriptive. Kripke also has some positive doctrines in mind, including the view that these terms are rigid, and that identity statements connecting two such expressions are supposed to be necessary, if true. This is illustrated in the next several pages after this passage, where Kripke goes on to give examples of such necessary truths involving natural kind terms.

7. Kripke, *Naming and Necessity*, p. 134. Emphasis added.

8. A more detailed and extensive discussion of the use of mass terms like *water* as predicates will be given in chapter 11.

9. Like the term *red*, which has a primary use as a predicate and a second-ary use as a name of a property (the color red), mass terms such as *water* and *H₂O* have primary uses in which they function as predicates, and secondary uses in which they are names of abstract kinds. The relevance of both uses for the analysis of sentences like *Water is H₂O*, and for the application of Kripke's doctrines to such sentences, will be carefully considered in chapter 11.

10. The use of the term *essentialist* to characterize this sort of predicate conforms to one common way in which the term is used in contemporary philosophy. However, more should not be read into it than this. I intend no suggestion that the main concerns of traditional metaphysicians like Aristotle with the notion of essence are fully or adequately characterized as involving a concern with essentialist predicates in this sense. For present purposes what is important is not the terminology used to pick out this class of predicates (or properties), but the obvious similarities between such predicates and rigid sin-gular terms.

11. Bold italics again indicate corner quotes. The need for the parenthe-sized clause in the case of singular terms, but not predicates, is a significant difference between the two cases. However, the similarity between the two cases is clear, and, it might be argued, the difference between them is just what one would expect, given the difference between singular terms and predicates.

12. One way of reading the passage on which Kripke need not be seen as running together (i) and (ii) of the previous paragraph has been suggested to me by David Lewis. On this interpretation, Kripke's comment *if something is a pain it is essentially so* is viewed as intended to defend the claim that the singular term *pain* rigidly designates a certain type of thing by rebutting one particular competing analysis according to which it nonrigidly designates dif-ferent types with respect to different worlds. The analysis to be rebutted holds that necessarily x is a pain iff x is an instance of whatever physical type is such that its instances play a certain functional role in our psychology. This is coupled with the thought that in different possible worlds, instances of different physical types play this role. Finally, the singular term *pain* is taken to be necessarily coextensive with the nonrigid designator *the physical type instances of which play such and such functional role in our psychology*, yielding the result that it is a nonrigid designator. Given that the predicate *is a pain* applies to something iff it is an instance of the kind designated by the singular term *pain*, and given further that the singular term picks out different physical types in different worlds, a proponent of this analysis will naturally conclude that being a pain is not an essential property of pains. For suppose that x is an instance of C-fiber stimulation, and that C-fiber stimulation plays the functional role in the actual world that makes it count as pain. Then x is both a pain and a C-fiber stimulation in the actual world. Next imagine that x exists in a differ-ent possible world w in which C-fibers are still stimulated, but such stimula-

tions don't play the functional role of pain; rather, instances of some other physical type do. The functionalist will describe this as a case in which something that is a pain in the actual world exists without being a pain. Thus, in asserting that being a pain is an essential property of anything that has it, Kripke may be seen as denying one particular way of analyzing the singular term *pain* as nonrigid—namely, by taking it to be necessarily equivalent to *the physical type instances of which play such and such functional role in our psychology*.

In considering this interpretation of the passage from Kripke, it is important to bear in mind that refuting one particular nonrigid analysis of the singular term *pain* is not equivalent to showing that it is rigid. Moreover, even if one accepts the claim that anything that is a pain is essentially so, one still might regard it as an open question whether the singular term *pain* is rigid. (It is possible for a singular term t to nonrigidly designate a kind, even though the predicate *is an instance of t* expresses an essential property of objects it applies to). Thus, if one thinks that Kripke's point in the passage cited (as well as in related passages) was merely to refute one particular nonrigid analysis of the term *pain*, then one must ask why he took it to be so obvious that such a refutation was tantamount to establishing the rigidity of the term. Apart from the connection that Kripke tries to make between rigidity and essentiality, the text does not provide a clear and unambiguous answer to this question.

13. See Kripke, *Naming and Necessity*, pp. 122–123, 125–126, 138. Kripke regards this sentence as expressing a necessary truth which, nevertheless, is an empirical discovery. On p. 125 he puts it "under the same sort of heading" as the sentence *gold is an element with atomic number 79*—that is, (5) in the original list of examples of theoretical identities. See also p. 138, where he compares (5) to *Cats are animals* and *Whales are mammals, not fish* as examples of necessary, a posteriori truths. Both (5) and the sentence about whales are viewed as being cases in which scientific investigation discovers necessary characteristics for being a member of the given kind (the species whale, the substance gold) that are better, for purposes of identification, than the original characteristics believed by speakers to characterize the sample (being a fish, being a yellow metal).

14. Note that the sentence *Lightning is electricity* cited above by Kripke should not to be taken as having the form $l = e$. For surely not all electricity is lightning, whereas Kripke takes the sentence to express a truth.

15. Kripke, *Naming and Necessity*, p. 138. Emphasis added.

16. Kripke, *Naming and Necessity*, p. 140.

17. Together with obvious semantic facts about the quantifiers, connectives, and the necessity operator.

18. Strictly speaking, (11d) is a consequence of (11a) and (11b) plus obvious semantic facts about the quantifiers, connectives, and the necessity operator.

19. This example is based on one originally suggested to me by Nathan Salmon.

20. Another example with the same moral can be given using the predicate *x is a sample of the colorless, odorless, thirst-quenching substance instances of which fall as rain, fill the lakes and rivers, and are necessary for human survival*, and the following pair of singular terms:

W1. The colorless, odorless, thirst-quenching substance instances of which . . .

W2. The property of being (a sample of) the colorless, odorless, thirst-quenching substance instances of which . . .

21. Fine made the observation in the Princeton seminar on this material jointly led by David Lewis and me in the spring of 2000.

22. In November 1997, I presented much of the material in chapters 9 and 10 in a lecture to the philosophy department at UCLA, which Saul Kripke attended. In the discussion period he expressed sympathy with this assessment of his use of the term 'rigid' in *Naming and Necessity* to talk about natural kind predicates. In particular he said that he had wanted to emphasize the similarity between proper names and natural kind terms, and that he may have used the notion of rigidity to do this without, as he now realizes, fully thinking through precisely what this was to mean in the case of expressions that are not singular terms.

23. Including singular definite descriptions, whether or not they are ultimately analyzed as generalized quantifiers.

Chapter 10

1. Kripke, *Naming and Necessity*, pp. 134–135. Boldface emphasis added.

2. This picture should not be credited to Kripke alone. Substantially the same picture was independently developed by Hilary Putnam. See in particular Putnam's "Is Semantics Possible?," in H. Kiefer and M. Munitz, eds., *Language, Belief and Metaphysics* (Albany: State University of New York Press, 1970); "Explanation and Reference," in G. Pearce and P. Maynard, eds., *Conceptual Change* (Dordrecht: Reidel, 1973); "Meaning and Reference," *Journal of Philosophy* 70 (1973): 699–711; "The Meaning of 'Meaning,'" in K. Gunderson, ed., *Language, Mind, and Knowledge*, Minnesota Studies in the Philosophy of Science, no. 7 (Minneapolis: University of Minnesota Press, 1975). All of these papers are reprinted in Hilary Putnam, *Philosophical Papers*, vols. 1 and 2 (Cambridge: Cambridge University Press, 1975).

3. It is conventional what proposition a sentence expresses. It is not conventional which propositions are necessary.

4. This involves a simplification. In reality the predicate *is a drop of water* is compound in virtue of individuating water by the drop. I ignore this for now, since it does not affect my present point. I will return to it in chapter 11, where I will discuss the semantics of mass terms like *water* in detail.

5. Nathan Salmon, *Reference and Essence* (Princeton, N.J.: Princeton University Press, 1981).

6. I am indebted to Professor Ali Kazmi for valuable discussion of the issues discussed in this section.

7. See, Jeff King, "Structured Propositions and Complex Predicates," *Nous* (1995): 29(4), 516–535; "Structured Propositions and Sentence Structure," *Journal of Philosophical Logic* (1996): 25(5), 495–521; and "What Is Philosophical Analysis?" *Philosophical Studies* (1998): 90(2), 155–179. Also see Mark Richard, "Analysis, Synonymy, and Sense," in C. A. Anderson and M. Zeleny, eds., *Logic, Computation and Meaning* (Kluwer, forthcoming); and "Articulated Terms," in J. Tomberlin, ed., *Philosophical Perspectives* 7 (Northridge, Calif.: Ridgeview, 1993).

8. Although the proposal is more in line with Richard's formalization than King's, no preference for one over the other is intended. I merely use the proposal to illustrate how the basic semantic idea might be expressed.

9. Like *water* and *gold*, *jade* is a mass term. In chapter 11 these terms are discussed in detail and distinguished from abstract singular terms, and from predicates that take count nouns as subjects.

10. See Mark Johnston, "Manifest Kinds," *Journal of Philosophy* (1997): 94(11) 564–583, footnote 3.

11. Johnston, "Manifest Kinds".

Chapter 11

1. In the case of the generic sentences, no precise analysis is intended. I wish merely to point out that we get essentially the same phenomena with mass terms as with count nouns.

2. Evidence that H_2O is a mass predicate is provided by the fact that it behaves like other mass predicates with respect to the points illustrated by (3b), (4c), and (7) above. Thus, corresponding to (3b) we have (i), corresponding to (4c) we have (ii), and corresponding to (7) we have (iii), which is equivalent to (iv).

   (i)   The stuff in the container is H_2O.
   (ii) A lot of H_2O, a little H_2O, some H_2O, not much H_2O, no H_2O
  (iii) H_2O is not found on the moon.
  (iv) No H_2O is found on the moon.

3. The extension of the expansive interpretation of *water* also includes individual water molecules—that is, molecules consisting of two hydrogen atoms and one oxygen atom.

4. Of course, different forms of coffee (beans, grounds, liquid) are not different (chemical) states of the same substance, as different forms of water (solid, liquid, gas) are. Still, there is a parallel in that *coffee*, like *water*, has both an expansive interpretation in which it applies to a range of different forms of the same stuff, and a more restricted interpretation in which it applies only to the stuff in liquid form.

5. In discussing how some of these predicates—*ice*, *water vapor*, and *water* (on its expansive and restricted interpretations)—might be introduced ostensively, while the other predicates might be defined in terms of them, I have, for simplicity's sake, reverted to the model in which speakers introducing the terms have explicit intentions about substances—that is, physically constitutive kinds—that govern the introductions of the terms. However, this is only a matter of convenience. All of the qualifications mentioned in the section "The Role of Intention in Determining the Reference of Natural Kind Terms" of chapter 10 should be understood as applying here.

6. See Mark Johnston, "Manifest Kinds," 573–574.

7. Johnston gives this argument in "Manifest Kinds," pp. 574–575, where he says the following: "Eliot's yellow fog was an instance of the kind water vapor. It was also made up of a quantity of H_2O, an instance of the kind H_2O. But contrary to (21) [*For any x (if x is an instance of the kind water vapor, then x is an instance of the kind H_2O)*], these instances are distinct. Suppose the fog suddenly liquefies. Then we still have the very same quantity of H_2O as made up the fog, but now it is in a liquid form. (After all, part of the point of talking of a chemical kind like H_2O is to allow that particular quantities of it can first be in one state and then another.) Not so with the fog. When the fog liquefies, the fog is no more; just as when a gold ring is rolled into a ball, the ring is no more. The fog is not identical with the quantity of H_2O that makes it up and, since that is the relevant instance of the kind H_2O here, the fog is not identical with any instance of H_2O. So Eliot's fog is a counterexample that shows that (21) is false. Mutatis mutandis with snow and (20) [*For any x (if x is an instance of the kind snow, then x is an instance of the kind H_2O]*."

8. For a relevant discussion, see section III.3 of Kathrin Koslicki, "The Semantics of Mass Predicates," *Nous* 38 (1999): 46–91.

9. This claim is supported by the observation that each step in Johnston's argument (23) is either identical with the corresponding step in (25), or so closely analogous to it that the considerations that support that step in Johnston's argument can be extended so as to apply to the corresponding step in (25).

10. My rejection of (26b) carries with it a rejection of the identity axiom of (a tensed version of) the calculus of individuals proposed by Leonard and Goodman. For a good discussion of the issues, as well as a careful statement of the argument against the identity axiom, see Ali Akhtar Kazmi, "Parthood and Persistence," *Canadian Journal of Philosophy* supp. vol. 16 (1990): 227–250, especially section IV.

11. Johnston, "Manifest Kinds," p. 575, footnote 8.

12. Johnston, "Manifest Kinds," p. 575.

13. Johnston, "Manifest Kinds," p. 572.

14. As we will see in a moment, there are instances of H_2O that are not naturally categorizable as either solid, liquid, or gaseous. But they are unusual cases—the exception rather than the rule. What I find mysterious is the view that no instances of H_2O are solid, liquid, or gaseous. This makes H_2O seem rather like Aristotelian matter.

15. Johnston's failure to recognize these points also undermines a related argument he gives in "Manifest Kinds," p. 573.

> What about saying that each instance of snow, ice, water vapor, or liquid water is an instance of H_2O? No, that too would be false. Instances of H_2O are quantities of H_2O. One of these quantities—for example, a mole of H_2O—can first be in a powdery, then a solid, then a liquid, and finally, a vaporous form. But that is not true of any of the instances of snow, ice, water vapor, or liquid water. Their form is essential to their being the particular powders, solid, vapors, and liquids that they are.

Here again the correct assumption that some instances of H_2O can survive changes in chemical state is insufficient to establish Johnston's conclusion that neither snow, ice, water vapor, nor liquid water is (an instance of) H_2O. What he needs is the stronger assumption, for which no argument is given, that all instances of H_2O can survive changes in chemical state. If, as I maintain, some instances of H_2O have survival conditions requiring them to be in a particular chemical state, whereas others do not, then there is nothing to prevent the claims (I-17a–c) from being true.

16. Here, and throughout this chapter, I ignore worries about impurities and other issues mentioned in the section "Boundaries of Natural Kind Terms" of chapter 10.

17. The decision to count individual water molecules as instances of the expansive kind water creates a minor complication for (C-17a)—*For all x, if x is water, then x is constituted by (made up of) H_2O*—on the expansive interpretation of *water*. On this interpretation, the truth of this sentence requires the truth of *x is constituted by (made up of) H_2O*, even in cases in which a single H_2O molecule is assigned as value of *x*. What makes this a complication is that one might wonder whether a single such molecule is indeed constituted by

(made up of) itself. If it is, then (C-17a) may be accepted on this interpretation; if not, not. Since I don't see any substantial issue of principle here, I don't think a decision on this point matters very much. Even though it may sound odd to talk of an individual molecule being constituted by, or made up of, itself, perhaps there isn't any harm in taking this as the degenerate case of the constitution relation—in which case (C-17a) might be accepted as true, even on the expansive interpretation of *water*.

18. The dispute between Johnston and me is not really about the semantic model of natural kind terms developed in chapter 10, but rather about the special features of *water*, *H_2O*, and related terms. Someone who adopted Johnston's position about the relationship between water and H_2O could accept the semantic model of chapter 10 by, for example, holding that the expansive term *water* is governed by the linguistic stipulation that it is to apply not to all and only instances of the substance of which most elements in the sample are instances, but to all and only those things constituted by instances of the substance—that is, physically constitutive kind—of which most elements in the sample are constituted. Other terms—like *ice*, the restricted term *water*, and *water vapor*—could be then defined in terms of this. (Alternatively, the restricted term *water* could be ostensively introduced by such a constitution stipulation, and related terms could be defined in terms of it.) Either way, the necessity of the sentences in (C-17) could be derived from their truth, plus the semantics of their natural kind terms, in accord with the model of chapter 10.

19. If *water* were a name for a single scattered object which is the totality of all actually existing quantities of water, then sentences like *Water weighs more than a billion tons* would be straightforwardly and unproblematically true, which they are not. Moreover, if *water* and *H_2O* did name concrete totalities of this sort, then they would not be rigid designators, since the concrete totalities of water/H_2O may differ radically from possible world to possible world. For example, if w is a possible world containing very much more water than exists in the actual world, very much less water, or water made up of entirely different H_2O molecules than those that make up water in the actual world, then presumably the concrete totality of all water existing in w will not be identical with the concrete totality of all water existing in the actual world. Thus, if *water* and *H_2O* were singular terms naming concrete totalities, then they would not be rigid designators, and Kripke's doctrine about the necessity of identity sentences containing rigid designators would then be irrelevant to the presumed necessity of (33).

Although *water* is not a name for the totality of all actually existing instances of water, it is a predicate that applies to all such instances, including, I suppose, an exhaustive instance of water that includes all others as parts. This fact, together with the fact that *water* is grammatically singular, may have encouraged some to think that it must be a name of a concrete totality. This is a mistake. As I emphasized in the text, *water* behaves like a predicate in several respects: (i) it occurs in ordinary predicative position (see (3)); (ii) it combines with quantificational expressions to form quantifiers (see (4)); and (iii) it has bare, unquantified occurrences the interpretations of which parallel those of bare, unquantified plural count nouns that function as predicates (see (5)–(8)). If one were to try to analyze these predicative features of the use of *water* as in terms of its being a name for a concrete totality, one would presumably have to view many occurrences of *water* as being implicitly prefixed by the relational expression *a bit (or instance) of.* Thus, *the stuff in the glass is water* might be treated as short for *the stuff in the glass is a bit (or instance) of water.* Similarly, *all water* might be understood as *all bits (or instances) of water,* and so on. However, there is a problem in characterizing the relation expressed by _____ *is a bit (or instance) of* _____.The natural thought is that the relation in question is the parthood relation—a bit or instance of water is a part of the water totality. But, as Koslicki ("The Semantics of Mass Predicates") points out, this can't be right; individual hydrogen atoms are parts of that totality, but they are not water. Intuitively, one wants to say that a bit or instance of water is a part of the water totality that is itself water. Although this may be true, it is no analysis of a predicative use of *water,* since it relies on an unanalyzed use of precisely this sort. Thus, it seems, there is no analyzing the predicative use of *water* in terms of an allegedly prior use of it as a name of a concrete totality. But once we have the mass predicate *water* applying to all instances of water, there is no reason to view it as a name of a concrete totality of all such instances.

20. In fact, the abstract singular term *water,* like the corresponding predicate, is Millian; it has no meaning apart from the kind it designates. By contrast, on the view of the abstract singular term H_2O on which it designates the intension of the associated predicate, it is natural to suppose that it has a semantically complex, descriptive meaning related to the meaning of the corresponding predicate.

21. Although I have provided a positive model on which *water* is nondescriptional, I haven't gone through the objections to descriptive conceptions of the term. For the most part I have simply taken for granted the success of the kinds of objections given in by Kripke in lectures 2 and 3 of *Naming and Necessity* to descriptive analyses of natural kind terms. For that reason, it may be useful for me to say a brief word here about some of the problems encountered by descriptive analyses of *water.* First, we can put aside analyses that treat it as having a semantic content incorporating the content of a description containing the actuality operator (or related rigidifiers), for the same reasons we rejected this view of proper names in chapter 2. Second, when we consider ordinary (nonrigidified) descriptions, we find that most of them express properties of water which, though familiar, are not semantically associated with the

term. Virtually all of the common knowledge we have about water—such as that it is thirst-quenching, that it falls from the sky as rain, that it fills the lakes and rivers, that it is necessary for our survival as well as the survival of plants and animals—is straightforward empirical, nonsemantic knowledge. One could understand both the predicate and the abstract singular term *water* without knowing these things. Imagine, for example, someone brought up in an extremely restricted environment in which he is acquainted with water, and perhaps uses it for washing things, but in which he never drinks it or uses it for cooking, or for any other purpose. We might even imagine that this person has never been outside, that he has never seen rain, lakes, or rivers, and doesn't know what liquid makes them up; nor does he know that water is necessary for survival. Such a person might nevertheless use the word *water* as a predicate applying to all and only instances of the substance—water—that he is familiar with, or as a singular term for that substance. If he does, then it would seem that he understands the word in the same sense that ordinary speakers of English do, and that he would be correctly described by us as believing that water can be used for washing things, but as not believing that water is thirst-quenching, that water falls from the sky as rain and fills the lakes and rivers, or that water is necessary for survival. This would not be so if the semantic content of either the singular term, or the predicate, *water* were analyzed as containing substantial descriptive content of this sort.

In this respect the term *water* is rather like the proper name *Bill Clinton*. Although there are lots of properties that speakers standardly associate with these terms, virtually none of these properties have to be grasped in order to understand them. As a result, virtually none of these properties are included in their semantic contents. However, since the properties are in fact associated with the terms by so many speakers, assertive utterances of sentences containing the terms often result in assertions the contents of which include these properties.

Index

Printed in the United States
24567LVS00004B/4-9

9 780195 145298